COMPARATIVE

WAGES, PRICES,

AND

COST OF LIVING.

[FROM THE SIXTEENTH ANNUAL REPORT OF THE
MASSACHUSETTS BUREAU OF STATISTICS
OF LABOR, FOR 1885.]

BY

CARROLL D. WRIGHT,

CHIEF OF THE BUREAU OF STATISTICS OF LABOR.

REPRINTED IN ACCORDANCE WITH THE PROVISIONS OF CHAP. 7,
RESOLVES OF 1888.

BOSTON:
WRIGHT & POTTER PRINTING CO., STATE PRINTERS,
18 POST OFFICE SQUARE.
1889.

With compliments of

Horace G. Wadlin,

Chief of Bureau of Statistics of Labor.

CONTENTS.

HISTORICAL REVIEW OF WAGES AND PRICES. 1752–1860.

CONTENTS.

CONTENTS.

CONTENTS.

HISTORICAL REVIEW

OF

WAGES AND PRICES.

1752-1860.

HISTORICAL REVIEW OF WAGES AND PRICES.

1752-1860.

The Bureau has, from time to time, devoted considerable attention to the important subject of wages and cost of living.

The chapters upon this topic presented in the annual report for 1879, and in subsequent issues, have quite fully covered the period between 1860 and 1884.

It was determined, therefore, to collect during the current year all available data respecting wages and prices in the early part of the century, and to bring the investigation forward to 1860 so as to connect such data with that already published.

Statistics of this sort seemed necessary properly to complete the history of the industrial development of Massachusetts, and the work, if undertaken at all, demanded immediate action, as the information, scattered through old account books, bills and miscellaneous papers, was rapidly passing out of existence.

The present Part contains the results of the work of the Bureau in this direction, the tabular matter relating to wages and prices being accompanied by such historical, explanatory, and comparative statements as are deemed proper adequately to portray the social conditions surrounding the laborer to-day and in the past.

In treating the subject historically, the industrial progress of Massachusetts, like that of the whole country, naturally falls into three periods. First, the early industrial period prior to the introduction of machinery and the factory system, and which may be said to close about the year 1815; secondly, the period of transition, marking the change from the old to the

modern industrial system, and comprising the years between 1815 and 1830; and, lastly, the present industrial period, from 1830 to the present time. In this order we proceed.

THE EARLY INDUSTRIAL PERIOD.

The early industrial period was that prior to 1815. The subjects considered are as follows: what industries had been established; how the industries were conducted; what machines had been introduced; hours of labor; household comforts possessed by the laborer; educational and social advantages; means of transportation, — facilities possessed by the workingman for changing his location; wages, and the purchase power of money.

WHAT INDUSTRIES HAD BEEN ESTABLISHED.

At the close of the Revolution several important industries had been placed upon a permanent basis, but the manufacturing interests of the country were still exceeded by its agricultural and commercial interests. Such manufactures as existed were largely confined to a system of isolated and household manual operations. Those were most prosperous which required the least outlay of capital and the least expenditure of labor.

The rich deposits of iron ore existing in the country had been profitably attacked, and several trades dependent on iron were fairly prosperous. The home production of nails, for instance, was nearly sufficient to supply the domestic market. Agricultural implements, edge tools, and hollow ware were beginning to be made. The war had created a demand for firearms and gunpowder which was met for the most part by private enterprise, government manufactories of such articles not having acquired much importance until after 1795.

Copper, like iron, could be found in considerable quantities, and being easily and cheaply worked the manufacture of copper and brass goods was among the most extensive of the infant industries.

American tanners were becoming able to meet successfully their foreign competitors. Extensive distilleries were in operation. Malt liquors were made in quantity nearly commensurate with the home demand.

Paper making, one of the earliest industries attempted in the colonies, was now one of the most prosperous and successful. Printing presses were sufficiently numerous in the United States to render us independent of foreign nations in respect to the manufacture of books.

Mills for the production of sawed lumber, flour, and meal abounded. Bricks were extensively made. Sugar refining and the manufacture of chocolate were among the leading industries.

Manufactories of cotton goods established at Beverly, Mass., and at Providence, R.I., were just overcoming the obstacles to success. Elsewhere this industry was struggling for a foothold. The printing of cotton fabrics was hardly more than attempted.

Manufactures of wool were almost entirely confined to the family. The making of wool hats, however, could no longer be classed among the household industries and the industry was in a thriving condition. At Hartford, Conn., before 1790, a woollen factory had been established, an enterprise that promised success. Small quantities of silk stockings, handkerchiefs and trimmings of silk were made, but the industry had scarcely emerged from the experimental state.

Shipbuilding was flourishing. Manufactories of rope and cordage, also, were prosperous. A single establishment at Boston making sail cloth was doing well. One at Ipswich for the manufacture of lace was noteworthy. In 1795 the shoe industry at Lynn employed about 200 master workmen with numerous apprentices, the annual product being about 300,000 pairs.

This list, meagre as it is, is practically exhaustive. Placed in opposition to the wide range of manufactures brought to view in the U. S. Census of 1880 it sinks into insignificance. It affords a background to the picture of industrial growth which the present century unfolds. It comprises industries near to the simplest needs of life and calculated to supply the most primitive social wants. Metallic implements and utensils of the crudest sort; arms for personal defence; ships for the navy and for commercial intercourse; paper and the printing press; brick, lumber, flour, and meal; liquors; coarse textiles, and a limited number of food products complete the list.

66662

These, and substantially these only, were the avenues open to mechanical skill in America in 1800. The condition of labor in these industries forms the starting point in our inquiry.

How the Industries were Conducted.

The factory system had not yet displaced the domestic or individual system of labor. Nothing was known of the development of special skill by the subdivision of labor and the confinement of each workman to one particular step in a series of progressive operations, an expedient by which the productive capacity of the modern operative has been brought to the maximum and the time required to complete the product reduced to the minimum.

The apprentice system was in vogue, and all parts of a trade were then taught where it is now usual and needful to teach but a single branch. The youth who aspired to become a shoemaker might, for instance, during his period of apprenticeship, acquire a knowledge of every step from the tanning of the leather to its embodiment in the finished shoe, and this illustration is applicable to other industries as well.

The modern artisan is, to a great or less extent, a specialist. He does one or a few things extremely well and very rapidly by the concentration of his power. He forms one of a company of specialists, each being a link in an industrial chain, and each, like himself, confined to a particular field of effort. His predecessor covered a wider range of industrial knowledge, but at a loss of time and skill. Hence a waste of productive force was contingent upon the industrial system, and the loss occasioned by this waste was borne partly by the laborer in the form of a lower wage for a given outlay of time and effort, and partly by the consumer in the form of a higher priced product.

The system permitted a more intimate relation between employer and employed than is usual to-day. Industrial operations were not then conducted by corporations. It was common for workmen in all industries to board with their employers. In country districts and small towns this may be said to have been the rule for unmarried men. Capital had not then turned to real estate operations as a channel of investment. It was too scarce and too much in demand for other enterprises. The

building of tenements for lease as an independent business venture was rarely undertaken. Men with families, who were drawn to a particular locality by the establishment there of some special industry, often lived in tenements belonging to their employers, the rental forming part of their wages.

WHAT MACHINES HAD BEEN INTRODUCED.

Manual labor was but little aided by the application of natural forces. The tools at the command of the laborer were few, and very crude in form. Neither the skill nor the appliances existed for the manufacture of machines. It is said that when Fairbairn, the distinguished English machinist, began his career, the human hand unaided was the sole reliance in such work. The early inventors were often obliged not only to construct the machines they devised, but to invent the tools for making them. The essential textile machines first went into operation in England, but it was not till 1790, as we shall hereafter show, that, under the direction of Samuel Slater, the first successful application was made of the English inventions to American textile manufacture. Slater's great difficulty was to find skilled workmen to carry out his ideas.

Just prior to 1800, Bentham, in England, was putting in practical form the essential wood-working machines, but it was many years before their influence was felt. In metal working, the lathe was still in its primitive state; the planing machine, which of itself revolutionized the manufacture of tools and machines of metal, was unknown, and the steam hammer was not yet perfected. The paper machine, also, was still an experiment.

Prior to 1800 steam was not applied to industry in America, though in 1789 the first engine for cotton spinning had been set up at Manchester, England. Water power was utilized in grist mills and for sawing lumber, but the wheels in use were very wasteful and not to be compared with the modern turbine.

Many things easily accomplished by the modern mechanic were simply impossible in the state of the arts then existing, and what was then done was accomplished at an expenditure of time and manual labor that to-day would not be required in the manufacture of the most complicated mechanism. Here, once more, was a waste of productive force, resulting

from not knowing the best way to do what was needed, and from the lack of proper tools to aid the hand of the workman.

The great inventions in agricultural implements that were to aid the laborer by cheapening the price of breadstuffs were then unknown.

During the early years of the century, then, we find little mechanical skill, and crude and imperfect machines. Muscle was essential to the workman, and what he accomplished was secured by purely manual, frequently monotonous and irksome labor, resulting in a product generally substantial, but often clumsy, and exhibiting, as a rule, little economy in the use of material or science in the adjustment of its parts. If the absence of machinery was a blessing to the laborer, then in that respect the early American artisan was in an ideal state.

HOURS OF LABOR.

The hours of labor in nearly all industries were measured by the sun, from sunrise to sunset constituting the working day. Not until 1824 was the subject of shorter hours agitated, and not until 1840 were shorter hours adopted to any extent; it was several years after that date before ten hours became the rule in the mechanic trades, while in the textile ind   the ten hour system is a modern innovation, as yet   d only in Massachusetts, so far as America is concerne

HOUSEHOLD COMFORTS POSSESSED BY THE LABORER.

Laborers at the beginning of the century had few of the comforts and conveniences now common in the poorest families. China, glassware, and carpets, to say nothing of the numberless contrivances now in use for facilitating household labor, were then practically out of reach. Dwellings were warmed by open fires of wood, while churches were not warmed at all. The iron cook stove for economically and efficiently aiding the culinary operations of the family had not yet appeared. Anthracite coal, though for fifteen years in use on blacksmiths' forges in the coal region, was unavailable for household purposes and in 1806 the first freightage of a few hundred bushels was brought down to Philadelphia, and there used experimentally with indifferent success.

The artisan's food was simple, often coarse, and in fact confined to the bare necessities of life. The wide range of products which now enrich the workingman's table, brought to him from all the markets of the world by the modern system of rapid transportation, were many of them unknown, or if known were expensive luxuries only obtainable by the favored few.

" Among the fruits and vegetables of which no one had then even heard, are cantaloupes, many varieties of peaches and pears, tomatoes and rhubarb, sweet corn, the cauliflower, the egg-plant, head lettuce, and okra.

* * * * * * * *

If the food of an artisan would now be thought coarse, his clothes would be thought abominable. A pair of yellow buckskin or leathern breeches, a checked shirt, a red flannel jacket, a rusty felt hat cocked up at the corners, shoes of neat's skin set off with huge buckles of brass, and a leathern apron, comprised his scanty wardrobe." *

The wealthy and more genteel wore silks, velvets and broadcloth of foreign manufacture, but the laboring classes were confined to coarse fabrics of home production.

EDUCATIONAL AND SOCIAL ADVANTAGES.

At the beginning of the century the educational advantages surrounding the workingman were few. Although common schools were early established in Massachusetts, yet judged by modern standards they were poor indeed. Hard by the church stood the school, but hard by the school on every village green stood, through all the early years, the gallows, stocks, and whipping post, and within, the rooms were bare and unattractive, and unprovided with apparatus for aiding the teacher's work. In school government the rod played an important part.

No systematic training for teaching as an independent profession was known. Indeed, such a profession as a distinct and honorable calling hardly existed. The instructors were, in many cases, young persons temporarily engaged while preparing for other pursuits, or the school dames and village pedagogues whose characteristics have been only too faithfully portrayed in story. Under these circumstances community of interests,

* McMaster. A History of the People of the United States. Vol. 1 — p. 97.

such as is now common among those engaged in teaching, was out of the question, and mutual action among those having the schools in charge, through conventions and institutes of instruction in which matters affecting the progress of education are discussed, was impossible. No rational methods of primary instruction were pursued. The range of text books was very limited and their typography beneath criticism. In some of the larger towns private academies were established in which, for a tuition fee, some attempt was made to overcome the deficiencies of the public schools.

The first educational association in the country * had just been formed and the first step taken which was to lead to important results. We shall hereafter see that the revival of education in Massachusetts, as in other States, was contemporaneous with the inception of the factory system and the introduction of machinery as an industrial force. But prior to 1820, although attention was gradually concentrating upon the public schools and plans were maturing for improving them, but little was actually accomplished and, consequently, the educational opportunities open to the children of the wage laborer were limited.

The opportunities for social enjoyment were no broader. An extensive inquiry into the social life of workingmen at the present day, undertaken by the Bureau in 1879, † showed the existence in Massachusetts of large numbers of social, farmers', and mechanics' clubs; base ball, rowing, and sailing clubs; secret societies offering social opportunities to members; literary and debating societies; musical societies; halls for dancing, billiard rooms, and bowling alleys, and other avenues of enjoyment practically open to all and utilized by a considerable number. A similar inquiry at any time during the first quarter of the century would have disclosed few such social institutions. The industrial population was too much diffused, the character of the labor too severe, and the hours of labor too long to permit of their existence.

It is frequently said that there were fewer class distinctions and greater social equality in early New England life than now. This is undoubtedly true if by social equality is meant equality

---

* Middletown, Conn., 1799. See Barnard's History of Education in Conn.
† See Eleventh Annual Report, pp. 239–293.

of condition. But the same causes that have operated to separate society into classes have, as we shall show, placed at the command of the manual workman opportunities for mental growth and social enjoyment unknown to the most favored in the early days. These opportunities have become his permanent possession. They constitute his environment. In modern society not only are all classes united by ties which cannot be broken except through revolution, and each class dependent upon every other to a degree never before known, but the social privileges of the present are open to the many and can no longer be monopolized by the few.

MEANS OF TRANSPORTATION. FACILITIES POSSESSED BY THE WORKINGMAN FOR CHANGING HIS LOCATION.

Transportation upon water was confined to sailing vessels, and upon land to wagons. The roads were very poor, although after 1800 the construction of turnpikes improved the means of communication between the larger towns. These were introduced by corporations, at first operated as toll roads, and finally assumed by the towns.

Canals, primitive in construction and crudely operated, were coming to be relied upon as avenues of internal commerce. These afterward reached a high point of development until superseded by the railway. Neither upon sea nor land in 1800 was steam employed in transportation. The experiments of Fulton, Fitch, and others culminated in the Clermont in 1807, but from 1807 to 1820 inclusive only 128 steamers were built. During the next decade 385 were added. On the western rivers, before 1820, only 71 steamboats were in use.

It was not till 1817 that a steamer was afloat in Boston harbor, and this proved a failure. It was 1824 before there was a regular line between Boston and Eastern ports, and at that time 17 hours were required for the trip from Boston to Portland, the fare being $5 including meals, and even this rate was one-half that charged upon the stages.

The commerce of the great lakes was exclusively confined to sailing craft till 1816, and it was three years later before the first steamer crossed the Atlantic.

The postal service was insufficient and far from rapid, while the rates were extremely high. Nine different rates were

established in 1792, varying from six cents for thirty miles to twenty-five for four hundred and fifty miles and over, and this schedule continued in force for many years. Missives were as frequently sent by private carriers as otherwise, and sometimes weeks would elapse in the transit between places no farther apart than Boston and Philadelphia. On the average each person in the country, for the period of five years ending with 1799, sent but $1\frac{4}{10}$ missives by the mails, while for the single year 1875 the average was $23\frac{1}{2}$ per person, or at the rate of $117\frac{1}{2}$ for five years, and the use of the mails has since increased, and is increasing. Nothing could better show the change in public importance of the mail service than the enormous increase here indicated.

The railroad, telegraph, and telephone are all comparatively modern inventions. By means of steam and electricity London, Liverpool, and San Francisco are to-day nearer Boston for all practical business purposes than were New York or Philadelphia at any time prior to 1820.

The comparative isolation of business centres and the lack of facilities for rapid communication between them materially affected the condition of the wage laborer. The risks of business were greater, and no industry could be considered permanent when it was impossible to forecast the state of the market; for instance, the manufacturer in Massachusetts was for weeks ignorant of affairs in centres of distribution like Philadelphia which might materially affect the price of his product. All commerce and manufacturing were then of the nature of a venture, and the labor dependent upon industrial operations thus limited remained more or less uncertain of employment.

The same conditions, which prevented the free and rapid exchange of products, raised the price and limited the variety of articles for household consumption, except such supplies as eggs, corn and rye meal, etc., which could be easily and cheaply procured on the farms near the consumer; and, beyond all, the laborer could not easily change his environment. Once located it was difficult for him to remove to other industrial neighborhoods, and this frequently operated to his disadvantage by limiting his employment and reducing his wage.

WAGES, AND THE PURCHASING POWER OF MONEY.

A system of barter was common in business transactions. Money was scarce and wages were frequently paid in groceries or clothing, or in orders for such commodities, the orders passing from hand to hand as currency. Of actual money the workingmen had little, and, when cash became absolutely necessary, they were often obliged to exchange store orders therefor at considerable discount.

Employers kept stores of groceries, clothing, boots and shoes, hats, and particularly liquors and tobacco, and it is evident from the inspection of old account books that a liberal share of the wages of labor was paid in rum and gin.

This payment of wages in necessaries, known as the " truck system," the prices being controlled by the employer, has fortunately practically passed away in Massachusetts. It arose from the inability of the employer to pay cash and the consequent impossibility of the workman buying for cash elsewhere. It enabled the employer to reap a double profit, but it frequently kept the workman poor. Very few were able to keep out of debt. The balance of the account was generally against the workman. This was a force sufficient in itself to prevent the free mobility of labor. In many cases the workman, especially if a man of family, was bound to the soil. There exists an isolated factory village in Massachusetts where the owners of the mills controlled the single store upon which the operatives were dependent for their supplies. For years the employés were at the mercy of the employers. Many came there poor, perhaps in debt for transportation thither. Once there, they remained poor. Every pay day found a balance against them. Reductions of wages must be submitted to, and exorbitant charges were irremediable. Unfortunately, such instances were not rare.

From the testimony of old men, and from such records of the times as have come into the possession of the Bureau, the fact appears that there was little or no variation in the rate of money wages paid laborers or mechanics between 1800 and 1815.

THE PERIOD OF TRANSITION.

We have thus summarized the conditions surrounding the laborer prior to 1815. We now pass to a consideration of the transition period, beginning with the introduction of the factory system in that year and ending with 1830 when the factory system in the great textile industry had become well established and was slowly but quite surely transforming other industries. Machinery, essential to the modern system of labor, had then become an important factor in the industrial problem.

The transition proceeded by degrees. In Massachusetts the cotton industry held the front rank, and it was the results achieved by the more perfect organization of labor in this industry that led to the adoption of similar methods in other branches of manufacture.

From 1733, the date of John Kay's invention of the fly shuttle, up to 1788, the introduction of the labor saving machines essential in the manufacture of textiles had proceeded in England. These inventions comprised the carding machine, the spinning-jenny, Arkwright's combined carding, drawing and spinning machines, Crompton's mule, Cartwright's power loom, Watt's improvements in the steam engine, and the cylinder calico printing machine, and to these should be added Berthollet's improvements in bleaching.

The exportation of machinery was forbidden by the English law, but in 1786 Massachusetts granted Thomas Somers, an Englishman, and Messrs. Robert and Alexander Barr, who were Scotchmen acquainted with the progress of English inventions, aid to enable them to construct spinning machinery, which, under the patronage of Col. Hugh Orr, of Bridgewater, was used experimentally at East Bridgewater. Soon after came the Beverly factory before alluded to, and, after experiments elsewhere, the successful application by Samuel Slater at Providence, in 1790–91, of water frame spinning on the Arkwright plan.

Until 1812 most factories employed the so-called water frame introduced by Slater. As early as 1808, however, throstle frame spinning had been introduced.

This is not the place for a detailed account of the commercial restrictions which grew out of the complicated foreign relations of the United States between 1808 and 1812. Such an account forms part of the political history of the country. It is sufficient for our present purpose to note that because of these restrictions prices of imported goods were raised, and, consequently, American manufactures stimulated. The expansion of the cotton industry was especially marked. Cotton mills which in 1803 were but four in number throughout the United States had in 1810 increased to 226, distributed as follows :

Number of Cotton Mills in the United States in 1810.

STATES.	No. of Mills.	STATES.	No. of Mills.
Massachusetts,	54	Delaware,	3
Vermont,	1	Maryland,	11
Rhode Island,	28	Ohio,	2
Connecticut,	14	Kentucky,	15
New York,	26	Tennessee,	4
New Jersey,	4		
Pennsylvania,	64	Total,	226

The war of 1812 still further expanded domestic production. English cotton goods advanced from 17 @ 20 cents to 75 cents per yard.

The principle of corporate action whereby small amounts of capital in many hands could be aggregated, and, under the control of a few, be profitably employed in industrial operations began to be utilized. Between 1806 and 1814 fifty companies were organized and incorporated in Massachusetts for the manufacture of textiles. In the latter year alone thirty corporations were authorized, including not only cotton and woollen companies but those for the manufacture of glass, files, wire, etc. Labor was in demand, wages advanced, and profits were large.

After the declaration of peace came the inevitable reaction. Unlimited foreign importations prostrated those industries which restricted commerce had fostered. American manufacturers were overwhelmed by the influx of English goods. Not only this, but the foreign demand for American cotton raised its price from 13 cents in 1814 to 20 cents in 1815, and 27

cents in 1816.   All industries were affected.   Everything was
at a standstill.   Much suffering was felt by the workingmen.

Then began the effort for a protective tariff which was
partially successful in the passage of the act of 1816.   From
thence to 1824 American manufacturers were struggling for a
foothold, their greatest obstacle being the commercial policy of
Great Britain, by whom the products of Northern factories
were rigidly excluded while the raw cotton of the South was
admitted, wrought into cloth, and poured into the American
market.

It was not a theoretical discussion of the respective merits of
free trade and protection that then interested the American
manufacturer and his employés.   It was a most practical problem that presented itself.   American manufactures had early
been advocated from a patriotic standpoint.   To be independent industrially as well as politically was the early argument.   It now assumed a different phase.   The war had
created a demand for domestic goods which had to be met.
Capital had been diverted from commercial into industrial
channels.   To allow the industries that the restrictions of war
had fostered to be overcome by the free commerce of returning
peace meant financial ruin to every manufacturer and distress
to every artisan.   With the patriotic argument was thus joined
every consideration of self-interest.   Until the question was
definitely settled great uncertainty attended manufacturing
enterprises, and the condition of the workingman was precari-
ous.   Finally, the revision of the tariff in 1824 and 1828 gave
the needed relief.   The latter law, bitterly opposed by the
commercial interests and in the non-manufacturing States,
especially in the cotton growing districts, was regarded by the
manufacturers as the first really protective measure enacted by
Congress.

Besides the influence of tariff legislation machinery now
·assisted the development of American manufactures.   The
liberal patent system of the United States stimulated American
ingenuity.   The impetus in this direction once given improvements of every sort quickly followed.   By 1817 steam was in
general use for spinning yarn and wool, and in breweries.
The first railway act was passed in Pennsylvania, March 31st,

1823, and 1827 witnessed the beginning of railway enterprises in America.

Until 1814 American textiles were generally woven upon the hand loom. In that year the American power loom of Francis C. Lowell went into operation at Waltham, Mass. This, together with subsidiary inventions by the ingenious Paul Moody, and the arrangements of Mr. Lowell for co-ordinating the processes of preparation, spinning, weaving and finishing within the same building, perfected the American factory system of textile manufacture, revived the cotton industry, and laid the foundation of its subsequent growth and prosperity.

Between 1820 and 1824 Massachusetts authorized $6,840,000 additional corporate capital. The factory system, the growth of manufacturing corporations, and the introduction and improvement of machinery by means of which the factory system was made effective, led to the foundation of factory villages such as Lowell, Fall River, Taunton, and Chicopee.

New industries, among others the manufacture of straw hats and bonnets, began to widen the avenues of employment. By 1829 Massachusetts contained 235 incorporated companies manufacturing cotton goods, woollen goods, iron, glass, hair, leather, wire, files, lead, duck, pins, soapstone, cordage, salt, calico, brass, copper, lace, umbrellas, linen, hose, ale, beer, type, cotton cards, gin, glass bottles, lead pipe, etc. There were sixty paper mills, six using machinery. The shoe industry at Lynn was thriving, the annual product being from 1,200,000 to 1,400,000 pairs, averaging in value 75 cents per pair. The females employed received $60,000 in wages annually. The woollen industry in the towns of Mendon, Uxbridge, Northbridge, and Grafton was also prosperous. Fitchburg, Leicester, Oxford, Dudley, Southbridge, and other Worcester County towns were coming forward in this industry.

In Lowell, in 1828, seven mills were in operation, giving employment to 1,200 females, while 500 were employed in the manufacture of lace at Ipswich.

By 1830, as we have said, the factory system of labor in the textile industries, and to a partial extent in other industries, was firmly established in Massachusetts. Its influence was felt in various ways. Employment became more constant. The laborer began to have savings. The savings bank, an

institution unknown in former years, was established. The
congregation of labor in factory towns led to a community of
interests among the wage classes. In 1824 agitation began
in behalf of shorter working time. The condition of the
laborer before the law began to demand reform. The onerous
requirements of military service, imprisonment for debt, and the
lack of a lien law, were among the topics discussed. After
the discussion began it never stopped till reform was secured.

The growth of an ever increasing industrial population
threw upon the employer class the responsibility of providing
for their mental and moral culture. Public opinion demanded
this at their hands. The factory was on trial, and the conditions surrounding it were jealously watched. It was with
some concern, and no little foreboding, that many viewed its
gradual supersession of the old system of labor. Its material
benefits might perhaps be admitted, though even these remained
to be proved, but what was most feared was the moral degra-
dation of the community. If this was to be the price of industrial progress, New England of all places would reject it.
To overcome these doubts and justify the new system by its
results, both financial and social, was the chief desire of the
manufacturer. The sabbath school established by Samuel
Slater in connection with his factories in Rhode Island, though
not first in America in point of date, as has been claimed, was
undoubtedly first in influence, and formed a precedent for such
institutions elsewhere.

The effort to surround the operatives in Lowell with a favor-
able moral atmosphere was a distinct advance, and attracted
wide notice.

The improvement of the common schools became an object
of solicitude. Primary schools were made part of the public
school system. Between 1826 and 1830 the governors of the
New England States, and some others, directed particular
attention to educational improvement. The education of the
artisan was felt to be essential. The establishment of Mechanics' Institutes in 1821, and the introduction of the Lyceum,
with free or popular scientific lectures, in 1826, indicate the
tone of public sentiment. Modified plans of higher education
which should give the artisan class a wider opportunity were
eagerly discussed, and technical schools, notably the Rensselaer

Institute at Troy, were founded, in which science as applied to the useful arts should form the basis of instruction.

These are all features contemporary with the change in the industrial system. Let it not be supposed that in 1830 much that was definite had been accomplished. Though the workman was better clothed, better fed, had more constant employment, had a broader outlook and a brighter hope for the future than in 1800, yet fifty years of industrial progress were necessary to the realization of many things then suggested for his relief. His sure guarantee for their final accomplishment lay in the fact that they had come to be suggested, and that discussion had largely turned from theological or political subjects to those departments of social and industrial life in which he had an ever present and vital interest. We merely point out in passing that coeval with the change in the industrial system and the introduction of machinery the workman began to rise in importance as a social factor. The impetus was given. The results we shall summarize hereafter.

The new system of production exerted an immediate and continued influence to increase the productive capacity of the workmen and to decrease the price of product to the consumers, of whom the workmen formed no inconsiderable part.

At Newburyport in hosiery weaving, by the use of the power stocking loom, the capacity of the female operative was increased ten times.

In textiles the greatest advance was made. In 1833 a weaver fifteen years of age, with a young assistant, could perform nine times as much work in a given time as could be performed by a man in 1803. Merrimac prints, which in 1825 averaged 25.07 cents per yard at the factory, declined to 16.36 cents by 1830. The cotton fabric made at Waltham, a staple article, bears the following quotations for the years succeeding the introduction of the power loom:

Year.		Price per yard.
1816,	. . . .	30 cents.
1819,	. . . .	21 cents.
1826,	. . . .	13 cents.
1829,	. . . .	8½ cents.

It was destined to decline to 6½ cents by 1843.*

* Cf. "The Introduction of the Power Loom," by Nathan Appleton.

The introduction of the brick machine made it possible to produce with one machine 25,000 bricks in 12 hours ready for the kiln.

By the pin machines the labor of 59 persons was saved through ingenious self-acting mechanism by which one operative performed the work of sixty unaided hands.

Paper was cheapened and improved by several inventions. Machinery had not yet affected the boot and shoe industry, which was one of the last to come under its influence.

The cost of a musket at the Springfield armory was reduced over 13 per cent between 1815 and 1829. The price of hooks and eyes was in 30 years reduced from $1.50 per gross to 15 @ 20 cents.

In the manufacture of machinery, also, increased skill and improved facilities had cheapened the product. Thus cotton machinery cost in the United States, in 1810, four times as much as in England, but in 1826 its cost was but 50 or 60 per cent more.

The early factory buildings often comprised six or seven stories, each story being low and poorly ventilated. Stoves were used for heating. The arrangements for artificial lighting were poor, although gas was now coming into general use. In the artisan's home anthracite coal was displacing wood as fuel, grates for its use having been introduced between 1825 and 1830.

Though the rate of wages during this transition period may show an apparent increase over that prior to 1815, it should be borne in mind that in the years immediately following the peace of 1815 the tenure of employment was very insecure and the annual earnings of the workingmen seriously affected. The relation of prices to money wages in each year should also be noted in any comparative estimate of the wage earner's condition.

We have already alluded to the distress among workingmen owing to the unsettled state of manufactures between 1815 and 1824. In connection with the wages and prices, given in the succeeding tables, it is proper to note more in detail the effect produced upon them by the disturbed industrial conditions.

The excess of importations over exports after the peace caused an efflux of specie, which, together with the violent contraction of paper currency between 1815 and 1819, its

volume being reduced about 59 per cent, and the prevailing depression in manufacturing on account of unlimited imports, combined to greatly reduce prices. As an instance, flour, a leading staple, fell from about $15 in 1817 to about $6 in 1819.

In Rhode Island, Pennsylvania, and New York the suffering among workingmen was most felt, although the depression was universal. The following from the report of a committee of the citizens of Philadelphia, October, 1819, throws some light on the state of affairs in that vicinity:

"In thirty out of sixty branches of manufacture there had been a reduction from the average of 1814 and 1816, in the number of persons employed, from 9,425 to 2,137; in their weekly wages, from $58,340 to $12,822; and in their annual earnings from $3,033,799 to $666,744. The actual loss of wages was therefore $2,366,935 per annum; and supposing the materials equal to their wages, the loss of productive industry in a single district, not forty miles in diameter, was $7,333,870.

"In the cotton manufacture the hands were reduced from 2,325 in 1816 to 149; in book printing, from 241 to 170; in the potteries, from 132 to 27; in the woollen branch, from 1,226 to 260; in iron castings, from 1,152 to 52; in paper hangings and cards, from 189 to 82. In the paper manufacture in their vicinity the hands were reduced from 950, in 1816, to 175, and their annual wages from $247,000 to $45,900; the annual production from $760,000 to $136,000." *

A committee of citizens of Pittsburgh, in December, 1819, reported:

"The whole number of hands employed in that town and vicinity, in 1815, to have been 1,960, and the value of their manufactures $2,617,833. In 1819 the hands numbered only 672 and the value of their manufactures was $832,000. In the steam engine factories the workmen were reduced from 290 to 24, and the value of their work from $300,000 to $40,000. In glass works and glass cutting the hands were reduced from 169 to 40, and the product from $235,000 to $35,000; the reduction in flint glass alone having been $75,000. In the manufacture of cotton, wire, umbrellas, yellow queensware, pipes, and linen, there was no longer a single hand employed." †

After the tariff act of 1824, however, a revival of manufacturing took place.

The following comparative showing exhibits wages in England, France, and the United States, in certain employments in

* History of American Manufactures. Bishop. Vol. II., p. 250.
† Ibid.

825, and also the average price of wheat per bushel in each country. It is taken from White's Memoir of Samuel Slater, and is said to have been compiled with great care from the results of personal inquiries:

Comparative Wages in England, France, and the United States.

1825.

[Expressed in United States money.]

EMPLOYMENTS.	Basis.	ENGLAND.	FRANCE.	UNITED STATES.
Common laborer,	day	$0.74	$0.37 to 0.40	$1.00
Carpenter,	"	.97	.55 to .75	1.45
Mason,	"	1.10	.60 to .80	1.62
Farm laborer (with board),	mo.	6.50	4.00 to 6.00	$8.00 to 10.00
Domestic servant (female, with board),	wk.	.67	– –	1.00 to 1.50
Machinists and forgers (best),	day	1.94	– –	1.50 to 1.75
Machinists and forgers (ordinary),	"	1.10	.92	1.25 to 1.42
Mule spinners (cotton),	"	1.02	.80 to .90	1.08 to 1.40
Spinners (woollen),	"	.94	.40 to .50	1.08
Weavers (on hand looms),	"	.74	.37 to .50	.90
Boys (age 10 to 12 years),	wk.	1.30	.85 to 1.00	1.50
Females (in cotton mills, average),	"	1.96	1.48 to 2.00	2.00 to 3.00
Females (in woollen mills, average),	"	1.96	1.50	2.50
Price of wheat (average),	bush.	$1.79	$1.17	$0.96* @ $0.49†

* New York.   † Pittsburgh.

Before leaving this period, it should be noted that after 1820 foreign immigration became active. The growth of the population from this source has had a marked effect on the condition of labor in America.

The following table shows the progress of immigration in the United States, and, for convenience, is carried forward to 1850:

Progress of Immigration in the United States.*

PERIODS.	Number of Immigrants arriving during period specified.	Estimated Increase of Immigrants and Descendants during period specified.	Estimated Increase during period specified of Immigrants and Descendants arriving in previous periods.	Total Immigrants and Descendants in country at end of each period.
1790–1810,	120,000	47,560	–	167,560
1810–1820,	114,000	19,000	58,450	359,010
1820–1830,	203,979	35,728	134,130	732,847
1830–1840,	762,369	129,602	254,445	1,879,263
1840–1850,	1,521,850	183,942	719,361	4,304,416

* From data contained in "Progress of the United States of America," by R. S. Fisher.

THE PRESENT INDUSTRIAL PERIOD.

The period since 1830 presents two important features:

I.   The first to be considered is the development of invention.   This is manifested in two directions, i. e., the application of natural forces in labor saving machines, and the adaptation of natural products to human wants.   The results of invention in this latter direction have much enlarged the comforts of life by increasing the range of products available for food and clothing.   Of this class of inventions among the leading, if not themselves the chief examples in industrial importance, are those which utilized caoutchouc gum.   The rubber industry arose soon after 1830, and in its various branches has become of considerable importance.   Six rubber companies were in existence in Massachusetts in 1835.   The state of the industry from 1855 to 1875 was as follows, all values being in gold:

YEARS.	EMPLOYÉS.	CAPITAL.	PRODUCT.
1855, ...	462	$438,000	$968,000
1865, ...	1,055	1,019,108	1,788,736
1875, ...	1,054	1,596,166	3,021,246

The United States Census of 1880 disclosed in Massachusetts 27 establishments manufacturing rubber and elastic goods, the invested capital being $3,077,000; the product for the census year was $6,990,856, representing the work of 3,494 employés who were paid $1,145,170 in wages.

In another direction this branch of invention has done much to prevent waste by utilizing refuse products, such, for instance, as the residuum of gas works; each new invention forming the basis of a new industry, besides enlarging the range of articles available for the uses of man.

In the application of natural forces in labor saving machinery, the introduction of the sewing machine was in many respects the most important epoch of this period.   This invention in its practical form belongs to the decade following 1840, and the manufacture of the machines alone added $5,605,345 to the product returned in the National Census of 1860.

The industrial effect of this invention, and in varying degrees of all similar machines, was well set forth by Mr. Kennedy, the Superintendent of the Eighth Census of the United States, in his preliminary report, as follows :

"It has opened avenues to profitable and healthful industry for thousands of industrious females to whom the labors of the needle had become wholly unremunerative and injurious in their effects. Like all automatic powers, it has enhanced the comforts of every class by cheapening the process of manufacture of numerous articles of prime necessity, without permanently subtracting from the average means of support of any portion of the community. It has added a positive increment to the permanent wealth of the country by creating larger and more varied applications of capital and skill in the several branches to which it is auxiliary. * * * * * * * Among the branches of industry which have been signally promoted by the introduction of the sewing machine is the manufacture of men's and women's clothing. * * * * * The increase of this manufacture has been general throughout the Union, and in the four cities of New York, Philadelphia, Cincinnati and Boston, amounted in value to nearly forty and one-quarter millions of dollars, or over 83 per cent of the product of the whole Union in 1850."

This meant more employment for labor, and greater variety in the wardrobe at lower prices for the public.

Improvements in printing presses also had a direct effect in extending the use of books and newspapers, and therefore upon the paper and printing industries. In 1860, Massachusetts alone produced paper of the value of $5,968,469, or 58 per cent of the product of the whole country in 1850. The value of book, job and newspaper printing in New England, the Middle and Western States, in 1860, reached $39,428,043, while the product of the same industries for the same states in 1850 was but $11,586,549.

The following table shows the wonderful increase in inventions during this period. It exhibits the business of the United States patent office from 1837 to 1860.

YEARS.	Applications filed.	Caveats issued.	Patents issued.
1837–1840,	–	–	1,853
1841–1845,	4,718	1,750	2,547
1846–1850,	8,579	2,785	3,916
1851–1855,	15,329	4,431	6,773
1856–1860,	28,973	5,158	18,479
Totals,	57,599	14,124	33,568

We have not the space, nor is this the place, to follow the course of invention farther, but it is pertinent to our subject to notice the effect of machinery, and of the modern industrial system which has been made possible by the aid of machinery, upon the condition of labor. This can be most clearly seen in the two leading industries, boots and shoes, and cotton goods.

The boot and shoe industry was one of the latest to come under the influence of machinery, but the change wrought by its introduction has been complete.

The entire shoe was formerly made by the same artisan, a small group of men often working together in a little one-story shop. Piece work was the custom, and it still prevails. In early times workmen were paid 15, 20, 25, or 30 cents a pair, according to the kind of shoe, and even higher prices for extra quality work. The average workman by twelve hours' labor could earn about a dollar. Women closers and binders working by hand could average about twenty cents a day.

Men living in towns adjacent to Lynn, then as now a centre of the industry, would walk to their employer's place of business for stock and in about a week return the finished shoes, frequently receiving their wages in store orders. The wages earned continually fluctuated, being always subject to individual bargains with employers.

The introduction of machinery occurred about 1860. The industry is now conducted in large, well lighted, thoroughly ventilated factories, equipped with a number of ingenious inventions, each shoe being the result of the successive operations of numerous workmen.

In 1845 the labor of each operative employed in Massachusetts produced slightly more than 455 pairs of boots and shoes. In 1875 the labor of each operative produced 1,205 pairs. In 1850 the average annual wage paid each operative in the United States was $205.43; in 1870 the average wage had become $370.81 gold; in 1875, in Massachusetts, $362.30 gold; in 1880, in the United States, $381.07 gold; in Massachusetts in the same year, $397.70; the average in each case being based upon the total amount of wages paid to the total number of operatives.

In 1855 hand workmen earned from six to seven and a half

dollars a week when constantly employed. In 1860, after the advent of machinery, it has been shown by a special investigation of this Bureau that the average weekly wages of workmen were from $10.50 to $18.00, and of women from $5.50 to $8.25 ; in 1872, of men from $14.22 to $22.22, and of women, $8.89 ; in 1878, of men from $8.00 to $19.50, of women, $7.33 to $8.00.

Since 1878 a slight decrease is observable in the rate of average weekly wages, as compared with 1860, owing partly to the fact that the sudden expansion of the trade in the years immediately following the introduction of machinery carried wages to an exceptionally high point. In 1850, 105,254 persons were employed in the industry in the United States, 32,949 being females. In 1880, 133,819 found employment, 29,798 being females and children.

In this branch of manufacture, therefore, more persons are employed than before the era of machinery, female labor has diminished, wages have been raised, and the productive capacity of the operatives largely increased, while working time has been diminished and the surroundings of the workmen improved.

Certain hand workmen, who have been unable to adapt themselves to the new conditions, have of course suffered. They have found it more difficult to obtain work and have had their wages reduced from year to year, as the machine-made shoes have gradually monopolized the market. Respecting the condition of the industry in the aggregate, however, our summary is conclusive.

Turning now to the cotton industry, we present in the following table statistics of its progress from 1831 to 1880 in the States of Maine, New Hampshire, Massachusetts, Rhode Island, and Connecticut.

These five States are the manufacturing States of New England, which is the leading cotton manufacturing district of the United States. The statistics for 1831 are from the report of a convention which secured data during that year on the manufactures of the country, while those for 1880 are from the United States census, except the statistics of wages, which are averages from returns covering 18 leading mills in Maine ; 6 in New Hampshire ; 25 in Massachusetts ; 10 in

Rhode Island, and 37 in Connecticut, secured during a special investigation undertaken by the Bureau in 1880.

Progress of the Cotton Industry: 1831 to 1880.

CLASSIFICATION.	Maine.	New Hampshire.	Massa-chusetts.	Rhode Island.	Connecticut.
1831.					
Capital invested, . . .	$765,000	$5,300,000	$12,891,000	$6,262,340	$2,825,000
Number of spindles, . . .	6,500	113,776	339,777	235,753	115,528
of looms, . . .	91	3,530	8,981	5,773	2,609
Product in pounds,* . . .	525,000	7,255,060	22,108,428	9,271,481	6,099,900
Men employed, ...	84	875	2,665	1,731	1,399
Average wages per week, .	$5.50	$6.25	$7.00	$5.25	$4.50
Women employed, . . .	205	4,090	10,678	3,297	2,477
Average wages per week, .	$2.33	$2.60	$2.25	$2.20	$2.20
Children { Under 12 years of employed, { age, . . . }	–	60	–	3,472	439
Average wages per week, .	–	$2.00	–	$1.50	$1.50
1880.					
Capital invested, . . .	$15,292,078	$19,877,084	$72,291,601	$28,047,331	$20,310,500
Number of spindles, . . .	695,924	944,053	4,236,084	1,764,569	936,376
of looms, . . .	15,971	24,299	95,321	29,669	18,261
Product in pounds, . . .	44,352,698	63,881,540	219,160,105	60,905,642	42,285,517
Men employed, { 16 years of age and over, . }	3,149	3,917	18,700	6,690	5,363
Average wages per week, .	$7.43	$7.41	$8.31	$9.05	$7.71
Women em- { 15 years of age ployed, { and over, . }	6,481	9,594	31,496	9,199	5,434
Average wages per week, .	$5.91	$5.45	$5.68	$6.37	$5.40
Children { Males under 16, . employed, { Females under 15, }	1,420	1,697	7,570	3,930	2,916
Average wages per week, .	$2.68	$3.08	$3.10	$3.30	$3.28

* Including yarn and cloth.

An analysis of this table affords some interesting results.

To bring these clearly before the reader we present a series of supplementary tables. The first of these relates to the productive capacity of the operatives at each period.

Productive Capacity of Cotton Mill Operatives.

STATES.	Number of Spindles per operative.			Product per operative, in pounds.		
	1831.	**1880.**	Percentage of Increase.	**1831.**	**1880.**	Percentage of Increase.
Maine, ...	22.5	63	180	1,817	4,014	121
New Hampshire, . . .	22.6	62.1	175	1,443	4,201	191
Massachusetts, . . .	25.5	73.3	187	1,656	3,794	129
Rhode Island, . . .	27.7	89	221	1,091	3,073	182
Connecticut, . . .	26.8	68	154	1,413	3,084	118
Average, . . .	25.02	71.08	184	1,484	3,633	145

By this table it appears that while in 1831 one operative was required on the average for every 25.02 spindles, in 1880, owing to perfected machinery, improved processes of manufacture and the development of individual skill, but one operative

was required for 71.08 spindles, being an increase of 184 per cent in the average number of spindles per operative during 50 years. The table also shows that, owing to this greater command of productive machinery, the product per operative, measured in pounds, has risen from an average of 1,484 pounds in 1831 to 3,633 pounds in 1880, an increase of 145 per cent.

The foregoing comparison of product is made on the basis of pounds, the pound being considered the fairest unit of measurement, inasmuch as it covers the entire product, whether sold as yarn or cloth, while the product in yards would cover cloth only. It is of course apparent that the weight of product resulting from a given output of labor would depend upon the fineness of the product spun or woven; hence, the comparisons of product in the table are of value as averages only, it being impossible to take into account the quality of the product.

The next table affords a comparison of the productive capacity of the operatives upon the more conclusive basis of value.

Increase of Product per Operative: 1850 to 1880.

STATES.	Net Product per Operative. 1850.	Net Product per Operative. 1880.	Percentage of Increase.
Maine, ...	$283 83	$510 18	80
New Hampshire, ...	331 82	476 15	43
Massachusetts, ...	351 73	592 62	68
Rhode Island, ...	276 91	499 84	81
Connecticut, ...	262 35	555 14	112
Average, ...	301 33	526 79	75

In this table the comparison is made between the years 1850 and 1880, as the value of product for 1831 is not obtainable; and *net* product, that is to say, the amount of product less the value of materials of manufacture, is taken as the basis of comparison. It will be noticed that the net product per operative, in 1880, with Massachusetts working under a ten-hour law, is greater in that State than in any of the others named, although the operatives in the other States work longer hours. This greater net product in 1880 is, of course, due to various influences, because the net product per operative in 1850 was greater in Massachusetts than in any other State

named. It is important, however, to know that Massachusetts by the adoption of the ten-hour law has not lost her rank in net product per operative.

This value of net product is divisible into the following items : rent, freights, insurance, interest on loans, interest on capital, commissions, wages, and the profits of the manufacturer.

In other words, in 1850, after deducting from the total value of product the cost of materials of manufacture, there remains a product value resulting from the labor of that year amounting on the average to $301.33 per operative. In 1880 this net product had risen to $526.79 per operative, showing an increase of 75 per cent in the productive capacity of the operative when the results of his labor are measured in dollars.

If this increase in the value created per operative over the cost of materials is shown between 1850 and 1880, a much greater increase would undoubtedly be shown between 1831 and 1880, inasmuch as the difference in skill, processes, and machinery is broader between the latter than between the former periods, and the results of this difference would therefore be more apparent. But assuming the increase between 1831 and 1880 to be identical with that between 1850 and 1880, — a fair assumption because manifestly within the limits of actual fact, let us next inquire what change has taken place in wages during this period. This query is answered by the data presented in the following table :

Percentages of Increase in Wages of Cotton Mill Operatives: 1831 to 1880.

STATES.	Men's Wages. Percentage of increase.	Women's Wages. Percentage of increase.	Children's Wages. Percentage of increase.	General Average. Percentage of increase.
Maine, ...	35	154	–	97
New Hampshire, . .	19	110	54	76
Massachusetts, ...	19	152	–	108
Rhode Island, ...	72	190	120	163
Connecticut, ...	71	145	119	104
Average, ...	38	149	115	115

Average Hours of Labor, 1831, — 12 hours 18 minutes.
1880, — 10 hours 52 minutes. Decrease, about 12 per cent.

From this table it is seen that, between 1831 and 1880, men's wages increased 38 per cent; women's wages 149 per cent; and

children's wages 115 per cent, or an average increase on all classes of labor of 115 per cent.

The average daily hours of labor, notwithstanding this increase in wages, have in the same time decreased about 12 per cent.

The average price of heavy sheetings per yard in 1829 was 8½ cents; of printed calicoes, 17 cents.* In 1880 heavy sheetings had declined to 7½ cents, a decrease of 11.8 per cent; printed calicoes to 7 cents, a decrease of 58.8 per cent.

Thus, to make a concise summary of the results brought out in these tables relating to the cotton industry in five leading cotton manufacturing States, it appears that since 1831 the productive capacity of the operative, measured in pounds of product, has increased 145 per cent; that this product is secured by the development of skill and by improved processes and machinery whereby 184 per cent more spindles are controlled by the average operative in 12 per cent less time, and that measured in net value of product the productive capacity of the operative has increased 75 per cent while the cost of product has been materially reduced to the consumer, and that, notwithstanding the decrease in working time, wages have increased 97 per cent.

The following table of general averages exhibits the increase in wages in nine leading industries, viz.: Agricultural implements; boots and shoes; cotton goods; carpentering; clothing; iron manufactures; paper; woollen goods; nails, tacks, and spikes. Each of these industries shows an increase in average money wages paid, the greatest increase appearing in the clothing trade, viz.: from $155.53 in 1850 to $282.79 in 1880. The percentage of net product paid to the workman as wages at each period is also shown by the table. It appears, for instance, that while 64.2 per cent of net product went to labor in the agricultural implement industry in 1850, but 35.3 per cent was thus apportioned in 1880, although the money wages of the laborer increased. Other industries exhibit the same feature of decrease in the percentage of net product paid as wages accompanied by an increase in money wages, but the ratio of decrease is different in each industry. Three in-

---

* Report on the Factory System of the United States, by Carroll D. Wright, in U. S. Census of 1880.

dustries, however, — carpentering, iron manufactures, and paper — show not only an increased average wage but also an increase in the share of net product paid out as wages.

Advance in Wages: 1850 to 1880.

INDUSTRIES.	Average Wages. 1850.	Average Wages. 1880.	Percentage of Net Product paid as Wages. 1850.	Percentage of Net Product paid as Wages. 1880.
Agricultural implements,	$368 04	$376 05	64.2	35.3
Boots and shoes,*	205 43	381 07	71.8	62.3
Cotton goods,	199 40	258 19	68.0	43.6
Carpentering,*	366 40	454 06	56.7	57.7
Clothing,*	155 53	282 79	66.6	27.8
Iron manufactures,	352 83	400 76	50.0	66.2
Paper,	221 32	345 18	34.3	41.3
Woollen goods,	228 71	315 69	62.1	43.3
Nails, tacks, and spikes,	343 47	414 69	61.9	56.9

* The statistics are for Massachusetts, except in respect to Boots and Shoes, Carpentering, and Clothing. For the latter industries the statistics for the United States are presented, the requisite data for Massachusetts alone not being available.

The next presentation exhibits the change in the amount of capital required per dollar of net product in the same industries.

Relation of Capital to Net Product: 1850 and 1880.

INDUSTRIES.	Amount of Capital per dollar of Net Product. 1850.	Amount of Capital per dollar of Net Product. 1880.	Percentage of Increase or Decrease.
Agricultural implements,	$1 20	$0 88	— 26.7
Boots and shoes,*	43	66	+ 53.5
Cotton goods,	3 38	1 01	— 70.1
Carpentering,*	33	46	+ 39.4
Clothing,*	55	47	— 14.5
Iron manufactures,	1 73	1 73	–
Paper,	1 66	1 96	+ 18.1
Woollen goods,	2 22	1 43	— 35.6
Nails, tacks, and spikes,	1 71	2 02	+ 18.1

* See note at foot of previous table.

It will be seen that in agricultural implements, cotton goods, clothing, and woollen goods, the ratio of capital to net product has decreased; in boots and shoes, carpentering, paper, and nails, tacks, and spikes it has increased, while in iron manufactures the ratio remains unchanged.

From these two tables it is shown that in boots and shoes, for instance, the average money wages of the laborer have increased from $205.43 to $381.07, while his share of net product has decreased from 71.8 per cent to 62.3 per cent. But the

relative amount of capital invested to secure this net product increased 53.5 per cent. While, therefore, the laborer received in 1880 a less share of net product, out of which both the laborer and the capitalist are remunerated, than he received in 1850, the decline in his share is partly offset by the increase of interest account, also paid from net product, which increase is made necessary by the relative increase of capital invested. The same thing is true in the manufacture of nails, tacks, and spikes, and in carpentering. In the manufacture of paper, however, not only have the laborer's money wages liberally increased but his relative share of net product has also increased, and this increase has taken place despite the fact that the capital invested for every dollar of this product in 1880 was more than 18 per cent more than that in 1850. In iron manufactures money wages and the laborer's share of net product have increased, while the ratio of capital to net product has not changed.

In cotton goods, on the contrary, although the money wages of the laborer have largely increased, a less relative share of the net product goes to wages than in 1850, although productive processes have been so perfected and machinery so ingeniously adjusted as to render it possible to make a dollar's worth of net product to-day with over 70 per cent less capital than was required to accomplish the same result in 1850. The same is true, in less degree, in agricultural implements, clothing, and woollen goods. The obvious inference is that in these industries the ratio of increase of profits outruns that of increase of wages.

Net product, or value of product remaining after deducting value of raw materials of manufacture, represents the direct result of the productive forces in the given industry; or, in other words, it represents the value created over and above the value of raw materials by the effective operation of labor and capital united.

The value of net product forms, as we have said, a fund divisible into interest on capital, interest on loans, insurance, freights, rents, commissions, wages, and profits. Now if the relative share paid to labor in the form of wages is decreased, it is, of course, obvious that the share remaining for the other purposes mentioned is increased. If capital is also relatively

decreased, then it is fair to suppose that the share chargeable to interest is also diminished. It is well known that the relative cost of freights and insurance has decreased. Allowing, then, for a possible increase in rents and commissions, it would seem probable that, in the industries last examined, the share drawn out as profits has relatively increased, though such an assumption is perhaps unwarranted in the absence of definite data. It is, however, clearly inferential from the tables.

It is well established that the proportionate cost of labor in the finished fabric has been greatly reduced through the use of machinery. This reduction of actual labor cost has been an important element, in reducing the price of product to the consumer, while permitting at the same time a liberal increase of wages to the laborer. An examination of these two tables would, we think, lead to the conclusion that although in every case money wages have considerably increased, yet in certain industries in which the principles of the factory system (i. e., sub-division of labor, co-ordination of processes, and the application of a series of mutually dependent and practically automatic machines) have been most effective, such, for instance, as in the cotton and woollen industries, the relative share of net product gained by the workman tends to decrease. That is to say, in these industries perfection of machines and processes constantly tends to create a larger product with less capital, and the ratio of increase in productive capacity tends to outrun the ratio of increase in wages, so that of this larger product labor obtains a less relative share, although it is produced at less expenditure of time and effort, and rewarded by a constantly increasing wage.

From the following presentation which exhibits the same data for all the industries in the United States, for 1850 and 1880, it appears that, when the field is broadened so as to include the entire manufacturing industries of the country, labor's share of net product has declined from 51 to 48.1 per cent. This slight decrease, however, is more than offset by the relative increase in capital.

Ratio of Wages to Net Product: 1850 and 1880.

THE UNITED STATES.	Average Wages. 1850.	Average Wages. 1880.	Percentage of net product paid as Wages. 1850.	Percentage of net product paid as Wages. 1880.
All industries, ...	$247.11	$346.91	51	48.1

Ratio of Capital to Net Product: 1850 and 1880.

THE UNITED STATES.	Amount of Capital per dollar of net product. 1850.	Amount of Capital per dollar of net product. 1880.	Percentage of Increase.
All industries, ...	$1.15	$1.41	22.6

It appears probable, then, that when all industries are considered money wages have not only increased, but that a slight increase has also taken place in the relative share of net product secured by labor after payment of interest on capital invested.

Through the introduction of machinery ignorant labor is utilized, not created, as some have supposed. That is, opportunity is made for the entrance into higher and better paid employments of those who before were confined to the lowest grade of purely manual labor. The lowest industrial class is thus raised in the social scale, for, as it is congregated in factory towns, it is brought into a new intellectual and moral atmosphere. The children of such a class are under these influences given wider privileges.

This is not a matter of theory. The change has been completely shown in the development of the cotton industry in Massachusetts, and has often been pointed out. In the beginning the daughters of American farmers and mechanics formed a large proportion of the operatives. It opened up for them a chance for remunerative employment which they gladly embraced. They brought to the work a degree of intelligence and culture which their successors have not shown because it is not now demanded. As machinery became more automatic and greater perfection of processes was attained, an operative class of less general intelligence took their place, while the young American found employments requiring greater individual skill.

Speaking broadly, the textile factory population of the State

has in this way presented three successive phases as to nationality, first, American; second, Irish and English; third, and the present, French Canadian. Each class found the factory a rise in the scale of employment, and each, except of course the last, gradually passed from factory labor into other pursuits. In fact already French Canadians are found engaged in agriculture and many other callings outside of the factory.

The constant establishment of new industries under the influence of machinery has aided the mobility of labor here indicated; the increase in aggregate earnings, with its complement, the savings bank system, has enabled the operative class gradually to amass sufficient capital for the acquisition of land or for other profitable uses,* while the free educational system has raised the intelligence of the children and fitted them to pass from the factory to other and better paid pursuits.

The allegation often made that we have a fixed factory population as a result of the modern organization of labor is therefore neither fair nor philosophical. Labor to-day, under the conditions obtaining in the United States, is less fixed than ever before. The growth of the country through immigration certainly shows that with modern facilities for travel it is not fixed geographically, while as to employment, although it is undoubtedly true that of a given number of operatives few ever change their occupation, yet when periods are compared it is found that the status of the industrial population is constantly changing, the narrow stream entering at the bottom diffusing into broader channels at the top.

This mobility of labor, brought about by the rise in intelligence of the laboring class and the development of industrial skill by which new industries are originated, occurring at a time

---

* The following, based upon data contained in the report of the Commissioners of Savings Banks, shows the condition of such banks in Massachusetts in 1884:

Number of open accounts on books of savings banks,	826,008
Amount of deposits,	$262,720,146.97
Average for each account,	$318.06
Estimated population of Massachusetts, 1884,	2,000,000
Number of persons to each open account,	2.42
Average deposit for each person in the Commonwealth,	$131.36

The amount thus deposited in savings institutions has been loaned in part to aid small owners to build houses, and in part to manufacturing companies as working capital. Post office banks if established might, equally with savings banks, induce savings, but the *lending* feature of our savings bank system is of the greatest importance socially and industrially. This, however, seldom attracts attention. — *Edward Atkinson.*

when, as in the United States, land is easily obtainable, is a marked characteristic of the present century, and that this mobility is secured together with increased wages to the workman and cheaper product to the consumer is a sufficient indication of industrial progress.

But, it may be asked, if the lowest labor is constantly being raised under the modern industrial system, will not a dearth arise of workmen willing to remain in the lowest employments? In reply it should be said that machinery constantly tends to narrow the range of purely manual labor. While certain operations can never be performed by machines, these are operations requiring a high, not a low grade of skill. The irksome labor of the world is largely coming to be performed by machinery. It is just here that its labor saving power is most apparent. Invention has not abolished labor. On the contrary, it has created new industries by stimulating new wants. But to a great degree it has overcome the necessity for a purely manual class. The hewing of wood, the drawing of water, the making of brick, tunnelling, dredging, all employments in the past restricted to laborers weak in intelligence and strong in muscle have now come under its influence. The demand for a purely manual class is constantly decreasing.

II. The second important feature of the period from 1830 to 1860 is the change that has taken place in the status of the laborer before the law. We have elsewhere given a complete summary of labor legislation in Massachusetts from 1833 to 1875 * and shall here present a digest merely, without detailing the discussions which preceded or the immediate causes which led to the passage of the various acts. The legislation embraces the following subjects : —

Abolishment of imprisonment for debt; various acts providing for the instruction of youth employed in manufacturing establishments ; various acts to secure to mechanics and laborers their payment for labor by a lien on real estate ; fixing the hours of labor for women and certain minors in manufacturing establishments at 60 per week ; relating to contracts for labor ; requiring belting, dangerous machinery, and hatchways in fac-

* Seventh Annual Report. See also "Labor Laws of the Commonwealth of Massachusetts," compiled by the Bureau, containing the existing Statutes on the subject of labor.

tories to be guarded; fire escapes to be provided; unsafe eleva-
tors prohibited, and authorizing the appointment of inspectors
of factories; providing for weekly payments to laborers in the
employ of cities; requiring seats for the use of females
employed in manufacturing, mechanical, and mercantile establishments; limiting the contract employment of prisoners in
certain industries; exempting from attachment the tools of
mechanics to the amount of $300; regulating the employment
of children in manufacturing establishments; authorizing the
formation of co-operative associations and exempting from
attachment of shares therein to the amount of $20; exempting
the wages of wife and minor children from attachment;
appointing commissions to investigate the condition of the
industrial classes, and, finally, establishing the bureau of statistics of labor; providing for ventilation, fire escapes, etc., in
tenement and lodging houses; authorizing the establishment of
industrial schools; providing for cheap transportation on rail-
roads for workingmen; authorizing towns to support public
libraries; requiring the maintenance of evening schools in certain
towns; authorizing instruction in schools in the use of hand
tools; providing for free text books and supplies in the public
schools; incorporating an industrial school for girls; relating to
loan and fund associations and co-operative banks; relating to
a fund for the promotion of education and the mechanic arts;
incorporating labor reform, co-operative building, and industrial associations; modifying the apprentice law by repealing
imprisonment and substituting a bond; appropriating money
for the representation of the industries of the Commonwealth
at industrial expositions; appropriating money to aid a school
of industrial science, with a proviso for free instruction; preventing the appearance of children under 15 as acrobats, etc.;
providing for special statistics from time to time on industrial
subjects, and, by means of the census, for industrial statistics
at decennial periods; regulating deposits in savings banks;
preventing persons or corporations from making special contracts with employés by which the latter exempt their employers from liability in case of accident to themselves while at
work; requiring contractors on public buildings or works to
give bonds or security for themselves and sub-contractors that
materials and labor shall be paid for; forbidding detention in

city almshouses of children after they reach the age of four years; providing that in cases of insolvency the wages of clerks and servants, to the amount of $100, shall be paid in full; fixing the responsibility of railroad corporations for negligently causing the death of employés; prohibiting the locking of factory doors during working hours; requiring railroad companies to use safety couplers; regulating the use of explosive compounds in factories; and requiring the compulsory vaccination of operatives.

As the grand result of this legislation, the legal hours of employment for women, and minors under 18 years, in factories, are fixed at 60 per week; no child under ten is to be employed in any manufacturing, mechanical, or mercantile establishment, and no child under twelve during school hours; no minor under eighteen can be legally employed more than 60 hours per week in any mercantile establishment; imprisonment for debt is abolished; a lien law is provided; the necessary tools of a mechanic are exempted from attachment; the trustee process is curtailed; proper fire escapes are to be maintained in factories and tenements; co-operative associations are authorized; regulations for the protection of life and health in factories are provided, and the inspection of factories required; and, finally, educational facilities have been broadened and made perfectly free as regards both instruction and text books.

Without specific legislation ten hours have come to be the maximum day's work in most industries; the rule in a few industries is eight hours.

THE WAGES AND PRICES TABLES. 1752 to 1860.

In the tables which follow, wages and prices are given for the years included in the period from 1752 to 1860. As has been already stated at the beginning of this Part, these wages and prices were secured by an examination of a large number of bills, day-books, and ledgers, containing the accounts of the daily transactions of large country stores at different intervals; of memorandum, pass, and family account books; of general family expense books, farm accounts, and manuscript material obtained from original sources by agents of the Bureau, in various sections of the State.

Through the courtesy of the persons in whose possession these books of account were found, the greater part of this examination was made at this office, the books being loaned for the purpose, and an excellent opportunity was thus afforded for a most careful and systematic investigation and classification of wages and prices for the years named. In many instances, however, where it was not convenient to allow the use of these account books for office examination, agents of the Bureau were accorded the privilege of making copies of such portions of these old " accounts" as seemed necessary to ensure complete-ness of detail, and in this way, also, much valuable material was added to that already obtained from the sources referred to above.

From the great mass of material so courteously placed at the disposal of this office, only that portion was used which fur-nished perfectly plain statements of wages and prices for the years specified. The material used, however, fully covers the different periods comprehended by this investigation of wages and prices, and the results can be accepted as accurate and entirely trustworthy in their nature.

As indicating still further the thoroughness with which this investigation has been conducted, as well as the extent to which it has been carried, it may be well to say that the average wages and prices by years for the various occupations and arti-cles named are based upon over 4,600 statements representing over 9,000 original quotations of wages, and nearly 25,000 statements representing 120,000 original quotations of prices. Of course, as is well known, statistics of prices for any period are much easier to obtain than statistics of wages for the same period. These quotations of wages and prices were obtained from 116 books of account, the original property of individuals, or persons engaged in business at some time, in 56 different towns and cities in the State.

In the earlier years, these wages and prices were originally given, as was the custom at that time, either as " old tenor" or as " lawful money." In some cases, however, this dis-tinction was not carefully made, but the approximation of the amount given for any occupation or article on any given basis to a properly comparative amount given as either old tenor or lawful money will easily determine to which class the

amount in question really belongs, although the evidence was not at hand to enable us to state definitely in every case whether the quotations are given in old tenor or lawful money.

For the convenience of those persons who may wish to make such comparisons, and as a ready means for converting old tenor into lawful money, we reprint portions of a table published as a part of the " Collections of the New Hampshire Historical Society," for the year 1824 (volume I). This table purports to be " A correct Table to bring Old Tenor into Lawful Money, at the rate of dollars, at six shillings per piece, from one penny to twenty shillings Old Tenor." The table was first printed at Boston, in 1750, and is said to be " calculated with exactness, even to the fifteenth part of a farthing." We reprint only such portions as are necessary for the conversion of any number of shillings or pence, the table, as stated above, including all possible combinations of shillings and pence from one penny to twenty shillings Old Tenor. Such combinations, however, can easily be made from the data here given : —

Old Tenor.		Lawful Money.				Old Tenor.		Lawful Money.			
s.	d.	s.	d.	q.	15ths.	s.		s.	d.	q.	15ths.
	1 is				8	5 is			8		
	2			1	1	6			9	2	6
	3			1	9	7			11	0	12
	4			2	2	8		1	0	3	3
	5			2	10	9		1	2	1	9
	6			3	3	10		1	4		
	7			3	11	11		1	5	2	6
	7½		1			12		1	7	0	12
	8		1	0	4	13		1	8	3	3
	9		1	0	12	14		1	10	1	9
	10		1	1	5	15		2			
	11		1	1	13	16		2	1	2	6
1			1	2	6	17		2	3	0	12
2			3	0	12	18		2	4	3	3
3			4	3	3	19		2	6	1	9
4			6	1	9	20		2	8		

From this table we can find the relation which old tenor bears to lawful money. Taking lawful money as the unit, or 100, the ratio for old tenor then becomes as 13.33 is to 100, or, in other words, the relative value of old tenor is two-fifteenths of the value of lawful money.

For an exact comparison of the wages and prices given for the earlier years in pounds, shillings, and pence with those which for succeeding years are given in United States money,

it is necessary to know the equivalent, in dollars and cents, for any value expressed in pounds, shillings, and pence.

It is a matter of history that the colonists at a very early date, while retaining the English form of money, ceased to use the pound sterling as a basis for reckoning. Although their books were still kept in pounds, shillings, and pence, the value of which was variously denominated either as lawful money, or as new, middle, or old tenor to distinguish the forms of the successive issues of colonial paper money, their bills were always made payable in Spanish milled dollars, which, as early as 1652, took the place of English sterling as the money of account. The value of the Spanish dollar, in the colonial currency of the times, varied greatly for the several colonies, the rate for Massachusetts being estimated, in 1782, at six shillings for a silver dollar. In computations of exchange with England, the Spanish dollar was uniformly estimated at 4s. 6d., or fifty-four pence sterling.*

At the establishment of the national mint, by Act of April 2, 1792, the unit of value, or dollar, was made to conform, so far as possible, to the average coin value of the Spanish dollar at that time, which dollar had continued to circulate as the principal money of account and was generally accepted as the standard in all money transactions. By Act of July 31, 1789, by which the values of foreign coins were regulated, the pound sterling was reckoned as $4.44, as compared with the Spanish dollar, this being the exact ratio at which the Spanish dollar was valued at the London mint. The union, therefore, between the values of the Spanish dollar, which had been the colonial money of account, and the dollar adopted by the United States government, in 1792, is complete.

Knowing the proportionate relation of old tenor to lawful money to be as 13.33 is to 100, or two-fifteenths in value, and knowing, also, that lawful money, expressed in shillings, represents six shillings to the Spanish dollar, which coin is the exact equivalent of the unit of value, or dollar, authorized by the United States, in 1792, we find the value of a shilling old tenor to be 2.22 cents, and of a shilling lawful money to be 16.7 cents, in United States currency of the present time.

* H. Linderman, on "Money and Legal Tender."

In that part of the tables devoted to wages, the amounts given for any occupation are, unless otherwise specified, the average wages paid to male day workers. In the "basis" column, however, the fact is always stated whether the amount given represents the work of a person in the occupation specified for a day, week, month, or year, as the case may be. The fact, also, of the wage being "with board" in any instance is so stated; in all other cases, the wages are the amounts received without regard to board.

In the same way, all prices given are average retail prices for the articles named, unless otherwise specified.

The term "wholesale" is used to distinguish the price paid for large quantities of any given article bought at any one time (not necessarily to be sold again) from the strictly retail price paid for the same article, this retail price being the "average" price obtained by the aggregation of a large number of quotations of prices for small quantities of the same article.

In the presentation of both wages and prices, the occupations and articles are arranged alphabetically, this arrangement furnishing the easiest means of comparison from year to year for any given occupation or article.

All "amounts" are average wages or prices for any given "basis," the recognized abbreviation being used, in each instance, to designate the particular time or quantity.

Wages and prices, when graded, are so indicated, the designation "high," "medium high," "medium," "medium low," or "low" being used to mark the comparative grade. Graded prices, however, for certain articles, when they appear in the tables, do not mean always that the range of price was alone due to the varying quality of the article named, for any given basis, but may have been caused wholly by the fluctuation of the price during the year, the difference in price at different periods of the year being so great as to necessitate the division into grades to bring out this point distinctly.

In the tables of wages and prices which follow, wages and prices are given for the following occupations and articles : —

Index to Occupations and Articles.

OCCUPATIONS.
Agricultural laborers.
Blacksmiths.
Bookbinders.
Brewery and distillery employés.
Butchers.
Carpenters.
Carriage makers.
Clockmakers.
Clothing makers.
Cordage makers.
Glass makers.
Gold and silver workers.
Harness makers.
Hat makers.
Laborers.
Machinists.
Masons.
Metal workers.
Millwrights.
Nail makers.
Painters.
Paper mill operatives.
Printers.
Ship and boat builders.
Shoemakers.
Stone quarrymen and cutters.
Tanners and curriers.
Teachers.
Teamsters.
Watchmen.
Wooden goods makers.
Woollen mill operatives.

ARTICLES.
Agricultural Products.
Apples.
Barley.
Beans.
Buckwheat.
Corn.
Cranberries.
Flax.
Flaxseed.
Hops.
Oats.
Onions.
Parsnips.
Peas.
Potatoes.
Rice.
Rye.
Squashes.
Sweet potatoes.
Turnips.
Wheat.
Wool.

Boots, Shoes, and Leather.
Boots.
Buckles.†
Calamanco.
Leather.
Overshoes.†
Rubber boots.†
Rubbers.
Sandals.†
Shoes.
Slippers.
Taps.

Buttons and Dress Trimmings.
Braid.
Buttons.
Fringe.†
Galloon.
Moire antique trimming.†
Tape.

Carpetings.
Bocking.†
Carpetings.†
Mats.†
Oil-cloth.†
Rugs.†

Clothing.
Bonnets.†
Breeches.†
Cloaks.†
Coats.†
Gloves.
Handkerchiefs.
Hats.
Hose.
Mittens.
Mitts.
Overalls.
Overcoats.†
Pantaloons.†
Shawls.†
Socks.
Stockings.
Vests.
Waistcoats.

Cloths.
Broadcloth.
Cassimere.
Circassian cloth.
Cloth.†
Corduroy.
Doeskin.†
Duffel.†
Durant.
Elastic cloth.†
Erminet.
Florentine.
Forest cloth.†
Frieze.†
Frocking.†
Fustian.
Lambskin.
Mixed cloth.
Plain blue cloth.
Plain cloth.
Ratteen.
Sheep's gray cloth.†
Striped woollen cloth.†
Thickset.†
Vestings.†
Wild boar cloth.†

Cutlery.
Knives.†
Knives and forks.†
Knives, pocket.†
Knives, table.†

Dairy Products.
Butter.
Cheese.
Eggs.
Milk.

Dress Goods.
Alepine.
Alpaca.
Barège.
Batiste.
Beige.
Bombazet.
Bombazine.†
Brilliant.†
Calico.
Cambric.
Camlet.
Cashmere.
Cashmerette.†
Challis.†
Crape.

Debeige.†
Delaine.†
Dimity.
Foulard.†
Gauze.
Gingham.
Ladies' cloth.†
Lawn.
Linsey-woolsey.
Lustring.
Lyonese cloth.†
Marseilles.†
Merino.
Millinet.
Mode.
Moreen.
Muslin.
Muslin de laine.
Nankeen.
Plaid.
Poplin.
Sarcenet.
Satin.
Satinet.
Satin stripe.†
Serge.
Shalloon.
Silk.
Swan's-down.
Tammy.
Thibet.†
Velvet.
Velveteen.

Dry Goods.
Baize.
Binding.
Blankets.
Buckram.
Canvas.
Chintz.
Copperplate.
Cotton and linen cloth.†
Cotton batting.
Cotton cloth.
Cotton flannel.
Cotton wool.
Crash.
Damask.
Denim.
Diaper.
Dowlas.
Drilling.
Duck.
Everlasting.†
Flannel.
Holland.
Huckaback.
Jean.
Lasting.
Linen.
Lining.
Napkins.
Oiled silk.
Padding.†
Patch.
Sheetings.
Shirtings.
Silesia.
Ticking.
Tow cloth.
Towelling.
Wadding.†
Wigan.†

Fish.
Clams.
Cod.
Codfish.
Eels.
Fish.

Index to Occupations and Articles — Concluded.

Fish, salt.
Haddock.
Halibut.
Herring.
Mackerel.
Oysters.
Pollock.
Salmon.
Shad.

Flour and Meal.
Flour.
Flour, buckwheat.
Flour, graham.
Flour, rye.†
Meal.
Meal, bolted rye.
Meal, Indian.
Meal, rice.
Meal, rye.
Oatmeal.
Wheat bran.†
Wheat meal.†

Food Preparations.
Biscuit.
Bread.
Chocolate.
Cocoa.
Cocoa and shells.
Cocoa shells.
Coffee.
Corn starch.
Crackers.
Cream of tartar.
Farina.
Hominy.†
Honey.
Lard.
Macaroni.
Molasses.
Pearl barley.
Sago.
Saleratus.
Salt.
Soda.
Starch.
Suet.
Sugar.
Syrup.
Tapioca.
Tea.

Fruits.
Citron.
Currants.
Dried apple.
Figs.
Lemons.
Oranges.
Prunes.
Raisins.

Fuel.
Bark.
Charcoal.
Coal.
Wood.

Furniture.
Bed cords.†
Bedsteads.†
Bureaus.†
Chairs.†
Tables.†

Liquors and Beverages.
Aniseed.
Beer.
Brandy.
Cider.
Gin.
Rum.
Snakeroot.
Wine.

Lumber.
Boards.†
Clapboards.†
Joist.†
Plank.†
Shingles.
Timber.

Meats.
Bacon.
Beef.
Ham.
Lamb.
Mutton.
Pork.
Sausages.
Tongue.
Tripe.
Veal.

Nuts.
Almonds.
Filberts.
Walnuts.

Oils and Illuminating Fluids.
Burning oils and fluids.
Linseed oil.

Paper.
Letter paper.
Wrapping paper.

Poultry and Game.
Chicken.
Fowl.
Goose.
Poultry.
Turkey.

Ribbons and Laces.
Lace.
Ribbon.

Small Wares.
Cotton, knitting.
Cotton, sewing.
Needles.
Pins.
Silk, sewing and embroidering.

Thread (cotton and linen).
Twist.
Worsted.†
Yarn.†

Spices and Condiments.
Allspice.
Cassia.
Cinnamon.
Cloves.
Ginger.
Mace.
Mustard.
Nutmegs.
Pepper.
Pepper, cayenne.
Pimento.
Vinegar.

Tacks, Brads, and Nails.
Nails.†
Nails, 4d.
Nails, 6d.†
Nails, 8d.†
Nails, 10d.
Nails, 20d.
Tacks and brads.†

Tallow, Candles, Soap, etc.
Candles.
Soap.
Soap, castile.
Soap, soft.†
Spermaceti.†
Tallow.

Tobacco and Snuff.
Cigars.†
Snuff.
Tobacco.

Tools and Implements.
Files.
Hoes.
Scythes.
Shoe knives.
Shovels.
Spades.†

Not Classified.
Andirons.†
Brick.
Brooms.
Candlesticks.†
Clocks.†
Cotton.
Feathers.†
Iron.
Kettles, brass.†
Matches.
Tubs.†
Tumblers.
Wafers.
Watches, silver.†
Wine glasses.

We present tables of wages and prices, by name and by periods of years, for each of the occupations and articles named which are not otherwise marked. Those marked with the (*) will not be shown by name, and those marked with the (†) will not be shown by periods of years, wages for such occupations and prices for certain of the articles so marked being

given only for one year or for one period, and consequently supply no comparisons. In many instances, also, either from the nature of the article itself, or because of a material variation in the " basis " of price, certain other articles are omitted from the tables by periods of years, although included in the " articles " tables by name.

In the occupations and articles tables, by name, all amounts originally given, as explained on pages 39 and 40, *ante*, in pounds, shillings, and pence, have been converted into United States currency in accordance with the basis of value established on pages 41 and 42, *ante*.

In bringing forward amounts (expressed in pounds, shillings, and pence either as old tenor or as lawful money) from the original documents, to the occupations and articles tables, by name, where all values are brought to the common basis, or United States currency, it frequently happened that the amounts were very nearly and sometimes exactly the same. This was, also, oftentimes true when brought into comparison with amounts which were originally given in the same year, for the same occupation or article, in United States money. Wherever two values in any one year, when expressed in United States currency, very nearly or exactly agreed, but one amount is given in the tables of occupations and articles; in all other cases, the amounts have been graded and properly marked. It will be noticed, however, in many cases that the currency values given for an occupation or article, for the same year, are very close. This is due to the re-arrangement of values on a currency basis.

In the occupations and articles tables, by name, the general form of presentation used has been to state for each occupation and article the various years, in their order, for which wages or prices are given, the "basis" and corresponding "amount." Any description other than the name of the occupation or article itself immediately follows, in parenthesis, the year, together with such designations as may be needed to explain the given basis or amount. The "occupations" and "articles" will be presented in the order in which they are named in the " index," this classification having been adopted in order to bring together all related occupations and articles, either under one title as in the case of occupations, or under general headings as regards articles.

The Occupations and Articles Tables, By Name.

Wages: Agricultural Laborers.

Years.	Basis.	Amount.	Years.	Basis.	Amount.
1752,	day	$0.333	1800,	day	$0.424
1753,	day	.37	1801,	day	.577
1754,	day	.333	1802,	day	.622
1755,	day	.356	1803,	day	.517
1756,	day	.333	1804, (high)	day	1.00
(plowing greensward)	day	2.00	(low)	day	.612
1757,	day	.317	1805, (high)	day	1.33
(with oxen)	day	1.00	(medium)	day	1.00
1758,	day	.259	(med. low)	day	.883
1759,	day	.25	(low)	day	.617
(with oxen)	day	1.00	1806, (high)	day	1.17
1760,	day	.25	(medium)	day	1.00
1761,	day	.319	(low)	day	.625
1763,	day	.333	1807, (high)	day	.83
(with oxen)	day	2.00	(medium)	day	.667
1764, (high)	day	.389	(low)	day	.58
(low)	day	.333	1808, (high)	day	1.00
1765, (plowing)	day	1.33	(medium)	day	.844
1766,	day	.333	(low)	day	.75
1767,	day	.271	(boys)	day	.167
1770,	day	.336	1809, (high)	day	.58
1771,	day	.333	(low)	day	.50
(boys)	day	.167	1810, (high)	day	1.17
1772,	day	.333	(medium)	day	1.00
(boys)	day	.167	(low)	day	.639
1773,	day	.342	1811, (high)	day	.683
1774,	day	.356	(low)	day	.50
1775,	day	.344	(boys)	day	.25
	wk.	1.75	1812, (high)	day	1.25
1776, (high)	day	.50	(medium)	day	1.00
(medium)	day	.333	(med. low)	day	.667
(low)	day	.167	(low)	day	.50
1777,	day	.556	1813, (high)	day	1.25
(with oxen)	day	1.50	(low)	day	.667
1781, (high)	day	.444	1814, (high)	day	.792
(low)	day	.40	(low)	day	.607
1782, (high)	day	.483	(with double team)	day	3.00
(medium)	day	.389	1815,	day	.868
(low)	day	.333		mo.	13.50
1783, (high)	day	.423	(with board)	day	.56
(low)	day	.347	(with board and lodging)	mo.	8.00
1784,	day	.394	(with two meals a day) .	mo.	10.00
1785, (high)	day	.468	1816, (high)	day	.909
(low)	day	.351	(low)	day	.595
1786,	day	.333	(plowing with oxen)	day	1.50
1787, (high)	day	.56	1817,	day	.827
(low)	day	.392	1818,	day	1.49
1788, (high)	day	.444	1819,	day	.533
(medium)	day	.389	1820, (high)	day	1.00
(low)	day	.333	(medium)	day	.75
1789,	day	.423	(low)	day	.50
1790, (high)	day	.425	1821, (high)	day	1.00
(medium)	day	.333	(medium)	day	.664
(low)	day	.25	(low)	day	.447
1791,	day	.438	(with oxen)	day	2.00
1792, (high)	day	.403	(with oxen; with board)	day	1.50
(low)	day	.167	(with four oxen and		
1793,	day	.353	plow; high)	day	2.40
1794, (high)	day	.667	(with four oxen and		
(low)	day	.416	plow; low)	day	1.67
1795, (high)	day	.75	1822,	day	.771
(medium)	day	.57	1823, (high)	day	1.25
(med. low)	day	.416	(medium)	day	1.00
(low)	day	.393	(low)	day	.57
1796,	day	.487	(with oxen)	day	1.50
1797,	day	.436	1825, (high)	day	.992
1798, (high)	day	.833	(medium)	day	.74
(low)	day	.41	(low)	day	.50
1799, (high)	day	.528	(high)	mo.	18.00
(low)	day	.43	(low)	mo.	15.00

Wages: Agricultural Laborers — CONCLUDED.

YEARS.	Basis.	Amount.	YEARS.	Basis.	Amount.
1825, (with board, high) . .	day	$0.66	1835, (with board, low) . .	day	$0.50
(with board, low) . .	day	.50	(with two meals a day, high)	mo.	15.00
(with two meals a day, high)	mo.	15.00	(with two meals a day, low)	mo.	12.00
(with two meals a day, low)	mo.	12.00	(with board and lodging, high)	mo.	12.00
(with board and lodging, high)	mo.	12.00	(with board and lodging, low)	mo.	10.00
(with board and lodging, low)	mo.	10.00	1845, (high)	day	1.00
(with oxen) . . .	day	1.50	(low)	day	.90
1826, (high)	day	.784	(high)	mo.	20.00
(low)	day	.45	(low)	mo.	15.00
1827, (high)	day	1.00	(with board and lodging, high)	mo.	12.00
(medium) . . .	day	.80	(with board and lodging, low)	mo.	10.00
(low)	day	.628	(with two meals a day, high)	mo.	15.00
(shearing sheep) .	day	1.34	(with two meals a day, low)	mo.	12.00
1828, (high)	day	1.00	1860, (high)	day	1.12
(medium) . . .	day	.75	(low)	day	1.00
(low)	day	.575	(high)	mo.	25.00
1831, (high)	day	1.00	(low)	mo.	18.00
(low)	day	.75	(with board, high) .	mo.	12.00
1835, (high)	day	1.00	(with board, low) .	mo.	10.00
(low)	day	.75			
(high)	mo.	18.00			
(low)	mo.	15.00			
(with board, high) .	day	.60			

Wages: Blacksmiths.

YEARS.	Basis.	Amount.	YEARS.	Basis.	Amount.
1781, ...	day	$0.667	1838, (cotton mill; high) .	day	$2.00
1782, ...	day	.833	(cotton mill; low) .	day	1.00
1784, ...	day	.667	(machine shop) .	day	1.75
1787, ...	day	.636	1839, ...	day	1.51
1790, ...	day	.667	1840, (carriage; with board) .	mo.	20.00
1815, (horseshoers) . .	day	.90	(cordage works) .	day	1.42
(horseshoers; with board) . . .	day	.45	(stone)	day	1.52
(helpers) . . .	day	.625	1845, (high)	day	1.25
(wagon smiths) . .	day	1.00	(low)	day	1.00
(wagon smiths; with board) . . .	day	.625	(with board; high) .	day	.60
1825, (with board) . .	day	.50	(with board; low) .	day	.50
(helpers) . . .	day	1.00	(carriage; high) .	day	1.50
(carriages and wagons; high) . . .	day	1.33	(carriage; low) .	day	1.25
(carriages and wagons; low) . . .	day	1.25	(machine shop) .	wk.	8.00
(carriages and wagons; helpers) . . .	day	1.00	(shovel works) .	day	1.50
(horseshoers) . . .	day	1.00	(stone yard) . .	day	1.60
1832, (carriage; with board, high) . . .	mo.	18.00	(helpers) . . .	day	1.00
(carriage; with board, low) . . .	mo.	15.00	1850, (carriage; high) .	day	1.75
1835, (carriages and wagons; high) . . .	day	1.50	(carriage; low) .	day	1.50
(carriages and wagons; low) . . .	day	1.25	(carriage; piece work) .	day	2.00
(horseshoers; high) .	day	1.25	(cordage works) .	day	1.50
(horseshoers; low) .	day	1.00	(locomotive works; high)	day	1.94
(horseshoers; with board) . . .	day	.60	(locomotive works; medium) . . .	day	1.51
(helpers) . . .	day	1.00	(locomotive works; low)	day	1.17
1836, ...	day	1.75	(machine shop) .	wk.	9.00
1837, (carriages and wagons; high) . . .	wk.	9.00	(shovel works) .	day	1.78
(carriages and wagons; low) . . .	wk.	7.50	(stone yard; high) .	day	1.79
(cotton mill; high) .	day	2.00	(stone yard; low) .	day	1.54
(cotton mill; low) .	day	1.00	1855, (locomotive works; high) . . .	day	3.00
(machine shop) .	day	1.75	(locomotive works; med. high) . . .	day	2.50
1838, (carriages and wagons; high) . . .	wk.	9.00	(locomotive works; medium) . . .	day	2.28
(carriages and wagons; low) . . .	wk.	7.50	(locomotive works; med. low) . . .	day	1.77
			(locomotive works; low)	day	1.33
			(stone yard) . .	day	1.24
			1860, (high)	day	1.50
			(low)	day	1.25
			(carriage; high) .	day	2.00
			(carriage; medium) .	day	1.75
			(carriage; low) .	day	1.50
			(machine shop) .	wk.	10.50

Wages: Bookbinders.

Years.	Ba-sis.	Amount.	Years.	Ba-sis.	Amount.
1837, (high)	wk.	$10.50	1840, (collators; girls; high)	wk.	$5.00
(low)	wk.	6.00	(collators; girls; low)	wk.	4.00
(apprentices; high)	wk.	3.00	(finishers; high)	wk.	11.00
(apprentices; low)	wk.	2.00	(finishers; low)	wk.	10.00
(boys; high)	wk.	3.00	(folders; girls)	wk.	4.00
(boys; low)	wk.	1.50	(forwarders)	wk.	10.00
(foremen; high)	wk.	12.00	(pasters; girls)	wk.	3.00
(foremen; low)	wk.	7.00	(sewers; girls; high)	wk.	5.00
(folders; high)	wk.	5.50	(sewers; girls; low)	wk.	4.00
(folders; low)	wk.	3.25	1845, (finishers; high)	wk.	10.00
(sewers; high)	wk.	6.00	(finishers; low)	wk.	8.00
(sewers; low)	wk.	3.00	(forwarders; high)	wk.	9.00
1838, (high)	wk.	10.50	(forwarders; low)	wk.	8.00
(low)	wk.	6.00	1860, (collators; girls)	wk.	5.00
(apprentices; high)	wk.	3.00	(finishers; high)	wk.	12.00
(apprentices; low)	wk.	2.00	(finishers; low)	wk.	10.00
(boys; high)	wk.	3.00	(folders; girls; high)	wk.	5.00
(boys; low)	wk.	1.50	(folders; girls; low)	wk.	4.00
(foremen; high)	wk.	12.00	(forwarders; high)	wk.	12.00
(foremen; low)	wk.	7.00	(forwarders; low)	wk.	9.67
(folders; high)	wk.	5.50	(pasters; girls; high)	wk.	4.00
(folders; low)	wk.	3.25	(pasters; girls; low)	wk.	3.00
(sewers; high)	wk.	6.00	(sewers; girls; high)	wk.	6.00
(sewers; low)	wk.	3.00	(sewers; girls; low)	wk.	5.00

Wages: Brewery and Distillery Employés.

Years.	Ba-sis.	Amount.	Years.	Ba-sis.	Amount.
1840, (brewery; with board)	mo.	$20.00	1860, (distillery; low)	wk.	$10.00
(distillery; with board)	mo.	20.00	(fermenters, brewery; high)	wk.	14.00
1860, (cellar men, brewery; high)	wk.	14.00	(fermenters, brewery; low)	wk.	12.00
(cellar men, brewery; low)	wk.	12.00	(kettle men, brewery)	wk.	14.00
(distillery; high)	wk.	15.00	(wash house hands, brewery)	wk.	11.00
(distillery; medium)	wk.	12.00			

Wages: Butchers.

Years.	Basis	Amount.	Years.	Basis	Amount.
1771,	day	$0.333	1821,	day	$0.75
1775,	day	.333	1826,	day	1.00
1808,	day	.50	1827,	day	1.00
1819,	day	.75			

Wages: Carpenters.

Years.	Basis	Amount.	Years.	Basis	Amount.
1772,	day	$0.441	1792,	day	$0.583
1773,	day	.34	1793, (high)	day	.914
1774,	day	.359	(low)	day	.482
1778,	day	.395	1794, (high)	day	.924
1779, (high)	day	1.03	(low)	day	.649
(low)	day	.647	1795, (high)	day	.833
1780,	day	.444	(medium)	day	.75
1781, (high)	day	.619	(low)	day	.583
(low)	day	.444	1796, (high)	day	.958
1782, (high)	day	.667	(low)	day	.578
(low)	day	.444	1797, (high)	day	.84
1783, (high)	day	.574	(low)	day	.583
(low)	day	.489	1798, (high)	day	.833
1784,	day	.609	(low)	day	.75
1785,	day	.59	1799, (high)	day	.785
1786,	day	.538	(low)	day	.556
1787, (high)	day	.535	1800, (high)	day	1.00
(low)	day	.389	(low)	day	.836
1788,	day	.50	1801, (high)	day	.99
1789,	day	.564	(low)	day	.75
1790,	day	.59	1802,	day	.833
1791,	day	.549	1803, (high)	day	1.08

Wages: Carpenters — Concluded.

Years.	Basis.	Amount.	Years.	Basis.	Amount.
1803, (low)	day	$0.788	1835, (and joiners; summer; high)	day	$1.25
1804, (high)	day	1.16	(and joiners; summer; low)	day	1.12
(medium)	day	.954	(and joiners; summer; with board, high)	day	.90
(low)	day	.668	(and joiners; summer; with board, low)	day	.60
1805, (high)	day	1.75	(and joiners; winter; high)	day	1.12
(medium)	day	1.46	(and joiners; winter; low)	day	1.00
(med. low)	day	1.17	(and joiners; winter; with board, high)	day	.84
(low)	day	1.12	(and joiners; winter; with board, low)	day	.50
1806,	day	.994	(and joiners — foremen)	day	1.50
1807, (high)	day	1.50	1837, (cotton mill; high)	day	2.00
(medium)	day	1.17	(cotton mill; low)	day	1.33
(low)	day	1.00	(machine shop)	day	1.42
1808, (high)	day	1.75	1838, (cotton mill; high)	day	2.00
(medium)	day	1.00	(cotton mill; low)	day	1.33
(med. low)	day	.889	(machine shop)	day	1.42
(low)	day	.668	1845, (cordage works)	day	1.42
1809, (high)	day	1.33	(ship; high)	day	1.50
(low)	day	1.06	(ship; low)	day	1.25
1810, (high)	day	1.11	(and joiners; summer; high)	day	1.33
(low)	day	1.00	(and joiners; summer; low)	day	1.25
1811, (high)	day	1.58	(and joiners; summer; with board, high)	day	.90
(med. high)	day	1.24	(and joiners; summer; with board, low)	day	.75
(med. low)	day	1.00	(and joiners; winter; high)	day	1.12
(low)	day	.748	(and joiners; winter; low)	day	1.00
1812, (high)	day	1.40	(and joiners; winter; with board, high)	day	.84
(low)	day	1.00	(and joiners; winter; with board, low)	day	.50
1813, (high)	day	1.43	(and joiners — foremen)	day	1.50
(medium)	day	1.26	(cabinet makers; high)	day	1.50
(low)	day	1.00	(cabinet makers; low)	day	1.25
1814,	day	1.04	(stair builders; high)	day	1.50
1815, (ship)	day	1.25	(stair builders; low)	day	1.25
(and joiners; high)	day	1.00	1850, (cordage works)	day	1.50
(and joiners; low)	day	.75	(locomotive works; high)	day	1.58
(and joiners; with board)	day	.625	(locomotive works; low)	day	1.39
(and joiners; summer; with board, high)	day	1.25	(metal work)	day	1.50
(and joiners; summer; with board, low)	day	.625	1855, (locomotive works; high)	day	1.83
1816,	day	1.00	(locomotive works; med. high)	day	1.54
1817, (high)	day	1.42	(locomotive works; medium)	day	1.33
(low)	day	1.00	(locomotive works; med. low)	day	1.17
1819,	day	1.14	(locomotive works; low)	day	.917
1820,	day	1.00	(nail works)	day	1.75
1822,	day	.89	1857, (woollen mill; high)	day	1.50
1823,	day	1.00	(woollen mill; low)	day	1.00
1824,	day	.833	(foremen, woollen mill)	day	2.00
(cordage works)	day	1.33	1860, (high)	day	1.50
1825,	day	.75	(low)	day	1.25
(cordage works; high)	day	1.25	(foremen; high)	day	2.00
(cordage works; medium)	day	1.00	(foremen; low)	day	1.75
(cordage works; low)	day	.75	(linen mill)	day	1.75
(ship; high)	day	1.33	(cabinet makers; high)	day	2.00
(ship; low)	day	1.25	(cabinet makers; low)	day	1.50
(and joiners; summer; high)	day	1.33	(stair builders; high)	day	2.00
(and joiners; summer; low)	day	1.00	(stair builders; low)	day	1.75
(and joiners; winter; high)	day	1.25			
(and joiners; winter; low)	day	1.00			
(and joiners; summer; with board, high)	day	.84			
(and joiners; summer; with board, low)	day	.50			
(and joiners; winter; with board, high)	day	.75			
(and joiners; winter; with board, low)	day	.50			
1835, (cordage works)	day	1.33			
(ship; high)	day	1.50			
(ship; low)	day	1.25			

Wages: Carriage Makers.

Years.	Basis.	Amount.	Years.	Basis.	Amount.
1831, (wheelwrights; high) .	day	$1.50	1838, (wood-workers; high) .	wk.	$9.00
(wheelwrights; low) .	day	1.37	(wood-workers; low) .	wk.	7.00
1832, (and wheel makers; with board, high) .	mo.	18.00	1840, (with board) . .	mo.	20.00
(and wheel makers; with board, low) .	mo.	15.00	(body makers; with board) .	mo.	20.00
(body makers; with board, high)	mo.	18.00	(trimmers; with board) .	mo.	20.00
(body makers; with board, low) .	mo.	15.00	1845, (high) . . .	day	1.25
(trimmers; with board, high) . . .	mo.	18.00	(low) . . .	day	1.00
(trimmers; with board, low) .	mo.	15.00	1850, (high) . . .	day	1.75
1837, (wheelwrights; high) .	wk.	9.00	(low) . . .	day	1.50
(wheelwrights; low) .	wk.	7.00	(piece work) . .	day	2.00
(wood-workers; high) .	wk.	9.00	(trimmers; high) .	day	1.75
(wood-workers; low) .	wk.	7.00	(trimmers; low) . .	day	1.50
1838, (wheelwrights; high) .	wk.	9.00	(trimmers; piece work)	day	2.00
(wheelwrights; low) .	wk.	7.00	1860, (high) . . .	day	2.00
			(medium) . . .	day	1.75
			(low) . . .	day	1.50
			(trimmers; high) .	day	2.00
			(trimmers; low) . .	day	1.75

Wages: Clockmakers.

Years.	Basis.	Amount.	Years.	Basis.	Amount.
1815, ...	day	$1.13	1845, (low) . . .	day	$1.12
1825, (high) . . .	day	1.33	1860, (high) . . .	day	2.25
(low) . . .	day	1.25	(medium) . . .	day	1.75
1835, (high) . . .	day	1.50	(med. low) . . .	day	1.50
(medium) . . .	day	1.25	(low) . . .	day	1.25
(low) . . .	day	1.12	(foremen; high) .	day	3.00
1845, (high) . . .	day	1.50	(foremen; low) .	day	2.00
(medium) . . .	day	1.25			

Wages: Clothing Makers.

Years.	Basis.	Amount.	Years.	Basis.	Amount.
1803, (pantaloons; piece work)	pr.	$0.416	1837, (vests; low) . . .	wk.	$1.25
1814, (coats; piece work) .	p'ce	2.25	(vests; custom work; high) .	wk.	4.50
(pantaloons; piece work)	pr.	1.25	(vests; custom work; low) .	wk.	3.75
(pantaloons cutters; piece work) .	pr.	.25	1838, (coats; high) . .	wk.	7.50
(waistcoats; piece work)	p'ce	1.25	(coats; low) . .	wk.	5.00
1815, (tailors) . . .	wk	6.00	(coats; custom work; high) .	wk.	9.00
(tailors; with board) .	wk.	8.00	(coats; custom work; low) .	wk.	7.50
1825, (tailors; high) . .	wk.	8.00	(cutters; high) .	day	1.50
(tailors; low) . .	wk.	7.00	(cutters; low) .	day	1.00
(tailors; with board) .	wk.	3 00	(cutters; high) .	wk.	11.00
1828, (tailors) . . .	day	1.50	(cutters; low) .	wk.	7.00
1835, (tailors; high) . .	day	1.50	(frock coats; high) .	day	1.00
(tailors; low) . .	day	1.25	(frock coats; low) .	day	.83
1837, (coats; high) . .	wk.	7.50	(overalls) . . .	day	.195
(coats; low) . .	wk.	5.00	(pantaloons) . .	day	.15
(coats; custom work; high) .	wk.	9.00	(pantaloons; high) .	wk.	1.50
(coats; custom work; low) .	wk.	7.50	(pantaloons; low) .	wk.	1.00
(cutters; high) . .	day	1.50	(pantaloons; custom work; high) .	wk.	6.00
(cutters; low) . .	day	1.00	(pantaloons; custom work; low) .	wk.	4.50
(cutters; high) . .	wk.	11.00	(pressmen; custom work; high) .	wk.	8.00
(cutters; low) . .	wk	7.00	(pressmen; custom work; low) .	wk.	7.00
(frock coats; high) .	day	1.00	(vests; high) . .	wk.	1.75
(frock coats; low) .	day	.83	(vests; low) . .	wk.	1.25
(overalls) . . .	day	.195	(vests; custom work; high) .	wk.	4.50
(pantaloons) . .	day	.15	(vests; custom work; low) .	wk.	3 75
(pantaloons; high) .	wk.	1.50	1845, (tailors; high) . .	day	1.50
(pantaloons; low) .	wk.	1.00	(tailors; low) . .	day	1.25
(pantaloons; custom work; high) .	wk.	6.00	1860, (tailors; high) . .	day	1.75
(pantaloons; custom work; low) .	wk.	4.50	(tailors; low) . .	day	1.50
(pressmen; custom work; high) .	wk.	8.00			
(pressmen; custom work; low) .	wk.	7.00			
(vests; high) . .	wk.	1.75			

Wages: Cordage Makers.

Years.	Basis.	Amount.	Years.	Basis.	Amount.
1825, (hatchellers; high) . .	day	$1.17	1845, (boys; high) . . .	day	$1.25
(hatchellers; low) . .	day	.833	(boys; low) . . .	day	.792
(pattern makers) . .	day	2.50	(foremen) . . .	day	1.83
(reelers)	day	1.13	(spinners; high) . .	day	1.32
(spinners; high) . .	day	1.20	(spinners; medium) .	day	1.06
(spinners; medium) .	day	1.00	(spinners; low) . .	day	.856
(spinners; low) . .	day	.833	(spinners — foremen;		
(spinners; boys) . .	day	.25	high)	day	2.00
1826, ...	day	.667	(spinners — foremen;		
1830, (spinners; high) . .	day	1.33	low)	day	1.63
(spinners; med. high) .	day	1.25	1850, (hemp openers; high) .	wk.	6.00
(spinners; medium) .	day	1.11	(hemp openers; medium)	wk.	5.50
(spinners; med. low) .	day	1.00	(hemp openers; low) .	wk.	5.00
(spinners; low) . .	day	.88	(lappers; high) . .	wk.	6.00
(spinners — foremen;			(lappers; medium) .	wk.	5.50
high)	day	1.83	(lappers; low) . .	wk.	5.00
(spinners — foremen;			(layers; high) . .	wk.	15.00
low)	day	.958	(layers; low) . .	wk.	9.00
1835, (spinners; high) . .	day	1.17	(preparers; boys; high)	wk.	4.00
(spinners; medium) .	day	1.05	(preparers; boys; low)	wk.	2.00
(spinners; low) . .	day	.92	(preparers; girls) . .	wk.	2.00
(spinners — foremen;			(spinners; high) . .	day	1.50
high)	day	1.83	(spinners; med. high) .	day	1.36
(spinners — foremen;			(spinners; medium) .	day	1.25
low)	day	1.33	(spinners; med. low) .	day	1.13
1840, (hatchellers) . . .	day	1.17	(spinners; low) . .	day	1.00
(spinners) . . .	day	1.25	(spinners, hand hemp) .	wk.	7.50
(spinners — foremen;			(spinners, machine; high)	wk.	3.50
high)	day	2.00	(spinners, machine; low)	wk.	3.00
(spinners — foremen;			(spinners — foremen) .	day	2.00
low)	day	1.50	(spinners' helpers, hand		
(spinners, hand; women;			hemp; boys; high) .	wk.	1.50
high)	day	.584	(spinners' helpers, hand		
(spinners, hand; women;			hemp; boys; low) .	wk.	1.00
low)	day	.50	1855, (spinners — foremen) .	mo.	75.00

Wages: Glass Makers.

Years.	Basis.	Amount.	Years.	Basis.	Amount.
1822, (gaffers)	day	$2.04	1840, (journeymen) . . .	wk.	$9.81
(journeymen) . . .	day	1.05	(boys)	day	.555
(journeymen) . . .	wk.	6.40	(cutters)	day	2.22
(boys)	day	.54	1845, (gaffers)	wk.	19.38
(boys)	wk.	3.28	(journeymen) . . .	day	1.51
(cutters)	day	1.63	(women and girls) . .	day	.448
1830, (gaffers)	day	2.35	(boys)	day	.542
(journeymen) . . .	day	1.39	(cutters)	day	2.17
(journeymen) . . .	wk.	8.43	1850, (gaffers)	wk.	19.88
(boys)	day	.456	(journeymen) . . .	day	1.53
(cutters)	day	1.94	(women and girls) . .	day	.557
1835, (gaffers)	day	2.49	(boys)	day	.528
(journeymen) . . .	day	1.59	(cutters)	day	2.24
(journeymen) . . .	wk.	8.75	1855, (gaffers)	wk.	24.10
(boys)	day	.572	(journeymen) . . .	day	1.76
(cutters)	day	2.05	(women and boys) . .	day	.59
1840, (gaffers)	day	2.87	(boys)	day	.54
(journeymen) . . .	day	1.49	(cutters)	day	2.56

Wages: Gold and Silver Workers.

Years.	Basis.	Amount.	Years.	Basis.	Amount.
1839, (women)	day	$0.50	1845, (women; high) . . .	day	$0.667
(boys; high) . . .	day	.667	(women; low) . . .	day	.50
(boys; low) . . .	day	.563	(boys; high) . . .	day	.679
(overseers) . . .	day	1.46	(boys; medium) . .	day	.50
(die sinkers) . . .	day	1.50	(boys; low) . . .	day	.292
(platers — journeymen;			(overseers; high) . .	day	2.25
high)	day	1.22	(overseers; low) . .	day	2.00
(platers — journeymen;			(platers — journeymen;		
medium) . . .	day	1.00	high)	day	2.00
(platers — journeymen;			(platers — journeymen;		
low)	day	.883	medium) . . .	day	1.50

Wages: Gold and Silver Workers — CONCLUDED.

YEARS.	Ba-sis.	Amount.	YEARS.	Ba-sis.	Amount.
1845, (platers — journeymen; med. low) . . .	day	$1.23	1855, (boys; high) . . .	day	$1.25
(platers — journeymen;			(boys; medium) . .	day	1.00
low)	day	1.00	(boys; low) . . .	day	.765
1850, (women; high) . .	day	.881	(overseers; high) . .	day	3.00
(women; medium) . .	day	.75	(overseers; low) . .	day	2.00
(women; low) . .	day	.659	(casters)	day	1.83
(girls)	day	.374	(die sinkers) . . .	day	2.67
(boys; high) . . .	day	.908	(platers — journeymen;		
(boys; low) . . .	day	.75	high)	day	2.00
(overseers) . . .	day	1.33	(platers — journeymen;		
(casters)	day	1.67	medium) . . .	day	1.67
(die sinkers; high). .	day	2.25	(platers — journeymen;		
(die sinkers; low) . .	day	1.87	low)	day	1.32
(platers — journeymen;			(platers — overseers) .	day	2.25
high)	day	2.00	1857, (women; high) . .	day	.944
(platers — journeymen;			(women; low) . .	day	.574
med. high) . . .	day	1.67	(boys; high) . . .	day	1.04
(platers — journeymen;			(boys; medium) . .	day	.797
medium) . . .	day	1.38	(boys; low) . . .	day	.40
(platers — journeymen;			(overseers; high) . .	day	3.00
med. low) . . .	day	1.13	(overseers; low) . .	day	2.50
(platers — journeymen;			(die sinkers) . . .	day	3.00
low)	day	.833	(platers — journeymen;		
(platers — overseers;			high)	day	2.51
high)	day	2.67	(platers — journeymen;		
(platers — overseers;			med. high) . . .	day	2.07
low)	day	?	(platers — journeymen;		
1855, (women; high) . .	day	a	medium) . . .	day	1.79
(women; medium) . .	day	.?	(platers — journeymen;		
(women; low) . .	day	.53	med. low) . . .	day	1.54
(girls; high) . .	day	.433	(platers — journeymen;		
(girls; low) . .	day	.375	low)	day	1.27

Wages: Harness Makers.

YEARS.	Ba-sis.	Amount.	YEARS.	Ba-sis.	Amount.
1815, ...	day	$0.88	1845, (and saddle; low) . .	day	$1.25
(with board) . . .	day	.45	1850, (high)	day	1.75
1825, (high)	day	1.25	(low)	day	1.50
(low)	day	1.00	(piece work) . . .	day	2.00
(with board, high) . .	day	.50	1860, (high)	day	2.00
(with board, low) . .	day	.40	(low)	day	1.75
1835, ...	day	1.25	(country towns; high) .	day	1.33
1840, (carriage; with board) .	mo.	20.00	(country towns; low) .	day	1.25
1845, (high)	day	1.25	(piece work, high) . .	day	1.75
(low)	day	1.00	(piece work, low) . .	day	1.50
(and saddle; high). .	day	1.50	(and saddle) . . .	day	2.00

Wages: Hat Makers.

YEARS.	Ba-sis.	Amount.	YEARS.	Ba-sis.	Amount.
1845, (high)	day	$1.50	1860, (low)	day	$1.50
(low)	day	1.00	(body makers; high) .	wk.	16.00
1850, (body makers) . .	wk	12.00	(body makers; low) .	wk.	14.00
(curlers)	wk.	15.00	(curlers)	wk.	18.00
(finishers) . . .	wk.	12.00	(finishers; high) . .	wk.	16.00
1860, (high)	day	1.75	(finishers; low) . .	wk.	14.00

Wages: Laborers.

YEARS.	Ba-sis.	Amount.	YEARS.	Ba-sis.	Amount.
1752, ...	day	$0.333	1759, ...	day	$0.25
1753, ...	day	.333	1760, ...	day	.25
1754, ...	day	.333	1761, ...	day	.25
1755, ...	day	.333	1762, ...	day	.178
1756, ...	day	.167	(chopping wood) . .	day	.25
(sawing timber) .	day	.483	1763, (high)	day	.583
1757, ...	day	.168	(medium) . . .	day	.356
1758, ...	day	.25	(low)	day	.333

Wages: Laborers — Continued.

Years.	Basis.	Amount.	Years.	Basis.	Amount.
1764, (high)	day	$0.356	1797, (medium)	day	$0.667
(low)	day	.328	(low)	day	.209
1765,	day	.333	(carting timber)	day	1.83
1766, (high)	day	.337	1798, (high)	day	1.00
(low)	day	.25	(medium)	day	.719
	mo.	6.00	(low)	day	.50
1767,	day	.333	(on mill)	day	1.50
1768,	day	.35	1799, (high)	day	.617
1769,	day	.296	(low)	day	.50
1770,	day	.341		mo.	13.33
1771,	day	.339	(with two meals per day)	yr.	160.00
1772, (high)	day	.333	1800, (high)	day	.82
(boys)	day	.133	(med. high)	day	.75
1773,	day	.333	(medium)	day	.692
1774,	day	.353	(low)	day	.333
1775,	day	.383		mo.	13.33
1776, (high)	day	.562	1801, (high)	day	.899
(medium)	day	.415	(low)	day	.64
(med. low)	day	.245	1802, (high)	day	1.00
(low)	day	.159	(medium)	day	.833
1777, (high)	day	.50	(med. low)	day	.75
(med. high)	day	.452	(low)	day	.66
(medium)	day	.344	1803, (high)	day	.803
(low)	day	.222	(low)	day	.42
1778,	day	.388	1804, (high)	day	.884
1779,	day	.793	(low)	day	.667
1780,	day	.444	1805, (high)	day	1.02
1781,	day	.468	(med. high)	day	.837
1782, (high)	day	.556	(medium)	day	.774
(medium)	day	.426	(med. low)	day	.50
(med. low)	day	.372	(low)	day	.25
(low)	day	.333	1806, (high)	day	1.27
1783, (high)	day	.478	(med. high)	day	1.00
(medium)	day	.367	(medium)	day	.93
(low)	day	.314	(med. low)	day	.855
1784, (high)	day	.40	(low)	day	.594
(low)	day	.342	1807, (high)	day	1.00
1785, (high)	day	.556	(medium)	day	.75
(low)	day	.40	(med. low)	day	.652
1786, (high)	day	.667	(low)	day	.583
(medium)	day	.333		mo.	12.50
(low)	day	.311	1808, (high)	day	1.00
1787, (high)	day	.833	(medium)	day	.845
(medium)	day	.413	(med. low)	day	.597
(low)	day	.333	(low)	day	.50
1788,	day	.514		mo.	12.00
(with team)	day	1.43	(boys)	day	.25
1789,	day	.399	1809, (high)	day	1.67
(on schooner)	day	.50	(medium)	day	1.23
(with team)	day	1.22	(med. low)	day	.988
1790, (high)	day	.468	(low)	day	.611
(low)	day	.333	1810, (high)	day	1.33
(boys)	day	.167	(med. high)	day	1.10
1791, (high)	day	.50	(medium)	day	1.00
(low)	day	.426	(med. low)	day	.842
1792, (high)	day	.608	(low)	day	.505
(low)	day	.333	1811, (high)	day	1.00
1793, (high)	day	.979	(low)	day	.958
(med. high)	day	.667	(boys)	day	.25
(medium)	day	.539	1812, (high)	day	1.25
(med. low)	day	.274	(medium)	day	1 07
(low)	day	.167	(low)	day	.667
1794, (high)	day	.833	1813, (high)	day	1.33
(medium)	day	.571	(medium)	day	1.00
(med. low)	day	.321	(med. low)	day	.84
(low)	day	.222	(low)	day	.57
1795, (high)	day	1.15	1814, (high)	day	1.35
(med. high)	day	.685	(medium)	day	1.00
(medium)	day	.667	(low)	day	.781
(med. low)	day	.556	(with oxen)	day	1.50
(low)	day	.333	(young persons)	day	.784
1796, (high)	day	.90	1815, (high)	day	1.50
(medium)	day	.629	(medium)	day	.987
(low)	day	.50	(low)	day	.50
1797, (high)	day	1.00	(cutting wood)	day	.864

Wages: Laborers — Concluded.

Years.	Basis.	Amount.	Years.	Basis.	Amount.
1815, (in mill)	day	$1.02	1840, (cordage works; low)	day	$1.00
(on highways)	day	.60	(shovel works; high)	day	1.00
(on sloop)	day	1.25	(shovel works; med. high)	day	.84
1816, (high)	day	1.74	(shovel works; med. low)	day	.736
(medium)	day	1.07	(shovel works; low)	day	.60
(low)	day	.785	1845, (high)	day	1.25
1817,	day	1.00	(medium)	day	1.00
1818, (high)	day	1.00	(low)	day	.808
(medium)	day	.753	(metal work; boys; high)	day	.50
(med. low)	day	.583	(metal work; boys; low)	day	.306
(low)	day	.382	(paper mill; high)	day	1.00
1819, (high)	day	1.15	(paper mill; low)	day	.785
(medium)	day	.795	(shovel works; high)	day	.947
(low)	day	.50	(shovel works; low)	day	.773
(laying wall)	day	1.25	(stone)	day	.856
1820, (high)	day	1.00	1848, (paper mill)	day	.898
(medium)	day	.676	1850, (cordage works; high)	day	1.67
(low)	day	.502	(cordage works; low)	day	1.04
1821, (high)	day	1.00	(locomotive works; high)	day	1.02
(medium)	day	.75	(locomotive works; medium)	day	.871
(low)	day	.638	(locomotive works; low)	day	.50
	mo.	8.00	(metal work; high)	day	1.27
1822, (high)	day	.80	(metal work; med. high)	day	.903
(low)	day	.67	(metal work; medium)	day	.737
	mo.	13.00	(metal work; med. low)	day	.543
1823, (high)	day	1.00	(metal work; low)	day	.45
(low)	day	.732	(metal work; boys; high)	day	.75
1824, (high)	day	1.00	(metal work; boys; medium)	day	.50
(low)	day	.68	(metal work; boys; low)	day	.333
1825, (high)	day	.992	(nail works; high)	day	1.15
(medium)	day	.709	(nail works; low)	day	.989
(low)	day	.50	(paper mill)	day	1.00
(on highways; high)	day	.875	(shovel works; high)	day	1.00
(on highways; low)	day	.705	(shovel works; medium)	day	.871
(cordage works)	day	.87	(shovel works; low)	day	.722
1826, (high)	day	1.00	(stone yard)	day	.976
(medium)	day	.792	(woollen mill)	day	.84
(low)	day	.464	1852, (cordage works)	wk.	5.00
1827, (high)	day	1.25	1855, (locomotive works; high)	day	1.11
(med. high)	day	1.13	(locomotive works; medium)	day	1.00
(medium)	day	1.00	(locomotive works; low)	day	.841
(med. low)	day	.72	(nail works; high)	day	1.34
(low)	day	.433	(nail works; low)	day	1.11
1828, (high)	day	1.00	(paper mill; high)	day	1.00
(medium)	day	.69	(paper mill; low)	day	.667
(low)	day	.50	(stone work)	day	.875
(woollen mill)	day	.684	(woollen mill)	day	.90
1829,	day	.76	1857,	day	1.50
1830,	day	.735	(cordage works)	day	1.17
1833, (high)	day	1.00	(paper mill)	day	.971
(low)	day	.875	1858, (paper mill)	day	1.00
1834,	day	1.00	(woollen mill)	day	.96
1835, (high)	day	.825	1859, (paper mill)	day	1.00
(low)	day	.63	(woollen mill)	day	1.10
(paper mill)	day	1.00	1860,	day	1.00
(on wharf)	day	1.25	(linen mill)	mo.	20.00
1837, (cotton mill; high)	day	.87	(on wharf)	day	1.50
(cotton mill; low)	day	.75	(paper mill; high)	day	1.25
(woollen mill)	day	.75	(paper mill; low)	day	1.01
1838, (cotton mill; high)	day	.87	(woollen mill)	day	1.00
(cotton mill; low)	day	.75			
(woollen mill)	day	.75			
1840, (cordage works; high)	day	1.08			

Wages: Machinists.

Years.	Basis.	Amount.	Years.	Basis.	Amount.
1837,	day	$1.50	1839, (high)	day	$1.34
(cotton mill; high)	day	2.00	(medium)	day	1.17
(cotton mill; low)	day	1.33	(low)	day	1.00
1838,	day	1.50	1840, (high)	day	1.25
(cotton mill; high)	day	2.00	(medium)	day	1.00
(cotton mill; low)	day	1.33	(low)	day	.75

Wages: Machinists — CONCLUDED.

YEARS.	Basis.	Amount.	YEARS.	Basis.	Amount.
1840, (cordage works)	day	$1.33	1850, (locomotive works; low)	day	$1.17
1845, (high)	day	1.92	(metal work; high)	day	2.50
(medium)	day	1.69	(metal work; medium)	day	2.00
(low)	day	1.29	(metal work; low)	day	1.75
(foremen; high)	day	1.75	(shovel works)	day	1.50
(foremen; low)	day	1.50	(foremen)	day	1.84
(paper mill; high)	day	1.50	(helpers)	day	.784
(paper mill; low)	day	1.25	1855, (high)	day	2.50
1846,	day	1.33	(med. high)	day	2.20
(apprentices)	day	.608	(medium)	day	1.84
(helpers)	day	.817	(med. low)	day	1.54
1849,	day	1.75	(low)	day	1.22
1850, (high)	day	2.00	(apprentices)	day	.609
(medium)	day	1.75	(foremen)	day	2.16
(low)	day	1.50	(helpers)	day	.792
(cordage works)	day	1.67	1857, (gold and silver work;		
(gold and silver work;			high)	day	2.25
high)	day	2.25	(gold and silver work;		
(gold and silver work;			low)	day	1.68
medium)	day	2.00	(woollen mill; high)	day	1.50
(gold and silver work;			(woollen mill; low)	day	1.25
low)	day	1.67	(overseers, woollen mill)	day	2.50
(locomotive works;			1860, (high)	day	2.00
high)	day	2.50	(med. high)	day	1.75
(locomotive works; med.			(medium)	day	1.50
high)	day	1.85	(low)	day	1.25
(locomotive works; me-			(linen mill; high)	day	1.60
dium)	day	1.57	(linen mill; low)	day	1.50
(locomotive works; med.			(foremen; high)	day	2.50
low)	day	1.34	(foremen; low)	day	2.00

Wages: Masons.

YEARS.	Basis.	Amount.	YEARS.	Basis.	Amount.
1774,	day	$0.666	1825, (helpers; low)	day	$0.90
1788,	day	1.00	1828,	day	1.26
1803,	day	1.66	1835, (summer; high)	day	1.50
1809, (high)	day	1.75	(summer; low)	day	1.25
(low)	day	1.33	(summer; with board,		
1810, (high)	day	1.33	high)	day	.84
(low)	day	1.00	(summer; with board,		
1811,	day	1.50	low)	day	.66
1812,	day	3.25	(winter)	day	1.00
1813, (high)	day	1.74	(winter; with board,		
(low)	day	1.50	high)	day	.75
1815, (summer)	day	1.21	(winter; with board,		
(winter)	day	.88	low)	day	.50
(summer and winter;			(foremen; summer; high)	day	1.75
with board)	day	.628	(foremen; summer; low)	day	1.50
(foremen; winter)	day	1.17	(foremen; summer; with		
(foremen; summer and			board, high)	day	1.50
winter; with board)	day	.88	(foremen; summer; with		
(helpers)	day	.88	board, low)	day	1.00
1825, (summer; high)	day	1.50	(foremen; winter)	day	1.50
(summer; medium)	day	1.25	(foremen; winter; with		
(summer; low)	day	1.00	board)	day	1.00
(summer; with board,			(helpers; summer; high)	day	1.25
high)	day	.84	(helpers; summer; low)	day	1.00
(summer; with board,			(helpers; winter; high)	day	1.00
low)	day	.66	(helpers; winter; low)	day	.90
(winter; with board,			1845, (high)	day	1.50
high)	day	.75	(low)	day	1.00
(winter; with board,			(summer; with board)	day	.75
low)	day	.50	(foremen; high)	day	1.75
(foremen; summer and			(foremen; low)	day	1.50
winter)	day	1.50	(foremen; with board)	day	1.00
(foremen; summer and			(helpers; high)	day	1.25
winter; with board,			(helpers; low)	day	.967
high)	day	1.25	1860, (a d bricklayers; high)	day	1.60
(foremen; summer and			(and bricklayers; low)	day	1.25
winter; with board,			(and bricklayers — fore-		
low)	day	1.00	men)	day	2.00
(helpers; high)	day	1.13	(helpers)	day	1.00

Wages: Metal Workers.

Years.	Basis.	Amount.	Years.	Basis.	Amount.
1815, (foundrymen, skilled) .	day	$1.13	1845, (skilled workmen; medium)	day	$1.31
(foundrymen, unskilled)	day	.875	(skilled workmen; low)	day	.792
(pattern makers) . .	day	1.13	(copper and tinsmiths; high)	day	1.50
1825, (foundrymen, s k i l l e d; high)	day	1.50	(copper and tinsmiths; low)	day	1.25
(foundrymen, s k i l l e d; low)	day	1.25	(foundrymen, s k i l l e d; high)	day	1.50
(foundrymen, unskilled; high)	day	1.25	(foundrymen, s k i l l e d; low)	day	1.25
(foundrymen, unskilled; medium)	day	1.00	(foundrymen, unskilled; high)	day	1.25
(foundrymen, unskilled; low)	day	.84	(foundrymen, unskilled; low)	day	1.00
(pattern makers, foundry; high) . .	day	1.50	(pattern makers; high) .	day	1.50
(pattern makers; foundry; low) . .	day	1.25	(pattern makers; low) .	day	1.25
(pattern makers, machine shop) . .	day	1.25	(shovel makers, skilled; high)	day	1.73
1835, (foundrymen, s k i l l e d; high)	day	1.50	(shovel makers, skilled; med. high) . . .	day	1.50
(foundrymen, s k i l l e d; low)	day	1.25	(shovel makers, skilled; medium) . . .	day	1.37
(foundrymen, unskilled; high)	day	1.25	(shovel makers, skilled; med. low) . . .	day	1.14
(foundrymen, unskilled; low)	day	1.00	(shovel makers, skilled; low)	day	1.00
(pattern makers; high) .	day	1.50	(shovel makers—apprentices; men; high) .	day	.68
(pattern makers; low) .	day	1.25	(shovel makers—apprentices; men; low) .	day	.60
1837, (brass founders; high) .	wk.	10.50	(shovel makers—apprentices; boys) . .	day	.50
(brass founders; low) .	wk.	9.00	(shovel makers — handlers; high) . .	day	2.00
(coppersmiths; high) .	wk.	10.50	(shovel makers — handlers; low) . . .	day	1.47
(coppersmiths; low) .	wk.	9.00	(shovel makers — t r i p - hammermen) . .	day	2.12
(tinsmiths; high) . .	wk.	10.50	1850, (foremen; high) . .	day	2.50
(tinsmiths; low) . .	wk.	9.00	(foremen; med. high) .	day	2.25
1838, (brass founders; high) .	wk.	10.50	(foremen; medium) .	day	1.99
(brass founders; low) .	wk.	9.00	(foremen; low) . .	day	1.75
(coppersmiths; high) .	wk.	10.50	(skilled workmen; high)	day	2.00
(coppersmiths; low) .	wk.	9.00	(skilled workmen; med. high)	day	1.69
(tinsmiths; high) . .	wk.	10.50	(skilled workmen; medium)	day	1.50
(tinsmiths; low) . .	wk.	9.00	(skilled workmen; med. low)	day	1.34
1840, (foundrymen, unskilled; high)	day	1.00	(skilled workmen; low)	day	1.10
(foundrymen, unskilled; low)	day	.60	(apprentices, locomotive works; high) . .	day	.807
(shovel makers, skilled; high)	day	1.31	(apprentices, locomotive works; medium) .	day	.667
(shovel makers, skilled; medium) . . .	day	1.21	(apprentices, locomotive works; low) . .	day	.476
(shovel makers, skilled; low)	day	1.09	(heaters; high) . .	day	1.92
(shovel makers—apprentices; high) . . .	day	.68	(heaters; low) . .	day	1.75
(shovel makers—apprentices; low) . . .	day	.58	(iron slitters; high) .	day	1.33
(shovel makers — foremen)	day	1.75	(iron slitters; low) .	day	1.25
(shovel makers — handlers, skilled; high) .	day	2.00	(locomotive boiler makers; high) . .	day	2.50
(shovel makers — handlers, skilled; medium)	day	1.50	(locomotive boiler makers; medium) . .	day	1.52
(shovel makers — handlers, skilled; med. low)	day	1.21	(locomotive boiler makers; med. low) . .	day	1.23
(shovel makers — handlers, skilled ; low) .	day	1.00	(locomotive boiler makers; low) . .	day	1.00
(shovel makers — riveters)	day	1.00	(pattern makers, machine shop) . .	day	1.52
(shovel makers — shearers)	day	1.25	(shovel makers; high) .	day	2.00
(shovel makers — trip-hammermen; high) .	day	2.25	(shovel makers; med. high)	day	1.67
(shovel makers — trip-hammermen; low) .	day	2.00	(shovel makers; medium)	day	1.50
1845, (foremen)	day	1.67			
(skilled workmen; high) .	day	1.52			

Wages: Metal Workers—Concluded.

Years.	Basis.	Amount.	Years.	Basis.	Amount.
1850, (shovel makers; med. low) . . .	day	$1.24	1855, (apprentices, locomotive works; medium) .	day	$0.648
(shovel makers; low) .	day	1.00	(apprentices, locomotive works; low) . .	day	.498
(shovel makers—apprentices; men) .	day	.70	(iron slitters; high) .	day	1.83
(shovel makers—apprentices; boys) .	day	.50	(iron slitters; med. high) .	day	1.75
(shovel makers—foremen) . . .	day	2.50	(iron slitters; medium) .	day	1.67
(shovel makers—hammermen; high) . .	day	2.66	(iron slitters; low) .	day	1.50
(shovel makers—hammermen; low) . .	day	1.50	(locomotive boiler makers; high) . . .	day	3.00
(shovel makers—hammermen, with helpers)	mo.	109.80	(locomotive boiler makers; med. high) .	day	2.00
(shovel makers—handlers; high) . .	day	1.75	(locomotive boiler makers; medium) .	day	1.66
(shovel makers—handlers; medium) . .	day	1.39	(locomotive boiler makers; med. low) .	day	1.47
(shovel makers—handlers; low) . .	day	1.00	(locomotive boiler makers; low) . . .	day	1.19
(shovel makers—polishers; high) . .	day	1.25	(pattern makers) . .	day	2.12
(shovel makers—polishers; medium) . .	day	1.00	1860, (copper and tinsmiths; high) . . .	day	1.75
(shovel makers—polishers; low) . .	day	.68	(copper and tinsmiths; medium) . .	day	1.50
(shovel makers—trip-hammermen; high) .	day	2.67	(copper and tinsmiths; low) . . .	day	1.25
(shovel makers—trip-hammermen; low)	day	1.50	(foundrymen; high) .	day	1.50
(shovel makers—welders)	day	1.25	(foundrymen; low) .	day	1.25
1855, (apprentices, locomotive works; high) . .	day	.833	(moulders; high) .	day	2.00
			(moulders; low) . .	day	1.50
			(pattern makers, foundry; high) . .	day	2.00
			(pattern makers, foundry; low) . . .	day	1.50

Wages: Millwrights.

Years.	Basis.	Amount.	Years.	Basis.	Amount.
1799, (high)	day	$1.17	1835, (and machinists—foremen; high) . . .	day	$1.66
(low)	day	1.00	(and machinists—foremen; low) . . .	day	1.50
1815, (and machinists) .	day	1.13	1845, (paper mill) . . .	day	1.23
1825, (and machinists; high) .	day	1.25	1848, (paper mill) . . .	day	1.54
(and machinists; low) .	day	1.16	1857, (paper mill) . . .	day	1.76
1835, (and machinists; high) .	day	1.25	1858, (paper mill) . . .	day	1.67
(and machinists; low) .	day	1.16			

Wages: Nail Makers.

Years.	Basis.	Amount.	Years.	Basis.	Amount.
1781, ...	day	$0.481	1839, (cutters—shoe nails; low) . . .	mo.	$19.77
1817, (tacks) . . .	day	1.00	1850, (brads) . . .	mo.	35.36
(tacks) . . .	mo.	18.00	(shoe nails; high) .	mo.	53.87
1819, (tacks) . . .	day	1.00	(shoe nails; medium) .	mo.	45.01
1820, (tacks) . . .	day	1.00	(shoe nails; low) .	mo.	34.30
1822, (tacks; high) . .	day	1.52	(tacks; high) . .	mo.	78.89
(tacks; low) . .	day	1.25	(tacks; med. high) .	mo.	52.95
(tacks; piece work) .	M.	.028	(tacks; medium) .	mo.	38.91
1823, (tacks) . . .	day	1.51	(tacks; med. low) .	mo.	34.32
1824, (tacks) . . .	day	1.35	(tacks; low) . .	mo.	16.00
1829, (tacks) . . .	day	1.33	(brads, shoe nails, and tacks; foremen; high)	day	2.00
1831, (tacks) . . .	day	.539	(brads, shoe nails, and tacks; foremen; low)	day	1.00
1832, (tacks) . . .	day	1.18	(nailers; high) . .	mo.	60.24
1839, (tacks; high) . .	mo.	76.70	(nailers; med. high) .	mo.	51.38
(tacks; low) . .	mo.	56.36	(nailers; medium) .	mo.	44.15
(cutters—brads; high) .	mo.	44.88	(nailers; med. low) .	mo.	32.86
(cutters—brads; low) .	mo.	28.54	(nailers; low) . .	mo.	23.96
(cutters—shoe nails; high) . .	mo.	44.81	(puddlers; high) . .	mo.	81.68
(cutters—shoe nails; medium) . .	mo.	33.78			

Wages: Nail Makers — Concluded.

Years.	Ba-sis.	Amount.	Years.	Ba-sis.	Amount.
1850, (puddlers; low)	mo.	$74.81	1855, (cutters — tacks; high)	mo.	$99.34
1855, (cutters — brads)	mo.	38.44	(cutters — tacks; med. high)	mo.	78.83
(cutters — shoe nails; high)	mo.	87.84	(cutters — tacks; medium)	mo.	60.38
(cutters — shoe nails; medium)	mo.	72.85	(cutters — tacks; med. low)	mo.	40.32
(cutters — shoe nails; low)	mo.	52.18	(cutters — tacks; low)	mo.	28.89

Wages: Painters.

Years.	Ba-sis.	Amount.	Years.	Ba-sis.	Amount.
1801,	day	$0.625	1838, (carriages and wagons; high)	wk.	$9.00
1804,	day	1.33	(carriages and wagons; low)	wk.	7.00
1807,	day	1.50	1840, (carriage; with board)	mo.	20.00
1812,	day	1.50	1845, (carriage; high)	day	1.75
1815, (house)	day	1.13	(carriage; low)	day	1.25
(ship and sign)	day	1.38	(sign; high)	day	1.50
1825, (house; high)	day	1.25	(sign; low)	day	1.25
(house; low)	day	1.00	(and glaziers; high)	day	1.25
(ship and sign; high)	day	1.50	(and glaziers; low)	day	1.00
(ship and sign; low)	day	1.25	1850, (carriage; high)	day	1.75
1832, (carriage; with board, high)	mo.	18.00	(carriage; low)	day	1.50
(carriage; with board, low)	mo.	15.00	(carriage; piece work)	day	2.00
1835, (house; high)	day	1.25	1860, (carriage; high)	day	2.00
(house; low)	day	1.00	(carriage; low)	day	1.75
(sign; high)	day	1.50	(sign)	day	1.75
(sign; low)	day	1.25	(and glaziers; high)	day	1.75
1837, (carriages and wagons; high)	wk.	9.00	(and glaziers; medium)	day	1.50
(carriages and wagons; low)	wk.	7.00	(and glaziers; low)	day	1.25

Wages: Paper Mill Operatives.

Years.	Ba-sis.	Amount.	Years.	Ba-sis.	Amount.
1815,	day	$1.13	1848, (rag engine tenders)	day	$1.01
(women and girls; piece work)	wk.	6.50	1850, (bleachers; high)	day	1.25
1825, (high)	day	1.33	(bleachers; medium)	day	1.00
(low)	day	1.00	(bleachers; low)	day	.667
(sorters; women and girls; piece work, high)	wk.	4.00	(finishers)	day	1.08
(sorters; women and girls; piece work, low)	wk.	3.00	(firemen)	day	1.25
1835, (machine men)	day	1.25	(foremen; high)	day	2.00
(sorters; women and girls; piece work, high)	wk.	4.00	(foremen; low)	day	1.75
(sorters; women and girls; piece work, low)	wk.	3.00	(lay girls)	day	.40
1837, (high)	day	1.25	(lay boys; high)	day	.833
(low)	day	1.00	(lay boys; low)	day	.343
1838, (high)	day	1.23	(machine tenders; high)	day	1.33
(low)	day	1.00	(machine tenders; low)	day	1.17
1845, (bleachers)	day	.863	(rag cutters)	day	1.04
(finishers)	day	1.16	(rag engine tenders)	day	1.32
(lay women)	day	.452	(sorters)	day	.50
(lay girls)	day	.334	1855, (bleachers; high)	day	1.17
(lay boys)	day	.468	(bleachers; medium)	day	1.10
(machine tenders)	day	1.19	(bleachers; low)	day	.834
(rag engine tenders)	day	1.00	(finishers)	day	1.25
(rag sorters; women and girls; high)	wk.	4.50	(finishers; boys)	day	.333
(rag sorters; women and girls; low)	wk.	3.00	(foremen; high)	day	2.00
1848, (finishers)	day	1.21	(foremen; low)	day	1.75
(lay women)	day	.451	(machine tenders)	day	1.17
(lay girls)	day	.36	(mechanics)	day	1.50
(lay boys)	day	.561	(rag cutters)	day	1.25
(machine tenders)	day	1 19	(rag engine tenders)	day	1.33
			(scourers and dyers)	day	.82
			1857, (bleachers)	day	1.12
			(finishers)	day	1.28
			(lay women)	day	.734
			(lay girls)	day	.465
			(lay boys)	day	.85
			(machine tenders)	day	1.58

Wages: Paper Mill Operatives—Concluded.

Years.	Basis.	Amount.	Years.	Basis.	Amount.
1857, (rag engine tenders) .	day	$1.15	1859, (rag room hands; high)	day	$1.29
1858, (boys)	day	.833	(rag room hands; low)	day	1.00
(girls)	day	.50	(rag room hands; girls)	day	.50
(bleachers; high) . .	day	1.19	(rag room hands — fore-		
(bleachers; low) . .	day	1.00	men)	day	1.38
(finishers; high) . .	day	1.67	(stockmen; high) . .	day	1.23
(finishers; low) . .	day	1.25	(stockmen; low) . .	day	1.00
(finishers; girls; high).	day	.48	1860, (high)	day	1.83
(finishers; girls; low) .	day	.26	(low)	day	1.06
(machine tenders; high)	day	1.98	(high)	wk.	16.00
(machine tenders; me-			(low)	wk.	9.00
dium)	day	1.42	(women)	day	.50
(machine tenders; low)	day	1.17	(bleachers; high) . .	day	1.23
(rag cutters; girls) .	day	.50	(bleachers; low) . .	day	1.13
(rag engine tenders; high)	day	1.25	(cutters; women; high)	day	.65
(rag engine tenders; low)	day	1.00	(cutters; women; low)	day	.50
(rag room hands; high)	day	2.01	(finishers; high) . .	day	1.68
(rag room hands; me-			(finishers; low) . .	day	1.25
dium)	day	1.37	(finishers; women) .	day	.50
(rag room hands; low)	day	1.08	(machine tenders; high)	day	1.98
(rag room hands; girls;			(machine tenders; me-		
high)	day	.703	dium)	day	1.55
(rag room hands; girls;			(machine tenders; low)	day	1.27
medium) . . .	day	.639	(rag engine tenders; high)	day	1.37
(rag room hands; girls;			(rag engine tenders; me-		
low)	day	.50	dium)	day	1.26
(rag room hands — fore-			(rag engine tenders; low)	day	1.01
men)	day	1.41	(rag room hands; high)	day	1.28
(stockmen; high) . .	day	1.23	(rag room hands; low).	day	1.04
(stockmen; low) . .	day	1.00	(rag room hands; wo-		
1859, ...	day	1.00	men; high) . . .	day	.542
(bleachers; high) . .	day	1.25	(rag room hands; wo-		
(bleachers; low) . .	day	1.03	men; low) . . .	day	.30
(cutters; girls) . .	day	.50	(rag room hands — fore-		
(finishers; high) . .	day	1.67	men)	day	1.45
(finishers; low) . .	day	1.25	(sorters; women and		
(finishers; women; high)	day	.50	girls; high). . .	wk.	5.00
(finishers; women; low)	day	.393	(sorters; women and		
(machine tenders; high)	day	1.98	girls; low) . . .	wk.	3.00
(machine tenders; low)	day	1.27	(stockmen; high) . .	day	1.19
(rag engine tenders; high)	day	1.24	(stockmen; low) . .	day	1.00
(rag engine tenders; low)	day	1.00			

Wages: Printers.

Years.	Basis.	Amount.	Years.	Basis.	Amount.
1815, ...	day	$1.13	1840, (compositors, job; me-		
1825, (compositors and press-			dium)	wk.	$10.00
men; high) . . .	day	1.50	(compositors, job; low)	wk.	8.00
(compositors and press-			(pressmen; high) . .	wk.	10.00
men; medium) . .	day	1.25	(pressmen; low) . .	wk.	8.00
(compositors and press-			(press feeders; girls;		
men; low) . . .	day	1.00	high)	wk.	6.00
1835, (compositors; high) .	day	1.66	(press feeders; girls; low)	wk.	5.00
(compositors; low) .	day	1.25	1845, (compositors; high) .	wk.	9.00
1837, (high)	wk.	8.00	(compositors; low) .	wk.	8.00
(low)	wk.	6.00	(press feeders; girls;		
(pressmen; high) .	wk.	10.00	high)	wk.	3.50
(pressmen; low) .	wk.	8.00	(press feeders; girls;		
1838, (high)	wk.	8.00	low)	wk.	2.50
(low)	wk.	6.00	1850, (high)	wk.	10.00
(pressmen; high) .	wk.	10.00	(low)	wk.	9.00
(pressmen; low) .	wk.	8.00	1860, (high)	day	3.00
1840, ...	wk.	8.00	(medium)	day	2.00
(compositors; high) .	wk.	10.00	(low)	day	1.63
(compositors; low) .	wk.	8.00	(compositors) . . .	wk.	10.00
(compositors, job; high)	wk.	12.00	(pressmen)	wk.	10.00

Wages: Ship and Boat Builders.

Years.	Basis.	Amount.	Years.	Basis.	Amount.
1789, (ship gravers) . . .	day	$0.889	1835, (boats; high) . . .	day	$1.33
1815, (boats) . . .	day	1.13	(boats; low) . . .	day	1.00
(boats; with board)	day	.50	(boats; with board)	day	.66
(ship gravers) . . .	day	1.38	(ship carvers; high)	day	1.66
(ship riggers) . . .	day	1.25	(ship carvers; low)	day	1.33
1825, (boats; high) . . .	day	1.25	1845, (boats; high) . . .	day	1.33
(boats; low) . . .	day	1.00	(boats; low) . . .	day	1.00
(boats; with board)	day	.50	(boats; with board, high)	day	.66
(ship gravers; high)	day	1.50	(boats; with board, low)	day	.50
(ship gravers; low)	day	1.25	(ship carvers; high)	day	1.75
1826, (caulkers) . . .	day	2.00	(ship carvers; low)	day	1.33

Wages: Shoemakers.

Years.	Basis.	Amount.	Years.	Basis.	Amount.
1754, (piece work) . . .	pr.	$0.601	1825, (shoe fitters; piece work)	pr.	$0.05
1798, ...	wk.	3.27	(shoe fitters; women; piece work) . . .	pr.	.05
1800, ...	wk.	5.52	(shoe fitters — brogans;		
(piece work) . . .	pr.	.234	women; piece work) .	pr.	.06
1803, (shoe binders; piece work) . . .	pr.	.042	1830, (piece work, high) . .	pr.	.417
(shoe binders; piece work, high; per dozen pair) . . .	doz.	.50	(piece work, low) . .	pr.	.295
			(brogans; piece work, high) . . .	pr.	.418
(shoe binders; piece work, low; per dozen pair) . . .	doz.	.222	(brogans; piece work, medium) . . .	pr.	.307
1810, (piece work) . . .	pr.	.20	(brogans; piece work, low) . . .	pr.	.203
1811, (piece work) . . .	pr.	.625	(nailed brogans; piece work) . . .	pr.	.236
1812, (piece work, high) . .	pr.	1.71	(pegged brogans; piece work, high) . . .	pr.	.42
(piece work, medium) .	pr.	1.17			
(piece work, low) . .	pr.	.373	(pegged brogans; piece work, medium) . .	pr.	.367
1813, (piece work, high) . .	pr.	.918	(pegged brogans; piece work, low) . . .	pr.	.189
(piece work, medium) .	pr.	.754			
(piece work, low) . .	pr.	.547	(sewed brogans; piece work, high) . . .	pr.	.62
(boot fitters; piece work, high)	pr.	1.00	(sewed brogans, piece work, medium) . .	pr.	.528
(boot fitters; piece work, low)	pr.	.46	(sewed brogans; piece work, low) . . .	pr.	.40
(boot makers; piece work, high) . .	pr.	1.26	(boots; piece work, high)	pr.	1.32
(boot makers; piece work, low) . .	pr.	1.13	(boots; piece work, low)	pr.	.559
1814, (piece work) . . .	pr.	.71	(sewed boots; piece work, high) . . .	pr.	1.75
1816, (piece work) . . .	pr.	.516	(sewed boots; piece work, medium) . .	pr.	1.08
1819, (piece work, high) . .	pr.	.655	(sewed boots; piece work, low) . . .	pr.	.62
(piece work, low) . .	pr.	.43	(nailed shoes; piece work)	pr.	.202
1823, (piece work, high) . .	pr.	.548			
(piece work, low) . .	pr.	.31	(sewed shoes; piece work)	pr.	.439
1825, (piece work, high) . .	wk.	7.00	(shoe fitters; piece work)	pr.	.055
(piece work, low) . .	wk.	6.00	(shoe fitters; women; piece work) . . .	pr.	.068
(piece work, high) . .	pr.	.35	1835, ...	day	1.00
(piece work, medium) .	pr.	.25	(piece work) . . .	wk.	6.00
(piece work, low) . .	pr.	.20	(boys' pegged brogans; piece work) . . .	pr.	.21
(brogans; piece work, high)	pr.	.514			
(brogans; piece work, low)	pr.	.25	(nailed brogans; piece work, high) . . .	pr.	.20
(boys' shoes; piece work, high)	pr.	.30	(nailed brogans; piece work, low) . . .	pr.	.16
(boys' shoes; piece work, low)	pr.	.20	(pegged brogans; piece work, high) . . .	pr.	.273
(nailed shoes; piece work)	pr.	.265	(pegged brogans; piece work, low) . . .	pr.	.20
(pegged shoes; piece work, high) . . .	pr.	.515	(pegged shoes; piece work)	pr.	.20
(pegged shoes; piece work, low) . . .	pr.	.20	(sewed brogans; piece work, high) . . .	pr.	.421
(sewed shoes; piece work)	pr.	.544			
(shoe cutters) . . .	day	.834			
(shoe cutters; piece work)	pr.	.02			

Wages: Shoemakers — CONCLUDED.

YEARS.	Basis.	Amount.	YEARS.	Basis.	Amount.
1835, (sewed brogans; piece work, low)	pr.	$0.28	1840, (nailed brogans; piece work, high)	pr.	$0.23
(sewed Oxfords; piece work)	pr.	.50	(nailed brogans; piece work, low)	pr.	.15
(sewed shoes; piece work, high)	pr.	.461	(pegged brogans; piece work, high)	pr.	.236
(sewed shoes; piece work, low)	pr.	.28	(pegged brogans; piece work, low)	pr.	.197
(No. 2 shoes; piece work)	pr.	.349	(sewed brogans; piece work, high)	pr.	.40
(shoe fitters; piece work)	pr.	.04	(sewed brogans; piece work, low)	pr.	.29
(shoe fitters and makers — brogans; piece work)	pr.	.20	(youths' brogans; piece work)	pr.	.14
1837, (high)	day	1.63	(slippers; piece work)	pr.	.35
(medium)	day	1.00	(boot fitters; women; piece work)	pr.	.13
(low)	day	.625	(shoe fitters — brogans; piece work)	pr.	.04
(high)	wk.	11.33	1845,	day	1.33
(medium)	wk.	6.38	(high)	wk.	7.00
(low)	wk.	3.64	(low)	wk.	6.00
(binders; women; high)	wk.	3.50	(sewed boots; piece work)	pr.	.75
(binders; women; medium)	wk.	3.00	(laced brogans; piece work)	pr.	.16
(binders; women; low)	wk.	2.50	(pegged brogans; piece work)	pr.	.229
(cutters)	day	1.25	(pegged brogans; boys; piece work)	pr.	.185
(cutters; high)	wk.	9.20	(pegged shoes; piece work)	pr.	.563
(cutters; low)	wk.	6.90	(pegged shoes; boys; piece work)	pr.	.20
(fitters; women; high)	day	.467	(shoe fitters; piece work)	pr.	.125
(fitters; women; low)	day	.25	(shoe fitters and makers; piece work)	pr.	.20
(fitters; women; high)	wk.	3.00	1847,	day	1.44
(fitters; women; low)	wk.	2.50	(finishers)	day	.962
1838, (high)	day	1.63	(shoe cutters; high)	day	1.33
(medium)	day	1.00	(shoe cutters; medium)	day	1.24
(low)	day	.625	(shoe cutters; low)	day	1.00
(high)	wk.	11.33	1848,	day	1.17
(medium)	wk.	6.38	1849, (high)	day	1.00
(low)	wk.	3.64	(low)	day	.82
(binders; women; high)	wk.	3.50	(shoe cutters)	day	1.09
(binders; women; medium)	wk.	3.00	(shoe heel cutters)	day	1.25
(binders; women; low)	wk.	2.50	1850, (high)	day	1.25
(cutters)	day	1.25	(medium)	day	.916
(cutters; high)	wk.	9.20	(low)	day	.564
(cutters; low)	wk.	6.90	(shoe cutters; high)	day	1.50
(fitters; women; high)	day	.467	(shoe cutters; medium)	day	1.34
(fitters; women; low)	day	.25	(shoe cutters; low)	day	1.25
(fitters; women; high)	wk.	3.00	1855,	day	1.25
(fitters; women; low)	wk.	2.50		wk.	2.50
1839, (light shoes; with board)	yr.	275.00	1856,	day	1 83
1840, (boots; piece work, high)	pr.	.68	1857,	day	1.50
(boots; piece work, low)	pr.	.40	(women)	day	.50
(pegged boots)	pr.	.50	(women)	wk.	3.75
(sewed boots)	pr.	1.00	(finishers)	day	3.50
(brogans; piece work, high)	pr.	.333	1858,	day	1.50
(brogans; piece work, low)	pr.	.19			
(boys' brogans; piece work)	pr.	.167			
(boys' pegged brogans; piece work)	pr.	.194			

Wages: Stone Quarrymen and Cutters.

YEARS.	Basis.	Amount.	YEARS.	Basis.	Amount.
1836, (cutters)	day	$1.43	1850, (cutters; high)	day	$1.74
1839, (cutters)	day	1.32	(cutters; low)	day	1.64
(quarrymen)	day	1.03	(quarrymen)	day	1.10
1840, (cutters)	day	1.49	1854, (hammerers)	day	1.75
(quarrymen)	day	1.20	(quarrymen)	day	1.21
1845, (cutters; high)	day	1.60	1855, (cutters)	day	1.88
(cutters; low)	day	1.47	(foremen)	day	1.75
(foremen)	day	1.41	(quarrymen)	day	1.19
(quarrymen)	day	1.19			

Wages: Tanners and Curriers.

Years.	Basis.	Amount.	Years.	Basis.	Amount.
1815, (curriers; high)	day	$1.25	1837, (whiteners; low)	day	$1.25
(curriers; medium)	day	1.00	(yard hands; high)	day	1.25
(curriers; low)	day	.75	(yard hands; low)	day	1.00
(tanners; high)	day	1.25	1838, (beamsters; high)	day	1.25
(tanners; medium)	day	1.00	(beamsters; low)	day	1.00
(tanners; low)	day	.75	(curriers; high)	wk.	10.00
1825, (curriers; high)	day	1.25	(curriers; low)	wk.	9.00
(curriers; low)	day	1.00	(knife men; high)	day	1.25
(tanners; high)	day	1.25	(knife men; low)	day	1.00
(tanners; low)	day	1.00	(scourers; high)	day	1.25
1835, (curriers; high)	day	1.25	(scourers; low)	day	1.00
(curriers; low)	day	1.00	(shavers; high)	day	2.00
(tanners; high)	day	1.25	(shavers; medium)	day	1.50
(tanners; low)	day	1.00	(shavers; low)	day	1.25
1837, (beamsters; high)	day	1.25	(splitters; high)	day	2.00
(beamsters; low)	day	1.00	(splitters; medium)	day	1.50
(curriers; high)	wk.	10.00	(splitters; low)	day	1.25
(curriers; low)	wk.	9.00	(stuffers; high)	day	1.25
(knife men; high)	day	1.25	(stuffers; low)	day	1.00
(knife men; low)	day	1.00	(table hands; high)	day	1.25
(scourers; high)	day	1.25	(table hands; low)	day	1.00
(scourers; low)	day	1.00	(tanners; high)	day	1.25
(shavers; high)	day	2.00	(tanners; low)	day	1.00
(shavers; medium)	day	1.50	(tanners; high)	wk.	7.00
(shavers; low)	day	1.25	(tanners; low)	wk.	6.00
(splitters; high)	day	2.00	(whiteners; high)	day	2.00
(splitters; medium)	day	1.50	(whiteners; medium)	day	1.50
(splitters; low)	day	1.25	(whiteners; low)	day	1.25
(stuffers; high)	day	1.25	(yard hands; high)	day	1.25
(stuffers; low)	day	1.00	(yard hands; low)	day	1.00
(table hands; high)	day	1.25	1845, (curriers; high)	day	1.25
(table hands; low)	day	1.00	(curriers; low)	day	1.00
(tanners; high)	day	1.25	(tanners; high)	day	1.25
(tanners; low)	day	1.00	(tanners; low)	day	1.00
(tanners; high)	wk.	7.00	1860, (curriers; high)	day	2.00
(tanners; low)	wk.	6.00	(curriers; low)	day	1.50
(whiteners; high)	day	2.00	(tanners; high)	day	1.75
(whiteners; medium)	day	1.50	(tanners; low)	day	1.50

Wages: Teachers.

Years.	Basis.	Amount.	Years.	Basis.	Amount.
1795,	yr.	$399.60	1805, (high)	mo.	$50.00
1796,	mo.	20.00	(low)	mo.	41.67
1797, (assistants)	mo.	20.00	1806, (high)	mo.	83.33
(principals)	yr.	450.00	(low)	mo.	32.50
1801,	mo.	30.00	1808,	wk.	6.56
1805,	day	1.11	1809,	wk.	6.00
	wk.	8.68			

Wages: Teamsters.

Years.	Basis.	Amount.	Years.	Basis.	Amount.
1836, (stone)	day	$1.13	1850, (stone)	day	$1.30
1837, (cotton mill)	day	1.14	1855, (stone)	day	1.26
1838, (cotton mill)	day	1.14	1857, (woollen mill)	day	1.25
1839,	day	1.17	1858, (paper mill)	day	1.34
1840, (stone)	day	1.25	1860, (brewery)	wk.	14.00

Wages: Watchmen.

Years.	Basis.	Amount.	Years.	Basis.	Amount.
1836, (woollen mill)	day	$0.805	1857, (woollen mill)	day	$1.00
1840, (woollen mill)	day	1.04	1858, (woollen mill)	day	.90
1855, (nail works)	day	.833	1859, (woollen mill)	day	1.10
(woollen mill)	day	.892	1860, (woollen mill)	day	1.00

Wages: Wooden Goods Makers.

Years.	Ba-sis.	Amount.	Years.	Ba-sis.	Amount.
1809, (coopers) . . .	day	$0.66	1845, (coopers; high) . .	day	$1.33
1815, (coopers) . . .	day	1.13	(coopers; low) . .	day	1.25
(coopers; piece work) .	day	1.38	1846, ...	day	.946
1823, (box makers) . .	day	1.00	1848, ...	day	1.01
1825, (coopers) . . .	day	1.25	1850, ...	day	1.00
(coopers; piece work) .	day	1.50	1855, ...	day	1.06
1835, (coopers; high) .	day	1.33	1860, ...	day	1.07
(coopers; low) . .	day	1.25	(coopers; high) . .	day	1.75
(coopers; piece work) .	day	1.50	(coopers; low) . .	day	1.33

Wages: Woollen Mill Operatives.

Years.	Ba-sis.	Amount.	Years.	Ba-sis.	Amount.
1828, ...	day	$0.504	1850, (card strippers; high) .	day	$0.84
(dye house) . . .	day	.769	(card strippers; low) .	day	.76
(overseers) . . .	day	1.50	(carding room) . .	day	.552
(carding overseers) .	day	1.25	(drawers) . . .	day	1.67
(dye house overseers) .	day	1.60	(dressers; high) . .	day	1.50
1832, ...	day	.431	(dressers; medium) .	day	1.25
(overseers) . . .	day	1.46	(dressers; low) . .	day	1.03
(carding overseers) .	day	1.25	(dressing room) . .	day	.387
(spinning overseers) .	day	1.00	(finishers; high) . .	day	1.00
1836, ...	day	.747	(finishers; low) . .	day	.76
(overseers) . . .	day	1.58	(finishing room) . .	day	.578
(finishing overseers) .	day	2.00	(fullers; high) . .	day	.84
(spinning overseers) .	day	1.34	(fullers; low) . .	day	.76
(weaving overseers) .	day	1.83	(giggers; high) . .	day	.84
(spinners) . .	day	1.42	(giggers; low) . .	day	.743
1837, (card room hands) .	day	.29	(machine shop) . .	day	1.13
(card tenders; high) .	wk.	2.50	(pickers; high) . .	day	.84
(card tenders; low) .	wk.	2.00	(pickers; low) . .	day	.76
(finishers) . .	wk.	6.00	(scourers and dyers) .	day	.84
(general hands) . .	wk.	6.00	(sorters) . . .	day	1.25
(overseers) . . .	day	1.00	(speckers) . . .	day	.50
(overseers) . . .	wk.	7.50	(spinners) . . .	day	1.00
(carding overseers) .	day	2.00	(spinning room) . .	day	.486
(carding overseers) .	wk.	9.00	(weavers) . . .	day	1.00
(spinning overseers) .	day	1.00	(weaving room) . .	day	.572
(weaving overseers) .	day	1.00	1855, (carders; high) . .	day	.70
(wool room overseers) .	day	1.00	(carders; low) . .	day	.57
(spinners) . . .	day	.85	(dressers; high) . .	day	1.12
(spinners) . . .	wk.	6.00	(dressers; low) . .	day	1.00
(weavers) . . .	day	.50	(fine drawers) . .	day	1.59
(weavers) . . .	wk.	6.00	(finishers; high) . .	day	.80
(wool washers) . .	wk.	6.00	(finishers; low) . .	day	.60
1838, (card room hands) .	day	.29	(fullers) . . .	day	.76
(card tenders; high) .	wk.	2.50	(giggers) . . .	day	.771
(card tenders; low) .	wk.	2.00	(pickers) . . .	day	.70
(finishers) . .	wk.	6.00	(sorters; high) . .	day	1.20
(general hands) . .	wk.	6.00	(sorters; low) . .	day	.884
(overseers) . . .	day	1.00	(spinners) . . .	day	.851
(overseers) . . .	wk.	7.50	(weavers; high) . .	day	.84
(carding overseers) .	day	2.00	(weavers; low) . .	day	.745
(carding overseers) .	wk.	9.00	1857, (men and women; piece		
(spinning overseers) .	day	1.00	work, high) . . .	mo.	28.00
(weaving overseers) .	day	1.00	(men and women; piece		
(wool room overseers) .	day	1.00	work, low) . . .	mo.	12.00
(spinners) . . .	day	.85	(burlers and speckers;		
(spinners) . . .	wk.	6.00	girls)	day	.50
(weavers) . . .	day	.50	(carders; girls) . .	day	.50
(weavers) . . .	wk.	6.00	(fullers; high) . .	day	1.50
(wool washers) . .	wk.	6.00	(fullers; low) . .	day	1.00
1840, ...	day	.569	(giggers; high) . .	day	1.00
(overseers) . . .	day	1.81	(giggers; low) . .	day	.83
(finishing overseers) .	day	2.00	(overseers) . . .	day	1.25
(spinning overseers) .	day	1.75	(carding overseers; high)	day	1.75
(weaving overseers) .	day	2.02	(carding overseers; low)	day	1.50
(spinners) . . .	day	1.36	(finishing overseers) .	day	2.50
1845, ...	day	.621	(picking overseers) .	day	1.50
(overseers) . . .	day	1.74	(spinning overseers) .	day	1.50
1850, (boys; high) . .	day	.45	(weaving overseers) .	day	1.50
(boys; low) . .	day	.30	(pattern makers) . .	day	2.00
(assorting room) .	day	.96	(picking hands) . .	day	.60

Wages (Concluded): **Woollen Mill Operatives** — Concluded.

Years.	Ba-sis.	Amount.	Years.	Ba-sis.	Amount.
1857, (finishing second hands)	day	$1.50	1859, (finishers) . . .	day	$0.82
(picking second hands) .	day	.83	(finishers; women) .	wk.	2.83
(weaving second hands)	day	1.25	(fullers) . . .	day	.76
(spinners; piece work, high) . . .	mo.	32 00	(giggers). . .	day	.83
			(repair hands) . .	day	1.38
(spinners; piece work, low) . . .	mo.	19.00	(spinners) . . .	day	.80
			(waste sorters) . .	day	.32
1858, (carders). . . .	day	.58	(weavers; women) .	wk.	4.40
(drawers; women; high)	wk.	5.31	(wool sorters) . .	day	1.19
(drawers; women; low)	wk.	4.50	1860, (carders)	day	.68
(dyers)	day	.82	(drawers; women) .	wk.	5.08
(finishers) . . .	day	.78	(dressers; women) .	wk.	4.55
(finishers; women) .	wk.	2.60	(dyers) . . .	day	.91
(fullers)	day	.74	(finishers) . . .	day	.88
(giggers). . . .	day	.72	(finishers; women) .	wk.	2.90
(repair hands) . .	day	1.25	(fullers) . . .	day	.81
(spinners) . . .	day	.78	(giggers) . . .	day	.84
(waste sorters) . .	day	.30	(pickers) . . .	day	.81
(weavers; women) .	wk.	3.96	(repair hands) . .	day	1.38
(wool sorters) . .	day	1.15	(spinners) . . .	day	.78
1859, (carders) . . .	day	.62	(waste sorters) . .	day	.34
(drawers; women) .	wk.	5.50	(weavers; women) .	wk.	4.18
(dressers; women) .	wk.	5.73	(wool sorters) . .	day	1.17
(dyers)	day	.82			

Prices: **Agricultural Products.**

Apples.			*Apples*—Con.		
1753, ...	bu.	$0.222	1837, (high)	pk.	$0.396
1758, ...	bu.	.416	(low)	pk.	.248
1763, ...	bu.	.167	1838, (high)	pk.	.36
1765, ...	bu.	.25	(low)	pk.	.20
1770, ...	bu.	.133		bu.	.58
1773, (sweet)	bu.	.156		bbl.	2.00
1777, ...	bu.	.147	1839, ...	pk.	.248
1781, ...	bu.	.167	1840, ...	bbl.	1.04
1782, ...	bu.	.167	1841, ...	pk.	.261
1785, ...	bu.	.167	(high)	bbl.	1.81
1790, ...	bu.	.177	(low)	bbl.	1.50
1792, ...	bu.	.278	(wholesale, high) .	bbl.	1.99
1795, (winter)	bu.	.25	(wholesale, low) .	bbl.	1.42
1797, ...	bu.	.25	1842, ...	bbl.	1.50
1807, ...	bbl.	1.50	(wholesale) . .	bbl.	1.00
1810, ...	bu.	.344	1843, (high)	pk.	.349
1812, ...	bu.	.36	(low)	pk.	.204
1813, ...	pk.	.075		bu.	.761
	bu.	.267	(high)	bbl.	2.29
1814, ...	bu.	1.00	(low)	bbl.	1.74
1816, ...	bu.	.50	1844, ...	bu.	.45
1817, ...	bu.	.50	(high)	bbl.	1.40
1818, ...	bbl.	2.50	(low)	bbl.	1.00
1821, (high)	bu.	.54	1845, ...	pk.	.227
(low)	bu.	.30		bbl.	1.72
1822, ...	pk.	.127	(wholesale) . .	bbl.	1.63
	bu.	.37	1846, (high)	pk.	.333
1823, ...	pk.	.131	(low)	pk.	.225
	bu.	.30	(high)	bbl.	2.00
1824, ...	pk.	.18	(low)	bbl.	1.56
(high)	bu.	.60	1847, (high)	pk.	.333
(low)	bu.	.44	(low)	pk.	.16
1827, ...	bu.	.351	(high)	bu.	1.25
1829, ...	bbl.	1.20	(low)	bu.	1.00
1830, (high)	pk.	.20	(high)	bbl.	2.62
(low)	pk.	.128	(low)	bbl.	2.12
(high)	bu.	.60	(wholesale) . .	bbl.	1 68
(low)	bu.	.45	1848, ...	pk.	.365
1831, ...	bu.	.25		bu.	1.00
1832, ...	bbl.	2.50	(wholesale, high) .	bbl.	1.84
1833, (high)	bu.	1.16	(wholesale, low) .	bbl.	1.25
(low)	bu.	.80	1849, ...	pk.	.17
1834, ...	pk.	.125		bu.	.67
	bu.	.75		bbl.	1.00

Prices: Agricultural Products — Continued.

Years.	Basis.	Amount.	Years.	Basis.	Amount.
Apples — Con.			*Beans* — Con.		
1849, (wholesale)	bbl.	$1.98	1807,	bu.	$1.69
1850, (high)	pk.	.412	(white)	bu.	1.75
(low)	pk.	.218	1808,	bu.	1.00
	bu.	1.00	1809,	pk.	.50
	bbl.	1.75		bu.	1.32
1851,	pk.	.221	1810,	pk.	.333
(high)	bbl.	2.00	1812, (high)	bu.	1.76
(low)	bbl.	1.75	(low)	bu.	1.33
(wholesale)	bbl.	1.59	1813,	bu.	3.00
1852,	bbl.	2.25	(white)	qt.	.09
(wholesale)	bbl.	1.16	1814,	pk.	.67
1853,	bbl.	2.25		bu.	2.34
(wholesale)	bbl.	1.16	(white)	pk.	.72
1854, (high)	pk.	.336	1815,	qt.	.079
(low)	pk.	.25		bu.	2.24
(wholesale)	bbl.	1.49	1816,	qt.	.098
1855, (high)	bbl.	2.25		bu.	2.50
(low)	bbl.	1.50	1817,	qt.	.187
(wholesale)	bbl.	1.57		bu.	4.00
1856, (wholesale)	bbl.	1.33	1818,	qt.	.091
1857, (high)	bu.	1.24		pk.	.557
(low)	bu.	.75	1819,	pk.	.646
(high)	bbl.	2.46	1820,	bu.	1.74
(low)	bbl.	1.75	1821,	bu.	1.20
1858,	bbl.	2.20	1822,	pk.	.25
(wholesale)	bbl.	1.32	1827,	qt.	.085
1859,	bbl.	2.00	1828,	pk.	.50
1860,	bbl.	1.13	(high)	bu.	1.76
			(low)	bu.	1.50
Barley.			1830, (high)	pk.	.66
1792,	bu.	.729	(medium)	pk.	.372
1793,	bu.	.667	(low)	pk.	.25
1795,	pk.	.209	1831,	pk.	.50
1798,	bu.	.667		bu.	1.42
1802,	pk.	.25	1832, (high)	bu.	1.50
	bu.	1.25	(low)	bu.	1.34
1803,	bu.	.50	(white)	qt.	.035
1805,	bu.	1.00	1834,	pk.	.75
1806,	bu.	1.11		bu.	1.25
1811,	bu.	1.00	1835,	qt.	.097
1812,	bu.	1.00	1837, (high)	qt.	.095
1813,	pk.	.50	(low)	qt.	.062
1815,	bu.	1.00	1838,	qt.	.094
1816,	bu.	1.00	(high)	bu.	2.80
1820, (wholesale)	bu.	.80	(low)	bu.	2.50
1824,	pk.	.18	1839,	qt.	.086
1859,	bu.	.80		pk.	.75
				bu.	2.58
Beans.			1840,	qt.	.10
1755, (white)	qt.	.033	1841,	qt.	.078
1759,	bu.	.80		bu.	2.00
1761, (white)	qt.	.042	1842,	qt.	.072
1763, (white)	qt.	.056		pk.	.50
1767,	pk.	.25		bu.	1.75
1768,	bu.	.80	1843,	qt.	.068
1770,	qt.	.027		pk.	.552
1778,	qt.	.042	(high)	bu.	2.14
1781,	qt.	.041	(low)	bu.	1.60
1782,	pk.	.33	1844,	pk.	.508
1783,	pk.	.506	1845,	pk.	.491
1785,	pk.	.33	1846,	pk.	.528
1792,	bu.	.896		bu.	2.00
1793,	qt.	.049	1847, (high)	pk.	.54
	bu.	1.01	(low)	pk.	.28
1794,	bu.	1.06	(high)	bu.	2.03
1797, (shell)	bu.	1.25	(low)	bu.	1.79
1798, (white; wholesale)	bu.	1.00	1848,	qt.	.062
1801,	pk.	.50		bu.	1.75
1802,	qt.	.06	1849,	qt.	.056
1804,	bu.	1.50		pk.	.50
1805, (high)	bu.	1.67	1850,	pk.	.532
(low)	bu.	1.33		bu.	2.00
(white)	qt.	.042	1851,	pk.	.574
1806,	bu.	1.57	1852,	qt.	.079

Prices: Agricultural Products — CONTINUED.

YEARS.	Basis	Amount.
Beans — Con.		
1854, .	qt.	$0.078
1855, .	qt.	.09
	bu.	2.50
1856, .	qt.	.096
	pk.	.50
1857, .	qt.	.083
1858, .	qt.	.082
	bu.	3.00
(high)		
(low)	bu.	1.87
1859, (high)	qt.	.12
(low)	qt.	.073
(high)	bu.	3.00
(low)	bu.	2.00
(wholesale)	bu.	.75
1860, (high)	bu.	3.00
(low)	bu.	2.80
Buckwheat.		
1847, .	bu.	.833
1850, .	bu.	.677
1859, .	bu.	1.00
Corn.		
1752, .	bu.	.778
1754, .	bu.	.555
1756, .	pk.	.222
1757, .	bu.	.444
1758, .	bu.	.444
1759, .	bu.	.555
1760, .	bu.	.667
1761, .	pk.	.167
	bu.	.667
1762, .	pk.	.167
	bu.	.667
1763, .	pk.	.167
1764, .	pk.	.167
1765, .	bu.	.556
1766, (high)	bu.	.538
(low)	bu.	.50
1767, .	bu.	.556
1768, (Indian) .	bu.	.483
1770, (Indian) .	bu.	.50
1772, (Indian) .	bu.	.667
1774, .	bu.	.555
1777, .	bu.	.903
(Indian) .	bu.	.667
1780, .	bu.	.723
1782, (high)	bu.	.911
(low)	bu.	.667
1783, (new)	bu.	.559
(old)	bu.	1.15
1784, .	bu.	.541
1785, .	pk.	.167
	bu.	.833
1786, .	bu.	.785
(Indian) .	bu.	.667
1787, .	bu.	.556
1788, (high)	bu.	.889
(low)	bu.	.667
1789, .	bu.	.528
1790, .	pk.	.167
	bu.	.667
1791, (high)	bu.	1.00
(low)	bu.	.556
(Indian) .	bu.	1.50
1792, (Indian) .	bu.	.692
1793, (Indian) .	bu.	.828
(Indian; wholesale)	bu.	.75
1794, .	bu.	.816
(Indian) .	bu.	.839
(Indian; wholesale)	bu.	.667

YEARS.	Basis	Amount.
Corn — Con.		
1795, (high)	bu.	$1.00
(low)	bu.	.556
1796, (Indian) .	bu.	1.10
(Indian; wholesale)	bu.	1.00
1797, (high)	bu.	1.11
(low)	bu.	.667
(Indian; wholesale)	bu.	1.00
1798, (high)	bu.	.958
(low)	bu.	.713
(wholesale)	bu.	.611
1799, (Indian; wholesale)	bu.	.802
1800, (high)	bu.	1.00
(low)	bu.	.833
(Indian) .	bu.	1.08
1801, (Indian) .	bu.	1.21
1802, .	bu.	.82
1803, (high)	bu.	.833
(low)	bu.	.75
1804, (Indian; wholesale)	bu.	.917
1805, .	pk.	.28
(high)	bu.	1.50
(low)	bu.	.987
(Indian; wholesale)	bu.	1.27
1806, (wholesale) .	bu.	1.00
(Indian; wholesale)	bu.	.785
1807, (high)	bu.	1.17
(low)	bu.	1.09
(wholesale)	bu.	.87
(Indian) .	bu.	1.00
1808, .	bu.	.971
(wholesale, high) .	bu.	.962
(wholesale, low) .	bu.	.751
1809, (Indian) .	bu.	1.01
(white) .	bu.	.85
1810, (high)	bu.	1.27
(low)	bu.	1 06
(Indian; wholesale)	bu.	1.03
1811, (Indian; wholesale, high)	bu.	1.45
(Indian; wholesale, medium)	bu.	1.17
(Indian; wholesale, low)	bu.	.973
1812, (high)	bu.	2.00
(medium)	bu.	1.58
(med. low)	bu.	1.25
(low)	bu.	1.17
(Indian) .	bu.	.916
1813, (high)	bu.	1.56
(low)	bu.	1.25
(Indian) .	bu.	2.00
(Indian; wholesale)	bu.	1.13
1814, (high)	bu.	1.70
(medium)	bu.	1.45
(low)	bu.	1.08
(Indian; wholesale)	bu.	1.75
1815, (high)	bu.	1.50
(low)	bu.	1.25
(Indian; wholesale)	bu.	1.08
1816, (high)	bu.	1.50
(low)	bu.	1.19
(cracked)	bu.	1.17
1817, (high)	bu.	1.68
(low)	bu.	1.25
(Indian) .	bu.	2.00
1818, (Indian; high)	bu.	1.28
(Indian; low) .	bu.	.95
(Indian; wholesale, high)	bu.	1.00
(Indian; wholesale, low)	bu.	.92
1819, .	bu.	1.16
(Indian) .	pk.	.28
(Indian; high) .	bu.	1.00
(Indian; medium) .	bu.	.89

Prices: Agricultural Products—CONTINUED.

YEARS.	Basis.	Amount.	YEARS.	Basis.	Amount.
Corn — Con.			*Corn — Con.*		
1819, (Indian; low).	bu.	$0.75	1857,	bu.	$0.95
1820, (high)	bu.	1.00	(wholesale)	bu.	.90
(low)	bu.	.80	(white)	bu.	1.04
(wholesale)	bu.	.66	1858, (high)	bu.	1.38
1821, (high)	bu.	1.00	(low)	bu.	.998
(low)	bu.	.672	(wholesale)	bu.	.956
(Indian)	bu.	.90	(white)	bu.	.793
(southern)	bu.	.63	1859,	bu.	1.12
1822, (high)	bu.	1.00	(white)	bu.	.952
(low)	bu.	.725	1860, (wholesale)	bu.	.804
(Indian)	bu.	.86			
(Indian; wholesale)	bu.	.718	*Cranberries.*		
1823, (high)	bu.	.90	1782,	pk.	.296
(low)	bu.	.65	1783,	pk.	.139
1824,	bu.	.816	1804,	pk.	.25
1825,	bu.	1.04	1805,	pk.	.375
(wholesale)	bu.	.50	1811,	pk.	.25
(yellow; wholesale)	bu.	.61	1821,	pk.	.25
1826, (high)	bu.	1.07	1822,	pk.	.32
(low)	bu.	.74	1828,	pk.	.25
1827,	bu.	.778	1832, (high)	pk.	.70
(new; wholesale)	bu.	.508	(low)	pk.	.38
(old; wholesale)	bu.	.58	1834,	bu.	2.26
1828, (high)	bu.	1.00	1837,	bu.	1.00
(medium)	bu.	.717	1838,	pk.	.50
(low)	bu.	.52	1839,	pk.	.50
(yellow; wholesale)	bu.	.361	1841,	bu.	1.34
1829, (high)	bu.	.92	1843,	bu.	2.00
(low)	bu.	.738	1845,	qt.	.125
1830,	bu.	.666	1846,	pk.	.40
1831, (high)	bu.	.83	1847,	bu.	2.00
(medium)	bu.	.697	1848,	pk.	.87
(low)	bu.	.556		bu.	2.25
1832, (high)	bu.	.894			
(low)	bu.	.75	*Flax.*		
1833,	bu.	.89	1767,	lb.	.139
1834,	bu.	.875	1768,	lb.	.124
1835,	bu.	1.00	1772,	lb.	.10
1840,	bu.	.724	1780,	lb.	.125
(yellow)	bu.	.60	1781,	lb.	.111
1841, (high)	bu.	.938	1782,	lb.	.178
(low)	bu.	.63	1783,	lb.	.143
1842, (high)	bu.	.825	1784,	lb.	.084
(low)	bu.	.688	1787,	lb.	.111
(wholesale, high)	bu.	.75	1794,	lb.	.167
(wholesale, low)	bu.	.606	1798,	lb.	.167
(white; wholesale)	bu.	.585	1799,	lb.	.174
1843,	bu.	.68	1802,	lb.	.20
(wholesale)	bu.	.50	1807,	lb.	.224
1844,	bu.	.62	1811,	lb.	.25
(wholesale)	bu.	.555	1814,	lb.	.20
(white)	bu.	.518	1815,	lb.	.20
1845,	bu.	.601	1817,	lb.	.20
(wholesale)	bu.	.502	1818,	lb.	.20
1846,	bu.	.901	1823,	lb.	.167
(wholesale)	bu.	.715	1826, (high)	lb.	.166
(white; wholesale)	bu.	.656	(low)	lb.	.124
1847,	pk.	.293			
	bu.	.847	*Flaxseed.*		
(wholesale, high)	bu.	1.14	1756,	bu.	.444
(wholesale, low)	bu.	.805	1787,	bu.	.185
1848,	bu.	.64	1790,	bu.	.599
(wholesale)	bu.	.56	1792,	bu.	.913
1849,	bu.	.73	1794,	pk.	.167
(wholesale)	bu.	.642	1796,	bu.	.958
1850,	bu.	.756	1821,	lb.	.247
(wholesale, high)	bu.	.737			
(wholesale, low)	bu.	.523	*Hops.*		
1851,	bu.	.769	1805,	lb.	.167
(wholesale)	bu.	.713	1806,	lb.	.166
1852, (white)	bu.	.749	1807,	lb.	.25
1853, (wholesale)	bu.	.69	1808,	lb.	.167
1855, (white)	bu.	1.17	1809,	lb.	.20
1856, (wholesale)	bu.	.712	1819,	lb.	.248
			1831,	lb.	.125

Prices: Agricultural Products — CONTINUED.

YEARS.	Basis.	Amount.	YEARS.	Basis.	Amount.
Hops — Con.			*Onions* — Con.		
1837,	lb.	$0.175	1843, (high)	pk.	$0.158
1838,	lb.	.163	(low)	pk.	.125
1839,	lb.	.173	1845,	pk.	.128
1842,	lb.	.25	1848,	pk.	.22
1843,	lb.	.168		bu.	.664
1845,	lb.	.168	1850,	bu.	.634
1847,	lb.	.169	1855, (high)	bu.	1.00
1848,	lb.	.186	(low)	bu.	.75
1850,	lb.	.189	1856,	pk.	.249
1851,	lb.	.181	1857,	bu.	1.06
1854,	lb.	.48	1858,	pk.	.25
1855,	lb.	.333		bu.	.942
1856,	lb.	.188	1859,	bu.	.95
1857, (high)	lb.	.34			
(low)	lb.	.25	*Parsnips.*		
1858,	lb.	.252	1756,	pk.	.167
			1761,	pk.	.126
Oats.			1839,	pk.	.193
1757,	bu.	.333	1843,	pk.	.17
1767,	bu.	.333			
1782,	bu.	.647	*Peas.*		
1783, (high)	bu.	.637	1768,	pk.	.277
(low)	bu.	.347	1771,	qt.	.055
1784,	bu.	.334	1783,	pk.	.514
1787,	bu.	.333	1804,	pk.	.31
1788,	bu.	.667		bu.	1.34
1793, (high)	bu.	.50	1805, (high)	pk.	.667
(low)	bu.	.333	(low)	pk.	.25
1798,	bu.	.555	1813,	pk.	.80
1800,	bu.	.416	1814, (high)	pk.	.80
1801,	bu.	.583	(low)	pk.	.45
1802,	bu.	.50	1819,	qt.	.06
1803,	bu.	.417	1821, (high)	bu.	1.50
1805,	bu.	.755	(low)	bu.	.68
1807,	bu.	.552	1835,	pk.	.20
1808,	bu.	.583	1841,	qt.	.06
1809,	bu.	.465	1843,	pk.	.248
1810,	bu.	.573	1846, (high)	pk.	.981
1811,	bu.	.613	(medium)	pk.	.758
(wholesale)	bu.	.40	(low)	pk.	.50
1814, (high)	bu.	1.13	(split)	qt.	.112
(low)	bu.	.67	1847,	bu.	2.52
1815,	bu.	.60	(split)	pk.	.75
1816,	bu.	.67	1850, (high)	pk.	.44
1821,	bu.	.35	(low)	pk.	.32
1822,	bu.	.50			
1823,	bu.	.498	*Potatoes.*		
1826,	bu.	.59	1752,	bu.	.40
1827, (wholesale)	bu.	.36	1754,	pk.	.083
1828,	bu.	.203		bu.	.333
1830,	bu.	.414	1755,	bu.	.389
1831,	bu.	.60	1756,	pk.	.111
1832,	bu.	.50	1759,	bu.	.333
1834,	bu.	.56	1760,	pk.	.10
1838,	bu.	.51		bu.	.40
1839, (high)	bu.	.66	1761,	pk.	.10
(low)	bu.	.50	1762,	pk.	.111
1840,	bu.	.48		bu.	.389
1841,	bu.	.55	1763,	bu.	.50
1842, (high)	bu.	.648	1764, (English)	bu.	.334
(low)	bu.	.45	1765, (high)	bu.	.333
1843,	bu.	.40	(low)	bu.	.27
1845,	bu.	.468	(English)	bu.	.40
1846, (high)	bu.	.64	1766,	bu.	.333
(low)	bu.	.515	1767,	bu.	.333
1847,	bu.	.63	1768, (English)	bu.	.40
1848,	bu.	.602	1770,	bu.	.25
1849,	bu.	.55	1771,	bu.	.204
			1772,	bu.	.176
Onions.			1773, (English)	bu.	.333
1768,	bu.	1.00	1774,	bu.	.231
1822, (high)	pk.	.26	1775,	bu.	.247
(low)	pk.	.18	1777,	bu.	.416
1841,	bu.	.63	1778, (English)	bu.	.333

Prices: Agricultural Products — Continued.

Years.	Basis	Amount.	Years.	Basis	Amount.
Potatoes — Con.			*Potatoes* — Con.		
1780,	bu.	$0.458	1826, (high)	bu.	$0.50
1781,	bu.	.333	(medium)	bu.	.42
1782,	bu.	.50	(low)	bu.	.34
1783, (high)	bu.	.556	1827,	bu.	.251
(low)	bu.	.333	1828,	bu.	.333
1784,	bu.	.167	1829,	pk.	.10
1785, (high)	bu.	.223	(early white)	bu.	1.00
(low)	bu.	.167	1830,	bu.	.249
1786, (high)	bu.	.296	1831,	bu.	.276
(low)	bu.	.223	1832, (high)	bu.	.397
1787,	bu.	.167	(low)	bu.	.30
1788, (high)	bu.	.333	1833, (high)	bu.	.40
(low)	bu.	.223	(low)	bu.	.32
1790, (high)	bu.	.222	1834,	pk.	.125
(low)	bu.	.167		bu.	.37
1791,	bu.	.18	1835,	pk.	.143
1792,	bu.	.25	(high)	bu.	.667
1793, (high)	bu.	.50	(low)	bu.	.40
(medium)	bu.	.167	(wholesale)	bu.	.25
(low)	bu.	.133	1836,	pk.	.31
1795,	bu.	.264		bu.	.75
1796,	bu.	.44	1837,	bu.	.75
1797,	bu.	.416	1838, (high)	bu.	.75
1798,	bu.	.256	(medium)	bu.	.50
1799,	bu.	.355	(low)	bu.	.30
1800,	bu.	.36	1839, (high)	bu.	.75
1802,	bu.	.33	(low)	bu.	.50
1803,	bu.	.355	1840, (high)	bu.	.60
1804, (high)	bu.	.583	(low)	bu.	.33
(low)	bu.	.33	1841, (high)	bu.	.50
1805, (high)	bu.	.563	(low)	bu.	.25
(low)	bu.	.333	(wholesale)	bu.	.375
(wholesale)	bu.	.631	1842,	bu.	.50
(early)	bu.	.74	(wholesale)	bu.	.30
1806,	pk.	.226	1843, (high)	bu.	.75
(high)	bu.	.993	(medium)	bu.	.471
(low)	bu.	.536	(low)	bu.	.33
(wholesale)	bu.	.285	1844,	bu.	1.00
1807,	bu.	.42	(wholesale)	bu.	.351
1808,	bu.	.322	1845, (high)	pk.	.375
1809, (high)	bu.	.714	(low)	pk.	.215
(low)	bu.	.483		bu.	.50
1810,	pk.	.167	(wholesale)	bu.	.333
(high)	bu.	.536	1846, (high)	bu.	1.10
(low)	bu.	.375	(medium)	bu.	.75
1811,	bu.	.353	(low)	bbl.	2.50
1812, (high)	bu.	.499	1847, (high)	pk.	.392
(medium)	bu.	.432	(medium)	pk.	.212
(low)	bu.	.333	(low)	pk.	.125
1813, (high)	bu.	.75	(high)	bu.	.90
(low)	bu.	.492	(medium)	bu.	.76
1814, (high)	bu.	.50	(low)	bu.	.608
(low)	bu.	.421	(wholesale)	bu.	.689
1815, (high)	bu.	.493	1848, (high)	pk.	.323
(low)	bu.	.336	(low)	pk.	.18
1816,	bu.	.451	(high)	bu.	1.25
1817, (high)	bu.	1.16	(low)	bu.	1.03
(medium)	bu.	.551	(wholesale, high)	bu.	.863
(low)	bu.	.33	(wholesale, low)	bu.	.548
(wholesale)	bu.	.28	1849,	pk.	.333
1818, (high)	bu.	.50	(high)	bu.	1.23
(low)	bu.	.334	(low)	bu.	.955
1819, (high)	bu.	.595	(wholesale)	bu.	.82
(low)	bu.	.406	1850, (high)	pk.	.38
1820, (high)	bu.	.50	(low)	pk.	.264
(low)	bu.	.254	(high)	bu.	1.25
1821, (high)	bu.	.488	(medium)	bu.	1.00
(low)	bu.	.197	(low)	bu.	.76
1822, (high)	bu.	.33	(wholesale)	bu.	.509
(low)	bu.	.213	1851,	pk.	.27
1823, (high)	bu.	.346	(high)	bu.	.80
(low)	bu.	.25	(low)	bu.	.678
1825, (high)	bu.	.375	1852,	pk.	.40
(low)	bu.	.25	(wholesale)	bu.	.573

Prices: Agricultural Products — Continued.

Years.	Basis.	Amount.	Years.	Basis.	Amount.
Potatoes — Con.			*Rice* — Con.		
1853, (wholesale, high)	bu.	$0.677	1829,	lb.	$0.043
(wholesale, low)	bu.	.406	1830,	lb.	.041
1854, (high)	pk.	.50	1831,	lb.	.047
(medium)	pk.	.362	1832, (high)	lb.	.06
(low)	pk.	.28	(low)	lb.	.045
(wholesale)	bu.	.755	1834, (high)	lb.	.05
1855,	pk.	.33	(low)	lb.	.04
(high)	bu.	.60	1835,	lb.	.043
(low)	bu.	.472	1836,	lb.	.051
(wholesale, high)	bu.	.851	1837, (high)	lb.	.113
(wholesale, low)	bu.	.682	(low)	lb.	.053
1856,	bu.	.459	1838,	lb.	.057
(wholesale, high)	bu.	.803	1839,	lb.	.059
(wholesale, low)	bu.	.437	1840,	lb.	.05
1857, (high)	bu.	1.56	1841,	lb.	.048
(med. high)	bu.	1.25	1842,	lb.	.045
(medium)	bu.	.997	1843,	lb.	.039
(low)	bu.	.777	1844,	lb.	.041
(wholesale)	bu.	.75	1845,	lb.	.047
1858, (high)	bu.	1.54	1846,	lb.	.053
(medium)	bu.	.821	1847,	lb.	.062
(low)	bu.	.605	1848,	lb.	.051
(wholesale)	bu.	.55	1849,	lb.	.049
1859, (high)	bu.	1.00	1850,	lb.	.05
(medium)	bu.	.777	1851,	lb.	.05
(low)	bu.	.599	1852,	lb.	.051
1860, (high)	bu.	1.00	1854,	lb.	.06
(low)	bu.	.68	1855,	lb.	.075
			1856,	lb.	.072
Rice.			1857,	lb.	.066
1783,	lb.	.055	1858,	lb.	.055
1792,	lb.	.034	1859,	lb.	.051
(wholesale)	lb.	.036			
1794,	lb.	.041	*Rye.*		
(wholesale)	lb.	.031	1752,	pk.	.195
1798, (wholesale)	lb.	.028	1753,	bu.	.80
1799,	lb.	.036	1754,	bu.	.511
1801,	lb.	.07	1755,	bu.	.806
(wholesale)	lb.	.066	1756,	bu.	.50
1802,	lb.	.071	1758,	bu.	.556
1803, (wholesale)	lb.	.057	1759,	bu.	.556
1804,	lb.	.055	1761,	bu.	.667
1805,	lb.	.064	1762,	bu.	.667
1806,	lb.	.053	1763,	bu.	.667
(wholesale)	lb.	.044	1764,	bu.	.889
1807,	lb.	.05	1765, (high)	bu.	.667
(wholesale)	lb.	.034	(low)	bu.	.633
1808, (wholesale)	lb.	.049	1766,	bu.	.667
1809, (wholesale)	lb.	.04	1767,	bu.	.667
1810,	lb.	.04	1770,	bu.	.444
1811,	lb.	.042	1780,	pk.	.25
1812,	lb.	.053		bu.	1.00
1813, (high)	lb.	.099	1782,	pk.	.33
(low)	lb.	.085	1783,	bu.	1.06
(by the cwt.)	lb.	.062	1784,	bu.	.997
1814,	lb.	.084	1785,	pk.	.25
(wholesale)	lb.	.07	1786,	bu.	1.00
1815,	lb.	.046	(wholesale)	bu.	.75
1816, (high)	lb.	.055	1788,	bu.	.944
(low)	lb.	.014	1790,	bu.	.833
1817,	lb.	.076	1791, (high)	bu.	1.00
(wholesale)	lb.	.061	(low)	bu.	.667
1818,	lb.	.071	1792,	bu.	.692
1819,	lb.	.071	1793,	bu.	1.67
(wholesale)	lb.	.049	(wholesale)	bu.	.836
1820, (wholesale)	lb.	.039	1794,	pk.	.25
1821,	lb.	.042	(high)	bu.	1.37
1822,	lb.	.043	(low)	bu.	1.03
1823,	lb.	.045	(wholesale)	bu.	.916
1824,	lb.	.042	1795,	bu.	1.42
1825,	lb.	.044	(wholesale)	bu.	1.17
1826,	lb.	.046	1796, (wholesale)	bu.	1.33
1827,	lb.	.046	1797,	pk.	.223
1828,	lb.	.045		bu.	1.33

Prices: Agricultural Products — CONTINUED.

Years.	Basis.	Amount.	Years.	Basis.	Amount.
Rye — Con.			*Rye* — Con.		
1800, (high)	bu.	$1.17	1827, (wholesale, medium) .	bu.	$0.60
(low)	bu.	1.03	(wholesale, low) . .	bu.	.48
	bag	2.50	1828, (high) . . .	bu.	1.03
1801, (high) . . .	bu.	1.46	(low) . . .	bu.	.82
(low) . . .	bu.	1.26	1829, ...	bu.	.935
1802, (high) . . .	bu.	1.17	1830, ...	pk.	.25
(low) . . .	bu.	1.11		bu.	.852
(wholesale) . .	bu.	.791	(wholesale) . . .	bu.	.735
1803, (high) . . .	bu.	1.08	1831, ...	bu.	1.10
(low) . . .	bu.	.903	1832, (high) . . .	bu.	1.13
1804, (high) . . .	bu.	1.67	(medium) . .	bu.	1.00
(med. high) . .	bu.	1.50	(low) . . .	bu.	.88
(medium) . .	bu.	1.04	1841, ...	bu.	1.00
(low) . . .	bu.	.761	1855, ...	bu.	1.50
1805, ...	pk.	.416			
(high) . . .	bu.	1.61	*Squashes.*		
(low) . . .	bu.	1.33	1845, ...	lb.	.02
(wholesale, high) .	bu.	1.72	1849, ...	lb.	.01
(wholesale, medium) .	bu.	1.57	1855, ...	lb.	.007
(wholesale, low) .	bu.	1.25	1858, ...	lb.	.025
1806, (high) . . .	bu.	1.57			
(low) . . .	bu.	1.30	*Sweet Potatoes.*		
(wholesale) . .	bu.	1.06	1840, ...	lb.	.023
1807, ...	bu.	1.29	1841, ...	pk.	.32
1808, ...	bu.	1.11	1842, ...	lb.	.02
(wholesale, high) .	bu.	.95	1843, ...	lb.	.025
(wholesale, low) .	bu.	.728	1845, ...	lb.	.026
1809, (high) . . .	bu.	1.53	(high) . . .	pk.	.327
(low) . . .	bu.	1.11	(low) . . .	pk.	.22
1810, (wholesale, high) .	bu.	2.00	1846, ...	lb.	.022
(wholesale, medium) .	bu.	1.56	1847, (high) . . .	lb.	.08
(wholesale, low) .	bu.	1.36	(low) . . .	lb.	.029
1811, (high) . . .	bu.	2.18		bu.	1.20
(medium) . .	bu.	1.64	1848, ...	lb.	.03
(low) . . .	bu.	1.44		pk.	.33
(wholesale) . .	bu.	.75	1849, ...	lb.	.03
1812, (high) . . .	bu.	2.50	1850, ...	lb.	.029
(medium) . .	bu.	1.83		pk.	.333
(med. low) . .	bu.	1.44	1854, ...	pk.	.647
(low) . . .	bu.	1.15	1855, ...	lb.	.029
(wholesale) . .	bu.	1.03	1857, ...	lb.	.036
1813, (high) . . .	bu.	1.50	1858, ...	lb.	.03
(low) . . .	bu.	1.33			
1814, ...	bu.	1.34	*Turnips.*		
1815, (high) . . .	bu.	1.42	1752, ...	bu.	.222
(medium) . .	bu.	1.32	1755, ...	bu.	.333
(low) . . .	bu.	1.09	1758, ...	bu.	.222
1816, (high) . . .	bu.	1.58	1759, ...	bu.	.25
(low) . . .	bu.	1.34	1760, ...	bu.	.278
1817, (high) . . .	bu.	2.00	(French) . . .	bu.	.266
(low) . . .	bu.	1.73	1762, ...	pk.	.063
1818, ...	pk.	.34	1763, (high) . . .	bu.	.333
(high) . . .	bu.	.95	(low) . . .	bu.	.223
(low) . . .	bu.	.85	1764, ...	bu.	.25
(wholesale) . .	bu.	.81	1765, ...	pk.	.083
1819, ...	pk.	.335	1766, ...	bu.	.278
(high) . . .	bu.	1.42	1767, ...	pk.	.083
(medium) . .	bu.	1.17	(high) . . .	bu.	.292
(low) . . .	bu.	.944	(low) . . .	bu.	.222
1820, ...	bu.	1.08	1770, ...	bu.	.25
1821, (high) . . .	bu.	1.00	1771, ...	bu.	.255
(low) . . .	bu.	.747	1775, ...	bu.	.249
1822, (high) . . .	bu.	1.00	1777, ...	pk.	.178
(medium) . .	bu.	.824	1781, ...	bu.	.20
(low) . . .	bu.	.68	1782, ...	bu.	.222
1823, (high) . . .	bu.	.96	1783, ...	bu.	.223
(medium) . .	bu.	.83	1784, ...	bu.	.244
(low) . . .	bu.	.635	1785, ...	bu.	.25
1824, ...	bu.	.82	1787, ...	bu.	.223
1825, ...	bu.	1.00	1790, ...	bu	.333
1826, (high) . . .	bu.	1.12	1798, ...	bu.	.50
(low) . . .	bu.	.74	1804, ...	pk.	.167
1827, ...	bu.	1.00	1807, ...	bu.	.333
(wholesale, high) .	bu.	.72			

Prices: Agricultural Products — Concluded.

Years.	Basis	Amount.	Years.	Basis	Amount.
Turnips — Con.			*Wheat.*		
1810,	bu.	$0.50	1770,	bu.	$0.999
1814,	bu.	.45	1774,	bu.	.999
1815,	bu.	.50	1775,	bu.	.832
1822,	bu.	.25			
(French)	bu.	.50	*Wool.*		
1824,	pk.	.07	1782, (high)	lb.	.416
(French)	bu.	.40	(low)	lb.	.333
1825,	bu.	.25	1784,	lb.	.226
1827,	bu.	.25	1802,	lb.	.416
1831,	bu.	.25	1803, (high)	lb.	.375
1841, (wholesale)	bu.	.20	(low)	lb.	.292
1847,	bu.	.335	1809,	lb.	.476
1848,	bu.	.33	1811, (lamb's)	lb.	.42
(wholesale)	bu.	.125	1812,	lb.	1.10
1853,	bu.	.42	1813,	lb.	.737
1854, (wholesale)	bu.	.494	1814, (high)	lb.	1.10
1858,	bu.	.25	(low)	lb.	.85
			1816,	lb.	.50

Prices: Boots, Shoes, and Leather.

Years.	Basis	Amount.	Years.	Basis	Amount.
Boots.			*Boots* — Con.		
1796,	pr.	$6.00	1850, (calf)	pr.	$2.62
1803, (high)	pr.	4.08	1854,	pr.	2.78
(low)	pr.	3.50	1855, (high)	pr.	4.25
1805,	pr.	2.00	(med. high)	pr.	3.47
1808,	pr.	3.50	(medium)	pr.	2.45
1809, (high)	pr.	7.00	(med. low)	pr.	1.25
(low)	pr.	5.00	(low)	pr.	.46
(short)	pr.	6.50	1856, (high)	pr.	3.52
1810,	pr.	4.00	(med. high)	pr.	2.76
1811, (high)	pr.	8.50	(medium)	pr.	1.91
(low)	pr.	8.00	(med. low)	pr.	1.29
(calf)	pr.	9.00	(low)	pr.	.573
(long-legged)	pr.	7.00	1857, (high)	pr.	4.00
1813,	pr.	4.00	(med. high)	pr.	3.41
(bootees)	pr.	1.75	(medium)	pr.	2.47
1814, (high)	pr.	9.00	(med. low)	pr.	1.31
(low)	pr.	8.00	(low)	pr.	.753
1816,	pr.	7.00	1858, (high)	pr.	3.75
1817, (small)	pr.	.75	(med. high)	pr.	3.13
1820,	pr.	4.50	(medium)	pr.	2.05
1821, (high)	pr.	7.00	(med. low)	pr.	1.28
(medium)	pr.	6.25	(low)	pr.	.64
(low)	pr.	4.25	1859, (high)	pr.	3.51
1822,	pr.	2.00	(med. high)	pr.	2.23
1828,	pr.	4.50	(med. low)	pr.	1.35
1830, (thin)	pr.	4.50	(low)	pr.	.704
1831,	pr.	4.50			
(sewed)	pr.	3.25	*Buckles.*		
1833,	pr.	4.00	1793, (plated)	doz.	3.50
1837, (calf)	pr.	4.00	1794, (knee)	pr.	.07
1838, (thick)	pr.	3.50	(plated)	doz.	4.00
1839,	pr.	4.50	(tin)	doz.	.778
1840, (high)	pr.	3.62			
(low)	pr.	2.38	*Calamanco.*		
1841,	pr.	2.88	1783,	yd.	.331
1843, (pegged)	pr.	2.37	1792, (wholesale)	yd.	.347
1844, (calf)	pr.	3.25	1793,	yd.	.457
1845, (calf)	pr.	2.75			
1847,	pr.	1.50	*Leather.*		
(cow-hide)	pr.	2.38	1792, (wholesale)	lb.	.203
1848, (high)	pr.	3.00	(sole; wholesale)	lb.	.187
(low)	pr.	2.42	1793, (wholesale)	lb.	.189
(boys')	pr.	1.75	1794,	lb.	.192
1849,	pr.	2.50			

Prices: Boots, Shoes, and Leather — Continued.

Years.	Basis.	Amount.
Leather — Con.		
1795,	lb.	$0.216
1797, (wholesale)	lb.	.20
1798,	lb.	.17
(wholesale)	lb.	.197
1799,	lb.	.198
1801,	lb.	.22
1810,	lb.	.25
1811, (sole; wholesale)	lb.	.21
1812, (high)	lb.	.25
(low)	lb.	.21
1813, (sole)	lb.	.187
1819, (sole)	lb.	.19
1820,	lb.	.20
1826, (sole)	lb.	.259
1830, (sole)	lb.	.25
Rubber Boots.		
1857, (high)	pr.	3.50
(med. high)	pr.	3.00
(med. low)	pr.	2.00
(low)	pr.	1.38
1858, (high)	pr.	3.18
(low)	pr.	1.50
1859, (high)	pr.	3.50
(medium)	pr.	2.25
(low)	pr.	1.72
Rubbers.		
1827,	pr.	1.38
1828, (India)	pr.	1.50
1830, (India; high)	pr.	1.25
(India; low)	pr.	.875
1832, (India)	pr.	1.25
1838,	pr.	1.25
1840,	pr.	1.00
1843,	pr.	.50
1844, (high)	pr.	.75
(low)	pr.	.625
1847,	pr.	1.00
1852,	pr.	1.00
1855, (high)	pr.	1.02
(medium)	pr.	.747
(low)	pr.	.552
1856, (high)	pr.	1.00
(medium)	pr.	.754
(low)	pr.	.50
1857, (high)	pr.	.98
(low)	pr.	.673
1858, (high)	pr.	.677
(low)	pr.	.437
1859,	pr.	.699
Sandals.		
1795, (wholesale)	pr.	.916
1814,	pr.	1.42
1816, (wholesale)	pr.	1.08
1817,	pr.	1.23
Shoes.		
1756,	pr.	1.00
1761,	pr.	1.11
1767,	pr.	1.11
1772, (high)	pr.	1.00
(medium)	pr.	.80
(low)	pr.	.709
1782,	pr.	.583
1783, (high)	pr.	1.57
(medium)	pr.	.907
(low)	pr.	.786
1784, (high)	pr.	.916
(medium)	pr.	.75
(low)	pr.	.444
1785,	pr.	1.17

Years.	Basis.	Amount.
Shoes — Con.		
1788,	pr.	$1.50
1791, (lasting)	pr.	.583
(satinet)	pr.	.702
1792, (high)	pr.	.938
(low)	pr.	.583
(wholesale, high)	pr.	.747
(wholesale, low)	pr.	.581
(calamanco; wholesale)	pr.	.629
(Florentine; wholesale)	pr.	.791
(girls' Florentine; wholesale)	pr.	.589
(lasting; wholesale)	pr.	.576
(leather; wholesale)	pr.	.764
(satinet; wholesale, high)	pr.	1.00
(satinet; wholesale, low)	pr.	.682
1793, (high)	pr.	1.09
(low)	pr.	.528
(wholesale)	pr.	.702
(calamanco; wholesale)	pr.	.653
(Florentine; wholesale, high)	pr.	.881
(Florentine; wholesale, low)	pr.	.782
(lasting; wholesale)	pr.	.593
(leather)	pr.	1.08
(leather; wholesale)	pr.	.648
(morocco)	pr.	.75
(satinet; wholesale, high)	pr.	.716
(satinet; wholesale, low)	pr.	.601
1794, (high)	pr.	.875
(low)	pr.	.667
(wholesale)	pr.	.716
(cloth)	pr.	.667
(Florentine)	pr.	.916
(Florentine; wholesale, high)	pr.	.897
(Florentine; wholesale, medium)	pr.	.764
(Florentine; wholesale, low)	pr.	.386
(lasting)	pr.	.601
(men's)	pr.	1.17
(men's leather)	pr.	.833
(misses' Florentine)	pr.	.652
(russet; wholesale)	pr.	.625
(satinet; wholesale)	pr.	.709
(silk)	pr.	1.08
1795, (high)	pr.	.889
(low)	pr.	.556
(Florentine; wholesale, high)	pr.	.868
(Florentine; wholesale, low)	pr.	.772
(lasting; wholesale)	pr.	.605
(russet; wholesale)	pr.	.667
(satinet; wholesale)	pr.	.699
1796, (high)	pr.	2.00
(low)	pr.	.90
(with English toes)	pr.	2.25
1797, (wholesale, high)	pr.	.723
(wholesale, low)	pr.	.333
1798, (wholesale, high)	pr.	.723
(wholesale, low)	pr.	.333
(buff; wholesale)	pr.	.333
(gum; wholesale)	pr.	.723
(morocco)	pr.	1.00
1799, (high)	pr.	1.11
(low)	pr.	1.00
1800, (high)	pr.	1.88
(medium)	pr.	1.50
(low)	pr.	1.00
(boys' thick)	pr.	.667
(men's thick)	pr.	.84
(stuff)	pr.	.75

Prices: Boots, Shoes, and Leather — CONTINUED.

YEARS.	Basis.	Amount.	YEARS.	Basis.	Amount.
Shoes — Con.			*Shoes* — Con.		
1801, (leather and stuff; wholesale)	pr.	$0.80	1815, (med. low)	pr.	$1.16
1802, (high)	pr.	2.00	(low)	pr.	.875
(low)	pr.	1.50	(boys')	pr.	1.00
1803, (high)	pr.	2.00	(women's)	pr.	1.50
(low)	pr.	1.50	1816, (high)	pr.	2.09
1804, (high)	pr.	1.22	(medium)	pr.	1.20
(medium)	pr.	.75	(med. low)	pr.	.897
(low)	pr.	.394	(low)	pr.	.508
(wholesale)	pr.	.917	(wholesale, high)	pr.	1.14
(calf-skin)	pr.	1.25	(wholesale, medium)	pr.	.927
1805, (high)	pr.	2.00	(wholesale, low)	pr.	.671
(med. high)	pr.	1.65	(Scotch ties; wholesale)	pr.	1.07
(medium)	pr.	1.56	(boys')	pr.	1.03
(med. low)	pr.	1.25	(cork)	pr.	1.67
(low)	pr.	.667	(kid; wholesale)	pr.	1.10
(morocco)	pr.	.96	(men's)	pr.	1.33
1806, (high)	pr.	2.00	(misses')	pr.	.50
(med. high)	pr.	1.50	(roan; wholesale)	pr.	.732
(medium)	pr.	1.25	(walking; wholesale)	pr.	1.15
(med. low)	pr.	.667	1817, (high)	pr.	2.25
(low)	pr.	.50	(med. high)	pr.	2.05
(wholesale)	pr.	.916	(medium)	pr.	1.29
1807, (high)	pr.	2.00	(med. low)	pr.	.961
(medium)	pr.	1.17	(low)	pr.	.50
(med. low)	pr.	.677	(wholesale, high)	pr.	1.11
(low)	pr.	.375	(wholesale, medium)	pr.	.90
1808, (high)	pr.	2.30	(wholesale, low)	pr.	.55
(med. high)	pr.	1.92	(kid; wholesale)	pr.	.971
(medium)	pr.	1.50	(morocco; wholesale, high)	pr.	.91
(med. low)	pr.	.849	(morocco; wholesale, low)	pr.	.80
(low)	pr.	.50	(pumps)	pr.	.916
1809, (high)	pr.	2.13	(roan)	pr.	.70
(medium)	pr.	1.25	(roan; wholesale)	pr.	.625
(med. low)	pr.	.969	(walking; wholesale)	pr.	1.13
(low)	pr.	.75	1818, (high)	pr.	2.22
(men's)	pr.	1.75	(med. high)	pr.	1.75
1810, (high)	pr.	2.13	(medium)	pr.	1.23
(med. high)	pr.	1.71	(low)	pr.	.662
(medium)	pr.	1.17	(small)	pr.	.42
(med. low)	pr.	.716	1819, (high)	pr.	2.25
(low)	pr.	.48	(med. high)	pr.	1.50
1811, (high)	pr.	2.00	(medium)	pr.	1.33
(med. high)	pr.	1.42	(med. low)	pr.	1.03
(medium)	pr.	1.19	(low)	pr.	.677
(med. low)	pr.	.813	1820, (high)	pr.	2.13
(low)	pr.	.656	(med. high)	pr.	1.71
(boys')	pr.	.83	(medium)	pr.	1.27
(children's)	pr.	.45	(med. low)	pr.	.739
(men's)	pr.	1.00	(low)	pr.	.525
(women's)	pr.	1.17	1821, (high)	pr.	2.50
1812, (high)	pr.	2.00	(med. high)	pr.	2.00
(med. high)	pr.	1.58	(medium)	pr.	1.32
(medium)	pr.	1.10	(med. low)	pr.	.875
(med. low)	pr.	.836	(low)	pr.	.58
(low)	pr.	.625	1822, (high)	pr.	2.00
(boys')	pr.	.92	(medium)	pr.	1.01
(men's)	pr.	1.38	(med. low)	pr.	.69
1813, (high)	pr.	2.00	(low)	pr.	.333
(med. high)	pr.	1.70	(kid)	pr.	1.34
(medium)	pr.	1.21	(walking)	pr.	1.44
(med. low)	pr.	.733	1823, (high)	pr.	1.28
(low)	pr.	.458	(medium)	pr.	.939
(girls')	pr.	1.25	(low)	pr.	.515
(walking)	pr.	1.50	(thin)	pr.	2.00
1814, (high)	pr.	2.08	1824, (high)	pr.	2.00
(medium)	pr.	1.56	(medium)	pr.	1.29
(med. low)	pr.	1.19	(low)	pr.	.873
(low)	pr.	.751	1825, (high)	pr.	1.56
(boys')	pr.	1.04	(medium)	pr.	1.08
(walking)	pr.	1.75	(low)	pr.	.58
1815, (high)	pr.	2.25	1826, (high)	pr.	2.00
(med. high)	pr.	1.98	(med. high)	pr.	1.62
(medium)	pr.	1.46			

Prices: Boots, Shoes, and Leather — CONCLUDED.

Years.	Basis.	Amount.	Years.	Basis.	Amount.
Shoes — Con.			*Shoes* — Con.		
1826, (medium)	pr.	$1.33	1846, (low)	pr.	$0.50
(med. low)	pr.	1.13	1847, (high)	pr.	1.12
(low)	pr.	.68	(low)	pr.	.518
1827, (high)	pr.	2.00	(ladies')	pr.	1.00
(med. high)	pr.	1.63	1848, (high)	pr.	.75
(medium)	pr.	1.14	(low)	pr.	.50
(med. low)	pr.	.665	1849, .	pr.	1.00
(low)	pr.	.50	1850, (high)	pr.	1.25
1828, (high)	pr.	2.13	(medium)	pr.	.92
(med. high)	pr.	1.78	(low)	pr.	.63
(medium)	pr.	1.36	1851, (high)	pr.	1.25
(med. low)	pr.	.999	(low)	pr.	.56
(low)	pr.	.625	1852, (high)	pr.	1.25
1829, (high)	pr.	1.90	(low)	pr.	.625
(medium)	pr.	1.02	1854, .	pr.	1.75
(low)	pr.	.62	1855, (high)	pr.	2.00
1830, (high)	pr.	2.00	(med. high)	pr.	1.55
(med. high)	pr.	1.42	(medium)	pr.	1.13
(medium)	pr.	1.25	(med. low)	pr.	.656
(med. low)	pr.	.967	(low)	pr.	.33
(low)	pr.	.625	1856, (high)	pr.	1.59
1831, (high)	pr.	1.92	(medium)	pr.	1.09
(medium)	pr.	1.30	(low)	pr.	.677
(low)	pr.	1.01	1857, (high)	pr.	1.75
1832, (high)	pr.	2.00	(med. high)	pr.	1.47
(medium)	pr.	1.32	(medium)	pr.	1.03
(low)	pr.	1.07	(med. low)	pr.	.68
1833, (high)	pr.	2.00	(low)	pr.	.37
(medium)	pr.	1.63	1858, (high)	pr.	1.71
(low)	pr.	1.13	(medium)	pr.	1.01
1834, (high)	pr.	1.42	(low)	pr.	.573
(medium)	pr.	1.03	1859, (high)	pr.	1.57
(low)	pr.	.542	(medium)	pr.	1.02
1835, (high)	pr.	2.00	(low)	pr.	.604
(medium)	pr.	1.38			
(low)	pr.	1.10	*Slippers.*		
(boys')	pr.	1.42	1792, (leather; wholesale)	pr.	.861
1836, (high)	pr.	2.00	1794, .	pr.	.556
(medium)	pr.	1.47	1795, (wholesale)	pr.	.556
(low)	pr.	1.00	1816, (kid and morocco; wholesale)	pr.	1.02
1837, (high)	pr.	2.00	(misses' kid and morocco; wholesale)	pr.	.60
(medium)	pr.	1.50			
(low)	pr.	1.14	1827, .	pr.	.75
1838, (high)	pr.	1.50	1830, .	pr.	1.12
(medium)	pr.	1.00	1833, .	pr.	.625
(low)	pr.	.75	1834, .	pr.	.531
(women's)	pr.	1.25	1836, (high)	pr.	1.25
1839, (high)	pr.	2.13	(low)	pr.	1.13
(medium)	pr.	1.38	1838, .	pr.	.62
(med. low)	pr.	1.03	1839, (high)	pr.	1.06
(low)	pr.	.62	(medium)	pr.	.75
1840, (high)	pr.	1.88	(low)	pr.	.50
(med. high)	pr.	1.50	1840, (high)	pr.	1.75
(medium)	pr.	1.21	(low)	pr.	1.25
(med. low)	pr.	.958	1841, .	pr.	1.00
(low)	pr.	.625	1854, .	pr.	.75
1841, (high)	pr.	1.50	1855, (high)	pr.	1.63
(medium)	pr.	1.25	(medium)	pr.	1.20
(low)	pr.	1.00	(low)	pr.	.657
1842, (high)	pr.	1.42	1856, (high)	pr.	1.17
(medium)	pr.	1.06	(low)	pr.	.765
(low)	pr.	.50	1857, (high)	pr.	1.07
1843, (high)	pr.	2.00	(low)	pr.	.667
(medium)	pr.	1.33	1858, (high)	pr.	1.25
(low)	pr.	1.00	(medium)	pr.	.953
1844, (high)	pr.	1.25	(low)	pr.	.574
(medium)	pr.	.906	1859, (high)	pr.	.976
(low)	pr.	.50	(low)	pr.	.627
1845, (high)	pr.	2.25			
(medium)	pr.	1.17	*Taps.*		
(low)	pr.	.50	1762, .	pr.	.167
1846, (high)	pr.	1.75	1766, .	pr.	.167
(med. high)	pr.	1.38	1798, .	pr.	.139
(medium)	pr.	1.00	1814, .	pr.	.12
(med. low)	pr.	.827			

Prices: Buttons and Dress Trimmings.

Years.	Basis.	Amount.	Years.	Basis.	Amount.
Braid.			*Buttons — Con.*		
1822,	yd.	$0.013	1816, (high)	doz.	$0.232
1830, (high)	p'ce	.125	(low)	doz.	.082
(medium)	p'ce	.069	1817, (high)	doz.	.333
(low)	p'ce	.04	(medium)	doz.	.242
1832,	p'ce	.04	(low)	doz.	.127
1855, (high)	yd.	.12	1818, (high)	doz.	.315
(low)	yd.	.016	(low)	doz.	.12
(by the stick; high)	ea.	.10	1819,	gro.	.124
(by the stick; low)	ea.	.06	(vest)	doz.	.62
1856,	p'ce	.05	1820, (high)	doz.	.20
	yd.	.03	(low)	doz.	.10
(wholesale)	yd.	.017	1821, (high)	doz.	.167
1857, (high)	p'ce	.10	(medium)	doz.	.125
(low)	p'ce	.056	(low)	doz.	.06
1858,	p'ce	.078	1822, (high)	doz.	.371
(by the stick)	ea.	.033	(low)	doz.	.084
1859,	yd.	.056	1823, (high)	doz.	.25
(high)	p'ce	.10	(low)	doz.	.099
(low)	p'ce	.053	1824, (high)	doz.	.254
			(medium)	doz.	.107
Buttons.			(low)	doz.	.033
1782, (high)	doz.	.628	1825, (high)	doz.	.20
(medium)	doz.	.254	(low)	doz.	.083
(low)	doz.	.153	1826,	doz.	.042
1783, (high)	doz.	.583	1827,	doz.	.066
(med. high)	doz.	.493	1828,	doz.	.333
(medium)	doz.	.291	1829,	doz.	.097
(med. low)	doz.	.136	1830, (high)	doz.	.125
(low)	doz.	.042	(low)	doz.	.04
1784, (high)	doz.	.916	1831,	doz.	.10
(low)	doz.	.14	1832,	doz.	.08
1786,	doz.	.083	(pearl)	doz.	.25
1787,	doz.	.213	(twist)	doz.	.42
1788,	doz.	.145	1833, (high)	doz.	.125
1791, (high)	doz.	.833	(low)	doz.	.052
(low)	doz.	.178	1835, (high)	doz.	.083
	gro.	3.33	(low)	doz.	.04
1792, (high)	doz.	.375	1837, (high)	doz.	.14
(low)	doz.	.083	(low)	doz.	.03
1793, (high)	doz.	.50	1838,	doz.	.17
(medium)	doz.	.284	1839, (high)	doz.	.248
(low)	doz.	.06	(low)	doz.	.043
(sleeve)	gro.	1.50	(bone)	doz.	.06
1794, (high)	doz.	.333	1840, (high)	doz.	.163
(low)	doz.	.167	(low)	doz.	.09
1795,	doz.	.083	1841,	doz.	.031
(high)	gro.	.833	1842,	doz.	.04
(low)	gro.	.482	1843,	doz.	.17
(plated)	gro.	1.50	1845,	doz.	.125
1800, (plated)	gro.	1.67	1846, (high)	doz.	.177
1801,	gro.	.583	(low)	doz.	.06
1802, (high)	gro.	.847	1855, (high)	doz.	.37
(low)	gro.	.50	(med. high)	doz.	.25
(metal)	doz.	.125	(med. low)	doz.	.124
(sleeve)	gro.	1.25	(low)	doz	.028
1803, (coat)	gro.	1.11	1856, (high)	doz.	.375
(gilt vest)	gro.	1.50	(medium)	doz.	.247
(vest)	gro.	.92	(low)	doz.	.071
1805,	doz.	.097	1857, (high)	doz.	2.00
	gro.	3.00	(med. high)	doz.	1.67
1806, (coat)	gro.	1.11	(med. low)	doz.	.457
(figured)	gro.	1.33	(low)	doz.	.109
1807,	doz.	.104	1858, (high)	doz.	.252
	gro.	1.75	(medium)	doz.	.115
1808,	doz.	.20	(low)	doz.	.033
1809,	doz.	.155	1859, (high)	doz.	.201
1810,	doz.	.167	(medium)	doz.	.12
1811,	doz.	.368	(low)	doz	.048
1812, (high)	doz.	.373			
(medium)	doz.	.231	*Fringe.*		
(low)	doz.	.125	1857, (high)	yd.	.164
1814,	doz.	.113	(low)	yd.	.071
1815, (high)	doz.	.782	1858, (high)	yd.	.50
(low)	doz.	.188	(medium)	yd.	.373

Prices: Buttons and Dress Trimmings — Concluded.

Years.	Basis.	Amount.	Years.	Basis.	Amount.
Fringe — Con.			*Tape* — Con.		
1858, (low)	yd.	$0.187	1820,	p'ce	$0.125
1859, (high)	yd.	.499	1821,	p'ce	.097
(low)	yd.	.179	1822, (high)	p'ce	.20
Galloon.			(low)	p'ce	.096
			1823, (high)	p'ce	.172
1807,	gro.	3.33	(low)	p'ce	.103
1810,	yd.	.042	1824, (high)	p'ce	.20
1816,	yd.	.051	(medium)	p'ce	.10
1841,	yd.	.03	(low)	p'ce	.026
1855,	yd.	.057	1825,	p'ce	.047
1857,	yd.	.057	1827, (high)	p'ce	.235
1858,	yd.	.054	(low)	p'ce	.068
1859,	yd.	.053	1829, (high)	p'ce	.115
			(low)	p'ce	.077
Moire Antique Trimming.			1832, (high)	p'ce	.10
1855, (high)	yd.	.167	(low)	p'ce	.067
(low)	yd.	.124	1834, (high)	p'ce	.063
1858,	yd.	.165	(low)	p'ce	.038
			1835, (high)	p'ce	.09
Tape.			(low)	p'ce	.05
1783,	yd.	.025	1836,	p'ce	.04
1784,	yd.	.017	1837, (high)	p'ce	.125
1805,	p'ce	.123	(low)	p'ce	.084
1806,	p'ce	.167	1838,	p'ce	.113
(ferret)	yd.	.041	1839,	p'ce	.08
1808,	p'ce	.20	1843,	p'ce	.043
1810, (high)	p'ce	.267	1845, (high)	p'ce	.083
(low)	p'ce	.104	(low)	p'ce	.05
1811,	p'ce	.116	1846,	p'ce	.05
(ferret)	yd.	.04	1851,	p'ce	.05
1812,	p'ce	.125	1855, (high)	p'ce	.08
(ferret)	yd.	.06	(low)	p'ce	.06
1814,	yd.	.063	1856,	p'ce	.049
1816,	p'ce	.09	1857, (high)	p'ce	.075
1817,	yd.	.02	(medium)	p'ce	.052
1818,	p'ce	.08	(low)	p'ce	.03
(silk ferret)	yd.	.083	1858,	p'ce	.059
1819, (high)	p'ce	.192	1859,	p'ce	.056
(low)	p'ce	.117			

Prices: Carpetings.

Years.	Basis.	Amount.	Years.	Basis.	Amount.
Bocking.			*Mats.*		
1821,	yd.	$0.667	1802, (high)	ea.	$0.75
1822,	yd.	.666	(low)	ea.	.188
1830,	yd.	.75	1804, (high)	ea.	.625
1843,	yd.	.417	(low)	ea.	.165
			1808,	ea.	.163
Carpeting.			1831, (entry)	ea.	1.00
1798,	yd.	.786	1847,	ea.	.92
1808,	yd.	1.25	1857,	ea.	1.00
1816,	yd.	1.50			
1821,	yd.	1.26			
1829, (high)	yd.	1.25	*Oil-cloth.*		
(low)	yd.	.725	1794,	yd.	.583
1830,	yd.	1.00	1807,	yd.	.611
1831, (Kidderminster)	yd.	1.33	1845,	yd.	.75
1837, (stair)	yd.	.167	1848,	yd.	.75
1838,	yd.	1.00	1856,	yd.	.511
1839, (high)	yd.	.373	1857,	yd.	.631
(low)	yd.	.20	1859,	yd.	.377
1842,	yd.	.625			
1851,	yd.	.873			
1852, (straw)	yd.	.247	*Rugs.*		
1854, (straw)	yd.	.37	1800,	ea.	.916
1856,	yd.	.171	1819, (Brussels)	ea.	14.50
1858,	yd.	.415			

Prices: Clothing.

Years.	Ba-sis.	Amount.	Years.	Ba-sis.	Amount.
Bonnets.			*Gloves* — Con.		
1820, (Leghorn)	ea.	$12.00	1822,	pr.	$0.62
1838, (high)	ea.	2.00	1823, (high)	pr.	.67
(low)	ea.	.75	(low)	pr.	.25
1839, (high)	ea.	2 00	1824, (high)	pr.	1.25
(low)	ea.	.833	(low)	pr.	.333
1840, (high)	ea.	1.25	1825,	pr.	.25
(medium)	ea.	1.00	(kid)	pr.	.583
(low)	ea.	.50	1826,	pr.	.54
1841, (high)	ea.	2.50	1827, (high)	pr.	.583
(low)	ea.	.75	(low)	pr.	.125
1842, (high)	ea.	3.00	1828, (high)	pr.	.62
(low)	ea.	1.00	(low)	pr.	.125
1849,	ea.	2.70	1829, (high)	pr.	.687
			(low)	pr.	.229
Breeches.			(kid)	pr.	.54
1783,	pr.	1.00	1830, (high)	pr.	.75
1791, (corded Nankeen)	pr.	3.75	(medium)	pr.	.58
(India Nankeen)	pr.	3.12	(low)	pr.	.42
			1832, (high)	pr.	.625
Cloaks.			(low)	pr.	.54
1845, (cashmere)	ea.	14.00	1833, (high)	pr.	.687
1848, (cashmere)	ea.	14.00	(low)	pr.	.291
			1834, (high)	pr.	.50
Coats.			(low)	pr.	.31
1783,	ea.	1.50	1835, (high)	pr.	.875
1804,	ea.	13.00	(low)	pr.	.40
1840,	ea.	25.62	1836, (high)	pr.	.75
1845,	ea.	1.75	(low)	pr.	.411
1855, (high)	ea.	12.50	1837,	pr.	.25
(med. high)	ea.	9.44	(kid)	pr.	.50
(medium)	ea.	6.98	1838, (high)	pr.	.717
(low)	ea.	4.33	(low)	pr.	.42
1857, (high)	ea.	8.75	1839, (high)	pr.	.50
(med. high)	ea.	7.50	(low)	pr.	.25
(medium)	ea.	6.67	1840, (high)	pr.	.42
(med. low)	ea.	5.58	(medium)	pr.	.25
(low)	ea.	4.29	(low)	pr.	.154
1858, (high)	ea.	12.75	1841, (high)	pr.	.75
(med. high)	ea.	9.00	(low)	pr.	.30
(medium)	ea.	6.56	1842,	pr.	.25
(med. low)	ea.	4.92	1843, (high)	pr.	.375
(low)	ea.	3.18	(low)	pr.	.25
(linen; high)	ea.	1.75	1844, (high)	pr.	.74
(linen; low)	ea.	1.25	(low)	pr.	.063
1859, (high)	ea.	8.80	1845, (high)	pr.	1.00
(med. high)	ea.	6.84	(low)	pr.	.08
(med. low)	ea.	4.14	1847, (high)	pr.	.47
(low)	ea.	1.76	(low)	pr.	.25
			1848, (high)	pr.	.663
Gloves.			(low)	pr.	.42
1782,	pr.	.347	1849,	pr.	.23
1783, (high)	pr.	.50	1850, (high)	pr.	.37
(medium)	pr.	.375	(low)	pr.	.25
(low)	pr.	.224	1851, (high)	pr.	.75
1784, (high)	pr.	1.08	(low)	pr.	.20
(low)	pr.	.257	1852,	pr.	.25
1793, (silk)	pr.	1.25	1854,	pr.	.50
(worsted)	pr.	.389	1855, (high)	pr.	1.04
1794,	pr.	.25	(medium)	pr.	.591
1805,	pr.	.666	(low)	pr.	.26
1806, (cotton)	pr.	.333	1856, (high)	pr.	.683
1807,	pr.	1.25	(medium)	pr.	.38
1808,	pr.	.50	(low)	pr.	.196
1815,	pr.	.46	1857, (high)	pr.	1.21
1816, (high)	pr.	.75	(medium)	pr.	.79
(low)	pr.	.473	(low)	Ba.	.291
1817, (high)	pr.	.398	(kid)	pr.	.855
(low)	pr.	.25	1858, (high)	pr.	1.12
1819, (high)	pr.	.688	(med. high)	pr.	.78
(low)	pr.	.272	(medium)	pr.	.575
1820,	pr.	.375	(med. low)	pr.	.407
1821, (high)	pr.	.50	(low)	pr.	.213
(low)	pr.	.20	(kid)	pr.	.838
(kid)	pr.	1.00	1859, (high)	pr.	1.12

Prices: Clothing — Continued.

Years.	Basis.	Amount.	Years.	Basis	Amount.
Gloves — Con.			*Handkerchiefs* — Con.		
1859, (med. high)	pr.	$0.783	1818, (cotton; low)	ea.	$0.042
(med. low)	pr.	.294	1819, (high)	ea.	.75
(low)	pr.	.136	(medium)	ea.	.25
Handkerchiefs.			(low)	ea.	.125
1767,	doz.	1.33	(silk)	ea.	1.95 =
(largest)	doz.	.622	1821,	ea.	.46
(smallest)	doz.	.888	(silk)	ea.	1.00
1774,	ea.	.40	1822, (high)	ea.	.25
1775,	ea.	.333	(low)	ea.	.165
1782, (high)	ea.	.244	1823, (high)	ea.	.412
(low)	ea.	.099	(low)	ea.	.125
1783, (high)	ea.	1.01	1824, (high)	ea.	.83
(medium)	ea.	.636	(medium)	ea.	.50
(low)	ea.	.357	(low)	ea.	.125
(gauze)	ea.	.517	1825, (high)	ea.	.50
1784, (high)	ea.	1.08	(low)	ea.	.167
(med. high)	ea.	.89	1826,	ea.	.113
(medium)	ea.	.706	(silk; high)	ea.	.92
(med. low)	ea.	.382	(silk; low)	ea.	.75
(low)	ea.	.25	1827, (high)	ea.	.67
1787,	ea.	.944	(low)	ea.	.145
(bandanna)	p'ce	11.25	1828, (high)	ea.	.75
(Barcelona)	doz.	15.32	(medium)	ea.	.50
1791, (black silk)	ea.	1.11	(low)	ea.	.147
(checkered)	doz.	3.66	1829, (high)	ea.	.355
(linen)	doz.	2.84	(low)	ea.	.214
1792, (bandanna)	p'ce	5.00	1830, (high)	ea.	.222
1793,	ea.	.944	(low)	ea.	.125
(bandanna)	ea.	1.07	(bandanna)	ea.	1.13
(linen; high)	ea.	.50	1831, (high)	ea.	.62
(linen; low)	ea.	.25	(medium)	ea.	.38
(silk)	ea.	.514	(low)	ea.	.211
(silk and cotton; high)	ea.	.667	(silk)	ea.	1.25
(silk and cotton; low)	ea.	.50	1832,	ea.	.56
1794,	doz.	2.00	1833, (high)	ea.	.52
(bandanna)	ea.	1.25	(low)	ea.	.193
(linen)	ea.	.181	1834, (high)	ea.	.63
(muslin)	ea.	.583	(medium)	ea.	.217
1795, (bandanna)	ea.	1.17	(low)	ea.	.04
1801, (Malabar)	doz.	4.00	(neck)	ea.	.333
(silk; high)	doz.	10.00	1835, (high)	ea.	.468
(silk; low)	doz.	8.67	(low)	ea.	.224
(white checked)	doz.	4.33	1836, (high)	ea.	.777
1803,	doz.	3.33	(low)	ea.	.28
1804,	ea.	.25	1837, (high)	ea.	.50
1805,	ea.	.75	(medium)	ea.	.347
(cotton)	doz.	2.67	(low)	ea.	.258
1807,	ea.	.313	1838, (high)	ea.	.675
1810, (high)	ea.	.75	(medium)	ea.	.417
(low)	ea.	.175	(low)	ea.	.243
1811, (high)	ea.	.25	(silk)	ea.	.625
(low)	ea.	.063	1839, (high)	ea.	.75
1812, (high)	ea.	.83	(med. high)	ea.	.50
(medium)	ea.	.67	(medium)	ea.	.302
(low)	ea.	.53	(low)	ea.	.117
(bandanna)	ea.	.75	1840, (high)	ea.	.38
1813,	ea.	.83	(low)	ea.	.25
(silk)	ea.	1.50	(silk)	ea.	.75
1815, (high)	ea.	1.25	1841, (high)	ea.	.571
(low)	ea.	.23	(medium)	ea.	.42
(bandanna)	ea.	1.50	(low)	ea.	.233
(silk)	ea.	.95	(Spitalfield)	ea.	1.13
1816, (high)	ea.	.67	1842, (high)	ea.	.75
(low)	ea.	.168	(low)	ea.	.25
1817, (high)	ea.	1.00	1843, (high)	ea.	.42
(med. high)	ea.	.67	(low)	ea.	.27
(medium)	ea.	.42	1844, (high)	ea.	1.00
(low)	ea.	.168	(med. high)	ea.	.75
(bandanna)	ea.	1.00	(medium)	ea.	.59
(silk)	ea.	1.00	(med. low)	ea.	.33
1818,	ea.	.50	(low)	ea.	.21
(cotton; high)	ea.	.292	1845, (high)	ea.	.50
(cotton; medium)	ea.	.125	(low)	ea.	.33
			(silk)	ea.	1.00

Prices: Clothing — CONTINUED.

YEARS.	Basis.	Amount.	YEARS.	Basis.	Amount.
Handkerchiefs — Con.			*Hats* — Con.		
1846, ...	ea.	$0.46	1806, (silk; low) . . .	doz.	$16.00
1847, ...	ea.	.125	(youths' camels hair) .	ea.	1.00
(silk) . . .	ea.	.67	1807, (men's; high) . .	ea.	2.67
1848, (high) . . .	ea.	.25	(men's; low) . .	ea.	1.50
(low) . . .	ea.	.154	(youths') . . .	ea.	.916
(silk; high) . .	ea.	.75	(youths' beaver) . .	ea.	2.25
(silk; medium) . .	ea.	.527	1808, ...	ea.	.92
(silk; low) . .	ea.	.37	(youths') . . .	doz.	7.00
1849, ...	ea.	.20	1809, (high) . . .	ea.	5.00
1850, ...	ea.	.50	(low) . . .	ea.	1.38
1851, ...	ea.	.125	(silk) . . .	ea.	2.50
1852, ...	ea.	.665	1810, (high) . . .	ea.	3.06
1854, (silk) . . .	ea.	.625	(medium) . . .	ea.	1.47
1855, (high) . . .	ea.	.725	(low) . . .	ea.	.583
(medium) . . .	ea.	.305	1811, ...	ea.	.75
(low) . . .	ea.	.15	1812, (high) . . .	ea.	2.00
(silk; high) . .	ea.	.80	(low) . . .	ea.	1.00
(silk; low) . .	ea.	.58	(beaver) . . .	ea.	7.00
1856, (high) . . .	ea.	.623	(youths') . . .	ea.	.583
(medium) . . .	ea.	.258	1813, (high) . . .	ea.	6.50
(low) . . .	ea.	.108	(low) . . .	ea.	1.00
(silk; high) . .	ea.	1.20	1814, (high) . . .	ea.	6.50
(silk; low) . .	ea.	.58	(medium) . . .	ea.	3.64
1857, (high) . . .	ea.	.50	(low) . . .	ea.	2.61
(medium) . . .	ea.	.36	(boys') . . .	ea.	.75
(low) . . .	ea.	.172	(felt; high) . .	ea.	1.00
1858, (high) . . .	ea.	.464	(felt; low) . .	ea.	.75
(medium) . . .	ea.	.236	(men's high) . .	ea.	5.50
(low) . . .	ea.	.113	(men's low) . .	ea.	1.00
1859, (high) . . .	ea.	.452	(men's broad brimmed;		
(medium) . . .	ea.	.286	high) . . .	ea.	3.00
(med. low) . .	ea.	.14	(men's broad brimmed;		
(low) . . .	ea.	.045	low) . . .	ea.	2.75
			(youths'; high) . .	ea.	3.00
Hats.			(youths'; low) . .	ea.	2.25
1764, ...	ea.	6.67	1815, (high) . . .	ea.	3.00
1783, (high) . . .	ea.	6.00	(low) . . .	ea.	1.00
(med. high) . .	ea.	4.66	(youths') . . .	ea.	3.00
(medium) . . .	ea.	3.51	1816, (high) . . .	ea.	7.00
(med. low) . .	ea.	.695	(med. high) . .	ea.	4.50
(low) . . .	ea.	.139	(medium) . . .	ea.	3.50
1784, (high) . . .	ea.	3.95	(med. low) . .	ea.	2.50
(med. high) . .	ea.	3.66	(low) . . .	ea.	1.00
(medium) . . .	ea.	1.96	(straw) . . .	ea.	.25
(med. low) . .	ea.	.354	1818, (high) . . .	ea.	2.00
(low) . . .	ea.	.139	(low) . . .	ea.	1.00
1792, ...	ea.	3.33	1822, (beaver) . . .	ea.	2.25
(castor), . . .	ea.	2.67	1824, ...	ea.	3.50
1793, (high) . . .	ea.	5.16	1825, (high) . . .	ea.	5.00
(med. high) . .	ea.	3.94	(low) . . .	ea.	.794
(medium) . . .	ea.	3.01	1828, (felt) . . .	ea.	1.50
(med. low) . .	ea.	1.18	1831, ...	ea.	4.00
(low) . . .	ea.	.667	1832, (fur) . . .	ea.	4.00
(boys') . . .	ea.	.50	1833, (high) . . .	ea.	6.00
(castor; high) . .	ea.	4.00	(medium) . . .	ea.	2.75
(castor; low) . .	ea.	3.00	(low) . . .	ea.	.25
(wool) . . .	ea.	.667	1836, ...	ea.	2.25
1794, (high) . . .	ea.	3.00	1838, ...	ea.	.169
(low) . . .	ea.	.667	(boys') . . .	ea.	2.00
(castor) . . .	ea.	5.00	(fur) . . .	ea.	6.00
1802, (beaver) . . .	ea.	5.50	1839, (high) . . .	ea.	3.50
1803, ...	ea.	.75	(low) . . .	ea.	.315
1804, ...	ea.	5.50	1841, (high) . . .	ea.	4.00
1805, (high) . . .	ea.	5.50	(low) . . .	ea.	1.75
(low) . . .	ea.	2.50	1844, ...	ea.	3.50
(silk) . . .	doz.	24.00	1845, ...	ea.	4.50
1806, (high) . . .	ea.	6.00	1846, ...	ea.	.25
(med. high) . . .	ea.	4.50	1847, (high) . . .	ea.	2.25
(medium) . . .	ea.	3.43	(low) . . .	ea.	.407
(med low) . . .	ea.	2.00	1848, (high) . . .	ea.	.298
(low) . . .	ea.	1.00	(low) . . .	ea.	.13
(boys' superfine; high) .	ea.	.653	1855, (high) . . .	ea.	3.00
(boys' superfine; low) .	ea.	.50	(medium) . . .	ea.	2.06
(silk; high) . .	doz.	17.00	(low) . . .	ea.	1.06

Prices: Clothing — CONTINUED.

Years.	Basis.	Amount.	Years.	Basis.	Amount.
Hats — Con.			*Hose* — Con.		
1856, (high)	ea.	$3.00	1822, (woollen)	pr.	$0.58
(medium)	ea.	1.37	1823, (high)	pr.	.70
(med. low)	ea.	.705	(low)	pr.	.50
(low)	ea.	.238	1824, (high)	pr.	1.13
1857, (high)	ea.	3.17	(medium)	pr.	.653
(med. high)	ea.	1.91	(med. low)	pr.	.45
(med. low)	ea.	.881	(low)	pr.	.25
(low)	ea.	.24	1825, .	pr.	.75
1858, (high)	ea.	3.54	1826, (high)	pr.	1.50
(med. high)	ea.	2.57	(medium)	pr.	.859
(medium)	ea.	1.57	(low)	pr.	.375
(med. low)	ea.	.888	1827, (high)	pr.	1.00
(low)	ea.	.258	(med. high)	pr.	.75
(ladies')	ea.	.75	(medium)	pr.	.622
(straw; high)	ea.	1.12	(med. low)	pr.	.267
(straw; medium)	ea.	.50	(low)	pr.	.063
(straw; low)	ea.	.185	1828, .	pr.	.583
1859, (high)	ea.	2.79	1829, (high)	pr.	.375
(medium)	ea.	1.73	(low)	pr.	.282
(med. low)	ea.	1.02	1830, (high)	pr.	.46
(low)	ea.	.331	(medium)	pr.	.389
			(low)	pr.	.25
Hose.			1831, (high)	pr.	.75
1787, (cotton)	pr.	.833	(medium)	pr.	.473
(worsted)	pr.	1.25	(low)	pr.	.283
1788, .	pr.	.416	1832, (high)	pr.	.918
1792, (high)	pr.	1.83	(medium)	pr.	.542
(low)	pr.	1.11	(low)	pr.	.375
1793, (high)	pr.	1.22	1833, .	pr.	.625
(low)	pr.	.89	1834, (high)	pr.	.75
1794, (high)	pr.	1.41	(low)	pr.	.65
(medium)	pr.	1.21	1835, (high)	pr.	.855
(low)	pr.	1.13	(low)	pr.	.625
1795, .	doz.	9.34	1836, (high)	pr.	.759
(ribbed)	doz.	12.00	(low)	pr.	.25
1797, (cotton; wholesale)	pr.	1.05	1837, (high)	pr.	.75
(silk)	pr.	3.33	(low)	pr.	.468
1800, (ribbed)	pr.	1.00	1838, .	pr.	.515
1801, (cotton)	pr.	1.00	1839, (high)	pr.	.666
(silk)	pr.	1.17	(low)	pr.	.17
(worsted)	pr.	.972	1840, (high)	pr.	.75
1802, (cotton)	pr.	1.33	(medium)	pr.	.625
1803, (silk)	pr.	1.75	(low)	pr.	.44
1804, (silk)	pr.	1.50	1841, .	pr.	.69
1805, (worsted)	pr.	.75	1842, (high)	pr.	.67
(worsted; wholesale)	pr.	.833	(medium)	pr.	.524
1806, .	pr.	1.42	(low)	pr.	.437
1807, .	pr.	1.18	1843, (high)	pr.	.50
(worsted; wholesale)	pr.	1.00	(low)	pr.	.27
1808, .	pr.	1.75	1846, (high)	pr.	.375
(worsted)	doz.	12.67	(medium)	pr.	.25
1809, (high)	pr.	1.50	(low)	pr.	.17
(low)	pr.	1.00	1847, (high)	pr.	.71
(cotton)	pr.	.75	(low)	pr.	.125
1810, .	pr.	1.84	1848, (high)	pr.	.33
1811, (high)	pr.	1.25	(medium)	pr.	.19
(low)	pr.	.438	(low)	pr.	.10
1812, (high)	pr.	2.25	1849, (high)	pr.	.25
(low)	pr.	1.00	(low)	pr.	.16
1815, .	pr.	1.29	1850, (high)	pr.	.50
1816, (high)	pr.	.957	(med. high)	pr.	.37
(low)	pr.	.833	(medium)	pr.	.25
1817, (high)	pr.	1.00	(low)	pr.	.143
(medium)	pr.	.88	1852, (high)	pr.	.75
(low)	pr.	.75	(low)	pr.	.125
1818, .	pr.	.75	1855, (high)	pr.	1.00
1819, (high)	pr.	1.00	(medium)	pr.	.448
(low)	pr.	.875	(low)	pr.	.176
1820, (high)	pr.	.664	1856, (high)	pr.	.467
(low)	pr.	.43	(medium)	pr.	.24
1821, (high)	pr.	1.09	(low)	pr.	.149
(low)	pr.	.333	1857, (high)	pr.	1.25
1822, (high)	pr.	.75	(med. high)	pr.	.625
(low)	pr.	.46	(medium)	pr.	.434

Prices: Clothing — CONTINUED.

YEARS.	Ba-sis.	Amount.	YEARS.	Ba-sis.	Amount.
Hose — Con.			*Overcoats* — Con.		
1857, (med. low)	pr.	$0.249	1857, (low)	ea.	$5.64
(low)	pr.	.142	1858,	ea.	5.50
(raw silk)	pr.	1.00			
1858, (high)	pr.	.596	*Pantaloons.**		
(medium)	pr.	.292	1783,	pr.	.416
(low)	pr.	.14	1798,	pr.	1.25
1859, (high)	pr.	.439	1799,	pr.	2.50
(medium)	pr.	.252	1805,	pr.	1.50
(low)	pr.	.135	1813, (high)	pr.	6.50
			(low)	pr.	3.50
Mittens.			(Nankeen)	pr.	2.50
1817,	pr.	.20	1838,	pr.	10.00
1824,	pr.	.12	1855, (high)	pr.	4.31
1830,	pr.	.321	(medium)	pr.	3.65
1837, (high)	pr.	.33	(low)	pr.	2.65
(low)	pr.	.25	1857, (high)	pr.	4.47
1838, (high)	pr.	.96	(med. high)	pr.	3.63
(low)	pr.	.20	(medium)	pr.	2.32
1839, (high)	pr.	.50	(low)	pr.	.85
(low)	pr.	.17	1858, (high)	pr.	4.03
1841, (high)	pr.	.72	(medium)	pr.	2.07
(medium)	pr.	.50	(low)	pr.	.74
(low)	pr.	.303	1859, (high)	pr.	4.02
1842,	pr.	.25	(medium)	pr.	2.34
1843,	pr.	.67	(low)	pr.	1.47
1844,	pr.	.20			
1845, (high)	pr.	.746	*Shawls.*		
(low)	pr.	.20	1791,	ea.	.916
1846, (high)	pr.	.657	1792,	ea.	.833
(medium)	pr.	.46	1794,	ea.	.60
(low)	pr.	.16	1795, (wholesale)	ea.	.556
1847, (high)	pr.	.562	1800,	doz.	7.59
(low)	pr.	.275	1801,	ea.	.75
1848, (high)	pr.	.662	1817,	ea.	2.50
(medium)	pr.	.415	1819, (cashmere)	ea.	5.00
(low)	pr.	.208	(long)	ea.	40.00
1849,	pr.	.50	1822, (crape)	ea.	6.00
1850,	pr.	.75	1824, (cashmere)	ea.	12.00
1852, (high)	pr.	.67	1825, (high)	ea.	7.75
(low)	pr.	.17	(low)	ea.	1.88
1854, (high)	pr.	1.12	1827,	ea.	3.00
(low)	pr.	.17	1830, (high)	ea.	3.75
1855, (high)	pr.	1.02	(low)	ea.	3.00
(med. high)	pr.	.713	1833, (high)	ea.	8.00
(med. low)	pr.	.46	(low)	ea.	1.00
(low)	pr.	.226	1836,	ea.	5.00
1856, (high)	pr.	1.00	1838,	ea.	.875
(medium)	pr.	.79	1840, (high)	ea.	10.00
(low)	pr.	.387	(low)	ea.	2.00
1857, (high)	pr.	1.05	1841, (high)	ea.	10.00
(medium)	pr.	.50	(low)	ea.	3.50
(low)	pr.	.25	1844, (high)	ea.	7.50
1858, (high)	pr.	.915	(low)	ea.	5.00
(medium)	pr.	.623	1846,	ea.	1.50
(low)	pr.	.291	1847,	ea.	.88
			1848,	ea.	1.00
Mitts.			1849,	ea.	7.50
1794, (silk)	pr.	.833	1850,	ea.	4.00
1850,	pr.	.75	1851,	ea.	3.50
1856,	pr.	1.00	1855, (high)	ea.	9.00
			(med. high)	ea.	7.38
Overalls.			(medium)	ea.	5.17
1844,	pr.	.70	(med. low)	ea.	2.50
1850,	pr.	.50	(low)	ea.	1.11
1855,	pr.	.464	1856, (high)	ea.	7.50
1857, (high)	pr.	.603	(medium)	ea.	3.50
(low)	pr.	.495	(low)	ea.	.83
1858,	pr.	.541	1857, (high)	ea.	8.00
1859,	pr.	.572	(med. high)	ea.	4.00
			(medium)	ea.	2.88
Overcoats.			(med. low)	ea.	1.75
1857, (high)	ea.	20.00	(low)	ea.	1.00
(medium)	ea.	12.50	1858, (high)	ea.	5.50

* Prices given in the earlier years for "trousers" are included under "pantaloons."

Prices: Clothing — CONCLUDED.

YEARS.	Basis.	Amount.	YEARS.	Basis.	Amount.
Shawls — Con.			*Stockings* — Con.		
1855, (med. high)	ea.	$3.84	1820,	pr.	$0.37
(medium)	ea.	2.35	1821,	pr.	.50
(low)	ea.	1.00	1832, (high)	pr.	.58
1859, (high)	ea.	11.00	(low)	pr.	.33
(medium)	ea.	4.83	1840,	pr.	.165
(med. low)	ea.	2.42	1841,	pr.	.58
(low)	ea.	.938	1845,	pr.	.32
			1848,	pr.	.279
Socks.					
1837, (high)	pr.	.50	*Vests.*		
(medium)	pr.	.333	1793,	ea.	2.23
(low)	pr.	.25	1811, (high)	ea.	5.00
1838,	pr.	.356	(low)	ea.	3.50
1843, (high)	pr.	1.00	(white)	ea.	5.00
(low)	pr.	.361	1847,	ea.	3.75
1847,	pr.	.33	1855, (high)	ea.	4.00
			(med. high)	ea.	3.00
Stockings.			(medium)	ea.	2.25
1764, (high)	pr.	1.33	(med. low)	ea.	1.64
(low)	pr.	.625	(low)	ea.	1.25
1782,	pr.	.625	1857, (high)	ea.	4.50
1783, (high)	pr.	.972	(medium)	ea.	3.09
(medium)	pr.	.785	(low)	ea.	1.78
(low)	pr.	.583	1858, (high)	ea.	3.50
1784, (high)	pr.	.667	(medium)	ea.	1.75
(low)	pr.	.472	(low)	ea.	.70
1794,	pr.	.972	1859, (high)	ea.	3.75
1800,	pr.	.75	(medium)	ea.	1.96
1801, (high)	pr.	1.03	(low)	ea.	1.36
(low)	pr.	.805			
1812, (high)	pr.	1.25	*Waistcoats.*		
(low)	pr.	1.00	1808,	ea.	2.33
1816,	pr.	.975	1810,	ea.	1.00
1819, (high)	pr.	1.25	1839,	ea.	1.38
(low)	pr.	.37			

Prices: Cloths.

YEARS.	Basis.	Amount.	YEARS.	Basis.	Amount.
Broadcloth.			*Broadcloth* — Con.		
1775,	yd.	$1.33	1803,	yd.	$6.00
1782,	yd.	2.50	1806,	yd.	4.00
1783, (high)	yd.	3.33	(wholesale, high)	yd.	2.21
(med. high)	yd.	2.95	(wholesale, low)	yd.	1.33
(medium)	yd.	2.17	1807, (high)	yd.	3.04
(med. low)	yd.	1.25	(low)	yd.	2.13
(low)	yd.	.889	1808,	yd.	3.33
1784, (high)	yd.	3.09	1809,	yd.	2.50
(medium)	yd.	1.83	1810, (high)	yd.	4.00
(low)	yd.	1.08	(low)	yd.	3.00
1787,	yd.	2.50	1811,	yd.	2.75
1788,	yd.	4.33	(mixed)	yd.	3.50
1791,	yd.	1.91	1812, (high)	yd.	11.00
1792, (high)	yd.	4.74	(medium)	yd.	4.21
(low)	yd.	2.46	(med. low)	yd.	2.75
1793, (high)	yd.	4.74	(low)	yd.	1.75
(medium)	yd.	3.82	1813,	yd.	8.00
(med. low)	yd.	2.62	(wholesale)	yd.	6.11
(low)	yd.	2.17	1814, (high)	yd.	8.00
1794, (high)	yd.	5.33	(medium)	yd.	6.82
(med. high)	yd.	4.29	(low)	yd.	5.00
(medium)	yd.	3.45	1815, (high)	yd.	7.39
(med. low)	yd.	2.32	(low)	yd.	7.00
(low)	yd.	1.58	1816, (high)	yd.	7.50
1795,	yd.	2.00	(med. high)	yd.	5.84
1799,	yd.	2.58	(medium)	yd.	3.99
1800, (high)	yd.	2.81	(med. low)	yd.	2.80
(medium)	yd.	1.00	(low)	yd.	1.25
(low)	yd.	.916	1817, (high)	yd.	6.06
(mixed)	yd.	4.15	(med. high)	yd.	4.95
1802, (high)	yd.	6.00	(medium)	yd.	2.17
(medium)	yd.	1.00	(low)	yd.	1.48
(low)	yd.	.76	1820,	yd.	5.50

Prices: Cloths — CONTINUED.

YEARS.	Basis.	Amount.
Broadcloth — Con.		
1821,	yd.	$6.00
1822,	yd.	6.00
1823,	yd.	4.58
1829,	yd.	2.58
1830, (high)	yd.	3.75
(low)	yd.	3.24
1831,	yd.	4.00
1832,	yd.	2.00
1837,	yd.	2.50
1856,	yd.	2.00
1857,	yd.	3.12
1858,	yd.	2.50
1859, (high)	yd.	2.24
(low)	yd.	1.29
Cassimere.		
1792,	yd.	2.33
1793,	yd.	2.33
1794,	yd.	2.30
1799,	yd.	2.00
1800, (high)	yd.	1.58
(low)	yd.	1.50
1801, (black)	yd.	2.04
1802, (high)	yd.	3.73
(low)	yd.	1.83
1803, (high)	yd.	2.50
(low)	yd.	1.50
1804, (high)	yd.	4.43
(low)	yd.	1.50
1805, (cotton)	yd.	.375
1806, (high)	yd.	2.67
(low)	yd.	1.75
1807,	yd.	1.29
1810, (high)	yd.	4.00
(low)	yd.	3.50
1811,	yd.	2.50
(cotton)	yd.	.25
(mixed)	yd.	2.00
1812, (high)	yd.	2.90
(low)	yd.	2.47
1813,	yd.	2.50
1814,	yd.	3.50
1815, (high)	yd.	2.75
(low)	yd.	1.46
1816, (high)	yd.	3.00
(medium)	yd.	1.25
(med. low)	yd.	.757
(low)	yd.	.267
1817, (high)	yd.	2.75
(medium)	yd.	1.61
(low)	yd.	.457
1820, (high)	yd.	2.88
(medium)	yd.	2.00
(low)	yd.	1.63
1821, (high)	yd.	2.44
(low)	yd.	1.25
1822,	yd.	2.75
1823,	yd.	.78
1824,	yd.	1.87
1825,	yd.	3.50
1826,	yd.	1.62
1827,	yd.	3.50
1828,	yd.	1.67
1829,	yd.	1.13
1830, (high)	yd.	1.50
(low)	yd.	.952
1831,	yd.	1.25
1832, (high)	yd.	1.37
(low)	yd.	.20
(Angola)	yd.	.92
1833, (high)	yd.	2.25
(low)	yd.	1.62
1834,	yd.	3.00
1836,	yd.	3.25

YEARS.	Basis.	Amount.
Cassimere — Con.		
1837,	yd.	$2.50
1838,	yd.	1.23
1839, (high)	yd.	4.52
(low)	yd.	2.75
(mixed)	yd.	1.00
1840,	yd.	1.05
1843,	yd.	1.37
1844, (high)	yd.	1.12
(low)	yd.	.875
1847, (high)	yd.	1.25
(low)	yd.	.90
1848,	yd.	1.25
1855, (high)	yd.	.89
(low)	yd.	.125
1858,	yd.	.125
1859,	yd.	.125
Circassian Cloth.		
1829,	yd.	.393
1830,	yd.	.588
1831,	yd.	.375
1833,	yd.	.417
Cloth.		
1762,	yd.	.267
1764,	yd.	.667
1782,	yd.	1.14
1783, (high)	yd.	2.67
(med. high)	yd.	2.15
(medium)	yd.	1.11
(med. low)	yd.	.416
(low)	yd.	.195
1784, (high)	yd.	2.33
(medium)	yd.	1.13
(med. low)	yd.	.396
(low)	yd.	.048
1788,	yd.	1.81
1792,	yd.	.75
1793, (high)	yd.	1.50
(low)	yd.	.833
1794, (high)	yd.	2.20
(medium)	yd.	1.76
(low)	yd.	.784
1804, (high)	yd.	1.33
(low)	yd.	.43
1805, (high)	yd.	1.42
(low)	yd.	.834
1806, (wholesale)	yd.	.96
1807,	yd.	3.03
1808,	yd.	1.50
1809, (high)	yd.	3.00
(low)	yd.	2.50
1810,	yd.	1.25
(wholesale)	yd.	.87
1813,	yd.	.167
1814, (high)	yd.	5.00
(low)	yd.	1.64
1815,	yd.	3.75
1816, (high)	yd.	6.00
(low)	yd.	.427
1817, (high)	yd.	5.00
(medium)	yd.	4.00
(low)	yd.	1.25
1821,	yd.	2.72
1824, (high)	yd.	1.75
(low)	yd.	1.25
1825, (high)	yd.	8.00
(low)	yd.	.255
1827,	yd.	9.00
1828, (high)	yd.	3.00
(low)	yd.	.125
1830,	yd.	.167
1831, (high)	yd.	1.25
(medium)	yd.	.833

Prices: Cloths — Concluded.

Years.	Basis.	Amount.	Years.	Basis.	Amount.
Cloth — Con.			*Frocking.*		
1831, (low)	yd.	$0.295	1855, ...	yd.	$0.58
1832, (high) . . .	yd.	.623	1857, ...	yd.	.58
(medium) . . .	yd.	.42	1858, ...	yd.	.58
(low) . . .	yd.	.20			
1833, (high) . . .	yd.	6.74	*Fustian.*		
(low) . . .	yd.	.961	1794, ...	yd.	.361
1834, ...	yd.	6.50	1801, ...	yd.	.375
1835, ...	yd.	.85	1802, ...	yd.	.392
1836, (high) . . .	yd.	6.00	1807, ...	yd.	.222
(low) . . .	yd.	.85	1824, ...	yd.	.30
1837, (high) . . .	yd.	.223			
(low) . . .	yd.	.165	*Lambskin.*		
1840, ...	yd.	5.00	1783, ...	yd.	1.13
			1784, ...	yd.	1.21
Corduroy.			1791, ...	yd.	1.17
1783, (high) . . .	yd.	.893	1792, (striped) . . .	yd.	1.50
(low) . . .	yd.	.814	1793, (high) . . .	yd.	1.41
1784, ...	yd.	.803	(low) . . .	yd.	.50
1785, ...	yd.	.833	1794, (high) . . .	yd.	1.00
1794, ...	yd.	.833	(low) . . .	yd.	.753
1799, (high) . . .	yd.	.83			
(low) . . .	yd.	.50	*Mixed Cloth.*		
			1793, ...	yd.	1.83
Doeskin.			1801, ...	yd.	1.08
1855, (high) . . .	yd.	1.16			
(low) . . .	yd.	.753	*Plain Blue Cloth.*		
1856, (high) . . .	yd.	1.10	1792, ...	yd.	.543
(low) . . .	yd.	.734	1803, (wholesale) . . .	yd.	1.00
1857, (high) . . .	yd.	1.12	1808, ...	yd.	.813
(low) . . .	yd.	.989	1810, (high) . . .	yd.	1.42
1858, ...	yd.	.876	(low) . . .	yd.	1.25
			1811, ...	yd.	1.25
Duffel.			1814, ...	yd.	1.42
1783, ...	yd.	1.33	1815, ...	yd.	1.42
1788, ...	yd.	1.11			
			Plain Cloth.		
Durant.			1792, ...	yd.	.861
1783, (high) . . .	yd.	.745	1793, ...	yd.	.528
(low) . . .	yd.	.374	1795, ...	yd.	2.16
1793, ...	yd.	.389	1808, ...	yd.	1.00
1794, ...	yd.	.444			
1797, ...	yd.	.333	*Ratteen.*		
			1784, ...	yd.	.969
Elastic Cloth.			1795, ...	yd.	.556
1792, ...	yd.	1.20	1803, ...	yd.	.50
1793, ...	yd.	1.20	1807, ...	yd.	1.42
Erminet.			*Sheep's Gray Cloth.*		
1843, ...	yd.	.664	1855, ...	yd.	.751
1856, ...	yd.	.35	1856, ...	yd.	.749
1858, ...	yd.	.417	1858, ...	yd.	.75
Florentine.			*Striped Woollen Cloth.*		
1792, (high) . . .	yd.	1.00	1792, ...	yd.	.278
(medium) . . .	yd.	.833	1793, ...	yd.	.529
(low) . . .	yd.	.723			
1793, (high) . . .	yd.	1.00	*Thickset.*		
(low) . . .	yd.	.782	1792, (twilled) . . .	yd.	1.08
1794, (high) . . .	yd.	.99	1793, ...	yd.	.961
(low) . . .	yd.	.715			
1795, ...	yd.	.531	*Vestings.*		
1811, ...	yd.	.761	1803, (high) . . .	yd.	1.56
			(low) . . .	yd.	.833
Forest Cloth.			1807, ...	yd.	1.50
1792, ...	yd.	1.08	1811, ...	yd.	.58
1793, (high) . . .	yd.	1.26	1830, (high) . . .	yd.	1.33
(low) . . .	yd.	.528	(low) . . .	yd.	.752
1794, (high) . . .	yd.	1.98			
(low) . . .	yd.	1.47	*Wild Boar Cloth.*		
			1792, ...	yd.	.375
Frieze.			1793, ...	yd.	.389
1783, ...	yd.	.385	1794, ...	yd.	.364
1784, ...	yd.	.333			
1805, ...	yd.	1.83			

Prices: Cutlery.

Years.	Basis.	Amount.	Years.	Basis.	Amount.
Knives.			*Pocket Knives.*		
1806,	doz.	$1.00	1801,	doz.	$2.25
1808,	doz.	2.08	1802,	doz.	1.04
Knives and Forks.			1830,	ea.	.25
1784,	set	.678			
1801,	gro.	13.33	*Table Knives.*		
1810,	doz.	4.00	1783, (high)	c'se	1.33
1820,	doz.	2.50	(low)	c'se	.522
1846,	set	1.00	1822, (tea)	set	1.17
1850,	doz.	1.25			
1857,	set	1.13			

Prices: Dairy Products.

Year	Basis	Amount	Year	Basis	Amount
Butter.			*Butter — Con.*		
1762,	lb.	$0.167	1817, (high)	lb.	$0.31
1771,	lb.	.101	(low)	lb.	.266
1772,	lb.	.109	(wholesale)	lb.	.27
1773,	lb.	.109	1818, (high)	lb.	.238
1774,	lb.	.103	(low)	lb.	.197
1777,	lb.	.125	1819, (high)	lb.	.28
1778,	lb.	.11	(low)	lb.	.215
1783,	lb.	.121	(wholesale)	lb.	.19
1786,	lb.	.111	1820, (high)	lb.	.204
1787,	lb.	.111	(low)	lb.	.163
1794,	lb.	.171	1821, (high)	lb.	.25
1796, (wholesale)	lb.	.153	(medium)	lb.	.20
1798, (wholesale)	lb.	.15	(low)	lb.	.152
1800,	lb.	.198	1822, (high)	lb.	.25
(wholesale)	lb.	.185	(medium)	lb.	.193
1801, (high)	lb.	.237	(med. low)	lb.	.16
(low)	lb.	.20	(low)	lb.	.132
1802, (high)	lb.	.215	1823, (high)	lb.	.20
(low)	lb.	.196	(low)	lb.	.176
(wholesale)	lb.	.181	(wholesale)	lb.	.154
1803,	lb.	.214	1824,	lb.	.162
(wholesale, high)	lb.	.163	1825, (high)	lb.	.232
(wholesale, low)	lb.	.125	(low)	lb.	.20
1804,	lb.	.245	1826, (high)	lb.	.216
1805,	lb.	.256	(low)	lb.	.181
(wholesale)	lb.	.207	(wholesale)	lb.	.10
1806, (high)	lb.	.282	1827,	lb.	.207
(medium)	lb.	.233	(wholesale)	lb.	.166
(low)	lb.	.174	1828, (high)	lb.	.20
(wholesale)	lb.	.212	(low)	lb.	.166
1807, (wholesale)	lb.	.20	(wholesale)	lb.	.148
1808,	lb.	.166	1829,	lb.	.159
(wholesale, high)	lb.	.179	(wholesale)	lb.	.125
(wholesale, low)	lb.	.143	1830, (high)	lb.	.192
1809, (high)	lb.	.20	(medium)	lb.	.159
(low)	lb.	.158	(low)	lb.	.109
1810,	lb.	.201	1831, (high)	lb.	.161
(wholesale)	lb.	.17	(low)	lb.	.124
1811, (high)	lb.	.243	1832, (high)	lb.	.211
(low)	lb.	.203	(low)	lb.	.177
(wholesale)	lb.	.169	1833, (high)	lb.	.255
1812, (high)	lb.	.26	(medium)	lb.	.191
(low)	lb.	.22	(low)	lb.	.166
1813, (high)	lb.	.30	1834, (high)	lb.	.236
(medium)	lb.	.249	(low)	lb.	.182
(low)	lb.	.221	1835, (high)	lb.	.254
(wholesale, high)	lb.	.20	(low)	lb.	.197
(wholesale, low)	lb.	.17	1836, (high)	lb.	.309
1814, (high)	lb.	.275	(low)	lb.	.257
(medium)	lb.	.249	1837,	lb.	.233
(low)	lb.	.166	1838,	lb.	.247
(wholesale)	lb.	.222	1839, (high)	lb.	.339
1815,	lb.	.253	(low)	lb.	.247
(wholesale)	lb.	.208	1840, (high)	lb.	.243
1816, (high)	lb.	.282	(medium)	lb.	.209
(low)	lb.	.245	(low)	lb.	.164

Prices: Dairy Products — Continued.

Years.	Basis.	Amount.	Years.	Basis.	Amount.
Butter — Con.			*Cheese* — Con.		
1841, (high)	lb.	.$0.252	1802, (medium)	lb.	$0.167
(low)	lb.	.206	(med. low)	lb.	.138
1842, (high)	lb.	.217	(low)	lb.	.098
(medium)	lb.	.179	1803, (wholesale)	lb.	.095
(low)	lb.	.11	1804,	lb.	.167
1843, (high)	lb.	.197	(wholesale)	lb.	.10
(low)	lb.	.156	1805,	lb.	.143
(wholesale, high)	lb.	.129	(wholesale)	lb.	.12
(wholesale, low)	lb.	.065	1806,	lb.	.161
1844, (high)	lb.	.196	(wholesale)	lb.	.118
(medium)	lb.	.162	1807,	lb.	.11
(low)	lb.	.11	(wholesale)	lb.	.094
1845, (high)	lb.	.232	1808,	lb.	.073
(medium)	lb.	.172	(wholesale)	lb.	.089
(low)	lb.	.13	1809,	lb.	.112
1846, (high)	lb.	.232	1810, (high)	lb.	.147
(medium)	lb.	.175	(low)	lb.	.102
(low)	lb.	.14	1811, (high)	lb.	.209
1847, (high)	lb.	.273	(low)	lb.	.139
(medium)	lb.	.213	(wholesale)	lb.	.102
(low)	lb.	.167	1812, (high)	lb.	.167
1848, (high)	lb.	.288	(low)	lb.	.114
(low)	lb.	.213	1813, (high)	lb.	.14
(by the tub; high)	lb.	.22	(medium)	lb.	.107
(by the tub; medium)	lb.	.185	(low)	lb.	.07
(by the tub; low)	lb.	.143	1814, (high)	lb.	.141
1849, (high)	lb.	.279	(low)	lb.	.088
(low)	lb.	.201	(wholesale, high)	lb.	.12
1850, (high)	lb.	.264	(wholesale, low)	lb.	.10
(medium)	lb.	.206	1815,	lb.	.144
(low)	lb.	.129	1816, (high)	lb.	.153
1851,	lb.	.206	(low)	lb.	.11
(wholesale)	lb.	.10	1817,	lb.	.144
1852,	lb.	.236	1818, (high)	lb.	.15
1853,	lb.	.25	(medium)	lb.	.127
1854,	lb.	.261	(low)	lb.	.098
1855,	lb.	.271	1819, (high)	lb.	.14
1856,	lb.	.265	(medium)	lb.	.105
1857,	lb.	.261	(low)	lb.	.05
1858, (high)	lb.	.40	1820, (high)	lb.	.14
(low)	lb.	.252	(medium)	lb.	.099
(wholesale)	lb.	.227	(low)	lb.	.06
1859, (high)	lb.	.28	1821, (high)	lb.	.127
(low)	lb.	.25	(medium)	lb.	.085
1860, (high)	lb.	.29	(low)	lb.	.04
(low)	lb.	.23	1822,	lb.	.089
			1823,	lb.	.103
Cheese.			(wholesale)	lb.	.08
1752,	lb.	.078	1824,	lb.	.102
1755,	lb.	.089	(wholesale)	lb.	.08
1762,	lb.	.087	1825,	lb.	.096
1779,	lb.	.133	1826,	lb.	.095
1782,	lb.	.083	(wholesale)	lb.	.065
1783, (high)	lb.	.139	1827,	lb.	.093
(medium)	lb.	.083	1828,	lb.	.088
(low)	lb.	.048	1829, (high)	lb.	.084
1784, (high)	lb.	.096	(low)	lb.	.04
(low)	lb.	.048	1830, (high)	lb.	.118
1785,	lb.	.083	(low)	lb.	.079
1787,	lb.	.077	1831, (high)	lb.	.091
1788,	lb.	.083	(low)	lb.	.066
1789,	lb.	.07	1832, (high)	lb.	.083
1790,	lb.	.083	(low)	lb.	.046
1792,	lb.	.086	1833,	lb.	.104
1793,	lb.	.125	1834,	lb.	.098
(wholesale)	lb.	.10	1835,	lb.	.108
1794, (high)	lb.	.118	1836,	lb.	.124
(low)	lb.	.083	1837, (high)	lb.	.123
(wholesale)	lb.	.104	(low)	lb.	.099
1797,	lb.	.091	1838, (high)	lb.	.122
1798,	lb.	.071	(medium)	lb.	.09
1800, (wholesale)	lb.	.105	(low)	lb.	.063
1801, (wholesale)	lb.	.105	1839,	lb.	.123
1802, (high)	lb.	.256	1840,	lb.	.097

Prices: Dairy Products — CONTINUED.

YEARS.	Ba-sis.	Amount.	YEARS.	Ba-sis.	Amount.
Cheese — Con.			*Eggs* — Con.		
1841,	lb.	$0.094	1838, (high)	doz.	$0.251
1842, (high)	lb.	.126	(low)	doz.	.179
(low)	lb	.09	1839, (high)	doz.	.271
1843,	lb.	.083	(low)	doz.	.182
1844,	lb.	.078	1840, (high)	doz.	.219
1845,	lb.	.091	(medium)	doz.	.169
1846,	lb.	.107	(low)	doz.	.127
1847,	lb.	.092	1841, (high)	doz.	.263
1848,	lb.	.10	(medium)	doz.	.158
1849,	lb.	.101	(low)	doz.	.10
1850,	lb.	.094	1842, (high)	doz.	.275
1851,	lb.	.094	(medium)	doz.	.219
(wholesale)	lb.	.081	(low)	doz.	.151
1852,	lb.	.099	1843, (high)	doz.	.236
1854,	lb.	.131	(medium)	doz.	173
1855,	lb.	.118	(low)	doz.	.142
1856,	lb.	.128	1844, (high)	doz.	.221
1857,	lb.	.122	(low)	doz.	.138
1858, (high)	lb.	.109	1845, (high)	doz.	.214
(low)	lb.	.061	(low)	doz.	.158
1859, (high)	lb.	.15	1846, (high)	doz.	.277
(low)	lb.	.118	(medium)	doz.	.209
1860,	lb.	.14	(low)	doz.	.146
			1847, (high)	doz.	.25
Eggs.			(medium)	doz.	.176
1758,	doz.	.078	(low)	doz.	.113
1773,	doz.	.056	1848, (high)	doz.	.258
1783, (high)	doz.	.114	(medium)	doz.	.192
(low)	doz.	.056	(low)	doz.	.163
1794,	doz.	.07	1849, (high)	doz.	.176
1802,	doz.	.183	(low)	doz.	.137
1803,	doz.	.24	1850, (high)	doz.	.232
1806,	doz.	.246	(medium)	doz.	.191
1807,	doz.	.27	(low)	doz.	.153
1813,	doz.	.18	1851,	doz.	.153
1814, (high)	doz.	.206	1852,	doz.	.162
(low)	doz.	.17	1853,	doz.	.254
1816,	doz.	.30	1854,	doz.	.223
1817,	doz.	.167	1855, (high)	doz.	.282
1819, (high)	doz.	.25	(low)	doz.	.235
(low)	doz.	.164	1856, (high)	doz.	.30
1820, (high)	doz.	.26	(medium)	doz.	.244
(low)	doz	.157	(low)	doz.	.172
1821, (high)	doz.	.228	1857, (high)	doz.	.248
(medium)	doz.	.131	(low)	doz.	.205
(low)	doz.	.091	1858, (high)	doz.	.26
1822, (high)	doz.	.17	(medium)	doz.	.205
(medium)	doz.	.139	(low)	doz.	.161
(low)	doz.	.10	1859, (high)	doz.	.252
1823,	doz.	.22	(low)	doz.	.172
1824,	doz.	.153	1860, (high)	doz.	.27
1825, (high)	doz.	.167	(low)	doz.	.17
(low)	doz.	.135			
1826,	doz.	.164	*Milk.*		
1827, (high)	doz.	.172	1774,	qt.	.022
(low)	doz.	.132	1780,	qt.	.036
1828, (high)	doz.	.154	1784,	qt.	.028
(low)	doz.	.10	1785,	qt.	.014
1829,	doz.	.144	1786,	qt.	.028
1830, (high)	doz.	.165	1788,	qt.	.028
(low)	doz.	.129	1790,	qt.	.028
1831, (high)	doz.	.15	1794,	qt.	.028
(low)	doz.	.122	1797,	qt.	.039
1832, (high)	doz.	.17	1801,	qt.	.035
(low)	doz.	.136	1802,	qt.	.056
1833, (high)	doz.	.236	1803,	qt.	.036
(low)	doz.	.157		gal.	.167
1834, (high)	doz.	.23	1804,	qt.	.031
(low)	doz.	.139	1805, (high)	qt.	.042
1835,	doz.	.173	(low)	qt.	.028
1836,	doz.	.20	1806, (high)	qt.	.05
1837, (high)	doz.	.277	(low)	qt.	.029
(medium)	doz.	.23	1807, (high)	qt.	.05
(low)	doz.	.184	(low)	qt.	.029

Prices: Dairy Products — Concluded.

Years.	Basis.	Amount.	Years.	Basis.	Amount.
Milk — Con.			*Milk* — Con.		
1808,	qt.	$0.06	1842,	qt.	$0.05
1809,	qt.	.06	(wholesale)	qt.	.04
1810, (high)	qt.	.056	1843,	qt.	.05
(low)	qt.	.029	(wholesale)	qt.	.04
1811,	qt.	.061	1844,	qt.	.05
1812, (high)	qt.	.052	(wholesale)	qt.	.04
(low)	qt.	.034	1845,	qt.	.05
1813, (high)	qt.	.053	(wholesale)	qt.	.04
(low)	qt.	.03	1846,	qt.	.051
1814,	qt.	.05	(wholesale, high)	qt.	.04
1815,	qt.	.05	(wholesale, low)	qt.	.028
1816, (high)	qt.	.05	1847,	qt.	.052
(low)	qt.	.03	(wholesale, high)	qt.	.04
1818,	qt.	.06	(wholesale, low)	qt.	.028
1820, (high)	qt.	.06	1848,	qt.	.05
(low)	qt.	.03	(wholesale)	qt.	.04
1821,	qt.	.05	1849,	qt.	.05
1822,	qt.	.04	(wholesale)	qt.	.038
1824, (high)	qt.	.06	1850,	qt.	.053
(low)	qt.	.03	(wholesale)	qt.	.037
1828,	qt.	.03	1851,	qt.	.051
1829,	qt.	.05	(wholesale)	qt.	.035
1830,	qt.	.05	1852,	qt.	.06
1833,	qt.	.048	(wholesale)	qt.	.037
1834,	qt.	.05	1853,	qt.	.05
1835,	qt.	.045	(wholesale)	qt.	.039
1836,	qt.	.046	1854, (wholesale)	qt.	.043
1837,	qt.	.05	1855, (wholesale)	qt.	.047
1838,	qt.	.05	1856, (wholesale)	qt.	.052
1839,	qt.	.05	1857, (wholesale)	qt.	.05
1840,	qt.	.05	1858,	qt.	.05
1841,	qt.	.041	1859,	qt.	.05

Prices: Dress Goods.

Years.	Basis.	Amount.	Years.	Basis.	Amount.
Alepine.			*Beige.*		
1839,	yd.	$1.98	1792,	yd.	$0.486
1855,	yd.	1.25	1793,	yd.	.361
			1810, (high)	yd.	1.00
Alpaca.			(low)	yd.	.33
1845,	yd.	.472	*Bombazet.*		
1846,	yd.	.41	1807,	yd.	.625
1848, (high)	yd.	.75	1810, (high)	yd.	.74
(low)	yd.	.247	(low)	yd.	.458
1849,	yd.	.42	1812,	yd.	.50
1850, (high)	yd.	1.00	1816, (high)	yd.	.625
(low)	yd.	.292	(medium)	yd.	.53
1855, (high)	yd.	.78	(low)	yd.	.412
(medium)	yd.	.455	1817, (high)	yd.	.53
(low)	yd.	.25	(low)	yd.	.293
1856, (high)	yd.	.80	1820,	yd.	.583
(low)	yd.	.213	1822, (high)	yd.	.625
1857, (high)	yd.	.503	(low)	yd.	.329
(low)	yd.	.295	1823, (high)	yd.	.64
1858, (high)	yd.	.75	(medium)	yd.	.394
(low)	yd.	.491	(low)	yd.	.249
1859, (high)	yd.	.488	1825,	yd.	.295
(low)	yd.	.294	1826, (high)	yd.	.376
			(low)	yd.	.29
Barège.			1827,	yd.	.25
1841,	yd.	.50	1828,	yd.	.271
1855,	yd.	.498	1830, (high)	yd.	.333
1856, (high)	yd.	.494	(low)	yd.	.20
(low)	yd.	.25	1833,	yd.	.54
1857,	yd.	.50	1835, (high)	yd.	.31
1858, (high)	yd.	.46	(low)	yd.	.18
(low)	yd.	.321	1839,	yd.	.50
1859, (high)	yd.	.479	1846,	yd.	.30
(low)	yd.	.107	*Bombazine.*		
Batiste.			1832,	yd.	.627
1829,	yd.	.623	1837,	yd.	1.02
1831,	yd.	.334	1839,	yd.	2.25

Prices: Dress Goods — CONTINUED.

Years.	Basis	Amount.	Years.	Basis	Amount.
Brilliant.			*Calico — Con.*		
1857,	yd.	$0.14	1830, (low)	yd.	$0.059
1858, (high)	yd.	.249	1831, (high)	yd.	.31
(low)	yd.	.132	(medium)	yd.	.20
1859,	yd.	.138	(low)	yd.	.141
			1832, (high)	yd.	.311
Calico.			(medium)	yd.	.182
1783,	yd.	.782	(low)	yd.	.125
1784,	yd.	.376	1833, (high)	yd.	.267
1791,	yd.	.374	(low)	yd.	.149
1793,	yd.	.429	1834,	yd.	.166
1794, (high)	yd.	.497	1835, (high)	yd.	.25
(low)	yd.	.333	(medium)	yd.	.212
1795,	yd.	.336	(low)	yd.	.158
1797, (wholesale)	yd.	.389	1836, (high)	yd.	.448
1800, (wholesale)	yd.	.385	(medium)	yd.	.26
1801, (wholesale)	yd.	.378	(low)	yd.	.125
1803,	yd.	.292	1837,	yd.	.176
1804,	yd.	.417	1838, (high)	yd.	.416
1805, (high)	yd.	.625	(medium)	yd.	.28
(low)	yd.	.42	(low)	yd.	.149
(wholesale)	yd.	.333	(French)	yd.	.426
1806,	yd.	.333	1839, (high)	yd.	.25
1807, (high)	yd.	.306	(low)	yd.	.166
(low)	yd.	.277	(French)	yd.	.442
1808,	yd.	.278	1840, (high)	yd.	.334
1810, (high)	yd.	.62	(medium)	yd.	.25
(medium)	yd.	.417	(low)	yd.	.134
(low)	yd.	.25	1841, (high)	yd.	.247
1813,	yd.	.375	(medium)	yd.	.139
1814,	yd.	.50	(low)	yd.	.083
1815, (high)	yd.	.375	1842, (high)	yd.	.25
(medium)	yd.	.328	(medium)	yd.	.148
(low)	yd.	.265	(low)	yd.	.083
1816, (high)	yd.	.45	(French; high)	yd.	.50
(medium)	yd.	.327	(French; low)	yd.	.337
(low)	yd.	.262	1843, (high)	yd.	.127
1817, (high)	yd.	.75	(low)	yd.	.071
(med. high)	yd.	.633	1844,	yd.	.136
(medium)	yd.	.448	1845, (high)	yd.	.28
(med. low)	yd.	.366	(low)	yd.	.109
(low)	yd.	.259	1846, (high)	yd.	.25
1818, (high)	yd.	.354	(medium)	yd.	.117
(low)	yd.	.248	(low)	yd.	.063
1819, (high)	yd.	.29	1847, (high)	yd.	.123
(medium)	yd.	.241	(low)	yd.	.091
(low)	yd.	.20	1848, (high)	yd.	.122
1820, (high)	yd.	.333	(low)	yd.	.076
(low)	yd.	.19	1849, (high)	yd.	.25
1821, (high)	yd.	.375	(low)	yd.	.116
(medium)	yd.	.315	1850, (high)	yd.	.122
(low)	yd.	.26	(low)	yd.	.07
(French)	yd.	1.00	1851,	yd.	.062
1822, (high)	yd.	.336	1853,	yd.	.106
(medium)	yd.	.253	1854,	yd.	.062
(low)	yd.	.212	1855,	yd.	.12
1823,	yd.	.28	1856, (high)	yd.	.116
1824,	yd.	.244	(low)	yd.	.063
1825, (high)	yd.	.591	1857,	yd.	.117
(medium)	yd.	.356	1858, (high)	yd.	.117
(low)	yd.	.25	(low)	yd.	.079
1826, (high)	yd.	.355	1859, (high)	yd.	.25
(low)	yd.	.25	(medium)	yd.	.11
1827, (high)	yd.	.37	(low)	yd.	.062
(medium)	yd.	.237			
(low)	yd.	.167	*Cambric.*		
1828, (high)	yd.	.302	1771,	yd.	1.02
(medium)	yd.	.231	1783, (high)	yd.	1.41
(low)	yd.	.139	(low)	yd.	1.06
1829, (high)	yd.	.175	1794,	yd.	2.33
(low)	yd.	.125	(sarcenet)	yd.	.361
1830, (high)	yd.	.37	1798,	yd.	1.67
(med. high)	yd.	.306	1799,	yd.	.75
(medium)	yd.	.196	1804,	yd.	2.00
(med. low)	yd.	.126	1805, (high)	yd.	1.00

Prices: Dress Goods — CONTINUED.

YEARS.	Basis.	Amount.	YEARS.	Basis.	Amount.
Cambric — Con.			*Cambric* — Con.		
1805, (medium)	yd.	$0.79	1843, (low)	yd.	$0.07
(low)	yd.	.306	1844, (high)	yd.	.183
1806, .	yd.	1.00	(low)	yd.	.103
(cotton)	yd.	.50	1845, (high)	yd.	.375
1808, .	yd.	.709	(low)	yd.	.114
(cotton)	yd.	.475	1846, (high)	yd.	.50
1809, (high)	yd.	.96	(medium)	yd.	.37
(low)	yd.	.60	(low)	yd.	.10
1810, .	yd.	.515	1847, .	yd.	.10
1811, (high)	yd.	.625	1848, (high)	yd.	.334
(low)	yd.	.384	(low)	yd.	.103
1812, (cotton)	yd.	.96	1849, (high)	yd.	.42
1813, (high)	yd.	1.25	(low)	yd.	.083
(low)	yd.	1.00	1850, .	yd.	.089
1814, (high)	yd.	1.25	1851, (cotton)	yd.	.052
(low)	yd.	.89	(linen)	yd.	.25
1815, (high)	yd.	.88	1853, .	yd.	.07
(low)	yd.	.696	1855, (high)	yd.	.40
1816, (high)	yd.	.765	(medium)	yd.	.23
(medium)	yd.	.629	(low)	yd.	.095
(low)	yd.	.335	1856, .	yd.	.126
1817, (high)	yd.	.76	1857, (high)	yd.	.311
(low)	yd.	.398	(low)	yd.	.105
1818, (high)	yd.	.484	1858, (high)	yd.	.375
(low)	yd.	.25	(medium)	yd.	.257
1819, .	yd.	.508	(low)	yd.	.071
(cotton; high)	yd.	.45	1859, (high)	yd.	.257
(cotton; low)	yd.	.28	(low)	yd.	.097
(linen)	yd.	4.00			
1820, (high)	yd.	.482	*Camlet.*		
(low)	yd.	.225	1783, (high)	yd.	.438
1821, (high)	yd.	.417	(low)	yd.	.251
(low)	yd.	.243	1784, (high)	yd.	.375
1822, (high)	yd.	.591	(low)	yd.	.25
(low)	yd.	.242	1794, .	yd.	.416
1823, (high)	yd.	.50	1795, .	yd.	.389
(medium)	yd.	.235	1810, .	yd.	.26
(low)	yd.	.167	1841, .	yd.	.624
1824, .	yd.	.475	1847, .	yd.	.50
1825, (high)	yd.	.625			
(low)	yd.	.211	*Cashmere.*		
1827, (high)	yd.	.25	1819, .	yd.	1.50
(medium)	yd.	.202	1855, (high)	yd.	1.12
(low)	yd.	.146	(low)	yd.	.753
1828, (high)	yd.	.31	1856, (high)	yd.	1.17
(low)	yd.	.125	(low)	yd.	.836
1829, (high)	yd.	.417	1857, .	yd.	1.12
(low)	yd.	.25	1858, .	yd.	1.13
1830, (high)	yd.	.926	1859, (high)	yd.	1.12
(medium)	yd.	.668	(low)	yd.	.92
(low)	yd.	.182			
1831, (high)	yd.	.651	*Cashmerette.*		
(medium)	yd.	.333	1855, .	yd.	.667
(low)	yd.	.162	1856, .	yd.	.521
1832, (high)	yd.	.171	1857, .	yd.	.642
(low)	yd.	.112	1858, (high)	yd.	.642
1833, (high)	yd.	.472	(low)	yd.	.42
(low)	yd.	.212	1859, .	yd.	.668
1834, .	yd.	.145			
1835, .	yd.	.125	*Challis.*		
1836, (high)	yd.	.389	1856, .	yd.	.202
(low)	yd.	.147	1857, .	yd.	.185
1837, (high)	yd.	.75	1858, .	yd.	.193
(medium)	yd.	.25			
(low)	yd.	.119	*Crape.*		
1838, .	yd.	.125	1806, .	yd.	.56
1839, (high)	yd.	.25	1821, .	yd.	.751
(low)	yd.	.136	(Canton)	yd.	1.00
1840, (high)	yd.	.16	1822, (Canton; high)	yd.	1.37
(low)	yd.	.119	(Canton; low)	yd.	1.00
1841, .	yd.	.12	1826, (high)	yd.	.875
1842, (high)	yd.	.46	(low)	yd.	.75
(low)	yd.	.083	1829, .	yd.	.742
1843, (high)	yd.	.20	1831, .	yd.	.74
			1840, .	yd.	.625

Prices: Dress Goods — Continued.

YEARS.	Ba-sis.	Amount.	YEARS.	Ba-sis.	Amount.
Debeige.			*Gingham — Con.*		
1855,	yd.	$0.25	1817, (low)	yd.	$0.286
1856, (high)	yd.	.36	1818, (high)	yd.	.343
(low)	yd.	.149	(low)	yd.	.168
1858, (high)	yd.	.413	1819, (high)	yd.	.443
(low)	yd.	.10	(low)	yd.	.246
Delaine.			1820, (high)	yd.	.379
1856,	yd.	.192	(low)	yd.	.224
1857, (high)	yd.	.455	1821, (high)	yd.	.472
(low)	yd.	.204	(medium)	yd.	.351
1858, (high)	yd.	.377	(low)	yd.	.241
(medium)	yd.	.223	1822, (high)	yd.	.407
(low)	yd.	.152	(medium)	yd.	.29
1859, (high)	yd.	.42	(low)	yd.	.205
(medium)	yd.	.206	1823, (high)	yd.	.572
(low)	yd.	.131	(medium)	yd.	.346
Dimity.			(low)	yd.	.20
1810,	yd.	.531	1824, (high)	yd.	.34
1811, (high)	yd.	.667	(medium)	yd.	.25
(low)	yd.	.50	(low)	yd.	.167
1815,	yd.	.958	1825,	yd.	.289
1816, (high)	yd.	.876	1826, (high)	yd.	.369
(low)	yd.	.46	(low)	yd.	.25
1817, (high)	yd.	.923	1827, (high)	yd.	.583
(low)	yd.	.41	(medium)	yd.	.271
1822,	yd.	.50	(low)	yd.	.169
1823,	yd.	.58	1828,	yd.	.23
1829,	yd.	.35	1829,	yd.	.246
1831,	yd.	.584	1830,	yd.	.417
1838,	yd.	.374	1831, (high)	yd.	.333
1853,	yd.	.374	(low)	yd.	.15
1858,	yd.	.50	1832,	yd.	.333
Foulard.			1833,	yd.	.25
1858,	yd.	.342	1834, (high)	yd.	.333
1859,	yd.	.272	(medium)	yd.	.241
Gauze.			(low)	yd.	.167
1783, (high)	yd.	.85	1837,	yd.	.268
(medium)	yd.	.583	1839,	yd.	.167
(low)	yd.	.416	1843,	yd.	.242
1784,	yd.	.464	1844,	yd.	.21
1793, (black)	yd.	.333	1845,	yd.	.125
1794, (black)	yd.	.333	1846,	yd.	.25
1798, (black)	yd.	.278	1847,	yd.	.125
1801,	yd.	.278	1848,	yd.	.185
1805,	yd.	.278	(linen)	yd.	.30
1807,	yd.	.50	1849,	yd.	.146
1825,	yd.	.98	1850,	yd.	.245
Gingham.			1855, (high)	yd.	.333
1797,	yd.	.556	(low)	yd.	.176
1798, (wholesale)	yd.	.556	1856, (high)	yd.	.23
1800, (wholesale)	yd.	.167	(low)	yd.	.141
1801,	yd.	.17	1857, (high)	yd.	.216
1807, (high)	yd.	.50	(low)	yd.	.144
(low)	yd.	.361	1858, (high)	yd.	.221
1808,	yd.	.403	(low)	yd.	.129
1809,	yd.	.289	1859, (high)	yd.	.215
1810,	yd.	.297	(low)	yd.	.11
1812, (high)	yd.	1 20	*Ladies' Cloth.*		
(low)	yd.	.455	1856,	yd.	2.00
1813,	yd.	.435	1859, (high)	yd.	2.02
1814, (high)	yd.	.568	(low)	yd.	1.25
(low)	yd.	.46	*Lawn.*		
(wholesale)	yd.	.409	1771,	yd.	.903
1815, (high)	yd.	.873	1783,	yd.	.734
(low)	yd.	.384	1817,	yd.	.538
1816, (high)	yd.	.55	1822,	yd.	.60
(medium)	yd.	.403	1828,	yd.	.50
(low)	yd.	.271	1829, (linen)	yd.	.833
1817, (high)	yd.	.517	1840, (high)	yd.	.668
(medium)	yd.	.372	(low)	yd.	.45
			1841,	yd.	.48
			1842,	yd.	.653
			1843,	yd.	.417

Prices: Dress Goods — Continued.

Years.	Basis.	Amount.	Years.	Basis.	Amount.
Lawn — Con.			*Moreen* — Con.		
1847, (high)	yd.	$0 50	1848,	yd.	$0.25
(low)	yd.	.20	1855,	yd.	.28
1848,	yd.	.46	1856,	yd.	.26
1856,	yd.	.124	1857,	yd.	.25
1857, (high)	yd.	.42	1858, (high)	yd.	.353
(low)	yd.	.14	(low)	yd.	.26
			1859,	yd.	.293
Linsey woolsey.					
1821,	yd.	.583	*Muslin.*		
1857, (plaid)	yd.	.20	1793,	yd.	.723
			1794,	yd.	.333
Lustring.			1801,	yd.	.52
1793,	yd.	1.11	1803,	yd.	.75
1794,	yd.	1.25	1804,	yd.	1.00
1803,	yd.	1.13	1805,	yd.	1.00
1819,	yd.	.668	(cambric)	yd.	.50
1830,	yd.	.708	1806,	yd.	1.24
1832, (Italian)	yd.	.762	(cambric)	yd.	.50
			1807, (high)	yd.	1.12
Lyonese Cloth.			(medium)	yd.	.75
1855, (high)	yd.	.488	(low)	yd.	.604
(low)	yd.	.369	1809, (high)	yd.	.968
1856,	yd.	.424	(low)	yd.	.50
1857,	yd.	.42	1810, (high)	yd.	1.03
1858, (high)	yd.	.92	(low)	yd.	.625
(low)	yd.	.42	1811, (high)	yd.	.50
1859,	yd.	.42	(low)	yd.	.25
			1813,	yd.	1.00
Marseilles.			(colonnade)	yd.	1.12
1857,	yd.	.333	1815,	yd.	.668
1858, (high)	yd.	.499	1816, (high)	yd.	1.00
(low)	yd.	.25	(medium)	yd.	.50
1859,	yd.	.50	(low)	yd.	.313
			(gurrah)	yd.	.334
Merino.			1817, (high)	yd.	.75
1832,	yd.	1.00	(medium)	yd.	.38
1833,	yd.	1.25	(low)	yd.	.25
1836, (French)	yd.	1.29	1818, (high)	yd.	1.20
1839,	yd.	.251	(low)	yd.	.42
1841, (high)	yd.	2.00	1819, (high)	yd.	1.25
(low)	yd.	.50	(med. high)	yd.	.89
1842,	yd.	1.00	(medium)	yd.	.58
1843, (high)	yd.	.592	(low)	yd.	.25
(low)	yd.	.25	1820, (high)	yd.	1.25
			(medium)	yd.	1.03
Millinet.			(low)	yd.	.696
1783,	yd.	.389	1821, (high)	yd.	1.37
1804,	yd.	.146	(low)	yd.	.606
1805,	yd.	.25	1822, (high)	yd.	1.00
1811,	yd	.25	(med. high)	yd.	.764
1821,	yd.	.25	(medium)	yd.	.552
1825,	yd.	.16	(med. low)	yd.	.419
1827,	yd.	.25	(low)	yd.	.24
			1823, (high)	yd.	.595
Mode.			(medium)	yd.	.25
1783,	yd.	.933	(low)	yd.	.10
1784, (high)	yd.	1.09	1824, (high)	yd.	.984
(low)	yd.	.667	(med. high)	yd.	.75
1793, (black)	yd.	.723	(medium)	yd.	.50
(black; wholesale)	ell	.678	(low)	yd.	.25
1794,	yd.	.75	1825, (high)	yd.	1.06
1798,	yd.	.639	(medium)	yd.	.713
1803,	yd.	.75	(low)	yd.	.332
1805,	yd.	1.17	1826, (high)	yd.	.96
(wholesale)	ell	.667	(low)	yd.	.613
1806,	yd.	.834	1827, (high)	yd.	1.33
1818,	yd.	1.00	(medium)	yd.	.75
1826,	yd	.75	(med. low)	yd.	.32
			(low)	yd.	.167
Moreen.			1828, (high)	yd.	.32
1783, (high)	yd.	.542	(medium)	yd.	.20
(low)	yd.	.196	(low)	yd.	.125
1784,	yd.	.50	1829,	yd.	.36
1846,	yd.	.344	1830, (high)	yd.	.875

Prices: Dress Goods — Continued.

Years.	Ba-sis.	Amount.	Years.	Ba-sis.	Amount.
Muslin — Con.			*Nankeen* — Con.		
1830, (low)	yd.	$0.458	1800, (wholesale)	yd.	$0.372
1831,	yd.	.613	1804,	yd.	.28
1832,	yd.	.56	1805,	yd.	.50
1833,	yd.	.50	1806,	yd.	.444
1834,	yd.	.31	1817, (high)	yd.	.333
1836, (high)	yd.	.67	(low)	yd.	.20
(low)	yd.	.473	1822,	yd.	.185
1837, (high)	yd.	1.00	1828,	yd.	.167
(medium)	yd.	.625	1855,	yd.	.135
(low)	yd.	.25	1856,	yd.	.124
1838, (high)	yd.	.75	1857,	yd.	.15
(low)	yd.	.56	1858,	yd.	.08
1839, (high)	yd.	.78	1859, (high)	yd.	.347
(medium)	yd.	.425	(low)	yd.	.25
(low)	yd.	.298			
1840,	yd.	.30	*Plaid.*		
1841, (high)	yd.	.75	1817, (high)	yd.	.75
(low)	yd.	.30	(low)	yd.	.551
1843, (cambric)	yd.	.627	1822,	yd.	.50
1844,	yd.	.25	1824,	yd.	.50
1845,	yd.	.25	1825,	yd.	.75
1846, (high)	yd.	.57	1827, (Scotch)	yd.	.40
(low)	yd.	.20	1835, (Scotch)	yd.	.507
1847, (high)	yd.	.25	1836,	yd.	.75
(low)	yd.	.15	1837,	yd.	.50
1849,	yd.	.25	1838, (Scotch)	yd.	.748
1851, (high)	yd.	.37	1840,	yd.	.333
(low)	yd.	.25	1855, (high)	yd.	.749
1855,	yd.	.26	(medium)	yd.	.542
1856, (high)	yd.	.379	(low)	yd.	.25
(low)	yd.	.157	1856, (high)	yd.	.591
1857, (high)	yd.	.376	(medium)	yd.	.381
(medium)	yd.	.25	(low)	yd.	.242
(low)	yd.	.143	1857, (high)	yd.	.826
(cambric)	yd.	.35	(medium)	yd.	.54
1858, (high)	yd.	.387	(low)	yd.	.294
(medium)	yd.	.233	1858, (high)	yd.	.867
(low)	yd.	.127	(medium)	yd.	.399
1859, (high)	yd.	.338	(low)	yd.	.199
(medium)	yd.	.191	1859, (high)	yd.	.814
(low)	yd.	.128	(medium)	yd.	.469
			(low)	yd.	.279
Muslin de Laine.					
1838, (high)	yd.	.749	*Poplin.*		
(low)	yd.	.51	1784,	yd.	.443
1840,	yd.	.25	1794,	yd.	.458
1841,	yd.	.625	1856,	yd.	.30
1842,	yd.	.25	1857,	yd.	.28
1843, (high)	yd.	.46	1858, (high)	yd.	.268
(low)	yd.	.375	(low)	yd.	.167
1844, (high)	yd.	.40			
(low)	yd.	.238	*Sarcenet.*		
1845,	yd.	.333	1784,	yd.	.50
1846, (high)	yd.	.333	1793,	yd.	.433
(low)	yd.	.232			
1847, (high)	yd.	.396	*Satin.*		
(medium)	yd.	.25	1773,	yd.	.731
(low)	yd.	.167	1783, (high)	yd.	1.47
1848,	yd.	.166	(low)	yd.	.75
1849,	yd.	.20	1784,	yd.	1.08
1850,	yd.	.14	1802,	yd.	3.00
1851,	yd.	.22	1804,	yd.	1.89
1852,	yd.	.143			
1853,	yd.	.133	*Satinet.*		
1855, (high)	yd.	.231	1787,	yd.	.75
(low)	yd.	.153	1792,	yd.	.782
			(wholesale)	yd.	.472
Nankeen.			1793, (high)	yd.	.712
1782,	yd.	.80	(low)	yd.	.548
1791, (striped)	yd.	.625	1794, (high)	yd.	1.04
1793,	yd.	.549	(low)	yd.	.681
(wholesale)	yd.	.416	1811,	yd.	1.88
1794,	yd.	.472	1814, (high)	yd.	2.50
1797, (twilled)	yd.	.50	(low)	yd.	1.26

Prices: Dress Goods — Continued.

Years.	Basis.	Amount.	Years.	Basis.	Amount.
Satinet — Con.			*Silk* — Con.		
1815, ...	yd.	$0.932	1819, (high) . . .	yd.	$0.917
1816, (high) . . .	yd.	1.75	(low) . . .	yd.	.751
(medium) . . .	yd.	1.33	(Canton) . . .	yd.	1.00
(low) . . .	yd.	1.00	1820, (high) . . .	yd.	.861
1817, (high) . . .	yd.	1.78	(low) . . .	yd.	.625
(medium) . . .	yd.	1.40	1822, (high) . . .	yd.	.84
(low) . . .	yd.	1.05	(low) . . .	yd.	.632
1819, (high) . . .	yd.	1.25	1824, . . .	yd.	.563
(medium) . . .	yd.	1.08	1826, (high) . . .	yd.	1.68
(low) . . .	yd.	.917	(medium) . . .	yd.	1.00
1820, . . .	yd.	.278	(low) . . .	yd.	.674
1822, (high) . . .	yd.	1.07	1827, (high) . . .	yd.	.909
(low) . . .	yd.	.92	(medium) . . .	yd.	.623
1823, (high) . . .	yd.	.748	(low) . . .	yd.	.458
(low) . . .	yd.	.50	1828, (high) . . .	yd.	.789
1824, . . .	yd.	.667	(low) . . .	yd.	.625
1830, (high) . . .	yd.	.771	1831, . . .	yd.	.693
(low) . . .	yd.	.54	1833, (high) . . .	yd.	.851
1832, . . .	yd.	.792	(low) . . .	yd.	.50
1835, . . .	yd.	.751	1838, . . .	yd.	.75
1840, . . .	yd.	.667	1839, . . .	yd.	.50
1841, . . .	yd.	.833	1841, . . .	yd.	.827
1846, . . .	yd.	.751	1843, . . .	yd.	.65
1855, . . .	yd.	.422	1844, (high) . . .	yd.	1.25
1859, . . .	yd.	.50	(low) . . .	yd.	.60
			1853, . . .	yd.	.50
Satin Stripe.			1855, (high) . . .	yd.	1.20
1858, (high) . . .	yd.	.375	(medium) . . .	yd.	.876
(low) . . .	yd.	.167	(low) . . .	yd.	.619
1859, (high) . . .	yd.	.274	1856, (high) . . .	yd.	1.33
(low) . . .	yd.	.167	(medium) . . .	yd.	1.08
			(low) . . .	yd.	.731
Serge.			1857, (high) . . .	yd.	1.62
1792, . . .	yd.	.916	(medium) . . .	yd.	1.13
1795, . . .	yd.	.75	(low) . . .	yd.	.721
1800, (wholesale) . . .	yd.	.764	(moire antique) . . .	yd.	.746
1801, (wholesale) . . .	yd.	.785	(watered) . . .	yd.	1.50
1805, (high) . . .	yd.	.75	1858, (high) . . .	yd.	1.47
(low) . . .	yd.	.666	(med. high) . . .	yd.	1.19
1806, . . .	yd.	1.00	(med. low) . . .	yd.	.805
1812, . . .	yd.	.833	(low) . . .	yd.	.58
1823, . . .	yd.	2.47	1859, (high) . . .	yd.	1.37
1832, (Victoria) . . .	yd.	1.13	(low) . . .	yd.	.665
1835, . . .	yd.	.42	(lining) . . .	yd.	.662
1836, . . .	yd.	.60			
1843, . . .	yd.	.333	*Swan's-down.*		
			1799, . . .	yd.	1.17
Shalloon.			1817, . . .	yd.	.375
1779, . . .	yd.	.40			
1783, (high) . . .	yd.	.64	*Tammy.*		
(low) . . .	yd.	.422	1771, . . .	yd.	.36
1784, . . .	yd.	.40	1783, . . .	yd.	.295
1788, . . .	yd.	.444	1784, . . .	yd.	.264
1806, . . .	yd.	.50			
1816, . . .	yd.	.625	*Thibet.*		
1832, . . .	yd.	.63	1857, . . .	yd.	1.34
			1858, (high) . . .	yd.	.971
Silk.			(low) . . .	yd.	.53
1782, . . .	yd.	1.00			
1783, (high) . . .	yd.	1.50	*Velvet.*		
(medium) . . .	yd.	.814	1787, . . .	yd.	.889
(low) . . .	yd.	.416	1792, . . .	yd.	1.11
1784, . . .	yd.	.611	1793, . . .	yd.	.837
1800, . . .	yd.	1.00	1794, (high) . . .	yd.	.972
1803, . . .	yd.	.833	(low) . . .	yd.	.667
1808, . . .	yd.	1.33	(wholesale, high) . . .	yd.	.833
1813, . . .	yd.	1.00	(wholesale, low) . . .	yd.	.639
1815, . . .	yd.	9.00	1795, . . .	yd.	1.00
1816, (high) . . .	yd.	1.25	1805, (high) . . .	yd.	3.74
(medium) . . .	yd.	1.00	(low) . . .	yd.	1.00
(low) . . .	yd.	.667	1806, (high) . . .	yd.	1.75
1817, (high) . . .	yd.	1.25	(low) . . .	yd.	1.58
(low) . . .	yd.	1.00	1807, . . .	yd.	.667
1818, . . .	yd.	1.27	1809, . . .	yd.	1.25

Prices: Dress Goods — CONCLUDED.

Years.	Basis.	Amount.	Years.	Basis.	Amount.
Velvet — Con.			*Velvet* — Con.		
1810,	yd.	$1.25	1848,	yd.	$0.68
1811,	yd.	1.13	1855,	yd.	.50
1822,	yd.	1.00	*Velveteen.*		
1831,	yd.	.50	1800,	yd.	1.33
1839, (cotton)	yd.	.56	1801,	yd.	.75
1840,	yd.	4.00	1807,	yd.	.861
1842,	yd.	.50	1808,	yd.	.873

Prices: Dry Goods.

Years.	Basis.	Amount.	Years.	Basis.	Amount.
Baize.			*Buckram* — Con.		
1783,	yd.	$0.40	1807,	yd.	$0.35
1784,	yd.	.552	1824,	yd.	.25
1787, (green)	yd.	.333	1826,	yd.	.36
1788,	yd.	.333	1827,	yd.	.25
1791,	p'ce	15.27	1828,	yd.	.251
1792,	yd.	.341	1832,	yd.	.20
1793,	yd.	.333			
1794,	yd.	.351	*Canvas.*		
1795,	yd.	.357	1832, (high)	yd.	.42
1805,	yd.	.333	(low)	yd.	.337
1811,	yd.	.378	1839,	yd.	.33
1812,	yd.	.287	1840,	yd.	.253
1838,	yd.	.46	1858,	yd.	.20
1844,	yd.	.28			
1846,	yd.	.31	*Chintz.*		
			1771,	yd.	.557
Binding.			1773,	yd.	.533
1787, (shoe)	gro.	1.25	1785,	yd.	.593
1800, (quality)	gro.	1.67	1792, (high)	yd.	.567
(shoe)	gro.	.888	(low)	yd.	.389
(quality shoe)	gro.	1.00	1793,	yd.	.647
1801, (quality)	gro.	1.67	1794,	yd.	.625
(quality shoe)	gro.	1.00			
1803, (quality)	gro.	1.67	*Copperplate.*		
1805, (quality)	gro.	1.67	1794,	yd.	.419
1807, (quality)	gro.	1.50	1819,	yd.	.25
1808, (quality)	gro.	1.67	1821,	yd.	.40
1816, (carpet)	yd.	.083			
1818, (quality)	yd.	.02	*Cotton and Linen Cloth.*		
			1792, (high)	yd.	.581
Blankets.			(low)	yd.	.243
1783,	ea.	1.25	1793, (high)	yd.	.833
1784,	ea.	1.34	(low)	yd.	.343
1789,	ea.	.916			
1792,	ea.	2.33	*Cotton Batting.*		
1793,	pr.	3.66	1779,	lb.	.277
(rose)	pr.	3.49	1830,	lb.	.11
1794,	pr.	5.00	1840,	lb.	.10
1797,	pr.	4.74	1844,	lb.	.105
1798, (high)	pr.	5.00	1847,	lb.	.114
(low)	pr.	3.91	1848,	lb.	.10
1800,	pr.	11.17	1850,	lb.	.10
1807,	pr.	7.50	1855,	lb.	.11
1817,	pr.	7.50			
1831, (high)	ea.	1.90	*Cotton Cloth.*		
(low)	ea.	1.65	1784, (high)	yd.	1.20
1841, (high)	pr.	5.50	(low)	yd.	.567
(low)	pr.	3.00	1793,	yd.	.472
1855,	pr.	3.50	(fine)	yd.	.389
1857,	ea.	1.00	(India; high)	yd.	.361
1858,	pr.	4.25	(India; low)	yd.	.271
			(striped)	yd.	.278
Buckram.			1794, (high)	yd.	.50
1783,	yd.	.26	(low)	yd.	.292
1784,	yd.	.231	(India)	yd.	.358
1791,	yd.	.153	1795,	yd.	.288
1792,	yd.	.333	(India)	yd.	.293
1793,	yd.	.333	1798, (India)	yd.	.229
1794, (high)	yd.	.333	1801, (India)	yd.	.20
(low)	yd.	.223	1803,	yd.	.343

Prices: Dry Goods—Continued.

Years.	Basis.	Amount.	Years.	Basis.	Amount.
Cotton Cloth — Con.			*Cotton Cloth* — Con.		
1804,	yd.	$0.375	1826, (high)	yd.	$0.264
(India)	yd.	.333	(low)	yd.	.14
1805,	yd.	.25	1827, (high)	yd.	.376
(India; high)	yd.	.333	(low)	yd.	.147
(India; low)	yd.	.219	1828, (high)	yd.	.20
1806, (high)	yd.	.556	(medium)	yd.	.154
(low)	yd.	.28	(low)	yd.	.125
(India)	yd.	.355	1829, (high)	yd.	.239
1808, (high)	yd.	.403	(medium)	yd.	.164
(medium)	yd.	.274	(low)	yd.	.116
(low)	yd.	.167	1830, (high)	yd.	.244
(India)	yd.	.25	(medium)	yd.	.169
1809,	yd.	.292	(low)	yd.	.105
(India)	yd.	.334	1831, (high)	yd.	.288
1810, (high)	yd.	.48	(medium)	yd.	.186
(low)	yd.	.24	(low)	yd.	.122
(British)	yd.	.551	(twilled)	yd.	.20
1811, (high)	yd.	.425	1833, (high)	yd.	.18
(medium)	yd.	.33	(low)	yd.	.114
(low)	yd.	.167	1834, (high)	yd.	.155
(British)	yd.	.54	(low)	yd.	.111
(India)	yd.	.62	1835, (high)	yd.	.20
1812, (high)	yd.	.50	(medium)	yd.	.159
(low)	yd.	.20	(low)	yd.	.10
(factory)	yd.	.94	1836,	yd.	.137
(India)	yd.	.272	1837, (high)	yd.	.162
1813, (high)	yd.	.756	(low)	yd.	.118
(low)	yd.	.443	1838, (high)	yd.	.251
1814, (high)	yd.	.50	(medium)	yd.	.143
(medium)	yd.	.425	(low)	yd.	.087
(low)	yd.	.35	(unbleached)	yd.	.083
(British; high)	yd.	.874	1839, (high)	yd.	.155
(British; low)	yd.	.625	(low)	yd.	.115
(checked)	yd.	.55	1840, (high)	yd.	.16
1815,	yd.	.30	(medium)	yd.	.104
(Bristol)	yd.	.44	(low)	yd.	.07
1816,	yd.	.55	1841, (high)	yd.	.334
(British)	yd.	.30	(medium)	yd.	.167
(factory; high)	yd.	.58	(low)	yd.	.092
(factory; medium)	yd.	.398	1842, (high)	yd.	.144
(factory; low)	yd.	.329	(low)	yd.	.089
(India)	yd.	.25	1843, (high)	yd.	.125
1817, (high)	yd.	.453	(low)	yd.	.074
(medium)	yd.	.356	1844, (high)	yd.	.157
(low)	yd.	.274	(medium)	yd.	.105
(factory; high)	yd.	.626	(low)	yd.	.066
(factory; med. high)	yd.	.425	1845,	yd.	.099
(factory; medium)	yd.	.318	1846, (high)	yd.	.18
(factory; low)	yd.	.20	(medium)	yd.	.128
(India)	yd.	.307	(low)	yd.	.093
1818, (high)	yd.	.386	1847, (high)	yd.	.115
(low)	yd.	.30	(low)	yd.	.062
1819, (high)	yd.	.25	1848,	yd.	.097
(low)	yd.	.143	1849, (high)	yd.	.282
(India)	yd.	.418	(low)	yd.	.086
1820, (high)	yd.	.26	1850,	yd.	.08
(low)	yd.	.194	1851,	yd.	.109
1821, (high)	yd.	.20	1852, (high)	yd.	.173
(medium)	yd.	.157	(low)	yd.	.083
(low)	yd.	.125	1854,	yd.	.09
1822, (high)	yd.	.386	1855, (high)	yd.	.129
(medium)	yd.	.28	(low)	yd.	.089
(low)	yd.	.17	1856, (high)	yd.	.18
1823, (high)	yd.	.333	(low)	yd.	.124
(medium)	yd.	.219	1857, (high)	yd.	.148
(low)	yd.	.16	(low)	yd.	.107
(British; high)	yd.	.30	1858, (high)	yd.	.122
(British; low)	yd.	.25	(low)	yd.	.09
1824, (high)	yd.	.247	1859, (high)	yd.	.126
(low)	yd.	.135	(low)	yd.	.085
(British)	yd.	.20	*Cotton Flannel.*		
1825, (high)	yd.	.334			
(medium)	yd.	.225	1830,	yd.	.22
(low)	yd.	.143	1831, (high)	yd.	.362

Prices: Dry Goods — CONTINUED.

YEARS.	Basis.	Amount.	YEARS.	Basis.	Amount.
Cotton Flannel — Con.			*Denim — Con.*		
1831, (low)	yd.	$0.20	1855,	yd.	$0.133
1832,	yd.	.166	1856,	yd.	.145
1834,	yd.	.145	1857, (high)	yd.	.175
1835,	yd.	.203	(low)	yd.	.125
1837,	yd.	.20	1858,	yd.	.157
1838,	yd.	.167	1859, (high)	yd.	.167
1839,	yd.	.167	(low)	yd.	.126
1841,	yd.	.105			
1845,	yd.	.124	*Diaper.*		
1846,	yd.	.125	1819,	yd.	.35
1847, (high)	yd.	.31	1847,	yd.	.21
(low)	yd.	.11	1859,	yd.	.167
1854,	yd.	.125			
1855,	yd.	.128	*Dowlas.*		
1856,	yd.	.12	1793,	yd.	.156
1857,	yd.	.132	1821,	yd.	.333
1858,	yd.	.128			
1859,	yd.	.121	*Drilling.*		
			1826, (Russia)	yd.	.75
Cotton Wool.			1827,	yd.	.625
1764,	lb.	.50	1830, (high)	yd.	.625
1775,	lb.	.666	(low)	yd.	.167
1783,	lb.	.43	1831, (high)	yd.	.637
1788,	lb.	.50	(low)	yd.	.46
1791,	lb.	.32	1832, (French)	yd.	.30
1804,	lb.	.222	1833,	yd.	.249
1812,	lb.	.125	1840,	yd.	.12
			1841,	yd.	.12
Crash.			(linen)	yd.	.468
1811,	yd.	.109	1851,	yd.	.091
1813,	yd.	.167	1855,	yd.	.124
1817, (high)	yd.	.167	1856,	yd.	.131
(low)	yd.	.125	1857,	yd.	.125
1819,	yd.	.133	1858,	yd.	.12
1822,	yd.	.14	1859,	yd.	.12
1823,	yd.	.125			
1824,	yd.	.125	*Duck.*		
1826,	yd.	.11	1792,	yd.	.278
1830,	yd.	.10	1793,	yd.	.298
1831,	yd.	.112	1810,	yd.	.416
1832,	yd.	.10	1811, (raven)	yd.	.42
1835, (high)	yd.	.166	1816,	yd.	.392
(low)	yd.	.085	1817, (cotton)	yd.	.40
1837,	yd.	.115	1822,	yd.	.34
1838,	yd.	.077	1823, (Russia)	yd.	.383
1839,	yd.	.113	1828,	yd.	.25
1840,	yd.	.115	(Russia)	yd.	.50
1843,	yd.	.091	1830,	yd.	.25
1845,	yd.	.083	1831,	yd.	.25
1847,	yd.	.077	1832,	yd.	.241
1849,	yd.	.094	1833,	yd.	.28
1855,	yd.	.105	1839,	yd.	.34
1856, (high)	yd.	.157	1842,	yd.	.20
(low)	yd.	.11			
1857,	yd.	.116	*Everlasting.*		
1858,	yd.	.106	1783, (high)	yd.	1.39
1859, (high)	yd.	.123	(low)	yd.	.605
(low)	yd.	.066	1784,	yd.	.584
Damask.			*Flannel.*		
1827, (linen)	yd.	.835	1792,	yd.	.452
1833,	yd.	.50	(wholesale)	yd.	.264
1837,	yd.	.667	1793,	yd.	.407
1842, (cotton)	yd.	.62	(wholesale)	yd.	.278
1857,	yd.	.876	1794,	yd.	.416
1858, (brown)	yd.	.583	(wholesale)	yd.	.333
1859, (high)	yd.	.948	1795,	yd.	.416
(low)	yd.	.497	(wholesale, high)	yd.	.382
			(wholesale, low)	yd.	.306
Denim.			1800, (wholesale, high)	yd.	.556
1783,	yd.	.144	(wholesale, low)	yd.	.375
1794,	yd.	.111	1801, (wholesale)	yd.	.374

Prices: Dry Goods — CONTINUED.

YEARS.	Ba-sis.	Amount.	YEARS.	Ba-sis.	Amount.
Flannel — Con.			*Flannel* — Con.		
1802,	yd.	$0.375	1855, (high)	yd.	$0.754
1804,	yd.	.625	(med. high)	yd.	.58
1805,	yd.	.626	(medium)	yd.	.319
1806, (high)	yd.	.554	(low)	yd.	.122
(low)	yd.	.467	1856, (high)	yd.	.651
1807, (high)	yd.	1.32	(medium)	yd.	.342
(low)	yd.	.66	(low)	yd.	.195
1808,	yd.	1.33	1857, (high)	yd.	.584
(wholesale)	yd.	.416	(low)	yd	.358
1810,	yd.	.463	1858, (high)	yd.	.612
1811, (high)	yd.	.80	(medium)	yd.	.351
(medium)	yd.	.666	(low)	yd.	.125
(low)	yd.	.50	1859, (high)	yd.	.538
1812, (high)	yd.	.748	(low)	yd.	.344
(low)	yd.	.697			
1813,	yd.	.76	*Holland.*		
1814, (high)	yd.	.931	1784, (high)	yd.	.756
(low)	yd.	.75	(low)	yd.	.363
1815, (high)	yd.	.848	1792, (brown)	yd.	.196
(low)	yd.	.556	1793, (brown)	yd.	.223
(wholesale)	yd.	.167	1805, (brown; high)	yd.	.333
(American)	yd.	.418	(brown; low)	yd.	.17
(wide)	yd.	1.25	1808,	yd.	.407
1816, (high)	yd.	.564	1809, (brown; wholesale)	yd.	.335
(low)	yd.	.456	1810, (brown)	yd.	.50
1817, (high)	yd.	.885	1812, (brown)	yd.	.42
(med. high)	yd.	.66	1815,	yd.	.50
(medium)	yd.	.517	1819,	yd.	.417
(low)	yd.	.259	1823,	yd.	.25
(twilled)	yd.	.627	1825,	yd.	.50
1819,	yd.	.458			
1820,	yd.	.70	*Huckaback.*		
(cotton and wool)	yd.	.25	1840,	yd.	.45
(twilled; high)	yd.	.832	1849, (high)	yd.	.333
(twilled; low)	yd.	.625	(medium)	yd.	.25
1821, (high)	yd.	1.13	(low)	yd.	.125
(medium)	yd.	.614			
(low)	yd.	.46	*Jean.*		
1822, (high)	yd.	.667	1783,	yd.	.351
(low)	yd.	.461	1797, (wholesale, high)	yd.	.411
1824,	yd.	.505	(wholesale, low)	yd.	.278
1826,	yd.	1.24	1799, (wholesale)	yd.	.416
1827,	yd.	.30	1807,	yd.	.445
1828,	yd.	.42	1811,	yd.	.75
1829,	yd.	.375	1820,	yd.	.24
1830, (high)	yd.	.624	1824,	yd.	.333
(medium)	yd.	.358	1829,	yd.	.261
(low)	yd.	.25	1831, (high)	yd.	.37
1831, (high)	yd.	.654	(low)	yd.	.16
(low)	yd.	.333	1834,	yd.	.15
1835,	yd.	.334	1835, (high)	yd.	.22
1837, (high)	yd.	.54	(low)	yd.	.143
(low)	yd.	.15	1839,	yd.	.14
1838,	yd.	.50	1857,	yd.	.237
1840,	yd.	.531	1858, (high)	yd.	.42
1841, (high)	yd.	1.00	(low)	yd.	.124
(med. high)	yd.	.751			
(medium)	yd.	.524	*Lasting.*		
(med. low)	yd.	.287	1783,	yd.	.695
(low)	yd.	.138	1791,	p'ce	12.50
1842,	yd.	.55	1792,	yd.	.455
1843, (high)	yd.	.432	1793,	yd.	.472
(medium)	yd.	.318	1794,	yd.	.472
(low)	yd.	.13	1827,	yd.	1.36
1844, (high)	yd.	.458	1829,	yd.	.746
(low)	yd.	.293			
1845, (high)	yd.	.40	*Linen.*		
(low)	yd.	.269	1783, (high)	yd.	.626
1846, (high)	yd.	.44	(low)	yd.	.272
(low)	yd.	.13	1791, (high)	yd.	.556
1847, (high)	yd.	.333	(medium)	yd.	.399
(low)	yd.	.22	(low)	yd.	.167
1848,	yd.	.307	1792, (high)	yd.	.436
1853,	yd.	.20	(low)	yd.	.234

Prices: Dry Goods — Continued.

Years.	Basis.	Amount.	Years.	Basis.	Amount.
Linen — Con.			*Linen* — Con.		
1792, (Irish)	yd.	$0.163	1829, (low)	yd.	$0.25
(printed)	yd.	.292	1830, (high)	yd.	.84
(striped)	yd.	.278	(medium)	yd.	.63
1793, (high)	yd.	.833	(low)	yd.	.33
(med. high)	yd.	.639	(Russia)	yd.	.125
(medium)	yd.	.485	1831, (high)	yd.	.62
(med. low)	yd.	.25	(medium)	yd.	.314
(low)	yd.	.167	(low)	yd.	.169
(brown)	yd.	.278	(Russia)	yd.	.125
1794, (high)	yd.	.534	1832, (high)	yd.	1.00
(medium)	yd.	.39	(medium)	yd.	.575
(low)	yd.	.213	(low)	yd.	.125
(wholesale, high)	yd.	.492	1833,	yd.	.75
(wholesale, medium)	yd.	.306	1835, (high)	yd.	.58
(wholesale, low)	yd.	.163	(low)	yd.	.28
(brown; wholesale)	yd.	.178	1836,	yd.	.374
1795, (high)	yd.	.542	1837, (high)	yd.	1.13
(low)	yd.	.223	(medium)	yd.	.534
(wholesale)	yd.	.49	(low)	yd.	.322
(brown; wholesale)	yd.	.209	1838,	yd.	.835
1798,	yd.	.306	1839, (high)	yd.	1.00
1801, (wholesale)	yd.	.778	(medium)	yd.	.686
(wholesale, high)	yd.	.513	(low)	yd.	.288
(wholesale, low)	yd.	.402	1840, (high)	yd.	1.13
1803,	yd.	.722	(medium)	yd.	.75
(brown)	yd.	.257	(med. low)	yd.	.625
1804, (high)	yd.	.75	(low)	yd.	.50
(low)	yd.	.50	1841, (high)	yd.	.729
(German)	yd.	.417	(medium)	yd.	.363
1805, (high)	yd.	.653	(low)	yd.	.20
(low)	yd.	.417	1842,	yd.	.92
1806,	yd.	.334	1843,	yd.	.268
1807, (high)	yd.	1.00	1844, (high)	yd.	.625
(medium)	yd.	.556	(low)	yd.	.211
(low)	yd.	.40	1845,	yd.	.25
1808,	yd.	1.25	1846,	yd.	.205
(wholesale)	yd.	.379	1847, (high)	yd.	.50
(brown)	yd.	.291	(medium)	yd.	.373
1809, (high)	yd.	1.06	(low)	yd.	.25
(low)	yd.	.58	1848, (high)	yd.	.333
(wholesale)	yd.	.416	(low)	yd.	.25
1810,	yd.	.50	1849, (high)	yd.	.492
1811,	yd.	.50	(low)	yd.	.30
1812,	yd.	.19	1850, (high)	yd.	.33
1813,	yd.	.42	(low)	yd.	.225
1815, (high)	yd.	1.04	1853,	yd.	.75
(low)	yd.	.386	1854,	yd.	.25
(brown)	yd.	.375	1855, (high)	yd.	.60
1816, (high)	yd.	.413	(low)	yd.	.24
(low)	yd.	.262	1856, (high)	yd.	.818
(brown)	yd.	.50	(medium)	yd.	.507
1817,	yd.	.68	(low)	yd.	.266
(table)	yd.	.667	1857, (high)	yd.	.874
1818,	yd.	.333	(medium)	yd.	.621
1819, (high)	yd.	1.25	(low)	yd.	.323
(low)	yd.	.417	1858, (high)	yd.	.739
1820,	yd.	.351	(medium)	yd.	.502
(German)	yd.	.625	(low)	yd.	.302
1821, (high)	yd.	.589	1859, (high)	yd.	.877
(medium)	yd.	.409	(medium)	yd.	.546
(low)	yd.	.334	(low)	yd.	.286
1822, (high)	yd.	.418			
(medium)	yd.	.333	*Lining.*		
(low)	yd.	.25	1783, (high)	yd.	.75
1823, (Russia table)	yd.	1.00	(medium)	yd.	.583
1824,	yd.	.374	(low)	yd.	.323
1825, (high)	yd.	.417	1784,	yd.	.376
(low)	yd.	.25	1794,	yd.	.361
1827, (high)	yd.	1.00	1798, (wholesale)	yd.	.306
(medium)	yd.	.425	1805, (cotton)	yd.	.42
(low)	yd.	.28			
1828, (high)	yd.	.625	*Napkins.*		
(low)	yd.	.333	1819,	ea.	.65
1829, (high)	yd.	.30	1826,	doz.	1.25

Prices: Dry Goods — CONTINUED.

YEARS.	Basis.	Amount.	YEARS.	Basis.	Amount.
Napkins — Con.			*Sheetings* — Con.		
1853, ...	doz.	$1.50	1824, (Russia) . . .	yd.	$0.417
(doylies) . . .	doz.	1.20	1825, ...	yd.	.18
1857, ...	doz.	2.75	1826, ...	yd.	.15
			1829, ...	yd.	.157
Oiled Silk.			1830, (high) . . .	yd.	.56
1828, ...	yd.	1.33	(low) . . .	yd.	.11
1843, ...	yd.	1.00	1831, (high) . . .	yd.	.60
			(medium) . .	yd.	.206
Padding.			(low) . . .	yd.	.135
1832, ...	yd.	.50	1832, ...	yd.	.121
1839, ...	yd.	.50	(Russia) . .	yd.	.22
1840, ...	yd.	.37	1833, (cotton) . .	yd.	.131
			(Russia) . .	yd.	.333
Patch.			1836, ...	yd.	.149
1791, ...	yd.	.583	1837, ...	yd.	.167
1819, (high) . . .	yd.	.458	1838, ...	yd.	.125
(low) . . .	yd.	.27	1840, (high) . . .	yd.	.167
1820, ...	yd.	.42	(low) . . .	yd.	.115
1830, (high) . . .	yd.	.26	1841, (high) . . .	yd.	.167
(low) . . .	yd.	.15	(low) . . .	yd.	.102
1835, ...	yd.	.25	1842, ...	yd.	.096
1837, ...	yd.	.13	1843, (high) . . .	yd.	.125
1840, ...	yd.	.167	(low) . . .	yd.	.089
1841, ...	yd.	.188	1844, ...	yd.	.111
1843, ...	yd.	.15	1845, ...	yd.	.103
1844, ...	yd.	.07	1846, (high) . . .	yd.	.116
1848, ...	yd.	.037	(low) . . .	yd.	.09
1850, ...	yd.	.115	1847, ...	yd.	.098
1854, ...	yd.	.25	1848, ...	yd.	.094
1855, . . / . .	yd.	.13	1849, ...	yd.	.075
1856, ...	yd.	.059	1850, (high) . . .	yd.	.12
1857, (high) . . .	yd.	.127	(low) . . .	yd.	.086
(low) . . .	yd.	.057	1853, ...	yd.	.11
1858, ...	yd.	.11	1854, ...	yd.	.11
1859, ...	yd.	.114	1855, (high) . . .	yd.	.178
			(medium) . .	yd.	.13
Sheetings.			(low) . . .	yd.	.093
1792, (Russia) . . .	yd.	.414	1856, (high) . . .	yd.	.166
1793, (high) . . .	yd.	.806	(medium) . .	yd.	.133
(low) . . .	yd.	.372	(low) . . .	yd.	.091
1794, ...	yd.	.457	1857, (high) . . .	yd.	.18
1795, ...	yd.	.458	(low) . . .	yd.	.10
1800, ...	yd.	.55	1858, (high) . . .	yd.	.128
1804, (Russia) . . .	yd.	.556	(low) . . .	yd.	.084
1805, ...	yd.	.267	1859, ...	yd.	.11
1806, (Russia; high) .	yd.	.575			
(Russia; low) . .	yd.	.47	*Shirtings.*		
1807, ...	yd.	.167	1802, ...	yd.	.278
1809, ...	yd.	.43	1805, ...	yd.	.541
1810, ...	yd.	.52	1806, ...	yd.	.439
1811, ...	yd.	.54	1807, ...	yd.	.50
(Russia) . . .	yd.	.625	1808, (cotton) . . .	yd.	.50
1812, (high) . . .	yd.	.625	1809, ...	yd.	.49
(medium) . .	yd.	.565	1811, ...	yd.	.50
(low) . . .	yd.	.50	1812, (high) . . .	yd.	.70
1813, ...	yd.	.667	(low) . . .	yd.	.48
1814, (high) . . .	yd.	.582	1813, ...	yd.	.398
(low) . . .	yd.	.40	1814, (high) . . .	yd.	.50
1816, (high) . . .	yd.	.747	(low) . . .	yd.	.433
(medium) . .	yd.	.529	(wholesale, high) .	yd.	.45
(low) . . .	yd.	.393	(wholesale, low) .	yd.	.36
(Russia) . .	yd.	.556	(cotton) . . .	yd.	.335
1817, (high) . . .	yd.	.561	1816, ...	yd.	.463
(low) . . .	yd.	.286	1817, (high) . . .	yd.	.44
1820, ...	yd.	.265	(medium) . .	yd.	.347
1821, (high) . . .	yd.	.375	(low) . . .	yd.	.23
(low) . . .	yd.	.208	1818, ...	yd.	.31
1822, (high) . . .	yd.	.458	1819, (high) . . .	yd.	.368
(medium) . .	yd.	.321	(low) . . .	yd.	.225
(low) . . .	yd.	.20	1820, (high) . . .	yd.	.275
1823, ...	yd.	.18	(low) . . .	yd.	.171
(Russia) . . .	yd.	.417	1821, (high) . . .	yd.	.27
1824, (high) . . .	yd.	.33	(low) . . .	yd.	.171
(low) . . .	yd.	.15	1822, (high) . . .	yd.	.30

Prices: Dry Goods — Concluded.

Years.	Basis.	Amount.	Years.	Basis.	Amount.
Shirtings—Con.			*Ticking*—Con.		
1822, (low)	yd.	$0.184	1845,	yd.	$0.18
1823, (wholesale)	yd.	.135	1846, (high)	yd.	.195
(cotton and linen)	yd.	.83	(low)	yd.	.12
1824, (high)	yd.	.28	1847,	yd.	.18
(medium)	yd.	.211	1848,	yd.	.18
(low)	yd.	.16	1850,	yd.	.167
1826, (high)	yd.	.32	1854,	yd.	.18
(low)	yd.	.167	1855,	yd.	.158
1827,	yd.	.132	1856,	yd.	.14
1828, (high)	yd.	.151	1857,	yd.	.157
(medium)	yd.	.123	1858,	yd.	.136
(low)	yd.	.096	1859, (high)	yd.	.20
1830, (high)	yd.	.111	(low)	yd.	.151
(low)	yd.	.068			
1831, (high)	yd.	.18	*Tow Cloth.*		
(low)	yd.	.116	1756,	yd.	.15
1832,	yd.	.099	1761,	yd.	.311
1835,	yd.	.087	1766,	yd.	.286
1837,	yd.	.176	1782,	yd.	.25
1838, (high)	yd.	.19	(wholesale)	yd.	.167
(low)	yd.	.10	1783,	yd.	.223
1839, (high)	yd.	.15	1784,	yd.	.17
(low)	yd.	.11	(wholesale)	yd.	.153
1840, (high)	yd.	.163	1792,	yd.	.175
(low)	yd.	.11	1793,	yd.	.237
1841, (high)	yd.	.16	1794,	yd.	.194
(low)	yd.	.09	1795,	yd.	.199
1842,	yd.	.09	1801, (wholesale)	yd.	.18
1843,	yd.	.12	1807,	yd.	.167
1844, (high)	yd.	.14	1808,	yd.	.389
(low)	yd.	.085	1811,	yd.	.25
1845,	yd.	.08	1812,	yd.	.30
1846,	yd.	.13	1814, (high)	yd.	.416
1847,	yd.	.124	(low)	yd.	.262
1849,	yd.	.114	1815,	yd.	.234
1850,	yd.	.125	1821,	yd.	.20
1855,	yd.	.12	1822,	yd.	.17
1856,	yd.	.085	1824,	yd.	.22
1857,	yd.	.125	1827,	yd.	.125
1858,	yd.	.091	1828, (high)	yd.	.19
1859,	yd.	.116	(low)	yd.	.13
			1830,	yd.	.176
Silesia.			1831,	yd.	.17
1838,	yd.	.20	1832,	yd.	.15
1840,	yd.	.222	1833,	yd.	.14
1847,	yd.	.127	1837,	yd.	.134
1848,	yd.	.13	1840,	yd.	.14
1849,	yd.	.124	1851,	yd.	.125
1850,	yd.	.11	1857,	yd.	.13
1851,	yd.	.11			
1855,	yd.	.122	*Towelling.*		
1856,	yd.	.124	1792,	yd.	.111
1857,	yd.	.124	1834,	yd.	.417
1858,	yd.	.12	1856,	yd.	.151
1859,	yd.	.12	1857,	yd.	.159
			1859,	yd.	.20
Ticking.					
1794, (Russia)	yd.	1.03	*Wadding.*		
1795,	yd.	.778	1816,	yd.	.375
1809,	yd.	.75	1832, (by the sheet)	ea.	.05
1811,	yd.	.605	1840, (by the sheet)	ea.	.013
1812,	yd.	.733	1844, (by the sheet)	ea.	.04
1817,	yd.	.62	1856,	yd.	.05
1818,	yd.	.50	1857,	yd.	.05
1821,	yd.	.50	1858,	yd.	.046
1822,	yd.	.416	1859,	yd.	.05
1828,	yd.	.27	(by the sheet)	ea.	.17
1830,	yd.	.28			
1840,	yd.	.254	*Wigan.*		
1843,	yd.	.15	1855,	yd.	.16
1844,	yd.	.18	1858,	yd.	.166

Prices: Fish.

Years.	Basis.	Amount.	Years.	Basis.	Amount.
Clams.			*Eels* — Con.		
1809, ...	pk.	$0.133	1819, ...	lb.	$0.066
1813, (high) . . .	pk.	.50	1820, ...	lb.	.067
(low) . . .	pk.	.16	1821, ...	lb.	.063
1814, ...	pk.	.125	1822, ...	lb.	.06
1823, ...	pk.	.168	1823, ...	lb.	.063
1825, ...	pk.	.17	1824, ...	lb.	.062
1827, ...	pk.	.125	1825, ...	lb.	.063
1828, ...	pk.	.20	1827, ...	lb.	.062
1829, (high) . . .	pk.	.25	1829, ...	lb.	.063
(low) . . .	pk.	.20	1830, ...	lb.	.061
1838, ...	pk.	.20	1831, ...	lb.	.061
1839, ...	pk.	.25	1832, ...	lb.	.063
1840, ...	pk.	.25	1834, ...	lb.	.062
1842, ...	pk.	.228	1835, ...	lb.	.06
1849, ...	pk.	.25	1836, ...	lb.	.08
Cod.			1837, ...	lb.	.083
1842, (high) . . .	lb.	.05	1840, ...	lb.	.062
(low) . . .	lb.	.03	1841, ...	lb.	.082
1844, ...	lb.	.037	1842, ...	lb.	.074
1846, ...	lb.	.038	1843, ...	lb.	.064
1848, ...	lb.	.04	1844, ...	lb.	.08
1856, ...	lb.	.05	1846, ...	lb.	.063
			1847, ...	lb.	.057
Codfish.			1849, ...	lb.	.08
1782, ...	lb.	.017	*Fish.*		
1783, ...	lb.	.05	1757, (by the 100 lbs.)	lb.	.004
1801, ...	lb.	.034	1763, (by the 100 lbs.)	lb.	.006
1803, (wholesale) . .	lb.	.041	1793, ...	lb.	.035
(by the quintal)	q't'l	4.50	1794, ...	lb.	.032
1805, (by the quintal) .	q't'l	5.34	(wholesale) . .	lb.	.02
1806, ...	lb.	.035	(by the quintal) .	q't'l	4.00
1807, ...	lb.	.032	1797, (by the quintal) .	q't'l	5.19
1808, ...	lb.	.038	1798, (by the quintal) .	q't'l	4.00
1809, ...	lb.	.032	1800, (by the quintal) .	q't'l	4.00
1810, ...	lb.	.034	1801, ...	lb.	.057
1811, ...	lb.	.037	1802, ...	lb.	.051
1812, ...	lb.	.03	(by the quintal; high) .	q't'l	5.66
(by the quintal)	q't'l	6.00	(by the quintal; medium)	q't'l	4.33
1813, ...	lb.	.029	(by the quintal; low) .	q't'l	2.94
1814, ...	lb.	.036	1804, ...	lb.	.049
1815, ...	lb.	.032	(by the quintal) .	q't'l	6.00
1816, ...	lb.	.037	1806, (wholesale) . .	lb.	.049
(by the quintal)	q't'l	5.00	1807, (wholesale) . .	lb.	.047
1817, ...	lb.	.039	1810, ...	lb.	.049
1818, ...	lb.	.029	1811, ...	lb.	.063
1819, ...	lb.	.03	1812, ...	lb.	.066
1820, ...	lb.	.031	(wholesale) . .	lb.	.054
1821, ...	lb.	.031	(by the quintal) .	q't'l	4.75
1822, ...	lb.	.034	1813, ...	lb.	.064
1823, ...	lb.	.03	1814, ...	lb.	.06
1824, ...	lb.	.03	(wholesale) . .	lb.	.031
1825, ...	lb.	.027	(by the quintal) .	q't'l	5.75
1826, ...	lb.	.029		bbl.	7.00
1827, ...	lb.	.03	1815, (high) . . .	lb.	.077
1828, ...	lb.	.037	(low) . . .	lb.	.041
1829, ...	lb.	.035	(by the quintal) .	q't'l	5.13
1830, ...	lb.	.029	1816, ...	lb.	.04
1831, ...	lb.	.031	(by the quintal) .	q't'l	5.50
1832, ...	lb.	.031	1817, ...	lb.	.051
1833, ...	lb.	.029	1819, ...	lb.	.05
1835, ...	lb.	.03	1820, (by the quintal) .	q't'l	3.50
1836, ...	lb.	.04	1821, ...	lb.	.04
1837, ...	lb.	.05	1823, (high) . . .	lb.	.05
1838, ...	lb.	.048	(low) . . .	lb.	.03
1839, ...	lb.	.04	(wholesale) . .	lb.	.04
1840, ...	lb.	.04	1824, ...	lb.	.05
1841, ...	lb.	.032	1825, ...	lb	.03
1847, ...	lb.	.035	1826, (high) . . .	lb.	.054
			(low) . . .	lb.	.032
Eels.			1828, ...	lb.	.034
1806, ...	lb.	.066	1830, ...	lb.	.033
1807, ...	lb.	.07	1831, ...	lb.	.03
1808, ...	lb.	.05	1832, ...	lb.	.032

Prices: Fish — Continued.

Years.	Basis.	Amount.	Years.	Basis.	Amount.
Fish — Con.			*Halibut* — Con.		
1834,	lb.	$0.028	1827,	lb.	$0.051
1837,	lb.	.055	1828,	lb.	.046
1838,	lb.	.051	1829,	lb.	.048
1839,	lb.	.05	1830,	lb.	.046
1840,	lb.	.043	1831,	lb.	.047
1841,	lb.	.038	1832,	lb.	.05
1842, (high)	lb.	.10	1833,	lb.	.051
(low)	lb.	.039	1834,	lb.	.053
1843,	lb.	.037	1835,	lb.	.056
(wholesale)	lb.	.02	1836, (high)	lb.	.062
1844,	lb.	.035	(low)	lb.	.038
1845,	lb.	.039	1837,	lb.	.058
1846, (high)	lb.	.08	1838,	lb.	.052
(low)	lb.	.034	1839,	lb.	.061
(wholesale)	lb.	.02	1840,	lb.	.058
1847, (high)	lb.	.12	1841,	lb.	.058
(low)	lb.	.05	1842, (high)	lb.	.07
1848,	lb.	.051	(low)	lb.	.052
(wholesale)	lb.	.03	1843,	lb.	.047
1849,	lb.	.045	1844,	lb.	.061
1850,	lb.	.042	1845,	lb.	.058
1851,	lb.	.042	1846,	lb.	.052
1852,	lb.	.045	1847,	lb.	.054
1854,	lb.	.052	1848,	lb.	.06
1855,	lb.	.052	1849,	lb.	.06
1856,	lb.	.054	1850,	lb.	.074
1858,	lb.	.048	1851,	lb.	.065
			1853,	lb.	.08
Haddock.			1856,	lb.	.122
1813,	lb.	.024	1857,	lb.	.12
1814,	lb.	.04	1858,	lb.	.12
1817,	lb.	.033	1859,	lb.	.12
1819,	lb.	.03			
1820, (high)	lb.	.063	*Herring.*		
(low)	lb.	.03	1761,	doz.	.25
1822,	lb.	.03	1785,	doz.	.083
1824,	lb.	.03	1798,	C.	.667
1825,	lb.	.03	1810,	doz.	.15
1826,	lb.	.03	1817,	doz.	.192
1827,	lb.	.03		C.	1.26
1829,	lb.	.03	1819,	doz.	.16
1830,	lb.	.02	1820,	C.	1.00
1833,	lb.	.028	1821,	C.	.64
1834,	lb.	.03	1827,	C.	.747
1839,	lb.	.04	1830,	doz.	.083
1846,	lb.	.04	1831,	doz.	.09
1847,	lb.	.04	1845,	doz.	.12
1848,	lb.	.035	1847,	doz.	.17
			1848,	doz.	.12
Halibut.			1850,	doz.	.06
1804,	lb.	.044	1857,	doz.	.08
1805,	lb.	.054			
1806,	lb.	.053	*Mackerel.*		
1807,	lb.	.04	1752,	doz.	.267
1808,	lb.	.038	1753,	bbl.	5.33
1809,	lb.	.039	1804,	lb.	.055
1810,	lb.	.049	1817,	lb.	.068
1811,	lb.	.04	1819,	bbl.	8.75
1812,	lb.	.044	(pickled)	lb.	.10
1813,	lb.	.041	1820,	bbl.	5.60
1814,	lb.	.052	1822,	lb.	.04
1815,	lb.	.053	1823, (high)	bbl.	5.25
1816,	lb.	.053	(low)	bbl.	4.25
1817,	lb.	.049	1825, (No. 1)	bbl.	5.50
1818,	lb.	.047	(No. 2)	bbl.	4.50
1819,	lb.	.05	(wholesale)	bbl.	2.43
1820,	lb.	.046	1826,	bbl.	6.00
1821,	lb.	.041	(No. 1)	lb.	.054
1822,	lb.	.044	(No. 2)	lb.	.044
1823,	lb.	.049	(No. 3)	lb.	.031
1824,	lb.	.048	1827,	lb.	.019
1825,	lb.	.048	1831,	lb.	.041
1826, (high)	lb.	.061	1833, (by the half barrel)	bbl.	6.66
(low)	lb.	.045	1837,	lb.	.07

Prices: Fish — Concluded.

Years.	Basis.	Amount.	Years.	Basis.	Amount.
Mackerel — Con.			*Salmon* — Con.		
1838,	lb.	$0.069	1849,	lb.	$0.20
1840,	lb.	.085	1850,	lb.	.32
1842,	lb.	.059	1855,	lb.	.126
1843, (high)	lb.	.12	1856,	lb.	.126
(low)	lb.	.07	1858,	lb.	.124
1844,	lb.	.069	1859,	lb.	.123
1845,	lb.	.075			
1846,	lb.	.07	*Salt Fish.*		
1847,	lb.	.071	1795,	lb.	.056
	kit	1.65	1799, (high)	lb.	.056
1848,	lb.	.065	(low)	lb.	.021
1849,	lb.	.057	1812,	lb.	.06
1850,	lb.	.058	1813,	lb.	.057
1851,	lb.	.06	1814,	lb.	.061
1852,	lb.	.061	1815,	lb.	.06
1855,	lb.	.088	1816,	lb.	.06
1856,	lb.	.08	1817,	lb.	.055
1857,	lb.	.096	1818,	lb.	.045
1858,	lb.	.085	1819,	lb.	.047
1859, (high)	lb.	.122	1820, (wholesale)	lb.	.045
(low)	lb.	.08	1821, (high)	lb.	.084
			(low)	lb.	.045
Oysters.			1824, (dun)	lb.	.06
1808,	pk.	.50	1826,	lb.	.07
1810,	pk.	.50	1827,	lb.	.06
1811,	pk.	.50	1829,	lb.	.07
1830,	pk.	.50	1830,	lb.	.041
1833,	qt.	.50	1831, (dun)	lb.	.065
1837,	pk.	.50	1832, (high)	lb.	.07
1846,	qt.	.265	(low)	lb.	.04
1848,	qt.	.20	1833,	lb.	.023
			1834,	lb.	.04
Pollock.			1835,	lb.	.046
1809,	lb.	.029	1836,	lb.	.058
1814, (by the quintal)	q't'l	3.50	(dun)	lb.	.06
1817,	lb.	.027	1840,	lb.	.048
1827, (by the 100 lbs.)	lb.	·017	1841, (English)	lb.	.05
1828,	lb.	.027	1842,	lb.	.05
1829,	lb.	.025	1843,	lb.	.04
1830,	lb.	.025	(dun)	lb.	.05
1831,	lb.	.024	1844,	lb.	.042
1832,	lb.	.026	1845,	lb.	.05
1833,	lb.	.027	(dun)	lb.	.05
			1846,	lb.	.04
Salmon.			(dun)	lb.	.05
1808,	lb.	.167	1847,	lb.	.047
1813,	lb.	.11	(dun)	lb.	.08
1818, (smoked)	lb.	.18	1848,	lb.	.047
1819, (smoked)	lb.	.20	1849, (dun)	lb.	.06
1829,	lb.	.20	1850,	lb.	.035
1831,	lb.	.20	1855,	lb.	.06
1840,	lb.	.238	1857,	lb.	.05
1841,	lb.	.206	1858,	lb.	.05
1842,	lb.	.183	1859,	lb.	.05
1843,	lb.	.208	1860,	lb.	.05
1844,	lb.	.08			
1845,	lb.	.272	*Shad.*		
1846,	lb.	.23	1814,	lb.	.03
1847,	lb.	.168	1840,	lb.	.167
1848,	lb.	.232	1841,	lb.	.167

Prices: Flour and Meal.

Years.	Basis.	Amount.	Years.	Basis.	Amount.
Bolted Rye Meal.			*Flour.*		
1802,	bbl.	$4.50	1754,	lb.	$0.045
1813,	bbl.	8.75	1760,	lb.	.042
1817,	bbl.	7.00	1782,	lb.	.069
1820,	bbl.	4.00	1783,	lb.	.055
1825,	bbl.	3.00	1784,	lb.	.029
			1785,	lb.	.036
Buckwheat Flour.				bbl.	6.50
1850,	lb.	.033	1786,	bbl.	5.41
1855,	lb.	.035	1791,	bbl.	5.66
1859,	lb.	.041	1792, (wholesale)	bbl.	5.09

Prices: Flour and Meal—Continued.

Years.	Basis.	Amount.	Years.	Basis.	Amount.
Flour — Con.			*Flour* — Con.		
1792, (superfine) . . .	bbl.	$5.33	1816, (medium) . . .	bbl.	$9.30
1793, ...	lb.	.083	(med. low) . . .	bbl.	7.33
(high)	bbl.	6.89	(low)	bbl.	5.83
(low)	bbl.	6.14	(by the half barrel; high)	bbl.	15.50
(wholesale) . . .	bbl.	5.35	(by the half barrel; low)	bbl.	11.07
1794, ...	lb.	.042	1817, (high)	lb.	.088
(wholesale, high) .	bbl.	7.42	(low)	lb.	.065
(wholesale, low) .	bbl.	5.91	(high)	bbl.	15.25
1795, ...	bbl.	9.25	(medium) . . .	bbl.	13.67
(fine)	bbl.	11.33	(low)	bbl.	10.92
1797, (superfine) . . .	bbl.	10.00	(by the half barrel; high)	bbl.	16.00
(wholesale) . . .	bbl.	8.25	(by the half barrel; medium)	bbl.	15.36
1798, ...	lb.	.063	(by the half barrel; low)	bbl.	12.62
	cwt.	5.33	1818, ...	lb.	.065
(high)	bbl.	8.25	(high)	bbl.	12.00
(medium) . . .	bbl.	7.25	(low)	bbl.	10.71
(low)	bbl.	6.00	(wholesale) . . .	bbl.	5.00
1799, ...	bbl.	10.00	1819, ...	lb.	.058
(superfine) . . .	bbl.	10.25	(high)	bbl.	10.00
1800, ...	lb.	.063	(medium) . . .	bbl.	8.25
	bbl.	10.86	(low)	bbl.	7.41
1801, (high)	lb.	.067	1820, ...	lb.	.05
(low)	lb.	.053	(high)	bbl.	6.62
	bbl.	6.50	(low)	bbl.	5.36
1802, ...	lb.	.052	1821, ...	lb.	.037
	bbl.	8.25	(high)	bbl.	7.28
1803, ...	bbl.	7.00	(medium) . . .	bbl.	5.25
1804, ...	lb.	.072	(low)	bbl.	4.43
(high)	bbl.	11.55	1822, ...	lb.	.04
(low)	bbl.	7.63	(high)	bbl.	8.11
1805, ...	lb.	.071	(low)	bbl.	7.25
	bbl.	11.97	1823, ...	lb.	.041
(by the half barrel)	bbl.	13.76		bbl.	8.04
1806, ...	lb.	.09	1824, ...	lb.	.043
(high)	bbl.	9.13	(high)	bbl.	7.50
(low)	bbl.	8.17	(low)	bbl.	6.63
1807, (high)	bbl.	9.00	1825, (high)	lb.	.04
(medium) . . .	bbl.	7.87	(low)	lb.	.023
(low)	bbl.	7.00	(high)	bbl.	6.46
1808, (high)	bbl.	7.50	(low)	bbl.	5.79
(low)	bbl.	6.25	1826, ...	lb.	.044
1809, ...	lb.	.065	(high)	bbl.	6.44
(high)	bbl.	8.75	(medium) . . .	bbl.	5.83
(low)	bbl.	7.71	(low)	bbl.	5.48
1810, ...	lb.	.053	1827, (high)	bbl.	6.49
	cwt.	7.33	(low)	bbl.	5.52
(high)	bbl.	11.25	(wholesale, high) .	bbl.	6.13
(low)	bbl.	8.67	(wholesale, low) .	bbl.	4.75
1811, ...	lb.	.078	1828, ...	lb.	.042
(high)	bbl.	11.15	(high)	bbl.	10.13
(low)	bbl.	10.17	(med. high) . . .	bbl.	9.38
(by the half barrel)	bbl.	10.58	(medium) . . .	bbl.	8.75
1812, (high)	lb.	.071	(med. low) . . .	bbl.	7.75
(low)	lb.	.06	(low)	bbl.	5.78
(high)	bbl.	11.20	1829, (high)	bbl.	10.00
(medium) . . .	bbl.	10.50	(med. high) . . .	bbl.	9.42
(low)	bbl.	9.25	(medium) . . .	bbl.	8.25
1813, ...	lb.	.093	(med. low) . . .	bbl.	7.25
(high)	bbl.	17.00	(low)	bbl.	6.29
(medium) . . .	bbl.	14.00	1830, ...	lb.	.035
(low)	bbl	12.75	(high)	bbl.	7.08
(by the half barrel; high)	bbl.	17.24	(medium) . . .	bbl.	6.21
(by the half barrel; low)	bbl.	15.00	(low)	bbl.	5.47
1814, ...	lb.	.087	1831, ...	lb.	.038
(high)	bbl.	15.50	(high)	bbl.	8.13
(low)	bbl.	15.00	(medium) . . .	bbl.	7.07
(by the half barrel; high)	bbl.	16.08	(low)	bbl.	6.13
(by the half barrel; low)	bbl.	15.00	1832, ...	lb.	.041
1815, ...	lb.	.058		bbl.	7.31
(high)	bbl.	8.28	(Genesee) . . .	bbl.	6.63
(low)	bbl.	7.50	1833, ...	lb.	.036
1816, ...	lb.	.065	(high)	bbl.	7.58
(high)	bbl.	12.00	(low)	bbl.	6.63
(med. high) . . .	bbl.	10.51			

Prices: Flour and Meal—Continued.

Years.	Basis.	Amount.	Years.	Basis.	Amount.
Flour—Con.			*Flour*—Con.		
1834,	lb.	$0.035	1855, (low)	bbl.	$9.80
(high)	bbl.	7.04	(by the half barrel ; high)	bbl.	11.24
(low)	bbl.	6.11	(by the half barrel ; low)	bbl.	10.76
1835,	lb.	.036	1856,	lb.	.054
(high)	bbl.	7.52	(high)	bbl.	11.75
(low)	bbl.	6.25	(med. high)	bbl.	10.86
1836, (high)	bbl.	10.75	(med. low)	bbl.	9.71
(low)	bbl.	8.38	(low)	bbl.	8.78
1837, (high)	lb.	.071	1857,	lb.	.048
(low)	lb.	.055	(high)	bbl.	9.45
(high)	bbl.	12.75	(medium)	bbl.	7.90
(medium)	bbl.	10.81	(low)	bbl.	6.75
(low)	bbl.	7.65	1858,	lb.	.038
(by the half barrel)	bbl.	10.00	(high)	bbl.	9.00
1838,	lb.	.051	(medium)	bbl.	7.42
(high)	bbl.	10.25	(low)	bbl.	5.50
(medium)	bbl.	9.37	1859,	lb.	.045
(low)	bbl.	8.57	(high)	bbl.	10.50
1839,	lb.	.05	(medium)	bbl.	8.87
(high)	bbl.	9.67	(low)	bbl.	7.96
(medium)	bbl.	8.37	1860, (high)	bbl.	9.50
(low)	bbl.	7.16	(low)	bbl.	8.75
1840,	lb.	.033			
	bbl.	5.76	*Graham Flour.*		
1841,	lb.	.04	1836,	bbl.	8.50
(high)	bbl.	7.42	1839,	bbl.	8.00
(medium)	bbl.	6.95	1849,	pk.	.48
(low)	bbl.	5.30	1850,	lb.	.035
1842,	lb.	.036		bbl.	7.24
(high)	bbl.	7.63	1851,	lb.	.036
(medium)	bbl.	6.78	1855,	lb.	.06
(low)	bbl.	5.29	(by the half barrel)	bbl.	11.50
1843,	lb.	.031	1856,	lb.	.058
(high)	bbl.	6.26		bbl.	9.50
(low)	bbl.	5.38	1857,	lb.	.049
1844,	lb.	.03	1858,	lb.	.04
(high)	bbl.	6.25		bbl.	7.50
(low)	bbl.	5.29	1859,	lb.	.046
1845,	lb.	.032			
(high)	bbl.	7.92	*Indian Meal.*		
(medium)	bbl.	6.33	1792,	bu.	.723
(low)	bbl.	5.54	1793,	bu.	.886
1846,	lb.	.036	1794,	bu.	.834
(high)	bbl.	7.00	1799,	bag	1.00
(medium)	bbl.	6.40	1801,	bu.	1.17
(low)	bbl.	5.50	1802,	bu.	.854
1847,	lb.	.042	1803,	bu.	.987
(high)	bbl.	10.25	1804, (high)	bu.	1.25
(medium)	bbl.	8.25	(low)	bu.	.976
(low)	bbl.	7.30	1806,	bu.	1.00
1848,	lb.	.04	1809,	bu.	1.12
(high)	bbl.	8.19	1810, (high)	bu.	1.23
(medium)	bbl.	7.35	(low)	bu.	1.16
(low)	bbl.	6.50	1811, (high)	bu.	1.42
1849,	lb.	.036	(low)	bu.	1.15
	bbl.	6.80	1812, (high)	bu.	1.33
1850,	lb.	.037	(low)	bu.	1.13
(high)	bbl.	6.97	1813, (high)	bu.	1.63
(low)	bbl.	6.03	(low)	bu.	1.38
(by the half barrel)	bbl.	7.50	1814, (high)	bu.	1.77
1851,	lb.	.036	(low)	bu.	1.37
(high)	bbl.	6.49	1815, (high)	bu.	1.46
(low)	bbl.	5.88	(low)	bu.	1.17
1852,	lb.	.035	1816,	lb.	.033
(high)	bbl.	6.38	(high)	bu.	2.00
(low)	bbl.	5.60	(med. high)	bu.	1.79
1853,	bbl.	6.25	(medium)	bu.	1.48
1854,	lb.	.059	(med. low)	bu.	1.25
(high)	bbl.	11.89	(low)	bu.	1.13
(medium)	bbl.	10.26	1817,	lb.	.044
(low)	bbl.	9.25	(high)	bu.	2.00
1855,	lb.	.05	(medium)	bu.	1.75
(high)	bbl.	12.23	(low)	bu.	1.36
(medium)	bbl.	10.89	1818,	pk.	.33

Prices: Flour and Meal — Continued.

Years.	Basis.	Amount.	Years.	Basis.	Amount.
Indian Meal — Con.			*Indian Meal* — Con.		
1818, (high)	bu.	$1.27	1849, (wholesale)	bu.	$0.63
(low)	bu.	1.09	1850,	lb.	.016
1819, (high)	bu.	1.20		pk.	.28
(medium)	bu.	1.08	(high)	bu.	1.58
(low)	bu.	.89	(low)	bu.	.762
1820, (high)	bu.	.90	1851,	lb.	.016
(low)	bu.	.711		bu.	.772
1821, (high)	bu.	.847	1852,	lb.	.017
(low)	bu.	.686		pk.	.217
1822,	bu.	.888		bu.	.79
1823, (high)	bu.	1.08	1853,	lb.	.02
(medium)	bu.	.814	1854,	lb.	.022
(low)	bu.	.652		bu.	1.02
1824, (high)	bu.	.75	1855,	lb.	.026
(low)	bu.	.564		pk.	.36
1825, (high)	bu.	.98		bu.	1.04
(medium)	bu.	.677	1856,	lb.	.019
(low)	bu.	.40		bu.	1.25
1826,	bu.	.965	1857,	lb.	.021
1827,	lb.	.016	1858,	lb.	.021
(high)	bu.	1.08		pk.	.44
(low)	bu.	.75		bu.	1.00
1828,	bu.	.683	1859,	lb.	.021
1829, (high)	bu.	.90		bu.	1.00
(low)	bu.	.764	1860, (wholesale)	bu.	.70
1830,	bu.	.703			
1831,	bu.	.821	*Meal.*		
1832, (high)	bu.	.978	1765,	qt.	.028
(low)	bu.	.75	1766,	qt.	.022
1833,	pk.	.27	1767,	qt.	.018
(high)	bu.	1.12		bu.	.50
(low)	bu.	.923	1777,	pk.	.25
1834,	pk.	.25	1782,	bu.	1.00
(high)	bu.	1.43	1784,	bu.	.556
(medium)	bu.	1.08	1785,	pk.	.209
(low)	bu.	.85	1794,	bu.	.778
1835,	pk.	.264	1795,	bu.	.778
(high)	bu.	1.20	1797,	bu.	1.00
(low)	bu.	.90	1800,	bu.	.833
1836,	bu.	1.09	1802,	bu.	.944
1837,	lb.	.016	1803, (high)	bu.	1.08
	bu.	1.31	(low)	bu.	.653
1838,	lb.	.024	(wholesale)	bu.	.916
(high)	bu.	1.12	1804,	bu.	1.09
(low)	bu.	.86	1805,	bu.	1.00
1839, (high)	bu.	1.27	(wholesale)	bu.	1.26
(low)	bu.	1.05	1806,	bu.	1.17
1840, (high)	bu.	.92	1807,	pk.	.30
(low)	bu.	.744		bu.	1.11
1841, (high)	bu.	.90	1808,	bu.	.935
(low)	bu.	.66	1809,	pk.	.40
1842,	lb.	.016	1810,	pk.	.373
	bu.	.735		bu.	1.00
1843,	lb.	.014	1812, (high)	bu.	1.56
	bu.	.697	(low)	bu.	1.18
1844,	lb.	.013	1813, (high)	bu.	1.81
(high)	pk.	.28	(low)	bu.	1.51
(low)	pk.	.18	1814,	pk.	.67
	bu.	.673	(high)	bu.	2.12
1845,	lb.	.015	(medium)	bu.	2.00
(high)	bu.	.933	(low)	bu.	1.64
(low)	bu.	.673	1815,	lb.	.027
1846,	lb.	.018		pk.	.35
	bu.	.834	1816,	bu.	1.34
1847,	lb.	.02	1817,	bu.	1.84
1848,	lb.	.017	1818,	lb.	.026
	pk.	.27		bu.	1.30
(high)	bu.	.91	(wholesale)	bu.	1.20
(medium)	bu.	.803	1819, (high)	bu.	1.32
(low)	bu.	.682	(low)	bu.	.96
1849,	lb.	.015	1824,	pk.	.26
(high)	pk.	.28	1825,	bu.	1.00
(low)	pk.	.17	1826, (high)	bu.	1.25
	bu.	.794	(low)	bu.	.92

Prices: Flour and Meal — CONTINUED.

Years.	Basis	Amount.	Years.	Basis	Amount.
Meal — Con.			*Rye Meal — Con.*		
1827,	bu.	$0.82	1794,	bu.	$1.07
1828,	bu.	.933	1801,	bu.	1.33
1829,	bu.	.95	1807,	bu.	1.00
1830,	lb.	.016	1808,	bu.	.961
	bu.	.822	1809, (high)	bu.	1.67
1831,	pk.	.23	(medium)	bu.	1.42
1837,	lb.	.026	(low)	bu.	1.26
1839,	bu.	1.21	1810, (high)	bu.	1.74
1842,	bu.	.80	(low)	bu.	1.50
1847,	pk.	.275	1811, (high)	bu.	1.69
(high)	bu.	1.12	(low)	bu.	1.21
(medium)	bu.	.894	1812, (high)	bu.	1.50
(low)	bu.	.46	(low)	bu.	1.25
1849,	pk.	.255	(wholesale)	bu.	1.15
	bu.	1.08	1813,	bu.	1.47
1855,	lb.	.024	1814,	lb.	.05
	bu.	1.14		bu.	2.25
1856,	lb.	.02	1815, (high)	bu.	1.75
	pk.	.36	(low)	bu.	1.34
(high)	bu.	1.11	1816,	lb.	.034
(low)	bu.	.784	(high)	bu.	1.75
1857,	lb.	.023	(medium)	bu.	1.50
	bu.	.985	(low)	bu.	1.25
1858, (high)	bu.	.956	1817,	lb.	.043
(low)	bu.	.808	(high)	bu.	1.75
1859,	lb.	.023	(medium)	bu.	1.50
	bu.	1.09	(low)	bu.	1.25
1860,	bu.	.85	1818, (high)	bu.	1.28
			(low)	bu.	1.08
Oatmeal.			1819,	pk.	.30
1802,	lb.	.125	(high)	bu.	1.13
1803,	lb.	.125	(low)	bu.	.977
1804,	qt.	.125	1820, (high)	bu.	.90
1805,	qt.	.13	(low)	bu.	.72
1810,	lb.	.125	1821, (high)	bu.	.876
1813,	lb.	.129	(low)	bu.	.647
1814,	lb.	.14	1822,	bu.	.928
1815,	lb.	.125	1823, (high)	bu.	.911
1816,	lb.	.12	(low)	bu.	.745
1817, (high)	lb.	.157	1824, (high)	bu.	.84
(low)	lb.	.125	(low)	bu.	.629
1820,	lb.	.123	1825, (high)	bu.	1.08
1838,	lb.	.124	(medium)	bu.	.733
1840,	lb.	.08	(low)	bu.	.375
1841,	lb.	.10	1826, (high)	bu.	.965
1842,	lb.	.10	(low)	bu.	.84
1843,	lb.	.11	1827,	lb.	.018
1845,	lb.	.098	(high)	bu.	1.09
1846,	lb.	.099	(low)	bu.	.812
1847, (high)	lb.	.10	1828, (high)	bu.	1.08
(low)	lb.	.06	(medium)	bu.	.85
1848,	lb.	.101	(low)	bu.	.725
1850,	lb.	.095	1829, (high)	bu.	1.08
1851,	lb.	.10	(low)	bu.	.863
1852,	lb.	.092	1830, (high)	bu.	1.00
1854,	lb.	.10	(low)	bu.	.84
1858,	lb.	.06	1831, (high)	bu.	1.07
			(low)	bu.	.883
Rice Meal.			1832,	bu.	1.05
1846, (wholesale)	bu.	.35	1833, (high)	bu.	1.20
1847, (wholesale)	bu.	.35	(low)	bu.	1.06
1849,	lb.	.011	1834,	pk.	.26
1859,	lb.	.011	(high)	bu.	1.03
1860, (wholesale)	lb.	.011	(low)	bu.	.89
			1835,	pk.	.29
Rye Flour.				bu.	.952
1835, (high)	bbl.	5.25	1837,	lb.	.03
(low)	bbl.	4.50	(high)	bu.	2.00
1836, (high)	bbl.	7.00	(low)	bu.	1.34
(low)	bbl.	6.13	1838, (high)	bu.	1.34
			(medium)	bu.	1.22
Rye Meal.			(low)	bu.	1.14
1777,	pk.	.167	1839,	lb.	.029
1793,	bu.	.986		bu	1.33

Prices: Flour and Meal — Concluded.

Years.	Basis.	Amount.	Years.	Basis.	Amount.
Rye Meal — Con.			*Rye Meal* — Con.		
1840, ...	bu.	$0.987	1849, ...	bu.	$0.957
1841, ...	lb.	.02	1850, ...	lb.	.021
(high) . . .	bu.	.978		pk.	.278
(low) . . .	bu.	.825	(high) . . .	bu.	.92
1842, (high) . . .	bu.	.891	(low) . . .	bu.	.796
(low) . . .	bu.	.70	1851, ...	lb.	.021
1843, ...	lb.	.017	1852, ...	lb.	.019
	bu.	.887		pk.	.273
1844, ...	bu.	.888	1854, ...	lb.	.031
1845, ...	lb.	.019	1855, ...	lb.	.032
	pk.	.266	1856, ...	lb.	.03
(high) . . .	bu.	.941	(wholesale) . .	lb.	.025
(low) . . .	bu.	.85		bu.	1.49
1846, ...	lb.	.022	1857, ...	lb.	.03
(high) . . .	bu.	1.09	(high) . . .	bu.	1.50
(low) . . .	bu.	.963	(low) . . .	bu.	1.14
1847, ...	lb.	.023	1858, ...	lb.	.024
	pk.	.30		bu.	1.01
(high) . . .	bu.	1.16	1859, ...	lb.	.022
(medium) . .	bu.	.943		bu.	1.04
(low) . . .	bu.	.50			
1848, ...	lb.	.022	*Wheat Bran.*		
	pk.	.34	1803, ...	bu.	.40
(high) . . .	bu.	1 17	1810, ...	pk.	.20
(medium) . .	bu.	1.04			
(low) . . .	bu.	.855	*Wheat Meal.*		
1849, ...	lb.	.022	1841, ...	lb.	.038
	pk.	.20	1847, ...	lb.	.055

Prices: Food Preparations.

Years.	Basis.	Amount.	Years.	Basis.	Amount.
Biscuit.			*Chocolate.*		
1773, ...	ea.	$0.009	1783, (high) . .	lb.	$0.393
1782, ...	ea.	.014	(low) . . .	lb.	.219
1783, ...	ea.	.014	1784, ...	lb.	.223
1784, ...	ea.	.01	1794, ...	lb.	.209
1794, ...	doz.	.111	1799, ...	lb.	.333
1820, ...	doz.	.10	(wholesale) . .	lb.	.236
			1800, ...	lb.	.33
Bread.			(No. 1; wholesale) .	lb.	.298
1802, (by the loaf) . .	ea.	.125	(No. 2; wholesale) .	lb.	.251
1806, (by the loaf) . .	ea.	.125	1801, (wholesale) . .	lb.	.255
1814, (by the loaf) . .	ea.	.18	1802, (high) . .	lb.	.375
1817, (by the loaf) . .	ea.	.14	(low) . . .	lb.	.29
1819, (by the loaf) . .	ea.	.125	1803, ...	lb.	.311
1823, (by the loaf) . .	ea.	.08	(wholesale) . .	lb.	.20
1830, (by the loaf) . .	ea.	.078	1804, (high) . .	lb.	.342
1833, (by the loaf) . .	ea.	.073	(low) . . .	lb.	.28
1834, (by the loaf) . .	ea.	.07	1805, ...	lb.	.375
1841, (by the loaf) . .	ea.	.061	(No. 2; wholesale) .	lb.	.27
1842, (by the loaf) . .	ea.	.06	1806, ...	lb.	.324
1843, (by the loaf; high) .	ea.	.09	1807, ...	lb.	.375
(by the loaf; low) .	ea.	.06	(wholesale, high) .	lb.	.32
1844, (by the loaf) . .	ea.	.057	(wholesale, low) .	lb.	.26
1845, (by the loaf) . .	ea.	.07	1808, ...	lb.	.32
1846, (by the loaf) . .	ea.	.069	1809, ...	lb.	.375
1847, (by the loaf; high) .	ea.	.10	(No. 1; wholesale) .	lb.	.306
(by the loaf; low) .	ea.	.07	(No. 2; wholesale) .	lb.	.254
1848, (by the loaf; high) .	ea.	.10	1810, (high) . .	lb.	.38
(by the loaf; low) .	ea.	.066	(low) . . .	lb.	.312
1849, (by the loaf) . .	ea.	.052	(wholesale, high) .	lb.	.284
1850, (by the loaf; high) .	ea.	.10	(wholesale, low) .	lb.	.23
(by the loaf; low) .	ea.	.05	1811, (high) . .	lb.	.35
1851, (by the loaf; high) .	ea.	.10	(low) . . .	lb.	.30
(by the loaf; low) .	ea.	.051	(wholesale, high) .	lb.	.28
1852, (by the loaf; high) .	ea.	.10	(wholesale, medium) .	lb.	.232
(by the loaf; low) .	ea.	.05	(wholesale, low) .	lb.	.194
1854, (by the loaf; high) .	ea.	.10	1812, (high) . .	lb.	.25
(by the loaf; low) .	ea.	.05	(low) . . .	lb.	.207
1855, (by the loaf; high) .	ea.	.10	1813, ...	lb.	.267
(by the loaf; medium) .	ea.	.075	(wholesale, high) .	lb.	.302
(by the loaf; low) .	ea.	.05	(wholesale, medium) .	lb.	.235

Prices: Food Preparations — Continued.

Years.	Basis.	Amount.	Years.	Basis.	Amount.
Chocolate — Con.			*Cocoa* — Con.		
1813, (wholesale, low)	lb.	$0.16	1840, (low)	lb.	$0.18
1814,	lb.	.30	1841, (high)	lb.	.25
(wholesale, high)	lb.	.25	(low)	lb.	.15
(wholesale, low)	lb.	.20	1842,	lb.	.248
(No. 1)	lb.	.25	1843, (high)	lb.	.25
1815,	lb.	.31	(low)	lb.	.15
(wholesale, high)	lb.	.28	1845, (high)	lb.	.249
(wholesale, medium)	lb.	.244	(low)	lb.	.15
(wholesale, low)	lb.	.20	1846, (high)	lb.	.26
1816,	lb.	.33	(medium)	lb.	.20
1817, (high)	lb.	.282	(low)	lb.	.15
(medium)	lb.	.229	1847,	lb.	.251
(low)	lb.	.18	1848, (high)	lb.	.249
1818,	lb.	.257	(low)	lb.	.15
(wholesale, high)	lb.	.23	1849,	lb.	.243
(wholesale, low)	lb.	.18	1850, (high)	lb.	.249
(No. 1)	lb.	.23	(low)	lb.	.14
(No. 2)	lb.	.212	1851,	lb.	.248
(No. 2; wholesale)	lb.	.18	1852, (high)	lb.	.241
1819,	lb.	.28	(low)	lb.	.165
(No. 1; wholesale)	lb.	.25	1854, (high)	lb.	.253
1820, (high)	lb.	.38	(low)	lb.	.146
(low)	lb.	.27	1856,	lb.	.147
1821, (high)	lb.	.33	1857,	lb.	.25
(medium)	lb	.279	1858,	lb.	.26
(low)	lb.	.21	1859,	lb.	.26
1823,	lb.	.27			
1826,	lb.	.262	*Cocoa and Shells.*		
1827,	lb.	.24	1847,	lb.	.148
1828,	lb.	.229	1848,	lb.	.188
1829,	lb.	.22	1849,	lb.	.145
1830,	lb.	.164	1851,	lb.	.118
1831,	lb.	.20			
1836,	lb.	.20	*Cocoa Shells.*		
1837,	lb.	.20	1794,	lb.	.10
1838,	lb.	.20	1802,	lb.	.25
1839,	lb.	.20	1803,	lb.	.12
1841,	lb.	.20	1804,	lb.	.183
1843,	lb.	.20	1805,	lb.	.197
1844,	lb.	.20	(wholesale)	lb.	.129
1845,	lb.	.20	1806,	lb.	.167
1846,	lb.	.20	(wholesale)	lb.	.13
1847,	lb.	.20	1807, (high)	lb.	.358
1848,	lb.	.20	(low)	lb.	.16
1849,	lb.	.20	(wholesale)	lb.	.124
1850,	lb.	.202	1808, (wholesale)	lb.	.125
1851,	lb.	.201	1809, (wholesale)	lb.	.13
1852,	lb.	.20	1810,	lb.	.18
1854,	lb.	.20	(wholesale)	lb.	.127
1855,	lb.	.30	1811,	lb.	.167
1856,	lb.	.18	(wholesale)	lb.	.123
1857,	lb.	.25	1812, (high)	lb.	.16
1858, (high)	lb.	.30	(low)	lb.	.12
(low)	lb.	.22	1813,	lb.	.167
1859,	lb.	.26	1814,	lb.	.236
			(wholesale)	lb.	.15
Cocoa.			1815, (high)	lb.	.25
1800, (wholesale)	lb.	.255	(low)	lb.	.20
1801, (wholesale, high)	lb.	.207	(wholesale)	lb.	.15
(wholesale, low)	lb.	.16	1816,	lb.	.14
1803, (wholesale)	lb.	.199	1817,	lb.	.167
1804, (wholesale)	lb.	.238	(wholesale)	lb.	.09
1805, (wholesale)	lb.	.197	1818,	lb.	.12
1808, (wholesale)	lb.	.18	1819,	lb.	.125
1809, (wholesale)	lb.	.169	1820,	lb.	.14
1810, (wholesale)	lb.	.16	1821,	lb.	.144
1814, (wholesale)	lb.	.179	1823,	lb.	.14
1816, (wholesale)	lb.	.16	1826,	lb.	.16
1820,	lb.	.334	1829,	lb.	.161
1837,	lb.	.25	1830,	lb.	.15
1838,	lb.	.25	1832,	lb.	.14
1839, (high)	lb.	.248	1833,	lb.	.15
(low)	lb.	.15	1836,	lb.	.166
1840, (high)	lb.	.25	1837,	lb.	.147

Prices: Food Preparations—Continued.

Years.	Basis.	Amount.	Years.	Basis.	Amount.
Cocoa Shells—Con.			*Coffee*—Con.		
1838, ...	lb.	$0.151	1812, (low)	lb.	$0.151
1839, (high) . . .	lb.	.145	1813, (high) . . .	lb.	.333
(low) . . .	lb.	.08	(low) . . .	lb.	.20
1840, (high) . . .	lb.	.167	1814, (high) . . .	lb.	.278
(low) . . .	lb.	.12	(low) . . .	lb.	.25
1841, ...	lb.	.157	1815, ...	lb.	.232
1842, (high) . . .	lb.	.167	1816, (high) . . .	lb.	.255
(low) . . .	lb.	.135	(low) . . .	lb.	.20
1843, (high) . . .	lb.	.153	1817, (high) . . .	lb.	.328
(medium) . .	lb.	.123	(low) . . .	lb.	.242
(low) . . .	lb.	.094	(wholesale) . .	lb.	.235
1844, ...	lb.	.16	1818, (high) . . .	lb.	.351
1845, ...	lb.	.135	(medium) . .	lb.	.30
1846, (high) . . .	lb.	.16	(low) . . .	lb.	.259
(low) . . .	lb.	.122	(wholesale) . .	lb.	.241
1847, ...	lb.	.15	1819, ...	lb.	.338
1848, ...	lb.	.148	1820, (high) . . .	lb.	.318
1850, ...	lb.	.135	(low) . . .	lb.	.271
1852, ...	lb.	.127	1821, (Java) . . .	lb.	.297
1854, ...	lb.	.127	(Mocha) . .	lb.	.334
1855, ...	lb.	.13	1822, (high) . . .	lb.	.296
1856, ...	lb.	.124	(low) . . .	lb.	.177
1857, ...	lb.	.25	1823, ...	lb.	.264
1858, ...	lb.	.239	1824, ...	lb.	.22
			1825, ...	lb.	.19
Coffee.			1826, (high) . . .	lb.	.25
1782, ...	lb.	.355	(low) . . .	lb.	.199
1783, ...	lb.	.167	1827, (high) . . .	lb.	.20
1784, ...	lb.	.167	(medium) . .	lb.	.161
1792, ...	lb.	.208	(low) . . .	lb.	.12
(wholesale) . .	lb.	.174	1828, ...	lb.	.16
1793, ...	lb.	.195	1829, ...	lb.	.147
1794, ...	lb.	.171	(wholesale) . .	lb.	.13
(wholesale) . .	lb.	.157	1830, (high) . . .	lb.	.145
1795, (wholesale) . .	lb.	.181	(low) . . .	lb.	.128
1796, (wholesale, high) .	lb.	.243	1831, ...	lb.	.133
(wholesale, low) .	lb.	.222	(wholesale) . .	lb.	.11
1797, (wholesale) . .	lb.	.223	1832, ...	lb.	.14
1798, (wholesale) . .	lb.	.23	(Java) . . .	lb.	.167
1799, (wholesale) . .	lb.	.284	1833, ...	lb.	.142
1800, ...	lb.	.279	1834, ...	lb.	.14
(wholesale) . .	lb.	.257	(Java) . . .	lb.	.166
1801, (high) . . .	lb.	.279	1835, ...	lb.	.131
(low) . . .	lb.	.23	1836, (Sumatra) . .	lb.	.12
(wholesale, high) .	lb.	.26	1837, ...	lb.	.124
(wholesale, low) .	lb.	.233	1838, ...	lb.	.137
1802, ...	lb.	.244	1839, ...	lb.	.139
(wholesale) . .	lb.	.20	(Java) . . .	lb.	.145
1803, (high) . . .	lb.	.312	1840, (high) . . .	lb.	.16
(med. high) . .	lb.	.277	(low) . . .	lb.	.12
(medium) . .	lb.	.23	1841, ...	lb.	.132
(low) . . .	lb.	.167	(wholesale) . .	lb.	.115
(wholesale, high) .	lb.	.297	1842, ...	lb.	.127
(wholesale, low) .	lb.	.26	(wholesale) . .	lb.	.11
1805, (high) . . .	lb.	.375	1843, (high) . . .	lb.	.113
(low) . . .	lb.	.328	(low) . . .	lb.	.08
(wholesale, high) .	lb.	.31	(wholesale) . .	lb.	.077
(wholesale, low) .	lb.	.26	1844, ...	lb.	.111
1806, ...	lb.	.334	1845, (high) . . .	lb.	.16
1807, (high) . . .	lb.	.305	(low) . . .	lb.	.107
(low) . . .	lb.	.22	1846, (high) . . .	lb.	.125
1808, ...	lb.	.276	(low) . . .	lb.	.107
(wholesale) . .	lb.	.24	1847, ...	lb.	.108
1809, ...	lb.	.279	(green) . . .	lb.	.08
1810, (high) . . .	lb.	.28	1848, ...	lb.	.109
(low) . . .	lb.	.238	1849, ...	lb.	.112
1811, (high) . . .	lb.	.25	1850, ...	lb.	.137
(medium) . .	lb.	.206	1851, ...	lb.	.147
(low) . . .	lb.	.166	1852, ...	lb.	.144
(wholesale, high) .	lb	.193	1854, (high) . . .	lb.	.20
(wholesale, medium) .	lb.	.167	(low) . . .	lb.	.149
(wholesale, low) .	lb.	.125	1855, (high) . . .	lb.	.15
1812, (high) . . .	lb.	.26	(low) . . .	lb.	.11
(medium) . .	lb.	.19	1856, (high) . . .	lb.	.20

Prices: Food Preparations — CONTINUED.

YEARS.	Basis.	Amount.	YEARS.	Basis.	Amount.
Coffee — Con.			*Hominy.*		
1856, (medium)	lb.	$0.153	1858,	lb.	$0.05
(low)	lb.	.103	1859,	lb.	.05
1857, (high)	lb.	.201	1860,	lb.	.05
(medium)	lb.	.163	*Honey.*		
(low)	lb.	.102	1804,	lb.	.167
1858, (high)	lb.	.176	1817,	qt.	.25
(low)	lb.	.118	1825,	lb.	.125
1859, (high)	lb.	.196	1830,	lb.	.125
(medium)	lb.	.153	1835,	lb.	.12
(low)	lb.	.109	*Lard.*		
1860, (high)	lb.	.22	1797, (wholesale)	lb.	.125
(low)	lb.	.18	1803, (wholesale)	lb.	.10
Corn Starch.			1805,	lb.	.125
1850,	lb.	.121	1813,	lb.	.193
1851,	lb.	.121	1814,	lb.	.202
1852,	lb.	.10	1815,	lb.	.20
1854,	lb.	.12	1817,	lb.	.223
Crackers.			1818,	lb.	.216
			1819,	lb.	.166
1813,	bbl.	6.44	1820,	lb.	.169
1822,	doz.	.105	1821,	lb.	.115
1830,	doz.	.06	1823,	lb.	.112
(wholesale)	doz.	.045	1824,	lb.	.10
1832,	doz.	.111	1825,	lb.	.12
	bbl.	3.25	1826, (high)	lb.	.125
1839,	lb.	.125	(low)	lb.	.094
1843,	bbl.	3.00	1827,	lb.	.125
1847,	bbl.	3.88	1828,	lb.	.124
(soda)	lb.	.10	1829,	lb.	.09
1850,	lb.	.08	1830, (high)	lb.	.111
(soda)	lb.	.10	(low)	lb.	.07
1851,	lb.	.085	1831,	lb.	.10
(soda)	lb.	.10	1832,	lb.	.10
1852,	lb.	.112	1833,	lb.	.117
1856,	lb.	.121	1834,	lb.	.126
1857,	lb.	.117	1835,	lb.	.124
1858,	lb.	.112	1837, (high)	lb.	.151
1859,	lb.	.123	(low)	lb.	.118
			1838, (high)	lb.	.149
Cream of Tartar.			(medium)	lb.	.113
1811,	lb.	.50	(low)	lb.	.079
1817,	oz.	.063	1839, (high)	lb.	.159
1822,	lb.	.657	(low)	lb.	.118
1829,	lb.	.32	1840,	lb.	.132
1832,	oz.	.04	1841,	lb.	.099
1837,	lb.	.28	1842,	lb.	.104
1840,	lb.	.36	1843,	lb.	.094
1841,	lb.	.32	(wholesale)	lb.	.06
1843,	lb.	.26	1844,	lb.	.089
1844,	lb.	.24	1845,	lb.	.097
1845,	lb.	.228	1846, (high)	lb.	.131
1846,	lb.	.238	(medium)	lb.	.097
1847, (high)	lb.	.28	(low)	lb.	.063
(low)	lb.	.251	1847, (high)	lb.	.122
1848,	lb.	.278	(low)	lb.	.097
1849,	lb.	.257	(wholesale, high)	lb.	.116
1850, (high)	lb.	.254	(wholesale, low)	lb.	.062
(low)	lb.	.20	1848,	lb.	.103
1851,	lb.	.254	1849,	lb.	.098
1852,	lb.	.251	1850, (high)	lb.	.098
1854, (high)	lb.	.68	(low)	lb.	.063
(low)	lb.	.48	1851,	lb.	.11
1855,	lb.	.40	1852,	lb.	.122
1856,	lb.	.402	1853,	lb.	.138
1857,	lb.	.398	1854,	lb.	.13
1858,	lb.	.401	1855,	lb.	.143
1859,	lb.	.394	1856,	lb.	.137
			1857,	lb.	.16
Farina.			1858,	lb.	.14
1850,	lb.	.12	1859,	lb.	.145
1851,	lb.	.121	1860,	lb.	.15
1852,	lb.	.119			
1854,	lb.	.14	*Macaroni.*		
1857,	lb.	.15	1837,	lb.	.17
1858,	lb.	.15	1858,	lb.	.167

Prices: Food Preparations — Continued.

Years.	Basis.	Amount.	Years.	Basis.	Amount.
Macaroni — Con.			*Molasses* — Con.		
1859, ...	lb.	$0.18	1814, (medium) . .	gal.	$1.24
1860, ...	lb.	.19	(med. low) . .	gal.	1.00
			(low) . . .	gal.	.794
Molasses.			1815, (high) . . .	gal.	1.50
1753, ...	gal.	.555	(low) . . .	gal.	.843
1762, ...	gal.	.50	1816, (high) . . .	gal.	.774
1765, ...	qt.	.111	(low) . . .	gal.	.636
1767, (by the hhd.) .	gal.	.201	1817, (high) . . .	gal.	.676
1773, ...	qt.	.083	(low) . . .	gal.	.575
1774, ...	qt.	.083	1818, ...	qt.	.175
1775, ...	gal.	.40	(high) . . .	gal.	.767
1779, ...	gal.	.389	(low) . . .	gal.	.622
1780, ...	gal.	.389	(New Orleans) .	gal.	.72
1782, ...	qt.	.205	1819, ...	qt.	.17
	gal.	.50	(high) . . .	gal.	.596
1783, ...	qt.	.122	(low) . . .	gal.	.502
(by the hhd.) . .	qt.	.083	(wholesale) . .	gal.	.45
1784, ...	qt.	.078	1820, ...	gal.	.378
1785, ...	gal.	.361	1821, ...	gal	.38
1786, ...	gal.	.333	(sugar) . . .	gal.	.50
1788, ...	gal.	.333	1822, ...	gal.	.383
1790, ...	qt.	.167	1823, ...	gal.	.329
1791, ...	gal.	.416	(wholesale) . .	gal.	.294
1792, (high) . . .	gal.	.566	1824, (high) . . .	gal.	.324
(low) . . .	gal.	.444	(low) . . .	gal.	.22
1793, ...	gal.	.50	1825, (high) . . .	gal.	.388
(wholesale) . .	gal.	.389	(low) . . .	gal.	.25
1794, ...	gal.	.712	1826, (high) . . .	gal.	.50
1795, ...	gal.	.556	(med. high) . .	gal.	.40
(wholesale) . .	gal.	.444	(medium) . .	gal.	.352
1798, ...	gal.	.778	(low) . . .	gal.	.233
(wholesale) . .	gal.	.639	(wholesale) . .	gal.	.29
1799, ...	qt.	.165	1827, ...	gal.	.384
(high) . . .	gal.	.723	1828, ...	gal.	.355
(low) . . .	gal.	.58	1829, (high) . . .	gal.	.411
1800, ...	qt.	.14	(low) . . .	gal.	.32
	gal.	.556	1830, (high) . . .	gal.	.90
(wholesale) . .	gal.	.48	(low) . . .	gal.	.319
1801, ...	qt.	.25	1831, ...	qt.	.10
(wholesale) . .	gal.	.523	(high) . . .	gal.	1.02
1802, ...	qt.	.13	(medium) . .	gal.	.60
(high) . . .	gal.	1.00	(low) . . .	gal.	.331
(medium) . .	gal.	.556	1832, ...	gal.	.332
(low) . . .	gal.	.50	1833, ...	gal.	.353
1803, ...	gal.	.51	1834, (high) . . .	gal.	.45
(wholesale) . .	gal.	.463	(low) . . .	gal.	.329
(sugar-bakers') .	gal.	.584	1835, ...	gal.	.348
1804, ...	qt.	.167	1836, ...	gal.	.463
(high) . . .	gal.	.602	1837, (high) . . .	gal.	.448
(low) . . .	gal.	.445	(medium) . .	gal.	.37
(wholesale) . .	gal.	.511	(low) . . .	gal.	.27
1805, ...	qt.	.156	1838, ...	gal.	.408
(high) . . .	gal.	.666	1839, ...	qt.	.105
(low) . . .	gal.	.525		gal.	.392
(wholesale) . .	gal.	.422	(sugar-bakers') .	gal.	.65
1806, ...	gal.	.50	1840, ...	gal.	.348
1807, ...	gal.	.50	1841, (high) . . .	gal.	.333
1808, (high) . . .	gal.	.72	(low) . . .	gal.	.289
(low) . . .	gal.	.575	1842, ...	gal.	.272
(sugar-bakers') .	gal.	.75	1843, (high) . . .	qt.	.11
1809, (high) . . .	gal.	.75	(low) . . .	qt.	.076
(medium) . .	gal.	.638	(high) . . .	gal.	.295
(low) . . .	gal.	.52	(low) . . .	gal.	.235
1810, ...	gal.	.673	(wholesale, high)	gal.	.24
(wholesale) . .	gal.	.56	(wholesale, low)	gal.	.18
1811, (high) . . .	gal.	1.07	1844, ...	gal.	.345
(low) . . .	gal.	.595	1845, ...	gal.	.33
1812, (high) . . .	gal.	.745	1846, (high) . . .	gal.	.294
(low) . . .	gal.	.641	(low) . . .	gal.	.24
1813, ...	qt.	.335	1847, (high) . . .	gal.	.342
(high) . . .	gal.	1.19	(medium) . .	gal.	.30
(low) . . .	gal.	.837	(low) . . .	gal.	.255
1814, (high) . . .	gal.	1.50	1848, ...	gal.	.293
(med. high) . .	gal.	1.37	1849, (high) . . .	gal.	.33

Prices: Food Preparations — CONTINUED.

YEARS.	Basis	Amount	YEARS.	Basis	Amount
Molasses — Con.			*Saleratus* — Con.		
1849, (low)	gal.	$0.279	1858,	lb.	$0.067
1850, (high)	gal.	.405	1859,	lb.	.07
(low)	gal.	.291	*Salt.*		
1851,	qt.	.11	1756,	bu.	.667
	gal.	.252	1757,	bu.	.80
(sugar-house)	gal.	.42	1758,	bu.	.833
1852, (high)	gal.	.44	1760,	pk.	.222
(low)	gal.	.25	1762,	qt.	.021
1854,	gal.	.302	1768,	bu.	.556
1855, (high)	gal.	.455	1779,	bu.	.50
(low)	gal.	.39	1782,	pk.	.064
1856,	gal.	.492		bu.	.833
1857, (high)	gal.	.746	1783,	pk.	.208
(medium)	gal.	.588	1784, (high)	pk.	.167
(low)	gal.	.375	(low)	pk.	.083
1858, (high)	gal.	.41	1785,	pk.	.195
(low)	gal.	.31		bu.	.556
1859, (high)	gal.	.44	1786,	bu.	.667
(low)	gal.	.321	1788,	bu.	.33
1860, (high)	gal.	.50	1790,	bu.	.667
(low)	gal.	.40	1793,	bu.	.916
Pearl Barley.			1794,	pk.	.278
1806,	lb.	.334		bu.	1.06
1815,	lb.	.375	1795,	qt.	.028
Sago.			(high)	bu.	1.17
1847, (pearl)	lb.	.10	(low)	bu.	1.00
1848, (pearl)	lb.	.10	1798,	hhd.	6.00
1849,	lb.	.122	1801, (high)	bu.	1.33
1851, (high)	lb.	.11	(low)	bu.	1.00
(low)	lb.	.08	(fine)	pk.	.333
1852,	lb.	.10	1802,	pk.	.183
1854,	lb.	.12		bu.	.83
1855,	lb.	.125	1803,	hhd.	5.00
1856,	lb.	.125	(fine)	pk.	.27
1857,	lb.	.12	(Lisbon)	pk.	.209
1858,	lb.	.074	1804,	bu.	.977
1859,	lb.	.103	1805,	bu.	.834
Saleratus.			1806,	pk.	.272
1830, (high)	lb.	.15	1807, (high)	pk.	.332
(low)	lb.	.115	(low)	pk.	.20
1831,	lb.	.10	1808, (high)	pk.	.50
1832, (high)	lb.	.117	(low)	pk.	.334
(low)	lb.	.063	(rock)	bu.	.90
1833,	lb.	.104	1809, (wholesale)	bu.	.60
1834,	lb.	.088	(rock; high)	bu.	1.25
1835,	lb.	.112	(rock; low)	bu.	1.00
1837, (high)	lb.	.109	1810,	pk.	.333
(low)	lb.	.06	1811, (high)	bu.	.80
1838,	lb.	.118	(low)	bu.	.56
1839, (high)	lb.	.118		bag	4.50
(low)	lb.	.08	1812, (high)	pk.	.40
1840,	lb.	.091	(medium)	pk.	.30
1841,	lb.	.095	(low)	pk.	.235
1842,	lb.	.097	1813,	bu.	.80
1843,	lb.	.098	1814,	pk.	.24
1844,	lb.	.079		bu.	1.00
1845,	lb.	.08	(coarse)	pk.	.276
1846, (high)	lb.	.08	1815, (high)	pk.	.42
(low)	lb.	.06	(low)	pk.	.265
1847,	lb.	.088	(high)	bu.	1.35
1848,	lb.	.098	(low)	bu.	1.00
1849,	lb.	.099	1816,	qt.	.05
1850,	lb.	.092	(high)	pk.	.347
1851,	lb.	.078	(low)	pk.	.17
1852,	lb.	.078	(high)	bu.	1.02
1854, (high)	lb.	.125	(low)	bu.	.793
(low)	lb.	.08	1817,	pk.	.32
1855, (high)	lb.	.11	(high)	bu.	1.00
(low)	lb.	.07	(low)	bu.	.825
1856,	lb.	.07	1818,	pk.	.34
1857,	lb.	.071	(high)	bu.	.83
			(low)	bu.	.64
			1819, (high)	pk.	.33

Prices: Food Preparations — CONTINUED.

YEARS.	Basis.	Amount.	YEARS.	Basis.	Amount.
Salt—Con.			*Salt*—Con.		
1819, (medium)	pk.	$0.25	1845, (fine)	qt.	$0.026
(low)	pk.	.17	1846,	bu.	.607
	bu.	.84	(fine)	pk.	.232
1820, (high)	bu.	.86	1847, (high)	bu.	.88
(low)	bu.	.70	(low)	bu.	.599
(fine; high)	bu.	1.16		bag	1.62
(fine; low)	bu.	1.00	(coarse)	qt.	.015
1821,	qt.	.065	(fine)	qt.	.032
(high)	pk.	.25	1848,	qt.	.03
(low)	pk.	.18		bu.	.606
(high)	bu.	.84	1849,	qt.	.011
(low)	bu.	.665		pk.	.138
1822,	pk.	.17	1850,	lb.	.01
(high)	bu.	.84		qt.	.023
(low)	bu.	.74		pk.	.127
(fine)	pk.	.246		bu.	.40
1823,	bu.	.86	1851,	qt.	.026
(coarse)	bu.	.66		pk.	.13
1824,	pk.	.213	1854,	pk.	.192
1825,	pk.	.21	(fine)	qt.	.031
(high)	bu.	.78	1855, (high)	bu.	.816
(low)	bu.	.64	(low)	bu.	.667
1826,	pk.	.20	1856,	pk.	.24
	bu.	.70	(high)	bu.	.835
1827,	pk.	.20	(low)	bu.	.661
	bu.	.604	1857, (high)	bu.	.84
1828,	qt.	.06	(low)	bu.	.61
	pk.	.193	(high)	bag	2.12
	bu.	.666	(low)	bag	1.34
1829,	pk.	.20	1858, (high)	bu.	.642
	bu.	.688	(low)	bu.	.502
1830,	pk.	.223	1859, (high)	bu.	.663
(high)	bu.	.768	(low)	bu.	.458
(low)	bu.	.59			
(coarse)	pk.	.16	*Soda.*		
1831,	pk.	.14	1836,	lb.	.113
(high)	bu.	.777	1837, (high)	lb.	.10
(low)	bu.	.60	(low)	lb.	.063
1832,	pk.	.20	1838,	lb.	.101
	bu.	.667	(wholesale)	lb.	.067
(rock)	bu.	.84	1839,	lb.	.101
1833,	pk.	.20	1840,	lb.	.08
1834,	qt.	.03	1841, (high)	lb.	.10
	pk.	.226	(low)	lb.	.05
	bu.	.60	1842,	lb.	.087
1835,	qt.	.027	1843, (high)	lb.	.098
	pk.	.14	(low)	lb.	.042
1836, (high)	pk.	.20	1844, (high)	lb.	.16
(low)	pk.	.14	(medium)	lb.	.08
1837,	qt.	.025	(low)	lb.	.05
	bu.	.621	1845, (high)	lb.	.16
1838,	bu.	.608	(low)	lb.	.08
(fine)	pk.	.216	1846, (high)	lb.	.12
1839,	qt.	.029	(low)	lb.	.08
	bu.	.632	1847, (high)	lb.	.079
(fine)	pk.	.20	(low)	lb.	.03
1840, (fine)	pk.	.191	1848, (high)	lb.	.12
1841,	qt.	.025	(low)	lb.	.065
	bu.	.60	1849,	lb.	.06
(fine)	pk.	.20	1850, (high)	lb.	.111
1842,	qt.	.03	(low)	lb.	.06
	pk.	.20	1851, (high)	lb.	.116
	bu.	.612	(low)	lb.	.06
1843,	qt.	.026	1852,	lb.	.12
(high)	bu.	.772	1854, (high)	lb.	.119
(low)	bu.	.544	(low)	lb.	.06
	bag	1.75	1859, (high)	lb.	.154
(fine)	qt.	.03	(low)	lb.	.069
(fine)	pk.	.20			
1844,	qt.	.03	*Starch.*		
	pk.	.165	1794,	lb.	.167
	bu.	.563	1799,	lb.	.328
(fine)	pk.	.20	1800,	lb.	.25
1845,	bu.	.565	1802,	lb.	.28

Prices: Food Preparations — CONTINUED.

YEARS.	Basis.	Amount.	YEARS.	Basis.	Amount.
Starch — Con.			*Sugar* — Con.		
1807, ...	lb.	$0.14	1794, (brown) . . .	lb.	$0.132
1811, (wholesale) . . .	lb.	.18	(loaf) . . .	lb.	.33
1814, ...	lb.	.264	(loaf; wholesale) . .	lb.	.264
1815, ...	lb.	.20	1795, (wholesale) . .	lb.	.11
1817, ...	lb.	.28	1796, (loaf) . . .	lb.	.287
1818, ...	lb.	.208	1797, (wholesale) . .	lb.	.144
1819, ...	lb.	.24	1798, (wholesale, high) .	lb.	.185
1820, (wholesale) . . .	lb.	.125	(wholesale, low) .	lb.	.133
1821, ...	lb.	.165	(loaf) . . .	lb.	.306
1822, (high)	lb.	.26	1799, (high) . . .	lb.	.167
(low)	lb.	.113	(low) . . .	lb.	.136
1824, ...	lb.	.15	(wholesale) . .	lb.	.139
1826, ...	lb.	.16	(loaf) . . .	lb.	.22
1828, ...	lb.	.10	1800, ...	lb.	.13
1830, (high)	lb.	.224	(wholesale) . .	lb.	.117
(low)	lb.	.105	(loaf) . . .	lb.	.27
1832, ...	lb.	.20	1801, ...	lb.	.131
1833, ...	lb.	.17	(wholesale, high) .	lb.	.126
1834, ...	lb.	.124	(wholesale, low) .	lb.	.101
1835, ...	lb.	.20	(India; wholesale) .	lb.	.133
1837, ...	lb.	.12	(loaf; wholesale) .	lb.	.27
1838, ...	lb.	.124	1802, (high) . . .	lb.	.166
1839, ...	lb.	.12	(medium) . . .	lb.	.126
1841, ...	lb.	.128	(low) . . .	lb.	.096
1842, ...	lb.	.12	(wholesale, high) .	lb.	.118
1843, ...	lb.	.118	(wholesale, low) .	lb.	.09
1844, (high)	lb.	.12	(brown) . . .	lb.	.135
(low)	lb.	.09	(loaf) . . .	lb.	.25
1845, ...	lb.	.107	(powdered) . .	lb.	.179
1846, ...	lb.	.111	1803, (high) . . .	lb.	.23
1847, ...	lb.	.119	(medium) . . .	lb.	.132
1848, ...	lb.	.111	(low) . . .	lb.	.107
1849, ...	lb.	.112	(wholesale, high) .	lb.	.115
1850, ...	lb.	.119	(wholesale, low) .	lb.	.038
1851, ...	lb.	.119	(brown) . . .	lb.	.121
1852, ...	lb.	.114	(loaf) . . .	lb.	.22
1854, ...	lb.	.125	(powdered) . .	lb.	.179
1855, ...	lb.	.123	(West India) . .	lb.	.131
1856, ...	lb.	.124	1804, ...	lb.	.16
1857, ...	lb.	.123	(wholesale) . .	lb.	.118
1858, ...	lb.	.121	(brown) . . .	lb.	.12
			(India) . . .	lb.	.143
Suet.			(India; wholesale) .	lb.	.134
1804, ...	lb.	.125	(loaf) . . .	lb.	.212
1808, ...	lb.	.10	(powdered) . .	lb.	.182
1814, ...	lb.	.11	1805, ...	lb.	.133
1817, ...	lb.	.152	(wholesale) . .	lb.	.108
1824, ...	lb.	.10	(brown) . . .	lb.	.139
			(brown; wholesale) .	lb.	.116
Sugar.			(India; wholesale) .	lb.	.144
1753, ...	lb.	.146	(loaf; wholesale) .	lb.	.227
1755, ...	lb.	.128	(powdered) . .	lb.	.179
1758, (loaf)	lb.	.187	1806, (wholesale) . .	lb.	.12
1759, ...	lb.	.071	(brown) . . .	lb.	.14
1761, ...	lb.	.111	(loaf; wholesale) .	lb.	.207
1771, ...	lb.	.091	(lump) . . .	lb.	.219
1773, (high)	lb.	.25	(powdered) . .	lb.	.166
(low)	lb.	.089	1807, (wholesale) . .	lb.	.102
1774, ...	lb.	.083	(brown) . . .	lb.	.128
1780, ...	lb.	.097	(India; wholesale) .	lb.	.113
1782, (high)	lb.	.143	(loaf; wholesale) .	lb.	.212
(low)	lb.	.083	(lump; wholesale) .	lb.	.201
1783, ...	lb.	.119	(powdered) . .	lb.	.158
1784, ...	lb.	.104	1808, ...	lb.	.143
1785, ...	lb.	.10	(wholesale, high) .	lb.	.12
1791, ...	lb.	.105	(wholesale, low) .	lb.	.094
1792, ...	lb.	.153	(loaf; wholesale) .	lb.	.182
1793, ...	lb.	.139	(powdered) . .	lb.	.157
(wholesale) . . .	lb.	.119	1809, (wholesale) . .	lb.	.12
1794, (high)	lb.	.135	(brown) . . .	lb.	.127
(low)	lb.	.107	(India; wholesale) .	lb.	.124
(wholesale, high) .	lb.	.126	(loaf) . . .	lb.	.20
(wholesale, low) .	lb.	.08	(loaf; wholesale) .	lb.	.173
			(lump; wholesale) .	lb.	.189

Prices: Food Preparations — Continued.

Years.	Basis.	Amount.	Years.	Basis.	Amount.
Sugar — Con.			*Sugar* — Con.		
1809, (powdered; wholesale) .	lb.	$0.143	1823, (loaf; high)	lb.	$0.21
1810, (wholesale)	lb.	.117	(loaf; low)	lb.	.163
(brown; wholesale)	lb.	.129	(white)	lb.	.179
(loaf; wholesale)	lb.	.167	1824, (high)	lb.	.143
(powdered)	lb.	.14	(low)	lb.	.105
1811, (high)	lb.	.236	(brown)	lb.	.108
(low)	lb.	.138	(loaf)	lb.	.20
(wholesale, high)	lb.	.192	(white Havana)	lb.	.16
(wholesale, low)	lb.	.111	1825,	lb.	.098
(brown)	lb.	.13	(brown; high)	lb.	.125
(loaf; wholesale)	lb.	.189	(brown; low)	lb.	.105
(lump; wholesale)	lb.	.171	(loaf)	lb.	.19
(white; wholesale)	lb.	.134	(powdered)	lb.	.155
1812, (high)	lb.	.155	1826, (high)	lb.	.12
(low)	lb.	.126	(low)	lb.	.105
(wholesale)	lb.	.141	(brown; high)	lb.	.13
(brown)	lb.	.13	(brown; low)	lb.	.114
(brown; wholesale)	lb.	.09	(loaf; high)	lb.	.219
(loaf)	lb.	.18	(loaf; low)	lb.	.194
(powdered)	lb.	.19	(powdered)	lb.	.15
1813, (high)	lb.	.23	1827, (brown)	lb.	.111
(medium)	lb.	.175	(loaf)	lb.	.166
(low)	lb.	.143	(powdered)	lb.	.15
(wholesale)	lb.	.153	(white)	lb.	.158
(brown Havana)	lb.	.162	1828,	lb.	.103
(loaf)	lb.	.28	(brown)	lb.	.119
1814, (high)	lb.	.28	(loaf)	lb.	.168
(medium)	lb.	.206	(New Orleans)	lb.	.105
(low)	lb.	.165	(white)	lb.	.174
(brown)	lb.	.193	1829,	lb.	.113
(loaf)	lb.	.342	(loaf)	lb.	.17
(powdered)	lb.	.214	(powdered)	lb.	.154
1815, (high)	lb.	.197	1830, (high)	lb.	.18
(medium)	lb.	.164	(medium)	lb.	.14
(low)	lb.	.137	(low)	lb.	.103
(brown)	lb.	.177	(loaf)	lb.	.167
(white)	lb.	.261	(powdered)	lb.	.15
1816, (high)	lb.	.173	1831,	lb.	.091
(low)	lb.	.138	(powdered)	lb.	.15
(brown)	lb.	.153	(white)	lb.	.17
(powdered)	lb.	.214	(white Havana)	lb.	.125
(white)	lb.	.232	1832, (high)	lb.	.13
1817, (high)	lb.	.163	(medium)	lb.	.107
(low)	lb.	.086	(low)	lb.	.089
(brown)	lb.	.13	(loaf; high)	lb.	.191
(loaf)	lb.	.23	(loaf; low)	lb.	.151
(powdered)	lb.	.197	(Santa Cruz)	lb.	.095
1818, (high)	lb.	.175	1833,	lb.	.10
(low)	lb.	.146	(loaf)	lb.	.15
(wholesale)	lb.	.10	(powdered)	lb.	.14
(powdered)	lb.	.19	(Santa Cruz)	lb.	.166
(white Havana)	lb.	.19	1834,	lb.	.10
1819, (high)	lb.	.199	(loaf)	lb.	.15
(low)	lb.	.145	(white Havana)	lb.	.125
(brown)	lb.	.249	1835,	lb.	.11
(India)	lb.	.139	(loaf)	lb.	.169
(loaf)	lb.	.26	(powdered)	lb.	.145
1820, (high)	lb.	.181	1836,	lb.	.10
(medium)	lb.	.158	(brown)	lb.	.12
(low)	lb.	.13	(powdered)	lb.	.18
(brown)	lb.	.11	1837, (high)	lb.	.105
(loaf)	lb.	.20	(low)	lb.	.072
1821, (high)	lb.	.16	(wholesale, high)	lb.	.103
(low)	lb.	.109	(wholesale, low)	lb.	.075
(brown)	lb.	.112	(brown)	lb.	.102
(loaf; high)	lb.	.222	(loaf)	lb.	.18
(loaf; low)	lb.	.18	(maple)	lb.	.20
1822, (high)	lb.	.143	1838,	lb.	.15
(low)	lb.	.115	(brown)	lb.	.10
(brown)	lb.	.10	(crushed)	lb.	.166
(loaf)	lb.	.213	(loaf)	lb.	.18
(powdered)	lb.	.157	(molasses)	lb.	.05
1823,	lb.	.139	(white Havana)	lb.	.179
(brown)	lb.	.102	1839,	lb.	.098

Prices: Food Preparations — CONTINUED.

YEARS.	Basis.	Amount.	YEARS.	Basis.	Amount.
Sugar — Con.			*Syrup* — Con.		
1839, (loaf; high)	lb.	$0.181	1857,	gal.	$0.76
(loaf; low)	lb.	.163	1858, (high)	gal.	.50
1840,	lb.	.095	(low)	gal.	.415
1841, (high)	lb.	.124	1859,	gal.	.451
(low)	lb.	.087			
(wholesale)	lb.	.075	*Tapioca.*		
(loaf)	lb.	.166	1835,	lb.	.10
(white)	lb.	.154	1837,	lb.	.10
1842,	lb.	.08	1843,	lb.	.122
(wholesale)	lb.	.068	1844,	lb.	.113
(loaf)	lb.	.165	1845,	lb.	.123
(white; high)	lb.	.15	1846,	lb.	.12
(white; low)	lb.	.106	1847,	lb.	.10
1843,	lb.	.083	1848,	lb.	.113
(loaf)	lb.	.16	1849,	lb.	.123
(white; high)	lb.	.143	1850,	lb.	.124
(white; low)	lb.	.09	1851,	lb.	.12
1844,	lb.	.083	1852,	lb.	.115
(loaf)	lb.	.156	1854,	lb.	.129
(white)	lb.	.14	1857,	lb.	.166
1845, (high)	lb.	.13	1858,	lb.	.17
(low)	lb.	.095	1859,	lb.	.168
(brown)	lb.	.072			
(loaf)	lb.	.16	*Tea.*		
(molasses)	lb.	.04	1756,	lb.	1.33
(white)	lb.	.143	1780,	lb.	.625
1846,	lb.	.094	1782,	lb.	1.63
(white)	lb.	.143	1783,	lb.	.983
1847,	lb.	.085	(wholesale)	lb.	.528
(crushed)	lb.	.125	1784,	lb.	.661
(loaf)	lb.	.133	1785, (high)	lb.	.667
(molasses)	lb.	.04	(low)	lb.	.541
(powdered; high)	lb.	.15	1788, (Bohea)	lb.	.50
(powdered; low)	lb.	.13	1792,	lb.	.423
(white)	lb.	.135	(wholesale)	lb.	.375
1848, (high)	lb.	.137	1793, (high)	lb.	.916
(low)	lb.	.077	(low)	lb.	.423
(wholesale)	lb.	.066	(Bohea; wholesale)	lb.	.361
(molasses; high)	lb.	.057	1794, (high)	lb.	1.04
(molasses; low)	lb.	.03	(low)	lb.	.556
(New Orleans)	lb.	.059	(wholesale)	lb.	.365
(white)	lb.	.111	(Bohea; wholesale)	lb.	.362
1849,	lb.	.078	(green)	lb.	1.25
(loaf)	lb.	.11	(Hyson)	lb.	1.11
(New Orleans)	lb.	.06	1795,	lb.	.50
1850, (high)	lb.	.078	(Bohea; wholesale)	lb.	.389
(low)	lb.	.05	1796,	lb.	.444
(white)	lb.	.106	1797, (wholesale)	lb.	.416
1851,	lb.	.082	(Bohea; wholesale)	lb.	.43
(white)	lb.	.104	1798, (wholesale)	lb.	.50
1852, (high)	lb.	.099	(Bohea; wholesale, high)	lb.	.722
(low)	lb.	.075	(Bohea; wholesale, low)	lb.	.597
(wholesale)	lb.	.073	(Hyson)	lb.	1.50
(maple)	lb.	.167	(Souchong)	lb.	1.07
1854,	lb.	.077	1799,	lb.	.799
(white)	lb.	.101	(Bohea)	lb.	.668
(white coffee)	lb.	.08	(Bohea; wholesale)	lb.	.552
1855, (high)	lb.	.103	(Souchong; wholesale)	lb.	1.17
(low)	lb.	.088	1800, (high)	lb.	.877
(molasses)	lb.	.04	(low)	lb.	.49
1856, (high)	lb.	.102	(Bohea)	lb.	.48
(low)	lb.	.043	(Bohea; wholesale)	lb.	.44
1857, (high)	lb.	.145	(Congo)	lb.	.62
(medium)	lb.	.113	(Hyson)	lb.	1.17
(low)	lb.	.082	(Souchong; wholesale)	lb.	1.14
1858, (high)	lb.	.15	1801,	lb.	.60
(medium)	lb.	.097	(Bohea)	lb.	.44
(low)	lb.	.025	(Congo; high)	lb.	.611
1859, (high)	lb.	.103	(Congo; low)	lb.	.487
(low)	lb.	.078	(Hyson; high)	lb.	1.50
1860, (high)	lb.	.11	(Hyson; medium)	lb.	1.42
(low)	lb.	.09	(Hyson; low)	lb.	1.16
			(Souchong; high)	lb.	1.11
Syrup.			(Souchong; low)	lb.	.973
1854,	gal.	.40	(young Hyson)	lb.	1.17
1856,	gal.	.88	1802, (high)	lb.	1.32

Prices: Food Preparations — CONTINUED.

YEARS.	Basis.	Amount.	YEARS.	Basis.	Amount.
Tea — Con.			*Tea* — Con.		
1802, (low)	lb.	$0.586	1814,	lb.	$1.75
(Bohea; high)	lb.	.422	(Hyson; high)	lb.	2.00
(Bohea; low)	lb.	.556	(Hyson; low)	lb.	1.33
(Congo)	lb.	.59	(Hyson skin)	lb.	1.60
(Hyson)	lb.	1.33	(Souchong; high)	lb.	1.59
(Hyson; wholesale)	lb.	1.10	(Souchong; low)	lb.	1.21
(Souchong; high)	lb.	1.00	(young Hyson)	lb.	1.33
(Souchong; low)	lb.	.75	1815, (high)	lb.	1.67
1803, (high)	lb.	1.05	(low)	lb.	1.13
(low)	lb.	.62	(wholesale)	lb.	.90
(Bohea)	lb.	.334	(Hyson)	lb.	1.45
(Hyson)	lb.	1.33	(Souchong; high)	lb.	1.26
(Souchong)	lb.	.834	(Souchong; low)	lb.	1.00
(Souchong; wholesale)	lb.	.721	1816, (high)	lb.	1.27
1804,	lb.	.985	(low)	lb.	.70
(Bohea)	lb.	.375	(Hyson; high)	lb.	1.55
(Hyson; wholesale)	lb.	1.25	(Hyson; low)	lb.	.80
(Souchong)	lb.	.906	(Sonchong; high)	lb.	1.03
(Souchong; wholesale)	lb.	.80	(Souchong; low)	lb.	.897
1805,	lb.	1.03	1817, (high)	lb.	1.68
(Hyson)	lb.	1.27	(med. high)	lb.	1.52
(Souchong)	lb.	.889	(medium)	lb.	1.20
(Souchong; wholesale, high)	lb.	.807	(med. low)	lb.	.912
(Souchong; wholesale, low)	lb.	.755	(low)	lb.	.758
			(Hyson; high)	lb.	1.68
1806, (Hyson)	lb.	1.26	(Hyson; medium)	lb.	1.42
(Hyson skin; wholesale)	lb.	.72	(Hyson; low)	lb.	1.15
(Souchong; high)	lb.	1.00	(Souchong; high)	lb.	1.12
(Souchong; low)	lb.	.848	(Souchong; medium)	lb.	.83
(Souchong; wholesale)	lb.	.70	(Souchong; low)	lb.	.722
1807, (high)	lb.	1.20	1818,	lb.	1.00
(low)	lb.	1.00	(Hyson; high)	lb.	1.50
(Hyson)	lb.	1.33	(Hyson; low)	lb.	1.33
(Hyson skin)	lb.	.65	(Hyson skin)	lb.	.795
(Souchong)	lb.	.787	(Souchong)	lb.	.713
1808, (Hyson)	lb.	1.29	(young Hyson)	lb.	1.25
(Hyson skin; wholesale)	lb.	1.05	1819,	lb.	.837
(Souchong; high)	lb.	.929	(Hyson; high)	lb.	1.50
(Souchong; low)	lb.	.775	(Hyson; low)	lb.	1 25
1809,	lb.	1.00	(Hyson skin)	lb.	.80
(Hyson; high)	lb.	1.50	(Souchong)	lb.	.724
(Hyson; low)	lb.	1.25	(Souchong; by the chest)	lb.	.58
(Hyson; wholesale, high)	lb.	1.07	1820,	lb.	.738
(Hyson; wholesale, low)	lb.	.75	(Hyson)	lb.	1.09
(Souchong)	lb.	.833	(Hyson skin)	lb.	.588
1810, (Hyson)	lb.	1.13	(Souchong)	lb.	.579
(Souchong; high)	lb.	.875	(young Hyson)	lb.	.868
(Souchong; low)	lb.	.667	1821,	lb.	.667
1811, (high)	lb.	1.45	(Hyson)	lb.	1.09
(low)	lb.	1.12	(Souchong)	lb.	.566
(wholesale)	lb.	.65	(young Hyson; high)	lb.	1.00
(Hyson)	lb.	1.03	(young Hyson; low)	lb.	.875
(Hyson skin)	lb.	.80	1822,	lb.	.753
(Souchong)	lb.	.649	(Hyson)	lb.	1.09
1812, (high)	lb.	.925	(Souchong)	lb.	.627
(medium)	lb.	.833	(young Hyson)	lb.	1.00
(low)	lb.	.608	1823, (Hyson; high)	lb.	1.09
(Hyson; high)	lb.	1.50	(Hyson; low)	lb.	.70
(Hyson; low)	lb.	1.01	(Souchong; high)	lb.	1.13
(Hyson skin; high)	lb.	.952	(Souchong; low)	lb.	.651
(Hyson skin; medium)	lb.	.833	(Souchong; wholesale)	lb.	.599
(Hyson skin; low)	lb.	.625	1824,	lb.	.52
(Souchong; high)	lb.	1.25	(Bohea)	lb.	.40
(Souchong; low)	lb.	.855	(Hyson)	lb.	1.10
1813, (high)	lb.	1.75	(Souchong)	lb.	.64
(medium)	lb.	1.44	1825, (Hyson)	lb.	1.11
(low)	lb.	.80	(Souchong; high)	lb.	1.12
(Hyson)	lb.	1.63	(Souchong; low)	lb.	.605
(Hyson skin)	lb.	1.16	1826, (high)	lb.	1.12
(Souchong; high)	lb.	1.60	(low)	lb.	.44
(Souchong; med. high)	lb.	1.34	(Hyson)	lb.	1.10
(Souchong; medium)	lb.	1.12	(Souchong; high)	lb.	.70
(Souchong; low)	lb.	.60	(Souchong; low)	lb.	.595
			(Souchong; wholesale)	lb.	.55

Prices: Food Preparations — Concluded.

Years.	Basis.	Amount.	Years.	Basis.	Amount.
Tea — Con.			*Tea* — Con.		
1827, (Hyson)	lb.	$1.11	1842, (low)	lb.	$0.536
(Souchong)	lb.	.589	(young Hyson)	lb.	.751
1828,	lb.	.61	1843, (high)	lb.	.756
(black)	lb.	.667	(med. high)	lb.	.637
(Hyson)	lb.	1.13	(medium)	lb.	.486
(Souchong)	lb.	.572	(low)	lb.	.386
(young Hyson)	lb.	.90	(Souchong; high)	lb.	.60
1829,	lb.	.68	(Souchong; low)	lb.	.485
(Hyson)	lb.	1.05	(young Hyson; high)	lb.	.712
(old Hyson)	lb.	1.12	(young Hyson; low)	lb.	.563
(Souchong)	lb.	.586	1844, (high)	lb.	.64
1830,	lb.	.64	(low)	lb.	.34
(Hyson)	lb.	1.06	(old Hyson)	lb.	.60
(old Hyson)	lb.	1.12	1845, (high)	lb.	.591
(Pouchong)	lb.	.667	(medium)	lb.	.438
(Souchong)	lb.	.573	(low)	lb.	.338
(young Hyson)	lb.	.895	(Hyson)	lb.	.727
1831,	lb.	.516	(Souchong; high)	lb.	.509
(black)	lb.	.64	(Souchong; low)	lb.	.35
(Hyson)	lb.	1.12	1846, (high)	lb.	.725
(Souchong)	lb.	.598	(medium)	lb.	.554
(young Hyson)	lb.	1.00	(med. low)	lb.	.338
1832, (high)	lb.	.66	(low)	lb.	.268
(medium)	lb.	.497	(old Hyson)	lb.	.66
(low)	lb.	.38	(young Hyson)	lb.	.59
(Hyson)	lb.	1.00	1847, (high)	lb.	.72
(Souchong; high)	lb.	.623	(med. high)	lb.	.583
(Souchong; low)	lb.	.481	(med. low)	lb.	.334
1833,	lb.	.54	(low)	lb.	.25
(Hyson)	lb.	.95	(Hyson)	lb.	.68
(old Hyson)	lb.	.88	(Ningyong)	lb.	.391
(Pekoe)	lb.	.46	(young Hyson; high)	lb.	.60
(Souchong; high)	lb.	.50	(young Hyson; low)	lb.	.50
(Souchong; low)	lb.	.412	1848, (high)	lb.	.785
(young Hyson)	lb.	.789	(medium)	lb.	.589
1834, (Souchong; high)	lb.	.391	(low)	lb.	.325
(Souchong; low)	lb.	.33	(Hyson)	lb.	.345
(young Hyson)	lb.	.60	(Ningyong)	lb.	.375
1835, (high)	lb.	.517	1849, (high)	lb.	.594
(low)	lb.	.374	(medium)	lb.	.415
(black)	lb.	.28	(low)	lb.	.305
(Hyson)	lb.	.75	(Hyson)	lb.	.78
(Souchong)	lb.	.30	1850, (high)	lb.	.772
1837, (high)	lb.	.624	(medium)	lb.	.51
(medium)	lb.	.361	(low)	lb.	.367
(low)	lb.	.25	1851,	lb.	.378
(Souchong)	lb.	.28	(green)	lb.	.58
1838, (high)	lb.	.847	(Hyson; high)	lb.	.759
(medium)	lb.	.625	(Hyson; low)	lb.	.502
(med. low)	lb.	.461	1852, (high)	lb.	.755
(low)	lb.	.28.	(medium)	lb.	.468
(Hyson)	lb.	.78	(low)	lb.	.338
(Pekoe)	lb.	.44	1853,	lb.	.25
(Souchong)	lb.	.38	1854, (high)	lb.	.707
1839, (high)	lb.	.876	(medium)	lb.	.502
(medium)	lb.	.68	(low)	lb.	.376
(low)	lb.	.373	1855, (high)	lb.	.62
(Pekoe; high)	lb.	.44	(medium)	lb.	.50
(Pekoe; low)	lb.	.38	(low)	lb.	.408
(Souchong)	lb.	.333	1856, (high)	lb.	.63
1840, (high)	lb.	.80	(medium)	lb.	.50
(medium)	lb.	.609	(low)	lb.	.41
(low)	lb.	.49	1857, (high)	lb.	.754
(Hyson)	lb.	.46	(medium)	lb.	.555
(Pekoe)	lb.	.44	(low)	lb.	.295
(Souchong)	lb.	.493	1858,	lb.	.564
1841, (high)	lb.	.82	1859, (high)	lb.	.747
(low)	lb.	.604	(medium)	lb.	.607
(Souchong)	lb.	.75	(low)	lb.	.50
1842, (high)	lb.	.76	1860,	lb.	.50

Prices : Fruits.

YEARS.	Basis.	Amount.	YEARS.	Basis.	Amount.
Citron.			*Dried Apple — Con.*		
1830,	lb.	$0.418	1807,	bu.	$1.00
1831,	lb.	.76	1810,	bu.	1.00
1841,	lb.	.34	1812,	bu.	1.17
1844,	lb.	.33	1828,	lb.	.042
1845,	lb.	.32	1829,	lb.	.055
1846, (high)	lb.	.33	1830,	lb.	.05
(low)	lb.	.24	1831, (high)	lb.	.062
1847,	lb.	.33	(low)	lb.	.034
1848,	lb.	.334	1832,	lb.	.07
1850, (high)	lb.	.301	1833,	lb.	.08
(low)	lb.	.24	1835,	lb.	.079
1851,	lb.	.30	1837,	lb.	.065
1852,	lb.	.318	1838,	lb.	.08
1854,	lb.	.339	1839,	lb.	.079
1855, (high)	lb.	.40	1843,	lb.	.044
(low)	lb.	.325	1845, (high)	lb.	.067
1856,	lb.	.34	(low)	lb.	.045
1857, (high)	lb.	.48	1846,	lb.	.069
(low)	lb.	.373	1847,	lb.	.069
1858, (high)	lb.	.357	1848,	lb.	.065
(low)	lb.	.26	1849,	lb.	.068
Currants.			1850, (high)	lb.	.138
1802,	lb.	.167	(low)	lb.	.059
1804,	lb.	.181	1851,	lb.	.07
1805,	lb.	.25	1852,	lb.	.089
1806, (high)	lb.	.28	1854,	lb.	.087
(low)	lb.	.166	1855,	lb.	.124
1807,	lb.	.146	1856,	lb.	.093
1808,	lb.	.167	1857,	lb.	.17
1809,	lb.	.125	1858,	lb.	.111
1810,	lb.	.167	1859,	lb.	.12
1811,	lb.	.163			
1813,	lb.	.167	*Figs.*		
1819,	lb.	.22	1805,	lb.	.25
1820,	lb.	.15	1806,	lb.	.25
1821,	lb.	.20	1816,	lb.	.25
1823,	lb.	.25	1817,	lb.	.20
1824,	lb.	.20	1818, (high)	lb.	.20
1825,	lb.	.25	(low)	lb.	.14
1828,	lb.	.18	1819,	lb.	.13
1829,	lb.	.20	1820, (wholesale)	lb.	.083
1830, (high)	lb.	.25	1826,	lb.	.10
(low)	lb.	.175	1828,	lb.	.08
1831, (high)	lb.	.165	1829,	lb.	.165
(low)	lb.	.122	1830,	lb.	.145
1832,	lb.	.125	1831,	lb.	.125
1837,	lb.	.14	1832,	lb.	.14
1838,	lb.	.118	1837,	lb.	.125
1839,	lb.	.168	1843,	lb.	.123
1840,	lb.	.163	1844,	lb.	.14
1841,	lb.	.159	1845,	lb.	.138
1843,	lb.	.123	1846,	lb.	.122
1844,	lb.	.14	1847,	lb.	.121
1845,	lb.	.14	1848,	lb.	.119
1846,	lb.	.14	1850,	lb.	.152
1847,	lb.	.141	1851,	lb.	.152
1848,	lb.	.123	1852,	lb.	.12
1850,	lb.	.123	1856,	lb.	.173
1851,	lb.	.123	1857,	lb.	.24
1852,	lb.	.123	1858,	lb.	.154
1854,	lb.	.30			
1855,	lb.	.251	*Lemons.*		
1856, (high)	lb.	.331	1783,	ea.	.05
(low)	lb.	.252	1802, (high)	doz.	.834
1857, (high)	lb.	.332	(low)	doz.	.416
(low)	lb.	.183	1803, (high)	doz.	.50
1858, (high)	lb.	.211	(low)	doz.	.416
(low)	lb.	.159	1804,	doz.	.334
1859, (high)	lb.	.20	1805, (high)	doz.	1.00
(low)	lb.	.157	(low)	doz.	.584
Dried Apple.			1806, (high)	doz.	.50
1791,	bu.	.833	(medium)	doz.	.38
1803,	bu.	1.08	(low)	doz	.25
			1807,	ea.	.031
			1808,	ea.	.083

Prices: Fruits — CONTINUED.

Years.	Ba-sis.	Amount.	Years.	Ba-sis.	Amount.
Lemons — Con.			*Oranges — Con.*		
1809,	ea.	$0.035	1837,	doz.	$0.50
1810, (high)	doz.	.50	1838,	doz.	.206
(low)	doz.	.125	1839, (high)	doz.	.30
1811,	doz.	.30	(low)	doz.	.24
1812,	doz.	.417	1843, (high)	doz.	.239
1813,	doz.	.50	(low)	doz.	.171
1816,	doz.	.50	1845, (high)	doz.	.60
1817,	doz.	.40	(medium)	doz.	.24
1819,	doz.	.60	(low)	doz.	.12
1820, (high)	doz.	.728	1846, (high)	doz.	.333
(low)	doz.	.448	(medium)	doz.	.221
1822,	ea.	.06	(low)	doz.	.12
	doz.	.33	1847, (high)	doz.	.242
1823, (high)	doz.	.50	(medium)	doz.	.197
(low)	doz.	.24	(low)	doz.	.12
1824,	doz.	.36	1848, (high)	doz.	.341
1825,	doz.	.50	(medium)	doz.	.233
1826,	doz.	.38	(low)	doz.	.168
	box	4.00	1849,	ea.	.026
1827,	doz.	.20	1850, (high)	doz.	.345
1828,	doz.	.30	(medium)	doz.	.239
1829,	doz.	.22	(low)	doz.	.15
1830, (high)	doz.	.166	1851, (high)	doz.	.358
(low)	doz.	.125	(low)	doz.	.244
1831,	doz.	.36	1852, (high)	doz.	.36
1833, (high)	doz.	.20	(low)	doz.	.241
(low)	doz.	.12	1859,	doz.	.20
1834, (high)	doz.	.375	*Prunes.*		
(low)	doz.	.125			
1835,	doz.	.25	1805,	lb.	.25
1837,	doz.	.221	1806,	lb.	.25
1838, (high)	doz.	.336	1846, (high)	lb.	.125
(low)	doz.	.23	(low)	lb.	.09
1839, (high)	doz.	.366	1848,	lb.	.12
(low)	doz.	.236	1851,	lb.	.122
1840, (high)	doz.	.30	1852,	lb.	.10
(low)	doz.	.22	1859,	lb.	.10
1841,	doz.	.24	*Raisins.*		
1842,	ea.	.019			
1843, (high)	doz.	.32	1782,	lb.	.306
(low)	doz.	.229	1783,	lb.	.143
1844, (high)	doz.	.24	1784,	lb.	.111
(low)	doz.	.173	1794,	lb.	.133
1845, (high)	doz.	.345	1801, (high)	lb.	.117
(low)	doz.	.21	(low)	lb.	.10
1846, (high)	doz.	.244	1802, (high)	lb.	.25
(low)	doz.	.183	(low)	lb.	.103
1847, (high)	doz.	.34	1803, (high)	lb.	.25
(low)	doz.	.226	(low)	lb.	.125
1848, (high)	doz.	.334	1804,	lb.	.25
(low)	doz.	.234	1805, (high)	lb.	.153
1849, (high)	doz.	.28	(low)	lb.	.125
(low)	doz.	.232	1806, (high)	lb.	.25
1850,	doz.	.213	(low)	lb.	.123
1851,	doz.	.221	1807, (high)	lb.	.25
1852,	doz.	.209	(low)	lb.	.125
1855, (high)	doz.	.36	1809,	lb.	.25
(low)	doz.	.248	1810,	lb.	.125
1856,	doz.	.224	1812,	lb.	.25
1857, (high)	doz.	.36	1813, (high)	lb.	.333
(low)	doz.	.236	(low)	lb.	.206
1858, (high)	doz.	.36	1814,	lb.	.323
(low)	doz.	.24	1815,	lb.	.375
1859, (high)	doz.	.36	1816,	lb.	.139
(low)	doz.	.233	1817,	lb.	.131
			1818,	lb.	.135
Oranges.			1819, (high)	lb.	.14
1818,	ea.	.062	(low)	lb.	.10
	doz.	.60	1820,	lb.	.094
1829,	doz.	.50	1821, (high)	lb.	.25
1831,	doz.	.42	(low)	lb.	.108
1832,	doz.	.50	1822, (high)	lb.	.20
1833,	doz.	.50	(low)	lb.	.103
1834,	doz.	.50	1823,	lb.	.09

Prices: Fruits — CONCLUDED.

YEARS.	Basis	Amount.	YEARS.	Basis	Amount.
Raisins — Con.			*Raisins — Con.*		
1824,	lb.	$0.095	1845, (high)	lb.	$0.139
1825,	lb.	.14	(medium)	lb.	.114
1826,	lb.	.10	(low)	lb.	.077
1827,	lb.	.18	1846, (high)	lb.	.124
1828,	lb.	.17	(low)	lb.	.092
1829,	lb.	.10	1847, (high)	lb.	.125
1830, (high)	lb.	.17	(low)	lb.	.084
(low)	lb.	.104	1848, (high)	lb.	.123
1831, (high)	lb.	.167	(low)	lb.	.085
(low)	lb.	.101	1849, (high)	lb.	.123
1832, (high)	lb.	.193	(low)	lb.	.082
(low)	lb.	.099	1850, (high)	lb.	.148
1833,	lb.	.08	(low)	lb.	.101
1834,	lb.	.08	1851, (high)	lb.	.141
1835,	lb.	.093	(low)	lb.	.10
1837, (high)	lb.	.12	1852, (high)	lb.	.117
(low)	lb.	.085	(low)	lb.	.08
1838,	lb.	.071	1854, (high)	lb.	.175
(layer)	lb.	.125	(low)	lb.	.133
1839, (high)	lb.	.124	1855, (high)	lb.	.167
(low)	lb.	.071	(low)	lb.	.113
1840, (high)	lb.	.12	1856, (high)	lb.	.20
(low)	lb.	.067	(low)	lb.	.168
1841, (high)	lb.	.10	1857, (high)	lb.	.228
(low)	lb.	.065	(low)	lb.	.129
1842, (high)	lb.	.10	1858, (high)	lb.	.14
(low)	lb.	.064	(low)	lb.	.09
1843, (high)	lb.	.121	1859, (high)	lb.	.167
(medium)	lb.	.091	(low)	lb.	.135
(low)	lb.	.065	1860, (high)	lb.	.16
1844,	lb.	.111	(low)	lb.	.125

Prices: Fuel.

YEARS.	Basis	Amount.	YEARS.	Basis	Amount.
Bark.			*Wood — Con.*		
1805,	cd.	$7.24	1754,	ft.	$0.194
1806,	cd.	6.07	1755,	ft.	.139
1808,	cd.	5.19	1756, (high)	ft.	.194
1810, (high)	cd.	6.94	(low)	ft.	.111
(low)	cd.	5.46	1757,	ft.	.118
1811,	cd.	7.00	1758,	ft.	.13
1812, (high)	cd.	8.50	1759,	ft.	.139
(med. high)	cd.	7.41	1760,	ft.	.167
(medium)	cd.	6.21	1761,	ft.	.167
(low)	cd.	2.00	1764,	ft.	.222
1820,	cd.	6.00	1765, (high)	cd.	1.78
1821,	cd.	6.00	(low)	cd.	1.50
			1777,	ft.	.189
Charcoal.			(walnut)	ft.	.333
1795,	bu.	.063	1780,	cd.	2 00
1801, (by the basket)	b'k't	.25	1782,	ft.	.201
1811, (by the basket)	b'k't	.26		cd.	.556
1814,	bu.	.163	1783,	cd.	1.33
1815, (by the basket)	b'k't	.25	1784,	cd.	.518
1816, (by the basket)	b'k't	.30	(oak)	cd.	1.17
			1785, (walnut)	ft.	.292
Coal.			1786, (pine)	cd.	.25
1782,	cwt.	1.03	1787,	cd.	5.00
1831,	ton	8.50	1788,	cd.	2.00
1832,	ton	9.50	(walnut)	ft.	.50
1833,	ton	7.00	1790,	ft.	.167
1835,	ton	7.50	1793,	cd.	3.17
1836,	ton	9.00	1794, (high)	cd.	3.42
1837,	ton	9.13	(low)	cd.	.667
1839,	ton	8.50	(pine)	cd.	1.17
1855,	bu.	.375	1795,	ft.	.209
1857,	ton	7.00	(pine)	cd.	1.00
			1796,	cd.	5.41
Wood.			1797, (wholesale)	cd.	3.07
1752,	ft.	.139	1798, (pine)	cd.	.667
1753,	ft.	.139	1799,	ft.	.833

Prices: Fuel — Concluded.

Years.	Basis.	Amount.	Years.	Basis.	Amount.
Wood — Con.			*Wood* — Con.		
1799, ...	cd.	$1.58	1817, (low)	cd.	$5.00
(wholesale) . .	cd.	1.33	(oak) . . .	cd.	4.90
1800, . . .	ft.	.416	(pine; high) . .	cd.	2.83
(high) . . .	cd.	4.33	(pine; low) . .	cd.	2.61
(low) . . .	cd.	3.33	1818, (oak) . .	ft.	.647
(oak) . . .	ft.	.375	(pine) . . .	ft.	.368
(walnut) . . .	ft.	.50	1819, (high) . .	cd.	5.95
1802, . . .	cd.	4.72	(low) . . .	cd.	4.00
(hard) . . .	cd.	3.94	(pine; high) . .	cd.	1.92
1803, . . .	cd.	3.97	(pine; low) . .	cd.	1.00
(hard) . . .	cd.	4.15	1820, . . .	cd.	4.00
1804, (high) . .	cd.	7.22	(oak) . . .	ft.	.873
(low) . . .	cd.	5.32	(oak) . . .	cd.	6.00
(hard) . . .	cd.	5.00	1821, . . .	ft.	.25
1805, . . .	ft.	.396	(high) . . .	cd.	5.67
(high) . . .	cd.	6.50	(low) . . .	cd.	3.00
(med. high) . .	cd.	6.31	(oak) . . .	cd.	4.00
(medium) . .	cd.	5.00	1822, . . .	ft.	.408
(low) . . .	cd.	3.66		cd.	3.86
1806, (high) . .	cd.	6.50	(oak) . . .	ft.	.438
(med. high) . .	cd.	6.21	(pine) . . .	cd.	2.00
(medium) . .	cd.	5.50	1823, (oak) . .	cd.	5.36
(low) . . .	cd.	4.89	1824, . . .	cd.	3.50
(pine) . . .	ft.	.229	(pine) . . .	ft.	.314
1807, (high) . .	cd.	6.51	(pine) . . .	cd.	2.00
(low) . . .	cd.	5.33	1825, . . .	ft.	.45
(hard) . . .	ft.	.37		cd.	5.00
(pine) . . .	ft.	.23	(pine) . . .	cd.	3.0
1808, (high) . .	cd.	5.00	1826, . . .	cd.	3.50
(low) . . .	cd.	3.97	(maple) . . .	ft.	.687
(pine) . . .	cd.	4.42	(pine; high) . .	cd.	2.84
1809, . . .	cd.	5.36	(pine; low) . .	cd.	2.25
(wholesale, high)	cd.	4.14	1827, (maple) . .	cd.	5.08
(wholesale, low)	cd.	2.30	(oak) . . .	cd.	3.50
(hard) . . .	cd.	5.83	(pine) . . .	ft.	.436
(pine) . . .	cd.	1.74	(pine) . . .	cd.	3.00
1810, (high) . .	ft.	.472	1828, . . .	ft.	.687
(low) . . .	ft.	.333	(maple) . . .	ft.	.524
(high) . . .	cd.	5.99	(oak) . . .	cd.	3.50
(low) . . .	cd.	4.93	(pine) . . .	cd.	2.75
(oak) . . .	cd.	4.00	1829, (pine) . .	ft.	.344
(pine) . . .	ft.	.229	1830, . . .	cd.	3.81
(spruce) . . .	cd.	3.00	1831, (high) . .	cd.	5.00
1811, . . .	ft.	.626	(low) . . .	cd.	3.37
(high) . . .	cd.	7.00	(pine) . . .	cd.	3.00
(low) . . .	cd.	6.44	1832, (oak; high) .	ft.	1.09
(wholesale) . .	cd.	5.12	(oak; low) . .	ft.	.563
(oak) . . .	ft.	.874	1833, . . .	cd.	3.50
(pine) . . .	ft.	.50	(hard) . . .	cd.	4.00
1812, . . .	ft.	.334	1834, . . .	cd.	3.74
(high) . . .	cd.	7.00	(pine) . . .	cd.	3.00
(medium) . .	cd.	6.10	1840, . . .	cd.	5.15
(low) . . .	cd.	5.76	(hard; high) . .	cd.	6.00
(wholesale, high)	cd.	4.22	(hard; low) . .	cd.	4.33
(wholesale, low)	cd.	1.67	(hemlock) . .	cd.	2.75
(maple) . . .	cd.	3.00	(pine; high) . .	cd.	3.50
(pine) . . .	cd.	1.25	(pine; low) . .	cd.	2.23
(slabs) . . .	cd.	1.25	1841, . . .	ft.	.61
1813, (high) . .	cd.	7.52	1845, (wholesale) .	cd.	1.79
(medium) . .	cd.	5.96	1846, . . .	cd.	2.94
(low) . . .	cd.	4.00	1847, (high) . .	cd.	5.00
1814, . . .	ft.	.375	(low) . . .	cd.	2.57
(high) . . .	cd.	6.00	(wholesale) . .	cd.	4.03
(low) . . .	cd.	1.00	1848, . . .	cd.	5.00
(birch) . . .	cd.	3.67	1850, (high) . .	cd.	4.97
(maple) . . .	cd.	4.17	(low) . . .	cd.	2.51
(oak) . . .	ft.	.416	(pine) . . .	cd.	4.50
(pine) . . .	ft.	.25	1851, (high) . .	cd.	7.40
(pine) . . .	cd.	2.67	(low) . . .	cd.	4.09
1815, . . .	ft.	.292	1852, . . .	cd.	5.00
(pine) . . .	cd.	2.34	1853, . . .	cd.	2.56
(walnut) . . .	cd.	6.00	1855, . . .	cd.	6.09
1816, . . .	cd.	6.89	1856, . . .	cd.	7.00
(pine; high) . .	cd.	4.00	1857, . . .	cd.	6.50
(pine; low) . .	cd.	1.95	1858, . . .	ft.	.751
1817, (high) . .	cd.	6.97		cd.	6.00

Prices: Furniture.

Years.	Basis.	Amount.	Years.	Basis.	Amount.
Bed Cords.			*Chairs.*		
1799,	ea.	$0.372	1792, (dining)	doz.	$14.00
1822,	ea.	.50	1793, (fanback)	doz.	10.00
1830, (high)	ea.	.58	1794,	ea.	2.00
(low)	ea.	.33	(birch)	doz.	20.00
1831,	ea.	.33	(easy)	ea.	11.00
			1796, (arm)	ea.	2.67
Bedsteads.			1812,	ea.	4.50
1792,	ea.	2.00	1814, (bamboo)	ea.	2.33
1793, (birch)	ea.	2.50	1820, (fancy)	doz.	48.00
1794,	ea.	15.00	(Grecian)	doz.	72.00
1796, (with sacking bottom)	ea.	16.00			
1814,	ea.	20.00	*Tables.*		
			1793, (card)	ea.	6.00
Bureaus.			(writing)	ea.	25.00
1794,	ea.	23.33	1814, (4 ft.)	ea.	12.00
1814,	ea.	25.00			

Prices: Liquors and Beverages.

Years.	Basis.	Amount.	Years.	Basis.	Amount.
Aniseed.			*Brandy — Con.*		
1803,	gal.	$0.75	1810, (high)	gal.	$1.75
1804,	gal.	.797	(low)	gal.	1.33
1805,	gal.	.80	1811,	gal.	1.70
1806, (high)	gal.	.81	(wholesale)	gal.	1.50
(low)	gal.	.60	1812,	qt.	.67
1807,	gal.	.60	1813,	gal.	2.32
1811,	gal.	.80	1814, (high)	gal.	3.00
1813,	qt.	.345	(low)	gal.	2.50
1814,	qt.	.36	1815, (high)	qt.	.81
			(low)	qt.	.50
Beer.			1816,	gal.	1.76
1807, (wholesale)	gal.	.192	1817,	gal.	2.24
1812,	gal.	.233	1819,	gal.	1.76
1831,	bbl.	7.00	1820,	gal.	1.32
1838,	qt.	.086	1824,	gal.	1.50
1839,	qt.	.085	1825,	gal.	1.50
1846,	gal.	.315	1826,	gal.	1.50
			1827,	qt.	.38
Brandy.			1828,	gal.	1.40
1782,	qt.	.422	(wholesale)	gal.	1.15
1783,	qt.	.272	(cognac)	qt.	.375
1784,	qt.	.25	1829, (cognac)	qt.	.38
1793,	gal.	1.30	1830,	qt.	.31
1794,	gal.	1.44	(cognac)	qt.	.38
(wholesale)	gal.	1.09	1831,	qt.	.33
1795,	gal.	1.67	(cognac)	qt.	.41
1797, (wholesale)	gal.	1.46	1832, (cognac)	qt.	.50
1798, (wholesale)	gal.	1 44	1833, (cognac)	qt.	1.00
1799,	qt.	.38	1845,	gal.	2.00
(wholesale)	gal.	1.58	1854,	qt.	.875
1800, (wholesale)	gal.	1.17			
1801,	qt.	.292	*Cider.*		
1802, (high)	gal.	2.00	1755,	bbl.	.889
(low)	gal.	1.50	1757,	bbl.	.667
1803,	gal.	1.46	1761,	bbl.	1.00
(wholesale)	gal.	1.33	1763,	bbl.	1.00
1804,	qt.	.416	1764,	bbl.	1.00
	gal.	1.44	1766,	bbl.	.667
1805, (high)	gal.	1.75	1767,	bbl.	1.00
(low)	gal.	1.33	1770, (high)	bbl.	1.22
1806,	gal.	1.40	(low)	bbl.	.933
(wholesale, high)	gal.	1.00	1771,	bbl.	1.15
(wholesale, low)	gal.	.762	1772, (high)	bbl.	.978
1807, (high)	gal	1.50	(low)	bbl.	.667
(low)	gal	1.00	1773,	bbl.	1.00
(cognac; wholesale)	gal.	1.20	1774,	bbl.	.667
1808, (high)	gal.	2.00	1775,	bbl.	.716
(low)	gal.	1.50	1779,	gal.	.089
1809, (high)	gal.	1.75	1782,	bbl.	1.00
(low)	gal.	1.46	1791, (wholesale)	gal.	.032
1810,	qt.	.408	1793,	bbl.	3.00

Prices: Liquors and Beverages — CONTINUED.

YEARS.	Basis.	Amount.	YEARS.	Basis.	Amount.
Cider — Con.			*Gin* — Con.		
1794,	gal.	$0.042	1814, (high)	gal.	$1.20
1795,	gal.	.083	(low)	gal.	.989
1797,	gal.	.096	1815, (high)	gal.	1.20
1798,	gal.	.025	(medium)	gal.	1.13
1800,	gal.	.034	(low)	gal.	.904
1801, (high)	bbl.	4.00	1816,	gal.	.917
(low)	bbl.	3.33	1821,	qt.	.125
1802, (high)	gal.	.111	1822,	qt.	.17
(low)	gal.	.063	1827, (Holland)	qt.	.30
	bbl.	3.00	1828, (Holland)	gal.	1.20
1807,	gal.	.08	1830, (Holland)	qt.	.30
1810,	gal.	.083	1831,	qt.	.12
1811,	gal.	.57	(Holland)	qt.	.31
(high)	bbl.	3.00	1832, (Holland)	qt.	.328
(low)	bbl.	1.50	1833, (Holland)	qt.	.324
1813, (high)	gal.	.167	1834,	qt.	.28
(low)	gal.	.123		gal.	1.30
	bbl.	2.50	1835, (Holland)	pt.	.14
1816,	gal.	.17	*Rum.*		
	bbl.	3.00			
1817, (high)	bbl.	2.00	1761,	gal.	.50
(low)	bbl.	1.66	1764,	pt.	.10
1818,	bbl.	2.50	1765,	pt.	.111
1821,	gal.	.20	1779,	gal.	.444
1830,	qt.	.04	1781,	gal.	.444
1834,	qt.	.03	1782,	qt.	.333
1835,	qt.	.033	1783,	qt.	.227
1837,	gal.	.153	1784, (high)	qt.	.213
1838,	gal.	.137	(low)	qt.	.111
1839, (high)	qt.	.063	(wholesale)	qt.	.108
(low)	qt.	.03	1785,	gal.	.369
1841,	gal.	.121	1792, (cherry)	gal.	1.33
1842,	gal.	.12	1793, (New England)	gal.	.667
1843,	qt.	.04	(West India)	gal.	1.08
(high)	gal.	.25	(West India; wholesale)	gal.	.821
(medium)	gal.	.183	1794, (wholesale)	gal.	.923
(low)	gal.	.12	(New England)	gal.	.798
1844,	qt.	.03	(West India)	gal.	1.00
1845,	gal.	.123	1798, (wholesale)	gal.	1.17
1846,	gal.	.153	1799,	pt.	.13
1847, (high)	gal.	.195	(wholesale)	gal.	1.25
(low)	gal.	.09	(New England)	qt.	.20
1848,	gal.	.188	(West India)	qt.	.277
1850,	qt.	.04	(West India; high)	gal.	1.38
1851,	qt.	.04	(West India; low)	gal.	1.08
1852,	qt.	.045	1800,	qt.	.15
1854,	qt.	.05	(high)	gal.	1.00
1858,	gal.	.10	(low)	gal.	.75
			(wholesale)	gal.	.875
Gin.			1801, (wholesale)	gal.	1.08
1784,	qt.	.443	(West India)	qt.	.292
1794,	gal.	1.17	1802, (New England)	gal.	.50
(wholesale)	gal.	.954	(West India; high)	gal.	1.25
1797, (wholesale)	gal.	.958	(West India; medium)	gal.	1.00
1798, (wholesale)	gal.	1.08	(West India; low)	gal.	.611
1799,	gal.	1.33	1803, (wholesale)	gal.	.962
1801, (wholesale)	gal.	1.20	(New England)	qt.	.145
1803, (wholesale)	gal.	1.13	(New England; wholesale)	gal.	.502
1804, (Holland)	gal.	.94	(West India)	gal.	1.00
1805, (wholesale)	gal.	.95	1804, (wholesale)	gal.	1.05
1806,	qt.	.333	(New England)	gal.	.629
(wholesale)	gal.	.995	(New England; wholesale)	gal.	.568
1807,	gal.	1.24	(West India)	gal.	1.00
(wholesale)	gal.	1.02	1805,	gal.	.667
1808,	gal.	1.50	(wholesale)	gal.	.89
(wholesale)	gal.	1.25	(New England; wholesale)	gal.	.526
1809, (wholesale)	gal.	1.10	(West India)	gal.	1.00
1810, (high)	gal.	1.52	1806, (New England)	gal.	.482
(low)	gal.	1.20	(West India)	gal.	1.00
(wholesale)	gal.	.90	1807,	gal.	1.25
1811, (American; wholesale)	gal.	.92	(wholesale)	gal.	.86
(New England; wholesale)	gal.	1.06			
1813, (wholesale)	gal.	.915			

Prices: Liquors and Beverages — CONTINUED.

YEARS.	Basis.	Amount.	YEARS.	Basis.	Amount.
Rum — Con.			*Rum* — Con.		
1807, (New England; wholesale)	gal.	$0.44	1825, (New England)	gal.	$0.40
(West India)	gal.	1.00	(West India)	gal.	1.00
1808, (cherry)	gal.	1.33	1826,	gal.	.35
(New England; wholesale)	gal.	.54	1827, (West India)	qt.	.225
(West India)	gal.	1.00	1828,	qt.	.25
1809, (high)	gal.	.95	(Jamaica)	gal.	1.19
(low)	gal.	.678	(New England)	gal.	.389
(New England)	gal.	.606	1829, (West India)	qt.	.25
(West India)	qt.	.354	1830, (high)	qt.	.19
(West India)	gal.	1.25	(low)	qt.	.10
1810, (Medford; wholesale)	gal.	.59	(New England)	gal.	.30
(New England; wholesale)	gal.	.623	(West India)	qt.	.25
(West India)	gal.	1.10	1832, (West India)	qt.	.25
(West India; wholesale)	gal.	.89	1834,	qt.	.111
1811,	qt.	.30	1835,	qt.	.11
(high)	gal.	1.05	(West India)	qt.	.26
(low)	gal.	.784			
(New England)	gal.	.704	*Snakeroot.*		
(New England; wholesale)	gal.	.598	1805, (wholesale)	gal.	.80
(West India; high)	gal.	1.24	1806,	gal.	.80
(West India; low)	gal	1.07	1812,	gal.	.90
1812, (wholesale, high)	gal.	1.15			
(wholesale, low)	gal	.95	*Wine.*		
(New England)	gal.	.871	1783,	qt.	.362
(New England; wholesale, high)	gal.	.749	1784,	qt.	.306
(New England; wholesale, low)	gal.	.583	1792, (Malaga)	gal.	1.11
(West India; wholesale)	gal.	1.25	1793, (sherry)	gal.	1.27
1813,	qt.	.248	(sherry; wholesale)	gal.	1.14
(high)	gal.	1 12	1794,	gal.	1.89
(low)	gal.	.85	(wholesale)	gal.	1.30
(New England; high)	gal.	1.44	1795, (high)	gal.	2.00
(New England; low)	gal.	1.03	(low)	gal.	1.67
(New England; wholesale, high)	gal.	.95	1796, (sherry)	gal.	1.08
(New England; wholesale, low)	gal.	.775	1797, (sherry; wholesale)	gal.	1.08
(West India)	qt.	.36	1798, (sherry; wholesale)	gal.	1.11
(West India)	gal.	1.25	1801, (sherry)	qt.	.416
(West India; wholesale, high)	gal.	1.20	1802,	gal.	1.17
(West India; wholesale, low)	gal.	1.13	(sherry)	gal.	1.50
1814, (New England)	gal.	1.00	1803,	gal.	1.68
(West India; high)	gal.	2.33	(Lisbon; wholesale, high)	gal.	1.40
(West India; low)	gal.	1.98	(Lisbon; wholesale, low)	gal.	1.25
1815, (West India; high)	gal.	1.90	(sherry)	gal.	1.42
(West India; low)	gal.	1.40	(sherry; wholesale)	gal.	1.33
1816, (New England; wholesale)	gal.	.62	1804,	gal.	1.67
(West India)	gal.	1.00	(Corsica; wholesale)	gal.	.90
1817, (high)	gal.	1.33	(Lisbon)	gal.	1.45
(low)	gal.	.748	(Lisbon; wholesale)	gal.	1.34
(New England)	gal.	.64	(Madeira; wholesale)	gal.	2.25
(West India; high)	gal.	1.33	(port; wholesale)	gal.	1.14
(West India; low)	gal.	1.00	(sherry; wholesale)	gal.	1.33
1818,	gal.	1.34	1805,	gal.	1.01
1819,	qt.	.16	(Corsica; wholesale, high)	gal.	.90
(New England)	gal.	.48	(Corsica; wholesale, low)	gal.	.749
(West India)	gal.	1.00	(Lisbon; wholesale)	gal.	1.30
1820, (wholesale)	gal.	.45	(sherry; wholesale)	gal.	1.25
(New England)	gal.	.37	1806, (wholesale)	gal.	1.30
1821, (West India)	qt.	.25	(Lisbon; wholesale)	gal.	1.33
1822, (Jamaica; high)	gal.	1.25	(sherry; wholesale)	gal.	1.25
(Jamaica; low)	gal.	1.00	1807,	gal.	1.67
(New England)	qt.	.105	(Lisbon; wholesale)	gal.	1.30
(West India)	qt.	.50	1808,	gal.	1.67
1823, (New England)	gal.	.54	1809,	gal.	2.00
(West India)	gal.	1.12	(Lisbon; wholesale)	gal.	1.33
			(sherry; wholesale)	gal.	1.33
			1810,	gal.	1.96
			(Lisbon; wholesale)	gal.	1.35
			1811,	gal.	1.98
			(Lisbon; wholesale)	gal.	1.33
			1812,	qt.	.53
			(Lisbon; wholesale, high)	gal.	1.67
			(Lisbon; wholesale, low)	gal.	1.50
			1813,	gal.	2.09
			(Lisbon; wholesale)	gal.	1.65

Prices: Liquors and Beverages — CONCLUDED.

YEARS.	Basis.	Amount.	YEARS.	Basis.	Amount.
Wine — Con.			*Wine* — Con.		
1813, (sherry)	gal.	$2.00	1830, (Lisbon)	gal.	$0.90
1814, (Lisbon)	gal.	1.80	(port)	qt.	.38
1815,	qt.	.63	(vidonia)	gal.	1.10
(Lisbon)	gal.	1.80	1831, (Sicily Madeira)	qt.	.33
1816, (Lisbon; high)	gal.	2.00	1832, (Madeira)	qt.	.31
(Lisbon; low)	gal.	1.40	1833, (Sicily Madeira)	qt.	.31
(sherry; high)	gal.	2.25	1837, (high)	qt.	.50
(sherry; low)	gal.	2.00	(low)	qt.	.318
1817, (sherry)	gal.	1.75	1838,	qt.	.275
1818, (Lisbon)	gal.	1.50	(port)	qt.	.50
(sherry)	gal.	1.75	1839, (high)	qt.	.50
1819, (Lisbon)	gal.	1.33	(low)	qt.	.276
(sherry)	gal.	1.60	1841, (port)	gal.	2.00
1820, (sherry)	gal.	1.84	1842, (high)	qt.	.507
(Sicily)	gal.	1.60	(low)	qt.	.25
(Sicily Madeira)	gal.	1.40	1843,	qt.	.248
1821, (Lisbon)	gal.	1.33		gal.	.50
(Sicily Madeira)	gal.	1.62	(port; high)	qt.	.62
1822,	qt.	.25	(port; low)	qt.	.50
(Lisbon)	gal.	1.50	(Sicily Madeira)	qt.	.249
(sherry)	gal.	1.50	1844,	qt.	.24
1824,	pt.	.18	1845,	qt.	.255
(Sicily)	gal.	1.37	(port)	qt.	.50
1828, (vidonia)	gal.	1.30	1846, (high)	qt.	.50
1830,	qt.	.20	(low)	qt.	.249
	gal.	1.33	1848,	qt.	.25
(currant)	qt.	.25			

Prices: Lumber.

YEARS.	Basis.	Amount.	YEARS.	Basis.	Amount.
Boards.			*Joist.*		
1805, (clear)	M.ft.	$22.03	1796, (wholesale)	C.ft.	$2.00
(merchantable)	M.ft.	13.00	1800,	M.ft.	11.00
(merchantable pine)	M.ft.	12.87	1805,	M.ft.	10.00
(refuse)	M.ft.	5.90	1809,	M.ft.	9.00
(spruce)	M.ft.	10.00	*Plank.*		
1806, (clear)	M.ft.	20.12	1757, (2½ inch)	ft.	.005
(merchantable)	M.ft.	13.00	1811, (ash)	M.ft.	35.00
(refuse)	M.ft.	6.48	1812, (2 inch)	C.ft.	2.51
1807, (merchantable)	M.ft.	12.50	(2½ inch)	C.ft.	3.50
(refuse)	M.ft.	6.02	(2 inch white oak)	C.ft.	3.00
1808, (clear)	M.ft.	17.00	1815,	C.ft.	2.00
(merchantable)	M.ft.	10.98	1828, (oak)	C.ft.	1.00
1809, (clear)	M.ft.	18.00	*Shingles.*		
1811, (clear)	M. t.	19.00	1793,	M.	2.30
(clear table)	C.ft.	30.00	1795,	M.	3.33
(merchantable)	M.ft.	10.50	1805,	M.	2.83
(refuse)	M.ft.	5.25	1808,	M.	2.70
1813,	C.ft.	1.50	1811,	M.	2.50
(pine)	M.ft.	14.00	1812,	M.	5.00
1814,	C.ft.	1.33	1828,	M.	2.00
1816, (20 feet long)	M.ft.	17.00	*Timber.*		
1818,	C.ft.	1.50	1800,	C.ft.	2.64
1823,	C.ft.	1.60	1802,	C.ft.	2.91
Clapboards.			1805,	C.ft.	3.50
1805,	M.	22.00	1823,	ft.	.048
1808,	M.	15.75			

Prices: Meats.

YEARS.	Basis.	Amount.	YEARS.	Basis.	Amount.
Bacon.			*Bacon* — Con.		
1811, (wholesale)	lb.	$0.167	1818, (low)	lb.	$0.129
1813,	lb.	.144	1819,	lb.	.17
1814,	lb.	.163	1821,	lb.	.10
(wholesale, high)	lb.	.14	1822,	lb.	.11
(wholesale, low)	lb.	.11	1823,	lb.	.094
1816,	lb.	.16	1824,	lb.	.10
1818, (high)	lb.	.161	1825, (high)	lb.	.125

Prices: Meats—CONTINUED.

YEARS.	Basis.	Amount.	YEARS.	Basis.	Amount.
Bacon—Con.			*Beef*—Con.		
1825, (low)	lb.	$0.099	1814, (high)	lb.	$0.083
1826,	lb.	.096	(low)	lb.	.069
1827,	lb.	.09	1815, (high)	lb.	.118
1828,	lb.	.102	(medium)	lb.	.087
1829,	lb.	.10	(low)	lb.	.064
1830,	lb.	.086	1816, (high)	lb.	.10
1831,	lb.	.124	(low)	lb.	.063
1832,	lb.	.10	(corned)	lb.	.10
1833, (high)	lb.	.105	1817, (high)	lb.	.139
(low)	lb.	.08	(medium)	lb.	.079
1834,	lb.	.10	(low)	lb.	.059
1835,	lb.	.10	1818, (high)	lb.	.128
1841,	lb.	.076	(medium)	lb.	.102
1843,	lb.	.091	(low)	lb.	.082
1845,	lb.	.105	1819, (high)	lb.	.125
1846,	lb.	.09	(low)	lb.	.084
			1820,	lb.	.073
Beef.			1821, (high)	lb.	.093
1752,	lb.	.033	(low)	lb.	.072
1753,	lb.	.033	(salt)	lb.	.06
1754,	lb.	.055	1822,	lb.	.066
1755,	lb.	.037	1823, (high)	lb.	.095
1756,	lb.	.012	(low)	lb.	.065
1757,	lb.	.022	(wholesale)	lb.	.05
1760,	lb.	.042	1824, (high)	lb.	.087
1761,	lb.	.039	(low)	lb.	.058
1762,	lb.	.034	1825, (high)	lb.	.085
1763,	lb.	.045	(low)	lb.	.053
1764,	lb.	.042	(wholesale)	lb.	.06
1766,	lb.	.048	1826, (high)	lb.	.09
1769,	lb.	.028	(low)	lb.	.061
1780,	lb.	.074	1827,	lb.	.091
1781,	lb.	.033	(wholesale)	lb.	.058
1782,	lb.	.078	(salt; wholesale)	lb.	.06
(wholesale)	lb.	.042	1828, (high)	lb.	.094
1785,	lb.	.042	(low)	lb.	.072
1786, (high)	lb.	.041	(wholesale)	lb.	.05
(low)	lb.	.031	1829, (high)	lb.	.10
1790,	lb.	.039	(low)	lb.	.071
1792,	lb.	.034	(wholesale)	lb.	.045
1793,	lb.	.036	1830, (high)	lb.	.10
1794, (wholesale)	lb.	.053	(medium)	lb.	.065
1795, (wholesale, high)	lb.	.056	(low)	lb.	.035
(wholesale, low)	lb.	.034	1831, (high)	lb.	.099
1797, (wholesale, high)	lb.	.07	(low)	lb.	.054
(wholesale, low)	lb.	.034	1832, (high)	lb.	.095
1798,	lb.	.07	(low)	lb.	.068
(wholesale)	lb.	.034	(wholesale)	lb.	.055
1799, (wholesale)	lb.	.042	1833, (high)	lb.	.101
1800, (wholesale)	lb.	.05	(medium)	lb.	.07
1802,	lb.	.076	(low)	lb.	.04
1803,	lb.	.082	1834, (high)	lb.	.098
1804, (high)	lb.	.08	(low)	lb.	.062
(low)	lb.	.045	(salt)	lb.	.06
1805, (high)	lb.	.083	(steak)	lb.	.06
(low)	lb.	.063	1835, (high)	lb.	.083
(wholesale)	lb.	.049	(low)	lb.	.059
1806, (high)	lb.	.15	1836, (high)	lb.	.116
(low)	lb.	.084	(low)	lb.	.087
1807, (high)	lb.	.099	1837, (high)	lb.	.10
(low)	lb.	.074	(low)	lb.	.036
1808,	lb.	.079	(salt)	lb.	.06
(wholesale)	lb.	.056	1838, (high)	lb.	.124
1809,	lb.	.083	(low)	lb.	.088
(wholesale)	lb.	.036	1839, (high)	lb.	.111
1810, (high)	lb.	.11	(low)	lb.	.09
(low)	lb.	.068	1840, (high)	lb.	.106
1811, (high)	lb.	.10	(low)	lb.	.065
(low)	lb.	.073	1841,	lb.	.111
1812, (high)	lb.	.08	1842, (high)	lb.	.084
(low)	lb.	.061	(low)	lb.	.054
(wholesale)	lb.	.052	1843, (high)	lb.	.10
1813, (high)	lb.	.10	(low)	lb.	.069
(low)	lb.	.074	(wholesale)	lb.	.04

Prices: Meats — Continued.

Years.	Basis.	Amount.	Years.	Basis.	Amount.
Beef — Con.			*Ham* — Con.		
1844, (high)	lb.	$0.102	1855,	lb.	$0.107
(low)	lb.	.064	1858,	lb.	.125
1845, (high)	lb.	.117	1859,	lb.	.125
(low)	lb.	.06	1860,	lb.	.14
1846, (high)	lb.	.116			
(low)	lb.	.065	*Lamb.*		
1847, (high)	lb.	.123	1796,	lb.	.072
(low)	lb.	.083	1802,	lb.	.076
(wholesale)	lb.	.057	(fore-quarter)	lb.	.072
1848,	lb.	.088	(loin)	lb.	.063
(wholesale)	lb.	.057	1803,	lb.	.066
1849, (high)	lb.	.125	1804,	lb.	.079
(low)	lb.	.09	1805,	lb.	.075
1850, (high)	lb.	.113	1806,	lb.	.073
(low)	lb.	.065	1807, (high)	lb.	.096
(wholesale)	lb.	.055	(low)	lb.	.065
1851,	lb.	.123	1808,	lb.	.063
(wholesale)	lb.	.06	1809,	lb.	.065
1852,	lb.	.125	1810,	lb.	.067
(wholesale)	lb.	.053	1811,	lb.	.062
1853, (high)	lb.	.14	1812, (high)	lb.	.065
(low)	lb.	.088	(low)	lb.	.041
(wholesale)	lb.	.07	1813, (high)	lb.	.10
1854,	lb.	.17	(low)	lb.	.062
(wholesale)	lb.	.079	1814, (high)	lb.	.072
1855, (high)	lb.	.134	(low)	lb.	.054
(low)	lb.	.075	1815,	lb.	.067
(wholesale)	lb.	.087	1816, (high)	lb.	.093
(corned)	lb.	.096	(low)	lb.	.049
1856,	lb.	.17	1817,	lb.	.074
(wholesale)	lb.	.09	1818, (high)	lb.	.10
1857, (wholesale)	lb.	.089	(low)	lb.	.071
1858, (corned)	lb.	.095	1819,	lb.	.069
(round)	lb.	.132	1820,	lb.	.058
(rump)	lb.	.125	1821, (high)	lb.	.06
(rump steak)	lb.	.185	(low)	lb.	.043
(sirloin, best cuts)	lb.	.17	1822,	lb.	.066
(sirloin, tips)	lb.	.125	1823,	lb.	.067
1859,	lb.	.10	1824,	lb.	.06
(wholesale, high)	lb.	.083	1825,	lb.	.064
(wholesale, low)	lb.	.06	1826,	lb.	.062
(corned)	lb.	.10	1827,	lb.	.054
(round)	lb.	.125	1828,	lb.	.058
(rump)	lb.	.125	1829,	lb.	.058
(rump steak)	lb.	.167	1830,	lb.	.058
(sirloin, best cuts)	lb.	.167	1831,	lb.	.05
(sirloin, tips)	lb.	.125	1832,	lb.	.072
1860, (wholesale)	lb.	.067	1833,	lb.	.06
(corned)	lb.	.10	1834,	lb.	.069
(round)	lb.	.10	1835,	lb.	.054
(rump)	lb.	.125	1836,	lb.	.093
(rump steak)	lb.	.18	1837,	lb.	.075
(sirloin, best cuts)	lb.	.167	1838, (high)	lb.	.125
(sirloin, tips)	lb.	.125	(low)	lb.	.085
			1839,	lb.	.086
			1840,	lb.	.071
Ham.			1841,	lb.	.081
1790,	lb.	.215	1842, (high)	lb.	.09
1824,	lb.	.10	(low)	lb.	.067
1826,	lb.	.09	1843, (high)	lb.	.10
1832,	lb.	.10	(low)	lb.	.075
1834,	lb.	.10	1844, (high)	lb.	.076
1837,	lb.	.104	(low)	lb.	.043
1843,	lb.	.09	1845,	lb.	.077
1845,	lb.	.106	1846,	lb.	.091
1846,	lb.	.10	1847, (high)	lb.	.087
1847,	lb.	.122	(low)	lb.	.063
(wholesale)	lb.	.107	1848,	lb.	.08
1848,	lb.	.103	1849,	lb.	.081
1849,	lb.	.112	1856,	lb.	.10
1850,	lb.	.103	1858, (hind-quarter)	lb.	.14
1851,	lb.	.117	1859, (hind-quarter)	lb.	.125
1852,	lb.	.13	1860, (hind-quarter)	lb.	.125
1854,	lb.	.125			

Prices: Meats—CONTINUED.

YEARS.	Basis.	Amount.	YEARS.	Basis.	Amount.
Mutton.			*Mutton — Con.*		
1760,	lb.	$0.056	1841, (low)	lb.	$0.069
1767,	lb.	.046	1842,	lb.	.09
1777,	lb.	.083	1843,	lb.	.071
1780,	lb.	.078	1844, (high)	lb.	.10
1783,	lb.	.043	(low)	lb.	.06
1791,	lb.	.035	1845, (high)	lb.	.086
1792,	lb.	.042	(low)	lb.	.053
1794,	lb.	.042	1846,	lb.	.08
1795,	lb.	.06	1847,	lb.	.076
1796,	lb.	.083	1848,	lb.	.08
1797,	lb.	.07	1849,	lb.	.066
1799,	lb.	.042	1851,	lb.	.076
1800,	lb.	.07	1858, (chops)	lb.	.125
1802,	lb.	.065	(leg)	lb.	.147
1803,	lb.	.063	1859, (chops)	lb.	.125
1804,	lb.	.07	(leg)	lb.	.125
1805, (high)	lb.	.10	1860, (chops)	lb.	.125
(low)	lb.	.066	(leg)	lb.	.125
1806,	lb.	.074			
1807,	lb.	.071	*Pork.*		
1808,	lb.	.07	1752,	lb.	.074
1809, (high)	lb.	.10	1754,	lb.	.089
(low)	lb.	.064	1759,	lb.	.078
1810,	lb.	.069	1765,	lb.	.091
1811,	lb.	.069	1766,	lb.	.081
1812, (high)	lb.	.062	1774,	lb.	.067
(low)	lb.	.037	1780,	lb.	.125
1813,	lb.	.065	1782,	lb.	.121
1814, (high)	lb.	.10	1785,	lb.	.097
(low)	lb.	.063	1788, (high)	lb.	.111
1815, (high)	lb.	.10	(low)	lb.	.083
(low)	lb.	.069	1790,	lb.	.111
1816,	lb.	.062	1791,	lb.	.078
1817, (high)	lb.	.094	(lean)	lb.	.028
(low)	lb.	.064	1793,	lb.	.111
1818, (high)	lb.	.10	1794,	lb.	.125
(medium)	lb.	.073	(wholesale)	lb.	.07
(low)	lb.	.05	1795,	lb.	.124
1819, (high)	lb.	.081	(wholesale)	lb.	.071
(low)	lb.	.044		bbl.	22.00
1820,	lb.	.044	1796, (whole hog)	lb.	.083
1821, (high)	lb.	.08	1797, (high)	lb.	.139
(low)	lb.	.047	(low)	lb.	.097
1822, (high)	lb.	.10	1798, (wholesale)	lb.	.07
(low)	lb.	.05	1799, (high)	lb.	.158
1823, (high)	lb.	.08	(low)	lb.	.08
(low)	lb.	.056	1800,	lb.	.153
1824, (high)	lb.	.075	(whole hog)	lb.	.058
(low)	lb.	.052	1802, (high)	lb.	.114
1825, (high)	lb.	.06	(low)	lb.	.07
(low)	lb.	.041	1803, (high)	lb.	.125
1826, (high)	lb.	.094	(low)	lb.	.067
(low)	lb.	.061	(whole hog)	lb.	.065
1827,	lb.	.057	1804,	lb.	.06
1828,	lb.	.066	1805, (high)	lb.	.164
1829, (high)	lb.	.06	(low)	lb.	.122
(low)	lb.	.046	(wholesale)	lb.	.078
1830, (high)	lb.	.08	(whole hog)	lb.	.065
(low)	lb.	.054		bbl.	25.50
1831, (high)	lb.	.075	(corned; wholesale)	lb.	.12
(low)	lb.	.052	1806, (wholesale)	lb.	.166
1832, (high)	lb.	.10	(whole hog; high)	lb.	.184
(low)	lb.	.07	(whole hog; low)	lb.	.107
1833,	lb.	.066	1807, (high)	lb.	.187
1834,	lb.	.064	(med. high)	lb.	.167
1835, (high)	lb.	.085	(medium)	lb.	.12
(low)	lb.	.058	(low)	lb.	.10
1836,	lb.	.056	(wholesale)	lb.	.06
1837,	lb.	.072	1808,	lb.	.087
1838,	lb.	.075	(whole hog)	lb.	.066
1840, (high)	lb.	.10	1809,	lb.	.083
(medium)	lb.	.061	1810, (high)	lb.	.168
(low)	lb.	.03	(low)	lb.	.094
1841, (high)	lb.	.10	1811, (high)	lb.	.142

Prices: Meats—CONTINUED.

YEARS.	Basis.	Amount.	YEARS.	Basis.	Amount.
Pork—Con.			*Pork*—Con.		
1811, (low)	lb.	$0.089	1830, (salt)	lb.	$0.10
(whole hog)	lb.	.085	(spare rib)	lb.	.07
(spare rib)	lb.	10	1831, (high)	lb.	.092
1812, (high)	lb.	.151	(low)	lb.	.055
(medium)	lb.	.097	(whole hog)	lb.	.07
(med. low)	lb.	.073	(fresh)	lb.	.07
(low)	lb.	.069	1832,	lb.	.074
(whole hog)	lb.	.075	(whole hog)	lb.	.067
1813, (high)	lb.	.178	1833, (fresh)	lb.	.08
(low)	lb.	.123	1834,	lb.	.108
(salt; high)	lb.	.162	(whole hog)	lb.	.075
(salt; low)	lb.	.147	(salt)	lb.	.125
(whole hog)	lb.	.09	1835, (salt)	lb.	.126
1814, (high)	lb.	.184	1837, (high)	lb.	.157
(medium)	lb.	.085	(low)	lb.	.108
(low)	lb.	.04	1838, (high)	lb.	.148
(wholesale)	lb.	.173	(medium)	lb.	.10
(whole hog)	lb.	.096	(low)	lb.	.06
(salt; high)	lb.	.195	1839, (high)	lb.	.15
(salt; low)	lb.	.178	(low)	lb.	.125
(spare rib)	lb.	.09	(wholesale)	lb.	.109
1815, (high)	lb.	.212	1840,	lb.	.103
(medium)	lb.	.18	(wholesale)	lb.	.07
(low)	lb.	.10	1841,	lb.	.085
(whole hog)	lb.	.10	(fresh; wholesale)	lb.	.064
1816, (high)	lb.	.181	1842, (high)	lb.	.09
(low)	lb.	.125	(low)	lb.	.077
(salt)	lb.	.197	(whole hog)	lb.	.049
(spare rib)	lb.	.10	1843,	lb.	.086
1817, (high)	lb.	.201	(wholesale, high)	lb.	.059
(low)	lb.	.102	(wholesale, low)	lb.	.03
(wholesale)	lb.	.122	1844, (high)	lb.	.10
(fresh)	lb.	.13	(medium)	lb.	.082
1818, (high)	lb.	.23	(low)	lb.	.06
(medium)	lb.	.198	(whole hog)	lb.	.055
(low)	lb.	.116	1845,	lb.	.087
(whole hog)	lb.	.125	(whole hog)	lb.	.064
	bbl.	35.00	1846,	lb.	.088
1819, (high)	lb.	.166	(wholesale, high)	lb.	.08
(medium)	lb.	.114	(wholesale, low)	lb.	.064
(low)	lb.	.074	1847,	lb.	.12
1820, (high)	lb.	.167	(wholesale)	lb.	.08
(medium)	lb.	.118	1848,	lb.	.109
(low)	lb.	.079	(whole hog)	lb.	.076
(whole hog)	lb.	.072	1849,	lb.	.105
1821, (high)	lb.	.105	(wholesale)	lb.	.069
(low)	lb.	.07	1850,	lb.	.094
(fresh)	lb.	.062	(wholesale)	lb.	.063
1822, (high)	lb.	.125	1851, (high)	lb.	.10
(low)	lb.	.09	(low)	lb.	.063
(whole hog)	lb.	.065	(whole hog)	lb.	.075
1823, (high)	lb.	.10	1852,	lb.	.115
(low)	lb.	.083	(whole hog)	lb.	.075
1824, (high)	lb.	.095	1853, (whole hog)	lb.	.086
(low)	lb.	.069	1854,	lb.	.123
(spare rib)	lb.	.06	(whole hog)	lb.	.089
1825,	lb.	.101	1855,	lb.	.14
(wholesale)	lb.	.07	(wholesale)	lb.	.085
(fresh)	lb.	.095	1856,	lb.	.137
1826, (high)	lb.	.099	(whole hog)	lb.	.101
(low)	lb.	.061	1857, (high)	lb.	.149
(whole hog)	lb.	.07	(low)	lb.	.10
1827,	lb.	.131	1858,	lb.	.107
1828, (high)	lb.	.124	(wholesale)	lb.	.081
(low)	lb.	.087	(fresh)	lb.	.09
(wholesale)	lb.	.065	(salt)	lb.	.14
(fresh)	lb.	.08	1859,	lb.	.112
1829,	lb.	.10	(whole hog)	lb.	.082
(fresh)	lb.	.07	(fresh)	lb.	.125
(salt)	lb.	.09	(salt)	lb.	.11
1830, (high)	lb.	.091	1860, (whole hog)	lb.	.09
(low)	lb.	.065	(fresh)	lb.	.125
(whole hog)	lb.	.07	(salt)	lb.	.10
(fresh)	lb.	.07			

Prices: Meats—CONTINUED.

YEARS.	Ba-sis.	Amount.	YEARS.	Ba-sis.	Amount.
Sausages.			*Veal*—Con.		
1813,	lb.	$0.125	1802, (shoulder)	lb.	$0.056
1814,	lb.	.14	1803,	lb.	.077
1822,	lb.	.109	1804,	lb.	.076
1824,	lb.	.123	(loin)	lb.	.083
1826,	lb.	.125	1805, (high)	lb.	.103
1830,	lb.	.10	(low)	lb.	.091
1831,	lb.	.10	(leg)	lb.	.089
1832,	lb.	.10	(loin)	lb.	.114
1837,	lb.	.127	1806,	lb.	.088
1838,	lb.	.128	(hind-quarter)	lb.	.09
1839,	lb.	.128	(loin)	lb.	.083
1841,	lb.	.094	1807,	lb.	.083
1842,	lb.	.087	(leg)	lb.	.10
1843,	lb.	.085	(loin)	lb.	.10
1844,	lb.	.08	1808,	lb.	.069
1845,	lb.	.082	(fore-quarter)	lb.	.07
1846,	lb.	.077	(leg)	lb.	.074
1847,	lb.	.098	(loin)	lb.	.092
1848,	lb.	.099	1809,	lb	.084
1851,	lb.	.10	(leg)	lb.	.07
1852,	lb.	.10	(loin)	lb.	.08
1856,	lb.	.14	1810,	lb.	.08
1858,	lb.	.10	(leg)	lb.	.088
1859,	lb.	.125	(loin)	lb.	.12
1860,	lb.	.125	1811, (high)	lb.	.12
			(low)	lb.	.089
			(loin)	lb.	.096
Tongue.			1812, (high)	lb.	.16
1804,	lb.	.083	(low)	lb.	.078
1805, (high)	lb.	.10	1813,	lb.	.078
(low)	lb.	.063	(loin)	lb.	.083
1809,	lb.	.08	1814,	lb.	.083
1816,	lb.	.10	(loin)	lb.	.098
1818,	lb.	.125	1815,	lb.	.08
1825,	lb.	.079	(loin)	lb.	.087
1826,	lb.	.124	1816,	lb.	.086
1828,	lb.	.083	(loin)	lb.	.10
1829,	lb.	.067	1817,	lb.	.096
1830,	lb.	.073	(loin)	lb.	.125
1831,	lb.	.075	1818,	lb.	.095
1832,	lb.	.074	(loin; high)	lb.	.125
1833,	lb.	.071	(loin; low)	lb.	.095
1846,	lb.	.124	1819,	lb.	.096
1848,	lb.	.10	1820, (high)	lb.	.084
			(low)	lb.	.058
Tripe.			(loin; high)	lb.	.13
1837,	lb.	.095	(loin; low)	lb.	.07
1838,	lb.	.10	1821,	lb.	.058
1839,	lb.	.10	(loin)	lb.	.076
1841,	lb.	.09	1822,	lb.	.05
1842,	lb.	.086	(loin)	lb.	.075
1843,	lb.	.085	1823, (high)	lb.	.102
1844,	lb.	.08	(low)	lb.	.071
1845,	lb.	.087	(loin)	lb.	.084
1846,	lb.	.08	1824, (high)	lb.	.09
1847,	lb.	.095	(low)	lb.	.058
1848,	lb.	.09	(loin)	lb.	.075
1850,	lb.	.078	1825,	lb.	.062
			(loin)	lb.	.083
Veal.			1826,	lb.	.059
1754,	lb.	.033	(loin)	lb.	.077
1757,	lb.	.022	1827, (high)	lb.	.082
1759,	lb.	.033	(low)	lb.	.058
1765,	lb.	.035	(loin)	lb.	.074
1777,	lb.	.039	1828, (high)	lb.	.106
1783,	lb.	.042	(low)	lb.	.072
1784,	lb.	.042	1829,	lb.	.06
1785,	lb.	.041	(loin)	lb.	.075
1793,	lb.	.089	1830, (high)	lb.	.11
1794,	lb.	.034	(low)	lb.	.063
1795,	lb.	.041	(loin)	lb.	.07
1799,	lb.	.056	1831,	lb.	.05
1800,	lb.	.07	(loin)	lb.	.07
1802,	lb.	.063	1832, (high)	lb.	.075
(loin)	lb.	.08			

Prices: Meats—CONCLUDED.

Years.	Basis.	Amount.	Years.	Basis.	Amount.
Veal—Con.			*Veal*—Con.		
1832, (low)	lb.	$0.052	1844, (loin)	lb.	$0.09
(loin)	lb.	.077	1845, (wholesale)	lb.	.075
1833, (high)	lb.	.089	(breast)	lb.	.083
(low)	lb.	.061	1846, (breast)	lb.	.091
(loin)	lb.	.076	(loin; high)	lb.	.101
1834, (high)	lb.	.072	(loin; low)	lb.	.07
(low)	lb.	.05	1847, (breast)	lb.	.091
(hind-quarter)	lb.	.07	(loin)	lb.	.096
(loin)	lb.	.08	1848, (breast)	lb.	.076
1835, (high)	lb.	.088	(loin)	lb.	.102
(low)	lb.	.065	1849, (breast)	lb.	.08
(loin)	lb.	.08	(loin)	lb.	.106
1836, (high)	lb.	.089	1850, (high)	lb.	.10
(low)	lb.	.055	(low)	lb.	.07
(loin)	lb.	.095	1851, (wholesale)	lb.	.082
1837, (high)	lb.	.133	1852, (wholesale)	lb.	.075
(low)	lb.	.10	1853, (wholesale)	lb.	.088
1838, (high)	lb.	.10	1854, (wholesale; high)	lb.	.104
(low)	lb.	.08	(wholesale; low)	lb.	.075
(breast and neck)	lb.	.095	1855,	lb.	.125
(leg)	lb.	.097	(wholesale; high)	lb.	.10
1839, (breast; high)	lb.	.145	(wholesale; low)	lb.	.082
(breast; low)	lb.	.099	1856, (wholesale)	lb.	.101
(leg)	lb.	.123	1857,	lb.	.105
1840,	lb.	.10	1858, (wholesale)	lb.	.097
(breast and neck)	lb.	.073	(cutlet)	lb.	.17
(leg)	lb.	.093	(shoulder)	lb.	.10
1841,	lb.	.088	1859, (wholesale; high)	lb.	.097
(wholesale)	lb.	.085	(wholesale; low)	lb.	.08
1842,	lb.	.099	(cutlet)	lb.	.18
(loin)	lb.	.082	(shoulder)	lb.	.125
1843,	lb.	.04	1860, (wholesale)	lb.	.087
(loin)	lb.	.073	(cutlet)	lb.	.18
1844, (breast)	lb.	.074	(shoulder)	lb.	.125

Prices: Nuts.

Years.	Basis.	Amount.	Years.	Basis.	Amount.
Almonds.			*Almonds*—Con.		
1805,	lb.	$0.626	1847,	lb.	$0.168
1806,	lb.	.25	1848,	lb.	.166
1807,	lb.	.50	1852,	lb.	.151
1808,	lb.	.25			
1809,	lb.	.25	*Filberts.*		
1810,	lb.	.64	1808,	lb.	.25
1817,	lb.	.22	1837,	lb.	.08
1822,	lb.	.20			
1829,	lb.	.38	*Walnuts.*		
1831,	lb.	.167	1806,	bu.	1.75
1832,	lb.	.25	1810,	bu.	1.00
1833,	lb.	.32	1817,	bu.	1.58
1835,	lb.	.10	1819,	bu.	2.21
1837,	lb.	.15	1821,	bu.	1.25
1842,	lb.	.167	1843,	qt.	.08
1843,	lb.	.15	1848,	lb.	.125

Prices: Oils and Illuminating Fluids.

Years.	Basis.	Amount.	Years.	Basis.	Amount.
Burning Oils and Fluids.			*Burning Oils and Fluids*-Con.		
1785,	gal.	$1.08	1806, (low)	gal.	$0.997
1794,	gal.	.778	(winter-strained)	gal.	.80
1798,	pt.	.22	1807,	gal.	1.00
1800, (sperm; wholesale)	gal.	.583	1808, (sperm; high)	gal.	1.00
1801, (sperm; wholesale)	gal.	.833	(sperm; low)	gal.	.75
1802, (lamp; high)	qt.	.50	(winter; wholesale)	gal.	1.00
(lamp; low)	qt.	.273	1809, (high)	gal.	1.34
1803,	gal.	1.17	(low)	gal.	1.06
1804,	gal.	1.29	(winter; wholesale)	gal.	.90
1805,	gal.	1.23	1810,	qt.	.44
1806, (high)	gal.	1.25	(high)	gal.	1.67

Prices: Oils and Illuminating Fluids — Concluded.

Years.	Basis.	Amount.	Years.	Basis.	Amount.
Burning Oils and Fluids-Con.			*Burning Oils and Fluids*-Con.		
1810, (med. high)	gal.	$1.39	1834,	gal.	$1.06
(medium)	gal.	1.04	(lamp)	qt.	.262
(low)	gal.	.67	1835, (lamp)	gal.	1.06
(wholesale)	gal.	.80	1836, (high)	gal.	1.25
(sperm; wholesale)	gal.	1.10	(low)	gal.	1.10
1811, (high)	gal.	1.67	1837, (high)	qt.	.345
(medium)	gal.	1.47	(low)	qt.	.20
(low)	gal.	1.16		gal.	1.12
(summer; wholesale)	gal.	1.00	1838, (high)	gal.	1.14
(winter; wholesale)	gal.	1.20	(low)	gal.	.993
1812, (high)	gal.	1.80	(winter)	gal.	1.17
(med. high)	gal.	1.60	1839, (high)	qt.	.274
(medium)	gal.	1.40	(low)	qt.	.15
(low)	gal.	1.14	(high)	gal.	1.33
1813,	gal.	1.23	(low)	gal.	1.17
1814,	gal.	1.75	1840, (high)	gal.	1.33
1815,	gal.	1.75	(medium)	gal.	1.25
1816, (high)	gal.	1.77	(low)	gal.	1.15
(low)	gal.	1.58	1841, (high)	gal.	1.25
1817, (high)	gal.	1.60	(medium)	gal.	1.15
(medium)	gal.	1.30	(low)	gal.	1.00
(low)	gal.	.902	1842,	qt.	.45
1818,	qt.	.315	(high)	gal.	1.23
(high)	gal.	1.33	(low)	gal.	.939
(low)	gal.	.982	1843, (high)	qt.	.281
1819, (high)	gal.	1.25	(low)	qt.	.223
(medium)	gal.	1.09	(high)	gal.	.905
(low)	gal.	.92	(low)	gal.	.826
1820, (high)	gal.	1.33	1844, (high)	gal.	1.20
(low)	gal.	1.13	(medium)	gal.	1.11
1821, (high)	gal.	1.34	(low)	gal.	.80
(medium)	gal.	1.00	1845,	qt.	.36
(low)	gal.	.762	(high)	gal.	1.12
(lamp)	qt.	.33	(medium)	gal.	.92
1822,	qt.	.375	(low)	gal.	.799
	gal.	.865	1846, (high)	gal.	1.12
(lamp)	qt.	.34	(medium)	gal.	.987
(lamp)	gal.	1.00	(low)	gal.	.805
1823, (high)	gal.	1.83	(sperm)	gal.	1.16
(low)	gal.	.60	1847, (high)	qt.	.28
(summer)	gal.	.50	(low)	qt.	.22
(winter)	gal.	.65	(high)	gal.	1.31
1824,	gal.	.50	(med. high)	gal.	1.16
1825, (high)	gal.	.75	(medium)	gal.	1.00
(low)	gal.	.50	(low)	gal.	.845
(wholesale)	gal.	.08	1848, (high)	gal.	1.34
(summer)	gal.	.45	(low)	gal.	.796
(winter)	gal.	.53	1849, (high)	qt.	.349
1826, (high)	gal.	.85	(low)	qt.	.214
(low)	gal.	.75	(high)	gal.	1.30
1827,	qt.	.238	(low)	gal.	1.20
	gal.	.662	1850, (high)	gal.	1.38
(summer; wholesale)	gal.	.05	(medium)	gal.	1.00
(winter)	gal.	.90	(low)	gal.	.793
1828, (high)	gal.	1.00	1851,	qt.	.225
(medium)	gal.	.85	1852, (high)	gal.	1.50
(low)	gal.	.725	(medium)	gal.	1.00
1829,	gal.	.767	(low)	gal.	.788
1830, (high)	gal.	1.00	1854,	qt.	.256
(medium)	gal.	.805	1855, (high)	gal.	1.14
(low)	gal.	.533	(low)	gal.	.998
(fall)	gal.	.88	(burning fluid)	qt.	.228
(lamp)	qt.	.22	1856,	gal.	1.06
(winter)	gal.	.98	1857, (high)	gal.	1.14
1831,	qt.	.215	(low)	gal.	.944
	gal.	.825	1858, (high)	gal.	1.49
(lamp; high)	qt.	.29	(medium)	gal.	1.06
(lamp; low)	qt.	.25	(low)	gal.	.719
(winter)	gal.	.562	1859, (high)	gal.	1.12
1832,	qt.	.33	(low)	gal.	.754
(high)	gal.	1.50			
(low)	gal.	8.79	*Linseed Oil.*		
(sperm)	gal.	1.00	1786,	gal.	1.27
(winter)	gal.	1.08	1792,	gal.	.771
1833,	gal.	1.01	1828,	qt.	.29
(lamp)	gal.	1.33			

Prices: Paper.

Years.	Basis.	Amount.	Years.	Basis.	Amount.
Letter Paper.			*Letter Paper — Con.*		
1783,	qr.	$0.202	1829, (low)	qr.	$0.20
(letter sheet)	ea.	.015		r'm	3.00
1784,	qr.	.166	1830,	qr.	.24
1793,	qr.	.209	1831,	r'm	2.63
1794,	qr.	.195	1833,	r'm	1.50
(letter sheet)	ea.	.01	1837,	qr.	.20
1795,	qr.	.195	1838,	qr.	.375
1799,	qr.	.221		r'm	.62
1800,	qr.	.22	1839, (high)	qr.	.38
(letter sheet)	ea.	.01	(medium)	qr.	.24
(blue)	r'm	1.50	(low)	qr.	.10
1801,	qr.	.20	1840,	qr.	.25
(high)	r'm	2.67	(high)	r'm	3.25
(low)	r'm	.875	(low)	r'm	2.75
1802,	qr.	.375	1841, (high)	qr.	.26
	r'm	3.00	(low)	qr.	.05
1803,	qr.	.313	(letter sheet)	ea.	.02
1804, (high)	qr.	.375	1843,	qr.	.24
(low)	qr.	.25		r'm	2.00
(wholesale)	qr.	.175	1845, (high)	qr.	.37
	r'm	1.25	(medium)	qr.	.25
1805, (high)	qr.	.45	(low)	qr.	.198
(low)	qr.	.28	1846,	qr.	.196
	r'm	1.25		r'm	2.00
1806,	qr.	.343	1847,	qr.	.21
(blue)	qr.	.625		r'm	2.50
1807,	qr.	.375	1848, (high)	qr.	.20
(wholesale)	r'm	.833	(low)	qr.	.125
1808, (high)	r'm	3.25	1850,	qr.	.20
(low)	r'm	1.00	(letter sheet)	ea.	.01
1809, (high)	r'm	2.88	1852,	qr.	.24
(low)	r'm	1.08	1855,	qr.	.38
1810, (high)	r'm	3.00	1856, (high)	qr.	.36
(low)	r'm	.916	(low)	qr.	.11
(blue)	r'm	1.25	(high)	r'm	1.96
1811, (blue)	r'm	1.25	(low)	r'm	1.12
1812,	qr.	.25	1857,	qr.	.137
1813,	qr.	.25	1858, (high)	qr.	.25
1816,	qr.	.061	(medium)	qr.	.13
(letter sheet)	ea.	.01	(low)	qr.	.035
1817,	qr.	.063	(letter sheet)	ea.	.01
	r'm	3.17	1859, (high)	qr.	.20
(letter sheet)	ea.	.013	(low)	qr.	.08
(French)	r'm	2.00	(letter sheet)	ea.	.01
1818,	r'm	3.00			
1820, (high)	r'm	2.50	*Wrapping Paper.*		
(low)	r'm	2.00	1798,	r'm	1.17
1823,	qr.	.20	1806, (brown)	qr.	.375
	r'm	.75	1808, (wholesale)	r'm	.80
1824,	r'm	4.50	1809,	r'm	.917
1825,	qr.	.50	1810, (high)	r'm	1.25
1827, (high)	r'm	3.50	(low)	r'm	1.00
(low)	r'm	3.00	1811,	r'm	1.00
1829, (high)	qr.	.34	1812,	r'm	.931

Prices: Poultry and Game.

Years.	Basis.	Amount.	Years.	Basis.	Amount.
Chicken.			*Fowl — Con.*		
1811,	lb.	$0.08	1845,	lb.	$0.139
1815,	lb.	.10	1846,	lb.	.099
1821,	lb.	.063	1848,	lb.	.145
1822,	lb.	.05			
1829,	lb.	.05	*Goose.*		
1830,	lb.	.069	1806,	lb.	.08
1831,	lb.	.063	1815,	lb.	.078
1834,	lb.	.11	1816,	lb.	.09
			1819, (high)	lb.	.109
Fowl.			(low)	lb.	.06
1758,	lb.	.111	1820,	lb.	.08
1830,	lb.	.08	1821,	lb.	.07
1839,	lb.	.125	1822,	lb.	.065

Prices: Poultry and Game—Concluded.

Years.	Basis.	Amount.	Years.	Basis.	Amount.
Goose — Con.			*Turkey* — Con.		
1825,	lb.	$0.07	1815,	lb.	$0.124
1827,	lb.	.05	1816,	lb.	.132
1830,	lb.	.07	1818,	lb.	.14
1832,	lb.	.07	1819,	lb.	.08
1833,	lb.	.08	1820,	lb.	.07
1835,	lb.	.08	1821, (high)	lb.	.085
1837,	lb.	.125	(low)	lb.	.05
1838,	lb.	.101	1822, (high)	lb.	.10
1841,	lb.	.07	(low)	lb.	.059
1842,	lb.	.06	1823,	lb.	.07
1845,	lb.	.06	1824,	lb.	.088
1848,	lb.	.104	1825,	lb.	.09
1849,	lb.	.096	1826,	lb.	.10
			1827,	lb.	.08
Poultry.			1828,	lb.	.12
1815,	lb.	.125	1830,	lb.	.074
1839,	lb.	.125	1832,	lb.	.104
1846,	lb.	.12	1838,	lb.	.141
			1840,	lb.	.11
Turkey.			1841,	lb.	.10
1758,	lb.	.055	1842, (high)	lb.	.153
1788,	lb.	.056	(low)	lb.	.08
1800,	lb.	.055	1844,	lb.	.125
1803,	lb.	.087	1845,	lb.	.116
1804,	lb.	.08	1848,	lb.	.124
1806,	lb.	.12	1855,	lb.	.17
1808,	lb.	.101	1857,	lb.	.16
1809,	lb.	.125	1858,	lb.	.147
1810,	lb.	.103	1859, (high)	lb.	.17
1811, (high)	lb.	.12	(low)	lb.	.125
(low)	lb.	.097	1860, (high)	lb.	.17
1812,	lb.	.10	(low)	lb.	.125
1814,	lb.	.10			

Prices: Ribbons and Laces.

Years.	Basis.	Amount.	Years.	Basis.	Amount.
Lace.			*Lace* — Con.		
1806,	yd.	$0.84	1851,	yd.	$0.30
1810,	yd.	.33	1855, (high)	yd.	.50
1813, (thread; high)	yd.	1.00	(medium)	yd.	.217
(thread; low)	yd.	.75	(low)	yd.	.05
1815,	yd.	.25	1856, (high)	yd.	.432
1820,	yd.	.833	(low)	yd.	.118
1822, (high)	yd.	1.00	1857, (high)	yd.	.506
(low)	yd.	.375	(medium)	yd.	.269
1823,	yd.	.125	(low)	yd.	.14
1824, (cotton)	yd.	.128	1858, (high)	yd.	.492
(thread)	yd.	.75	(low)	yd.	.258
1826,	yd.	.36			
1827,	yd.	.50	*Ribbon.*		
1828, (high)	yd.	1.37	1783, (high)	yd.	.333
(low)	yd.	1.07	(med. high)	yd.	.285
1829, (high)	yd.	1.28	(medium)	yd.	.161
(medium)	yd.	.333	(med. low)	yd.	.096
(low)	yd.	.08	(low)	yd.	.038
1830, (high)	yd.	.687	1784, (high)	yd.	.154
(low)	yd.	.273	(medium)	yd.	.103
1831, (high)	yd.	.75	(low)	yd.	.028
(low)	yd.	.08	1794,	yd.	.097
1833,	yd.	.09	1795,	yd.	.185
1837,	yd.	.124	1798, (high)	yd.	.916
1838,	yd.	.125	(low)	yd.	.083
1840, (high)	yd.	.25	1800, (China)	yd.	.093
(low)	yd.	.029	1801, (high)	yd.	.209
1841,	yd.	.03	(low)	yd.	.157
1842,	yd.	.62	1804, (high)	yd.	.167
1843, (high)	yd.	.70	(low)	yd.	.10
(low)	yd.	.053	1805, (high)	yd.	.20
1844,	yd.	.125	(medium)	yd.	.167
1846,	yd.	.32	(low)	yd.	.10
1847,	yd.	.08	1807, (high)	yd.	.50

Prices: Ribbons and Laces—Concluded.

Years.	Ba-sis.	Amount.	Years.	Ba-sis.	Amount.
Ribbon — Con.			*Ribbon* — Con.		
1807, (low)	yd.	$0.078	1834, (low)	yd.	$0.04
1808,	yd.	.042	(velvet)	yd.	.08
1810,	yd.	.16	1836,	yd.	.125
1812, (high)	yd.	.25	1838, (high)	yd.	.25
(low)	yd.	.083	(medium)	yd.	.18
1813,	yd.	.091	(low)	yd.	.123
1814, (high)	yd.	.50	1839, (high)	yd.	.291
(low)	yd.	.04	(low)	yd.	.08
1815, (high)	yd.	.20	(velvet)	yd.	.20
(low)	yd.	.063	1840, (high)	yd.	.375
1816, (high)	yd.	.20	(medium)	yd.	.167
(medium)	yd.	.136	(low)	yd.	.04
(low)	yd.	.061	1841, (high)	yd.	.25
1817, (high)	yd.	.25	(low)	yd.	.093
(medium)	yd.	.106	1842,	yd.	.25
(low)	yd.	.062	1843, (high)	yd.	.063
1818,	yd.	.167	(low)	yd.	.03
1819, (high)	yd.	.222	1844, (high)	yd.	.25
(medium)	yd.	.12	(low)	yd.	.056
(low)	yd.	.048	(velvet)	yd.	.168
1820, (high)	yd.	.211	1845,	yd.	.125
(medium)	yd.	.125	1847, (high)	yd.	.30
(low)	yd.	.068	(low)	yd.	.059
1821, (high)	yd.	.275	(velvet)	yd.	.10
(medium)	yd.	.17	1849,	yd.	.167
(low)	yd.	.058	(velvet)	yd.	.08
1822, (high)	yd.	.333	1850,	yd.	.13
(medium)	yd.	.135	1855, (high)	yd.	.317
(low)	yd.	.065	(med. high)	yd.	.243
1823,	yd.	.059	(medium)	yd.	.16
1824, (high)	yd.	.226	(med. low)	yd.	.101
(medium)	yd.	.169	(low)	yd.	.037
(low)	yd.	.054	(velvet; high)	yd.	.213
(velvet)	yd.	.167	(velvet; low)	yd.	.08
1825, (high)	yd.	.25	1856, (high)	yd.	.283
(medium)	yd.	.167	(low)	yd.	.106
(low)	yd.	.103	(velvet; high)	yd.	.316
1826, (high)	yd.	.162	(velvet; low)	yd.	.196
(low)	yd.	.05	1857, (high)	yd.	.32
1827, (high)	yd.	.204	(medium)	yd.	.186
(low)	yd.	.096	(low)	yd.	.057
1828, (high)	yd.	.373	(velvet; high)	yd.	.503
(medium)	yd.	.162	(velvet; medium)	yd.	.289
(low)	yd.	.049	(velvet; low)	yd.	.134
1829, (high)	yd.	.232	1858, (high)	yd.	.344
(medium)	yd.	.12	(low)	yd.	.082
(low)	yd.	.034	(velvet; high)	yd.	.984
1830, (high)	yd.	.25	(velvet; med. high)	yd.	.398
(medium)	yd.	.113	(velvet; medium)	yd.	.259
(low)	yd.	.067	(velvet; low)	yd.	.099
1831, (high)	yd.	.248	1859, (high)	yd.	.36
(low)	yd.	.04	(medium)	yd.	.184
1832, (high)	yd.	.50	(med. low)	yd.	.124
(medium)	yd.	.253	(low)	yd.	.066
(low)	yd.	.123	(velvet; high)	yd.	.25
1833,	yd.	.04	(velvet; low)	yd.	.11
1834, (high)	yd.	.125			

Prices: Small Wares.

Years.	Ba-sis.	Amount.	Years.	Ba-sis.	Amount.
Knitting Cotton.			*Needles.*		
1814, (high)	lb.	$1.72	1783,	doz.	$0.063
(low)	lb.	1.28	1801,	M.	2.00
1815,	lb.	1.72	1808,	C.	.332
1817, (high)	lb.	1.94	1809,	C.	.50
(low)	lb.	1.52	1810,	pap.	.10
1818,	lb.	1.30	1812,	C.	.50
1839, (high)	lb.	1.20		pap.	.125
(medium)	lb.	.936	1813,	C.	.50
(low)	lb.	.50	1814, (high)	C.	.666
1840,	lb.	.913	(low)	C.	.493

Prices: Small Wares — CONTINUED.

Years.	Basis.	Amount.
Needles — Con.		
1816,	C.	$0.50
1817,	C.	.40
1819,	C.	.44
1820,	C.	.40
1821,	C.	.40
1822,	ea.	.005
	C.	.40
1823,	C.	.28
1824,	C.	.32
1825,	C.	.40
1828,	C.	.40
1829,	C.	.38
1830,	C.	.347
1831, (high)	pap.	.17
(low)	pap.	.10
1832,	pap.	.08
1838,	pap.	.087
1839,	pap.	.02
1855, (high)	pap.	.10
(low)	pap.	.047
1856,	pap.	.05
1857,	pap.	.05
1858,	pap.	.05
1859,	pap.	.05
Pins.		
1782, (high)	row	.014
(low)	row	.01
	pap.	.212
1783,	row	.01
	pap.	.128
1784,	pap.	.083
1794,	pap.	.111
1800,	lb.	.833
1807,	pap.	.083
1809,	pap.	.25
1810,	pap.	.167
1811, (high)	pap.	.125
(low)	pap.	.08
1816, (high)	pap.	.187
(low)	pap.	.10
1817,	pap.	.10
1818, (high)	pap.	.123
(low)	pap.	.06
1820, (high)	pap.	.15
(low)	pap.	.10
1822, (high)	pap.	.125
(low)	pap.	.063
1823,	pap.	.125
(mixed)	lb.	.73
1824, (high)	pap.	.185
(low)	pap.	.125
1825,	pap.	.225
1827,	pap.	.225
1830, (high)	pap.	.25
(low)	pap.	.13
1831, (high)	pap.	.25
(low)	pap.	.112
1832,	pap.	.117
1834,	pap.	.17
1837,	pap.	.17
1838,	pap.	.12
1855,	pap.	.071
1856,	pap.	.072
1857, (high)	pap.	.17
(low)	pap.	.086
1858,	pap.	.068
1859,	pap.	.065
Sewing Cotton.		
1803,	lb.	1.83
1807,	sk.	.125
1809, (high)	sk.	.116

Years.	Basis.	Amount.
Sewing Cotton — Con.		
1809, (low)	sk.	$0.06
1809, (high)	lb.	2.24
(low)	lb.	1.84
1810,	sk.	.032
1811,	sk.	.125
	lb.	3.68
(No. 9)	lb.	.78
1812, (high)	sk.	.063
(low)	sk.	.04
	lb.	1.30
1814, (high)	sk.	.125
(low)	sk.	.03
	lb.	2.88
1815,	sk.	.03
(high)	lb.	3.58
(low)	lb.	2.04
1816, (high)	sk.	.125
(medium)	sk.	.049
(low)	sk.	.03
1817, (high)	sk.	.13
(medium)	sk.	.063
(med. low)	sk.	.043
(low)	sk.	.03
1819, (high)	sk.	.063
(low)	sk.	.027
1820, (high)	sk.	.056
(low)	sk.	.025
1821, (high)	sk.	.09
(low)	sk.	.02
1822,	sk.	.014
1823, (high)	sk.	.105
(low)	sk.	.015
1824, (high)	sk.	.10
(medium)	sk.	.06
(low)	sk.	.015
1825, (high)	sk.	.10
(low)	sk.	.01
1826,	sk.	.015
1827,	sk.	.063
	sp.	.124
(No. 20)	lb.	2.00
(No. 40)	lb.	3.20
1829, (high)	sk.	.084
(low)	sk.	.033
1830,	sk.	.08
(by the dozen skeins)	doz.	.094
(high)	sp.	.084
(low)	sp.	.05
1831,	sp.	.062
1834,	sp.	.063
1835,	sk.	.01
	sp.	.07
1836, (high)	sp.	.083
(low)	sp.	.026
1837, (high)	sp.	.08
(low)	sp.	.051
1838, (high)	sk.	.20
(low)	sk.	.057
	sp.	.06
	lb.	.87
1839,	sk.	.054
	sp.	.08
	lb.	1.24
1841,	sk.	.041
(high)	sp.	.08
(low)	sp.	.052
	lb.	.915
1842,	sk.	.04
	sp.	.063
(by the dozen spools)	doz.	.12
	lb.	.91
1843,	sk.	.041
	sp.	.08
1844, (high)	sk.	.05

Prices: Small Wares — Continued.

Sewing Cotton — Con.

Years.	Basis.	Amount.
1844, (low)	sk.	$0.037
(high)	sp.	.125
(low)	sp.	.04
1845,	sp.	.04
1846,	sp.	.04
1847,	sk.	.05
	sp.	.04
1848,	sk.	.04
	sp.	.047
1849,	sk.	.125
	sp.	.03
1850,	sk.	.06
1851,	sp.	.045
1853,	sp.	.014
1856,	sp.	.04
1857,	sp.	.038
1858,	sp.	.041
1859,	sp.	.041

Sewing and Embroidering Silk.

Years.	Basis.	Amount.
1783, (high)	sk.	.089
(medium)	sk.	.056
(low)	sk.	.031
1784, (high)	sk.	.083
(low)	sk.	.028
1791,	lb.	4.67
1792,	sk.	.056
	oz.	.31
1793,	sk.	.056
	lb.	4.88
1794,	sk.	.056
	lb.	4.96
1795, (high)	lb.	8.00
(low)	lb.	5.66
1797,	lb.	5.11
1798, (high)	lb.	4.57
(low)	lb.	3.33
1799, (Italian)	lb.	5.33
1800, (high)	lb.	6.67
(medium)	lb.	6.50
(low)	lb.	5.33
1801, (high)	lb.	6.66
(low)	lb.	3.67
1804,	sk.	.083
1805,	lb.	5.90
1806,	sk.	.063
	lb.	7.50
1807,	sk.	.075
1808,	sk.	.063
	lb.	6.67
1810, (high)	sk.	.125
(low)	sk.	.063
1811,	lb.	8.00
1812, (high)	sk.	.083
(low)	sk.	.063
1813,	sk.	.06
1814,	sk.	.125
	lb.	11.00
1816, (high)	sk.	.10
(low)	sk.	.062
	oz.	.516
	lb.	6.50
1817,	sk.	.062
	oz.	.50
1818,	sk.	.125
1819, (high)	sk.	.125
(low)	sk.	.072
1820,	sk.	062
1821,	sk.	.052
1822, (high)	sk.	.084
(low)	sk.	.049
1823, (high)	sk.	.055
(low)	sk.	.03

Sewing and Embroidering Silk — Con.

Years.	Basis.	Amount.
1823,	lb.	$2.00
1824,	sk.	.049
1825, (high)	sk.	.063
(low)	sk.	.04
1827,	sk.	.039
1828,	sk.	.047
1829,	sk.	.039
1830,	sk.	.041
1831,	sk.	.04
1832,	sk.	.042
	sp.	.063
1833,	sk.	.04
1834,	sk.	.04
1835,	sk.	.03
1838,	sk.	.05
1839,	sk.	.04
1840,	sk.	.05
1841, (high)	sk.	.08
(low)	sk.	.047
1843,	sk.	.045
1844,	sk.	.032
	oz.	.56
1845,	sk.	.04
1846,	sk.	.04
1847,	sk.	.04
1848,	sk.	.04
1853,	sk.	.028
1855,	sk.	.029
(high)	oz.	.75
(low)	oz.	.67
1856, (high)	sk.	.06
(low)	sk.	.029
1857,	sk.	.03
	oz.	.76
1858,	sk.	.03
(high)	oz.	.84
(low)	oz.	.736
1859,	sk.	.031
	oz.	.80

Thread (Cotton and Linen).

Years.	Basis.	Amount.
1771,	sk.	.018
1773,	sk.	.011
1783, (high)	sk.	.056
(medium)	sk.	.029
(low)	sk.	.022
1784,	sk.	.018
1792,	oz.	.153
	lb.	1.00
1793, (high)	sk.	.209
(low)	sk.	.01
	lb.	.667
1794,	sk.	.209
1795,	lb.	2.75
1797, (No. 13)	lb.	1.50
(No. 14)	lb.	1.58
(No. 30)	lb.	4.16
1800,	lb.	1.02
1801, (high)	lb.	1.33
(low)	lb.	1.00
(Nankeen)	lb.	.778
1802, (high)	oz.	.111
(low)	oz.	.056
1803, (wholesale)	lb.	.878
1804,	sk.	.011
1805,	lb.	1.13
(No. 12)	lb.	1.50
(No. 26)	lb.	3.66
1806,	lb.	1.50
(No. 12)	lb.	1.00
(No. 14)	lb.	1.17
1807,	lb.	.778
(No. 12)	lb.	1.50

Prices: Small Wares — Concluded.

Years.	Basis.	Amount.	Years.	Basis.	Amount.
Thread (Cotton and Linen) — Con.			*Worsted* — Con.		
			1856,	oz.	$0.232
1808,	lb.	$0.854	1857,	sk.	.01
1812,	sk.	.333	1858,	sk.	.01
1813,	sk.	.02	(high)	oz.	.19
1815,	oz.	.125	(low)	oz.	.11
1816,	sk.	.252	1859,	sk.	.01
1817,	lb.	.80	(high)	oz.	.223
(linen)	sk.	.252	(low)	oz.	.13
1818,	sk.	.032			
1819,	sk.	.062	*Yarn.*		
1832,	sk.	.01	1793,	sk.	.034
	sp.	.08	1794,	sk.	.039
1838,	lb.	1.32	1802, (cotton)	lb.	2.00
1839,	lb.	1.68	1812,	sk.	.063
1841,	oz.	.125	1813, (No. 9)	lb.	.75
1842,	lb.	.74	(cotton)	sk.	.03
1843, (unbleached)	lb.	.75	(woollen)	lb.	1.50
1855, (high)	sp.	.053	1815, (cotton)	lb.	1.50
(low)	sp.	.038	1816, (No. 7)	lb.	.69
1858,	sp.	.04	(No. 9)	lb.	.75
(linen)	sk.	.036	1817, (cotton)	lb.	1.76
			1828,	lb.	.375
Twist.			1829, (No. 8)	lb.	.25
1783, (by the stick)	ea.	.10	1831, (No. 12)	lb.	.30
1784, (by the stick)	ea.	.097	1832, (woollen)	sk.	.21
1791,	oz.	.416	1838,	sk.	.22
1792,	sk.	.056	1839,	sk.	.25
1793,	sk.	.046		lb.	1.22
1794, (by the stick)	ea.	.049	1840,	sk.	.21
	sk.	.056	1841,	lb.	.88
	oz.	.416	1842,	sk.	.21
1795,	sk.	.056		lb.	1.21
1800,	lb.	7.34	1843,	sk.	.14
1805,	sk.	.042	1844,	lb.	1.19
	lb.	8.00	1846,	lb.	.70
1806, (by the stick)	ea.	.053	1847, (high)	sk.	.28
1807, (by the stick)	ea.	.063	(low)	sk.	.158
1808, (by the stick)	ea.	.063	1848,	sk.	.165
	lb.	8.34	1849,	sk.	.165
1811, (by the stick)	ea.	.125		lb.	1.50
1816, (by the stick)	ea.	.06	1850,	sk.	.185
1823, (high)	sk.	.063	1851, (high)	sk.	.20
(low)	sk.	.04	(low)	sk.	.14
1827, (by the stick)	ea.	.20	1852,	sk.	.12
1828, (by the stick)	ea.	.06	1854,	sk.	.097
1830,	sk.	.05	1855, (high)	sk.	.15
1839, (by the stick)	ea.	.062	(medium)	sk.	.096
1843, (by the stick)	ea.	.04	(low)	sk.	.04
1844, (by the stick)	ea.	.06	(high)	oz.	.094
1855, (by the stick)	ea.	.06	(low)	oz.	.066
1857, (high)	sk.	.06	1856, (high)	sk.	.098
(low)	sk.	.03	(low)	sk.	.042
1858,	sk.	.06		oz.	.074
(by the stick; high)	ea.	.06	1857, (high)	sk.	.103
(by the stick; low)	ea.	.03	(low)	sk.	.048
1859, (by the stick)	ea.	.03	(high)	lb.	1.23
			(low)	lb.	1.00
Worsted.			1858, (high)	sk.	.101
1803,	sk.	.125	(low)	sk.	.04
1819,	sk.	.389		lb.	1.22
1823,	sk.	.05	1859, (high)	sk.	.112
1825,	lb.	2.48	(low)	sk.	.04
1846,	sk.	.31		lb.	1.30

Prices: Spices and Condiments.

Allspice.			Allspice — Con.		
1782,	oz.	$0.08	1799,	lb.	$0.32
1783,	oz.	.028	1803,	lb.	.332
1784,	oz.	.042	1805,	lb.	.50
1794,	lb.	.278	1807,	lb.	.50

Prices: Spices and Condiments — Continued.

Years.	Basis.	Amount.	Years.	Basis.	Amount.
Allspice — Con.			*Cassia* — Con.		
1808,	lb.	$0.40	1842, (high)	lb.	$0.48
1810,	lb.	.40	(low)	lb.	.40
1811,	lb.	.50	1843, (high)	lb.	.469
(wholesale)	lb.	.23	(low)	lb.	.28
1813,	lb.	.50	1844, (high)	lb.	.48
1815,	lb.	.46	(low)	lb.	.28
1818,	lb.	.40	1845, (high)	lb.	.466
1819, (high)	lb.	.40	(low)	lb.	.28
(low)	lb.	.28	1846, (high)	lb.	.467
1821, (high)	lb.	.50	(low)	lb.	.28
(low)	lb.	.38	1847, (high)	lb.	.476
1822,	lb.	.496	(low)	lb.	.40
1823,	lb.	.37	1848, (high)	lb.	.396
1824,	lb.	.37	(low)	lb.	.28
1826,	lb.	.40	1849, (high)	lb.	.398
1827,	lb.	.37	(low)	lb.	.306
1829,	lb.	.366	1850, (high)	lb.	.488
1830,	oz.	.025	(low)	lb.	.397
	lb.	.258	1851,	lb.	.484
1832,	lb.	.40	1852,	lb.	.478
1833,	lb.	.25	1854,	lb.	.492
1835,	lb.	.40	1855,	lb.	.432
1836,	oz.	.03	1856,	lb.	.435
	lb.	.25	1857,	lb.	.504
1837,	lb.	.20	1858, (high)	lb.	.49
1838,	lb.	.24	(low)	lb.	.40
1839,	lb.	.24	1859,	lb.	.482
1840,	oz.	.03			
	lb.	.20	*Cayenne Pepper.*		
1841,	lb.	.20	1826,	oz.	.10
1842,	lb.	.20	1828,	lb.	1.50
1844,	lb.	.20	1831,	lb.	.80
1845,	lb.	.213	1835,	lb.	.672
1846, (high)	lb.	.24	1843,	lb.	1.00
(low)	lb.	.20	1845,	lb.	.667
1847,	lb.	.24	1850,	oz.	.06
1848,	lb.	.234	1854,	lb.	.76
1849,	lb.	.24			
1850,	lb.	.24	*Cinnamon.*		
1851,	lb.	.24	1782,	oz.	.08
1852,	lb.	.24	1783,	oz.	.282
1854,	lb.	.223	1784,	oz.	.223
1855,	lb.	.231	1794,	oz.	.111
1856,	lb.	.229	1801,	oz.	.083
1857,	lb.	.24	1802, (high)	oz.	.25
1858,	lb.	.247	(medium)	oz.	.083
			(low)	oz.	.063
Cassia.			1805,	oz.	.25
1807,	lb.	.40	1806,	oz.	.25
1808,	oz.	.06	1807,	oz.	.063
(wholesale)	lb.	.45	1809,	oz.	.375
1809, (wholesale)	lb.	.625	1810,	oz.	.31
1810,	oz.	.06		lb.	.80
	lb.	.544	1811, (high)	oz.	.25
1813,	lb.	1.00	(low)	oz.	.05
1819, (high)	lb.	.80	1812,	lb.	.67
(low)	lb.	.499	1813, (high)	oz.	.25
1821, (high)	lb.	.80	(low)	oz.	.05
(low)	lb.	.68	1814,	oz.	.06
1822,	lb.	.68	1816,	lb.	2.50
1828,	lb.	.28	1819,	oz.	.073
(ground)	lb.	.33	1822,	oz.	.032
1830,	lb.	.455	(high)	lb.	.74
1831,	lb.	.48	(low)	lb.	.30
1832,	lb.	.28	1824,	lb.	1.00
1833,	lb.	.40	1828,	oz.	.04
1836,	lb.	.28	1829,	lb.	.64
1837,	lb.	.40	1830,	lb.	.33
1838,	lb.	.24	1832,	oz.	.25
1840, (high)	lb.	.32	1834,	oz.	.025
(low)	lb.	.24	1835,	lb.	.25
1841, (high)	lb.	.471	1837,	lb.	.36
(medium)	lb.	.32	1838,	lb.	.35
(low)	lb.	.20	1839,	lb.	.358

Prices: Spices and Condiments—CONTINUED.

YEARS.	Basis	Amount.	YEARS.	Basis	Amount.
Cinnamon — Con.			*Ginger* — Con.		
1840,	lb.	$0.32	1799, (wholesale)	lb.	$0.093
1841,	lb.	.48	1800,	lb.	.25
1843,	lb.	.48	1803,	lb.	.332
1847,	lb.	.24	1804, (wholesale)	lb.	.11
1850,	lb.	.50	1805,	lb.	.332
			(wholesale)	lb.	.102
Cloves.			1806,	lb.	.24
1783,	oz.	.049	(wholesale)	lb.	.10
1784,	oz.	.033	1807,	lb.	.17
1800,	oz.	.165	(wholesale)	lb.	.11
1804,	oz.	.125	1808, (wholesale)	lb.	.109
1805,	oz.	.125	1809,	lb.	.24
1806,	lb.	.50	(wholesale)	lb.	.10
1807,	oz.	.125	1810,	lb.	.166
1810,	lb.	1.50	(wholesale)	lb.	.101
1816,	lb.	1.25	1811, (wholesale)	lb.	.094
1818,	lb.	1.68	1812,	lb.	.334
1819,	lb.	1.26	(wholesale)	lb.	.127
1822,	oz.	.10	1814,	lb.	.48
1824,	lb.	1.36	1815,	lb.	.40
1827,	lb.	1.16	1816,	lb.	.50
1828,	oz.	.10	1818, (high)	lb.	.25
1830,	oz.	.10	(low)	lb.	.10
(high)	lb.	1.00	1819,	lb.	.167
(low)	lb.	.76	1821, (high)	lb.	.16
1831,	oz.	.05	(low)	lb.	.10
1834,	oz.	.06	1822, (high)	lb.	.24
1835, (high)	oz.	.06	(low)	lb.	.123
(low)	oz.	.03	1823,	lb.	.12
	lb.	.30	1824,	lb.	.128
1837,	oz.	.032	1825,	lb.	.12
	lb.	.40	1826, (high)	lb.	.20
1838,	lb.	.508	(low)	lb.	.12
1839, (high)	lb.	.501	1827,	lb.	.12
(low)	lb.	.40	1828, (high)	lb.	.20
1840,	oz.	.03	(medium)	lb.	.16
	lb.	.40	(low)	lb.	.12
1842, (high)	lb.	.48	1829,	lb.	.13
(low)	lb.	.40	1830, (high)	lb.	.162
1843, (high)	lb.	.477	(low)	lb.	.12
(low)	lb.	.415	1831,	lb.	.142
1844,	lb.	.48	1832, (high)	lb.	.20
1845, (high)	lb.	.464	(low)	lb.	.143
(low)	lb.	.20	1833, (high)	lb.	.20
1846, (high)	lb.	.479	(low)	lb.	.146
(low)	lb.	.40	1834, (high)	lb.	.15
1847, (high)	lb.	.481	(low)	lb.	.12
(low)	lb.	.42	1835, (high)	lb.	.16
1848,	lb.	.447	(low)	lb.	.124
1849,	oz.	.026	1836,	lb.	.14
	lb.	.32	1837, (high)	lb.	.20
1850, (high)	lb.	.481	(low)	lb.	.128
(low)	lb.	.399	1838,	lb.	.13
1851,	lb.	.485	1839,	lb.	.123
1852,	lb.	.465	1840,	lb.	.133
1854, (high)	lb.	.485	1841,	lb.	.14
(low)	lb.	.40	1842,	lb.	.12
1855, (high)	lb.	.40	1843,	lb.	.121
(low)	lb.	.34	1844,	lb.	.12
1856,	oz.	.03	1845,	lb.	.12
	lb.	.387	1846,	lb.	.121
1857, (high)	lb.	.474	1847,	lb.	.122
(medium)	lb.	.40	1848, (high)	lb.	.16
(low)	lb.	.34	(low)	lb.	.12
1858, (high)	lb.	.479	1849,	lb.	.12
(low)	lb.	.392	1850,	lb.	.124
1859, (high)	lb.	.39	1851,	lb.	.121
(low)	lb.	.208	1852,	lb.	.122
			1854,	lb.	.12
Ginger.			1855,	lb.	.12
1782,	oz.	.021	1856, (high)	lb.	.164
1783,	oz.	.022	(low)	lb.	.12
1784,	lb.	.333	1857, (high)	lb.	.17
1797, (wholesale)	lb.	.20	(low)	lb.	.124

Prices: Spices and Condiments — CONTINUED.

Years.	Basis.	Amount.	Years.	Basis.	Amount.
Ginger — Con.			*Nutmegs* — Con.		
1858,	lb.	$0.124	1814,	ea.	$0.10
1859, (high)	lb.	.157		oz.	.50
(low)	lb.	.12	1821, (high)	lb.	2.48
Mace.			(low)	lb.	2.00
1804,	oz.	.75	1822,	oz.	.185
1805,	oz.	.75	1824,	oz.	.15
1806,	oz.	.63	1826,	lb.	2.08
1830,	lb.	3.00	1830, (high)	oz.	.15
1831,	oz.	.25	(low)	oz.	.124
1832,	oz.	.25	1831,	oz.	.125
1844,	oz.	.125		lb.	1.68
1847,	lb.	2.64	1832,	oz.	.14
1848,	oz.	.15		lb.	2.00
	lb.	2.00	1833,	oz.	.12
1852,	lb.	1.48	1835,	lb.	2.00
1857,	oz.	.133	1837,	oz.	.128
1858,	lb.	1.94		lb.	1.85
Mustard.			1838,	oz.	.131
1802,	oz.	.031	1839,	oz.	.132
(high)	lb.	.50	(high)	lb.	2.00
(low)	lb.	.40	(low)	lb.	1.76
1805,	lb.	.56	1840,	oz.	.11
1806,	lb.	.48	1841,	oz.	.106
1809, (wholesale)	lb.	.35		lb.	1.52
1810,	lb.	.64	1842,	oz.	.10
1812,	lb.	.60	1843,	oz.	.106
1815,	lb.	.76		lb.	1.62
1817,	lb.	.64	1844,	oz.	.107
1818,	lb.	.55		lb.	1.44
1819,	lb.	.50	1845,	oz.	.114
1821,	lb.	.48		lb.	1.57
1824,	lb.	.48	1846,	oz.	.117
1826,	lb.	.40		lb.	1.83
1828,	lb.	.40	1847,	oz.	.11
1830,	lb.	.40	(high)	lb.	1.84
1833,	can	.25	(low)	lb.	1.64
	lb.	.56	1848,	oz.	.113
1837,	lb.	.38	1849,	oz.	.114
1838,	box	.178	1850,	oz.	.12
	lb.	.34		lb.	1.71
1839,	box	.17	1851,	oz.	.108
	lb.	.34	1852,	oz.	.108
1842,	box	.17	1854,	lb.	1.59
1843, (high)	lb.	.48	1855,	oz.	.097
(low)	lb.	.34	1856, (high)	lb.	1.60
1844,	box	.15	(low)	lb.	1.32
1845, (high)	lb.	.41	1857, (high)	lb.	1.58
(low)	lb.	.30	(medium)	lb.	1.33
1847,	lb.	.40	(low)	lb.	1.00
1848,	lb.	.404	1858,	oz.	.064
1850, (high)	lb.	.48	(high)	lb.	1.00
(low)	lb.	.40	(low)	lb.	.773
1851,	lb.	.40	1859,	oz.	.079
1854,	lb.	.414		lb.	.978
1859,	box	.16	*Pepper.*		
	lb.	.24	1782,	oz.	.111
Nutmegs.			1783,	oz.	.038
1782,	ea.	.098	1784,	oz.	.035
1783,	ea.	.062	1793, (wholesale)	lb.	.416
	oz.	.333	1794,	lb.	.556
1794,	ea.	.097	1799,	lb.	.50
1799,	lb.	5.00	(wholesale)	lb.	.416
1802,	oz.	.50	1800,	oz.	.04
1803,	lb.	6.00	1801,	lb.	.50
1804,	oz.	.50	1802,	lb.	.50
1805,	oz.	.50	1803,	lb.	.50
1806,	oz.	.458	(wholesale)	lb.	.29
1807,	oz.	.417	1804,	lb.	.434
1808,	oz.	.75	(wholesale)	lb.	.24
1809,	ea.	.078	1805, (wholesale)	lb.	.23
			1806,	lb.	.42
			1807,	lb.	.44

Prices: Spices and Condiments—Continued.

Years.	Basis.	Amount.	Years.	Basis.	Amount.
Pepper — Con.			*Pimento* — Con.		
1808, (wholesale)	lb.	$0.22	1804, (wholesale)	lb.	$0.215
1810,	lb.	.35	1806, (wholesale)	lb.	.37
1811, (wholesale)	lb.	.17	1807, (wholesale)	lb.	.354
1812,	lb.	.40	1820, (wholesale)	lb.	.28
1814, (high)	lb.	.68	1834,	oz.	.025
(low)	lb.	.493	1837,	lb.	.24
1815,	lb.	.48	1839,	lb.	.18
1816,	lb.	.40	1841,	lb.	.25
1817,	lb.	.40	1843,	lb.	.24
1818,	lb.	.40	1844,	lb.	.24
1819, (high)	lb.	.50	1845,	lb.	.24
(low)	lb.	.355	1846,	lb.	.24
1820, (high)	lb.	.28	1847,	lb.	.24
(low)	lb.	.23	1848,	lb.	.236
1821, (high)	lb.	.37	1850,	lb.	.24
(low)	lb.	.19	1851,	lb.	.24
1822,	lb.	.40	1857,	lb.	.244
1824,	lb.	.375	1858,	lb.	.245
1825,	lb.	.33			
1826,	lb.	.40	*Vinegar.*		
1827, (ground)	lb.	.33	1767,	gal.	.126
1828, (high)	lb.	.40	1777, (high)	gal.	.167
(low)	lb.	.17	(low)	gal.	.089
1829, (high)	lb.	.33	1780,	gal.	.111
(low)	lb.	.24	1783,	qt.	.053
1830, (high)	lb.	.387	1788,	qt.	.049
(low)	lb.	.25	1790,	gal.	.125
1831,	lb.	.40	1793, (high)	gal.	.25
(ground)	lb.	.26	(low)	gal.	.133
1832,	lb.	.34	1796, (wholesale)	gal.	.139
1834,	lb.	.20	1799,	gal.	.25
1835, (high)	lb.	.32	(wholesale)	gal.	.143
(low)	lb.	.17	1800,	gal.	.201
1837, (high)	lb.	.22	1802, (high)	qt.	.10
(low)	lb.	.16	(low)	qt.	.063
1838,	lb.	.231		gal.	.25
1839,	lb.	.233	1804,	gal.	.195
1840,	lb.	.16	1805,	gal.	.223
1841, (high)	lb.	.218	(wholesale)	gal.	.175
(low)	lb.	.16	1809,	gal.	.285
1842,	lb.	.224	1810,	gal.	.167
1843, (high)	lb.	.233	1811,	qt.	.07
(low)	lb.	.186		gal.	.25
1844, (high)	lb.	.24	1814, (high)	gal.	.32
(low)	lb.	.16	(low)	gal.	.248
1845, (high)	lb.	.228	(wholesale)	gal.	.165
(low)	lb.	.16	1817,	gal.	.30
1846, (high)	lb.	.60	1819,	gal.	.32
(medium)	lb.	.34	1823,	gal.	.168
(low)	lb.	.23	(wholesale)	gal.	.15
1847, (high)	lb.	.243	1826,	gal.	.20
(low)	lb.	.216	1828,	gal.	.20
1848, (high)	lb.	.231	1830,	qt.	.05
(low)	lb.	.16	1832,	qt.	.04
1849, (high)	lb.	.23	1834,	qt.	.052
(low)	lb.	.14	1835,	gal.	.239
1850, (high)	lb.	.226	1837,	gal.	.20
(low)	lb.	.14	1838, (high)	gal.	.201
1851,	lb.	.231	(low)	gal.	.153
1852,	lb.	.235	1839,	qt.	.05
1854, (high)	lb.	.216		gal.	.172
(low)	lb.	.14	1840,	gal.	.20
1855, (high)	lb.	.24	1841,	qt.	.05
(low)	lb.	.181		gal.	.186
1856,	lb.	.186	1842,	gal.	.187
1857, (high)	lb.	.249	1843,	gal.	.179
(low)	lb.	.20	1844, (high)	gal.	.18
1858, (high)	lb.	.234	(low)	gal.	.125
(low)	lb.	.123	1845, (high)	gal.	.173
1859,	lb.	.224	(low)	gal.	.134
			1846, (high)	gal.	.173
Pimento.			(low)	gal.	.125
1799, (wholesale)	lb.	.139	1847,	gal.	.198
1801, (wholesale)	lb.	.14	1848,	gal.	.185

Prices: Spices and Condiments — CONCLUDED.

YEARS.	Basis.	Amount.	YEARS.	Basis.	Amount.
Vinegar — Con.			*Vinegar — Con.*		
1849,	qt.	$0.044	1856,	gal.	$0.16
	gal.	.18	1857, (high)	gal.	.167
1850, (high)	gal.	.185	(low)	gal.	.112
(low)	gal.	.124	1858, (high)	gal.	.20
1851, (high)	gal.	.18	(low)	gal.	.16
(low)	gal.	.125	(wholesale)	gal.	.125
1852, (high)	gal.	.182	1859, (high)	gal.	.24
(low)	gal.	.13	(low)	gal.	.152
1854,	gal.	.20	(wholesale)	gal.	.125
1855,	gal.	.152	1860,	gal.	.20

Prices: Tacks, Brads, and Nails.

YEARS.	Basis.	Amount.	YEARS.	Basis.	Amount.
Nails.			*8d. Nails.*		
1802, (high)	lb.	$0.167	1819, (wrought)	lb.	$0.12
(low)	lb.	.13			
1812,	lb.	.18	*10d. Nails.*		
1813,	lb.	.124	1800, (by the cask)	M.	1.41
1814, (wrought)	lb.	.14	1805, (by the cask)	lb.	.115
1816,	lb.	.115	1807,	M.	1.46
1817,	lb.	.10	1808,	lb.	.10
1818,	lb.	.11	1810, (by the cask)	M.	1.46
1823,	lb.	.10	1811, (cut; by the cask)	lb.	.09
(cut)	lb.	.071	1813,	lb.	.09
1826,	lb.	.08	1815, (by the cask)	lb.	.112
1827,	lb.	.081	1819, (cut)	lb.	.08
1828,	lb.	.10	(wrought)	lb.	.10
1830, (high)	lb.	.13			
(low)	lb.	.07	*20d. Nails.*		
4d. Nails.			1800,	M.	2.25
1800, (by the cask)	M.	.32	1811, (wrought; by the cask)	lb.	.104
1801,	M.	.333	(wrought; by the cask)	M.	2.08
1805, (by the cask)	lb.	.10	1822,	lb.	.10
1807,	lb.	.11			
1808,	lb.	.11	*Tacks and Brads.*		
1809, (by the cask)	lb.	.11	1795, (tacks; wholesale)	gro.	.167
1810, (by the cask)	lb.	.11	1808, (2d. brads)	M.	.42
1811, (cut; by the cask)	lb.	.10	(4d. brads)	M.	.625
1815, (by the cask)	lb.	.11	(6d. brads)	M.	1.00
1830,	lb.	.08	1847, (tacks)	pap.	.12
6d. Nails.					
1819, (wrought)	lb.	.14			

Prices: Tallow, Candles, Soap, etc.

YEARS.	Basis.	Amount.	YEARS.	Basis.	Amount.
Candles.			*Candles — Con.*		
1758,	lb.	$0.122	1804,	lb.	$0.224
1760,	lb.	.093	(wholesale)	lb.	.20
1761,	lb.	.133	1805,	lb.	.234
1780,	lb.	.223	1806,	lb.	.195
1782,	lb.	.209	(wholesale)	lb.	.168
1783,	lb.	.281	1808, (wholesale)	lb.	.13
1793,	lb.	.167	1809,	lb.	.169
1794,	lb.	.174	(wholesale)	lb.	.143
1795, (wholesale)	lb.	.197	1810,	lb.	.198
1797, (wholesale)	lb.	.167	(wholesale)	lb.	.16
1798, (wholesale)	lb.	.138	1811,	lb.	.198
1799,	lb.	.254	(wholesale)	lb.	.16
1800,	lb.	.20	1812,	lb.	.194
(wholesale)	lb.	.167	1813, (high)	lb.	.42
1801,	lb.	.20	(low)	lb.	.188
(wholesale)	lb.	.167	(wholesale)	lb.	.147
1802,	lb.	.182	1814, (high)	lb.	.20
(wholesale)	lb.	.148	(low)	lb.	.18
(mould)	lb.	.25	1815,	lb.	.209
1803,	lb.	.139	1816,	lb.	.223
(wholesale)	lb.	.12	1817,	lb.	.209

Prices: Tallow, Candles, Soap, etc. — Continued.

Years.	Basis	Amount.	Years.	Basis	Amount.
Candles — Con.			*Soap* — Con.		
1817, (wholesale)	lb.	$0.174	1838, (low)	bar	$0.24
1818,	lb.	.172	1839,	lb.	.09
(sperm)	lb.	.50		bar	.26
1819,	lb.	.19	1840,	lb.	.09
1820, (wholesale)	lb.	.18	1841,	lb.	.079
1821,	lb.	.20		bar	.223
1822,	lb.	.20	1842,	lb.	.08
1824,	lb.	.16		bar	.227
1825,	lb.	.167	1843,	lb.	.07
1826,	lb.	.125	(high)	bar	.245
1830,	lb.	.127	(low)	bar	.21
1831,	lb.	.128	1844,	lb.	.079
1832,	lb.	.14		bar	.20
1834, (high)	lb.	.15	1845,	lb.	.078
(low)	lb.	.122	(wholesale)	lb.	.06
1835,	lb.	.123	(high)	bar	.226
1837,	lb.	.15	(low)	bar	.13
1840,	lb.	.16	1846,	lb.	.078
1841,	lb.	.147	(wholesale)	lb.	.06
1842,	lb.	.12		bar	.226
1843,	lb.	.15	1847,	lb.	.071
1844,	lb.	.14	(high)	bar	.227
1846,	lb.	.13	(low)	bar	.17
1847, (high)	lb.	.147	1848, (high)	lb.	.16
(low)	lb.	.10	(low)	lb.	.085
1848,	lb.	.141	(wholesale, high)	lb.	.067
(wholesale)	lb.	.12	(wholesale, low)	lb.	.03
1849,	lb.	.13	(high)	bar	.239
1851,	lb.	.14	(low)	bar	.173
1857, (high)	lb.	.333	(soda)	lb.	.10
(low)	lb.	.17	1849,	lb.	.068
1858,	lb.	.167	1850,	lb.	.081
1859, (high)	lb.	.618		bar	.235
(medium)	lb.	.33	1851,	lb.	.079
(low)	lb.	.16		bar	.237
			1852, (high)	lb.	.16
Castile Soap.			(low)	lb.	.109
1843,	lb.	.25		bar	.234
1851,	lb.	.147	1854,	lb.	.095
				bar	.248
Soap.			1855,	lb.	.108
				bar	.234
1783,	lb.	.196	1856,	lb.	.075
1784,	lb.	.173	(high)	bar	.241
1785,	lb.	.111	(low)	bar	.115
1792,	lb.	.083	1857, (high)	lb.	.184
1794,	lb.	.139	(low)	lb.	.076
1795, (wholesale)	lb.	.139		bar	.237
1806,	lb.	.10	1858, (high)	lb.	.173
1813,	lb.	.11	(low)	lb.	.089
1814,	lb.	.122	(high)	bar	.232
1815,	lb.	.109	(low)	bar	.099
1816,	lb.	.128	1859,	lb.	.111
(wholesale)	lb.	.10		bar	.243
1818,	lb.	.126			
1819,	lb.	.13	*Soft Soap.*		
1820, (wholesale)	lb.	.10	1774,	qt.	.033
1821,	lb.	.124	1780,	qt.	.083
1822,	lb.	.12	1830,	lb.	.02
1825, (high)	lb.	.10	1833,	bbl.	4.00
(low)	lb.	.082			
1826,	lb.	.12	*Spermaceti.*		
1829, (bar)	lb.	.125	1782,	oz.	.241
1830,	lb.	.095	1783,	oz.	.154
1831,	lb.	.10	1784,	oz.	.131
(white)	lb.	.11			
1832,	lb.	.087	*Tallow.*		
1834,	lb.	.10	1758,	lb.	.111
1835,	lb.	.10	1760,	lb.	.122
1837,	lb.	.083	1762,	lb.	.122
(wholesale)	lb.	.056	1780,	lb.	.111
1838, (high)	lb.	.235	1782,	lb.	.177
(medium)	lb.	.16	1783,	lb.	.17
(low)	lb.	.091	1794,	lb.	.139
(high)	bar	.35	1795, (wholesale)	lb.	.107

Prices: Tallow, Candles, Soap, etc. — Concluded.

Years.	Basis.	Amount.	Years.	Basis.	Amount.
Tallow — Con.			*Tallow* — Con.		
1800,	lb.	$0.167	1824,	lb.	$0.10
(wholesale)	lb.	.084	(wholesale)	lb.	.06
1813, (wholesale)	lb.	.11	1825, (high)	lb.	.15
1816,	lb.	.153	(low)	lb.	.07
1817,	lb.	.156	1826,	lb.	.10
1818,	lb.	.13	1827, (wholesale)	lb.	.06
1822, (bay)	lb.	.24	1834,	lb.	.06
1823,	lb.	.10	1841,	lb.	.08

Prices: Tobacco and Snuff.

Years.	Basis.	Amount.	Years.	Basis.	Amount.
Cigars.			*Tobacco* — Con.		
1806,	doz.	$0.25	1799,	lb.	$0.083
1807,	doz.	.25	1800, (wholesale)	pap.	.088
1809,	ea.	.02	(pigtail; wholesale)	lb.	.183
	C.	.314	1801, (pigtail; wholesale)	lb.	.174
1810,	C.	.225	1808,	lb.	.125
1811,	C.	2.00	1810, (wholesale)	lb.	.167
1813,	C.	2.00	1816, (high)	lb.	.32
1816,	C.	.75	(low)	lb.	.08
1817, (high)	C.	.90	(plug)	lb.	.40
(low)	C.	.75	1817, (plug)	lb.	.40
Snuff.			1819,	lb.	.32
1782,	oz.	.055	1821,	lb.	.24
1783,	oz.	.048	1822,	lb.	.248
(wholesale)	lb.	.389	1824,	lb.	.20
1784,	oz.	.048	1826,	lb.	.20
1794,	oz.	.028	1827,	lb.	.207
1822,	lb.	.40	1829,	lb.	.193
1830,	oz.	.015	1830, (high)	lb.	.188
1832,	lb.	.24	(low),	lb.	.12
1837,	lb.	.31	1831, (high)	lb.	.172
1838,	lb.	.317	(low)	lb.	.10
1839,	lb.	.31	1832, (high)	lb.	.166
1841,	lb.	.32	(low)	lb.	.107
1845,	lb.	.25	1833,	lb.	.18
1846,	lb.	.24	1834,	lb.	.17
1847,	lb.	.248	1837,	lb.	.201
1850,	lb.	.236	1838, (high)	lb.	.213
1851,	lb.	.248	(low)	lb.	.14
1852,	lb.	.248	1839, (high)	lb.	.273
1854,	lb.	.24	(low)	lb.	-.204
1856,	lb.	.251	1840,	lb.	.25
1857, (high)	lb.	.333	1841, (high)	lb.	.28
(low)	lb.	.256	(low)	lb.	.20
1858,	lb.	.257	1842,	lb.	.202
1859,	lb.	.248	1843, (high)	lb.	.247
			(low)	lb.	.20
Tobacco.			1844,	lb.	.20
1767,	lb.	.056	1845, (high)	lb.	.24
1770,	lb.	.063	(low)	lb.	.164
1771,	lb.	.056	1846, (high)	lb.	.30
1772,	lb.	.056	(medium)	lb.	.24
1774,	lb.	.056	(low)	lb.	.18
1775,	lb.	.089	1847, (high)	lb.	.252
1782,	lb.	.108	(low)	lb.	.125
1783,	lb.	.112	1848,	lb.	.251
1784,	lb.	.067	1849,	lb.	.253
1788,	lb.	.083	1850,	lb.	.285
1790,	lb.	.083	1851,	lb.	.34
1792,	lb.	.311	1852,	lb.	.229
1793,	lb.	.195	1854, (high)	lb.	.337
(pigtail; wholesale)	lb.	.125	(low)	lb.	.25
1794,	lb.	.083	1855,	lb.	.248
1795, (wholesale)	pap.	.093	1856,	lb.	.247
1797,	lb.	.119	1857,	lb.	.31
1798,	pap.	.125	1858,	lb.	.30
	lb.	.111	1859,	lb.	.30

Prices: Tools and Implements.

Years.	Basis.	Amount.	Years.	Basis.	Amount.
Files.			*Shoe Knives* — Con.		
1793,	doz.	$0.962	1801,	doz.	$0.625
1808,	doz.	.75	1802, (heel)	doz.	1.00
			1847,	doz.	1.60
Hoes.			*Shovels.*		
1802,	ea.	.63			
1805,	ea.	.50	1797,	doz.	7.50
1813,	ea.	.54	1798,	doz.	7.50
1830,	ea.	.334	1799, (iron)	ea.	1.08
(steel)	ea.	.60	1801,	doz.	9.00
1847,	ea.	.56	1805,	doz.	9.50
			1806,	doz.	8.50
Scythes.			1807,	doz.	10.00
1792,	ea.	.857	1810, (iron)	doz.	12.00
1794,	ea.	.916	1811,	doz.	11.00
1805, (high)	ea.	1.25	1817,	doz.	10.50
(low)	ea.	.75	1821,	ea.	.25
1808,	doz.	6.00	1847,	ea.	.88
1819,	ea.	.92	1855,	ea.	.96
1830,	ea.	1.00			
			Spades.		
Shoe Knives.			1801,	doz.	12.00
1795,	doz.	.875	1806,	doz.	12.00
(heel)	doz.	.916			

Prices: Not Classified.

Years.	Basis.	Amount.	Years.	Basis.	Amount.
Andirons.			*Brooms* — Con.		
1814, (brass)	pr.	$4.50	1827, (high)	ea.	$0.28
1815, (brass)	set	14.50	(low)	ea.	.184
			1828, (high)	ea.	.25
Brass Kettles.			(low)	ea.	.167
1799,	ea.	10.00	1830, (high)	ea.	.25
(17 lbs.)	ea.	9.92	(low)	ea.	.15
(11 lbs.)	ea.	6.39	1832,	ea.	.25
1814,	ea.	2.00	1833,	ea.	.125
			1835,	ea.	.27
Brick.			1836,	ea.	.20
1753,	M.	2.44	1837,	ea.	.203
1754,	M.	2.44	1838, (high)	ea.	.332
1757,	M.	1.33	(low)	ea.	.231
1764,	M.	2.50	1839, (high)	ea.	.38
1765,	M.	3.00	(low)	ea.	.256
1802,	C.	.835	1840, (high)	ea.	.33
1809,	M.	10.00	(medium)	ea.	.23
			(low)	ea.	.13
Brooms.			1841, (high)	ea.	.262
1783,	ea.	.129	(low)	ea.	.17
1801, (corn)	doz.	1.83	1842, (high)	ea.	.30
1802,	ea.	.23	(low)	ea.	.25
1803,	ea.	.167	1843, (high)	ea.	.227
1805,	ea.	.375	(low)	ea.	.156
1806,	doz.	2.25	1844,	ea.	.30
1809, (high)	doz.	4.50	1845, (high)	ea.	.50
(low)	doz.	2.17	(medium)	ea.	.33
1810,	ea.	.30	(low)	ea.	.19
1811, (high)	ea.	.33	1846, (high)	ea.	.33
(low)	ea.	.20	(medium)	ea.	.25
1812,	ea.	.18	(low)	ea.	.107
1813,	ea.	.18	1847, (high)	ea.	.205
1816,	ea.	.20	(low)	ea.	.127
1817,	ea.	.28	1848,	ea.	.249
1819,	ea.	.30	1849, (high)	ea.	.26
1820,	ea.	.166	(low)	ea.	.12
1821,	ea.	.17	1850, (high)	ea.	.25
1822,	ea.	.14	(low)	ea.	.12
(corn)	ea.	.17	1851, (high)	ea.	.251
1823, (high)	ea.	.25	(low)	ea.	.15
(low)	ea.	.10	1852, (high)	ea.	.25
1824,	ea.	.183	(low)	ea.	.12
1825,	ea.	.20	1854, (high)	ea.	.258
1826,	ea.	.20	(low)	ea.	.13

Prices: Not Classified — CONCLUDED.

YEARS.	Basis.	Amount.	YEARS.	Basis.	Amount.
Brooms — Con.			*Matches* — Con.		
1855, (high)	ea.	$0.27	1855,	¼gro.	$0.15
(low)	ea.	.10	1856,	¼gro.	.15
1856, (high)	ea.	.373	1857,	¼gro.	.15
(low)	ea.	.286	1858,	¼gro.	.15
1857, (high)	ea.	.50	1859,	¼gro.	.15
(medium)	ea.	.395	(wholesale)	gro.	.40
(low)	ea.	.238			
1858, (high)	ea.	.33	*Silver Watches.*		
(medium)	ea.	.244	1812,	ea.	15.00
(low)	ea.	.106	1817,	ea.	15.00
1859, (high)	ea.	.37			
(medium)	ea.	.264	*Tubs.*		
(low)	ea.	.12	1774,	ea.	.444
			1847, (high)	ea.	1.00
Candlesticks.			(low)	ea.	.75
1783,	ea.	.167			
1784,	ea.	.111	*Tumblers.*		
			1787, (large)	doz.	2.50
Clocks.			1809,	doz.	1.50
1795, (eight-day)	ea.	60.00	1810,	doz.	1.75
1799, (high)	ea.	60.00	1814,	ea.	.25
(low)	ea.	30.00	1815,	ea.	.138
1814,	ea.	10.00	1817,	doz.	2.25
			1820,	doz.	.40
Cotton.			1826, (high)	doz.	3.36
1787,	lb.	.50	(low)	doz.	.74
1791,	lb.	.223	1827,	doz.	1.00
1793,	lb.	.361	1837,	doz.	1.24
1794,	lb.	.403	1838, (high)	doz.	.955
(wholesale)	lb.	.317	(low)	doz.	.72
1795, (wholesale)	lb.	.292	1842,	doz.	.96
1801,	lb.	.42	1843, (high)	doz.	2.07
(wholesale, high)	lb.	.28	(low)	doz.	.96
(wholesale, low)	lb.	.235	1845, (high)	doz.	1.68
1802, (high)	lb.	.46	(low)	doz.	.96
(low)	lb.	.25	1846, (high)	doz.	1.63
1829,	lb.	.15	(low)	doz.	.96
			1847,	doz.	1.50
Feathers.			1848, (high)	doz.	1.48
1767,	lb.	.133	(low)	doz.	1.15
1796,	lb.	.667	1849,	doz.	1.50
1822,	lb.	.333	1850,	doz.	1.50
			1851, (high)	doz.	1.50
Iron.			(low)	doz.	.75
1752,	lb.	.055	1852, (high)	doz.	1.50
1759, (refined)	lb.	.055	(low)	doz.	.962
1762,	lb.	.045	1854,	doz.	1.05
1830,	lb.	.055	1856,	doz.	.634
			1857,	doz.	.616
Matches.			1858, (high)	doz.	.96
1837,	¼gro.	.175	(low)	doz.	.604
1840,	pap.	.02			
1841,	¼gro.	.46	*Wafers.*		
1842,	¼gro.	.40	1804,	lb.	1.50
1843,	¼gro.	.125	1819,	lb.	2.00
1846,	¼gro.	.18			
1847, (high)	¼gro.	.20	*Wine Glasses.*		
(low)	¼gro.	.17	1801,	doz.	.60
1848,	¼gro.	.16	1804,	doz.	1.00
1850,	¼gro.	.177	1807,	doz.	1.50
1851,	¼gro.	.173	1816,	doz.	1.00
1852,	¼gro.	.166	1817,	doz.	2 50
1854,	¼gro.	.165	1829,	doz.	.88

We have presented on pages 3 to 38, in the text preceding the statistical tables, a brief account of the rise and growth of the cotton industry, and, on pages 26 to 30, have made comparisons between early and late periods, showing the effect

upon production and wages of the changes which have taken place in this branch of manufacture.

The cotton industry has always been accepted as typical, in discussions of the factory system; the date and circumstances of its inception, the improvements and modifications of method that have influenced it, and its present condition are all well known, and the records to which recourse is had for facts concerning the industry are unusually complete and trustworthy. For these reasons, we have thus far omitted any reference to it in the preceding tables of wages, preferring to treat it in a special supplementary table, which we now present, containing wages of cotton mill operatives for various years from 1828 to 1860. The statistics for the years subsequent to 1860, which statistics have appeared in detail in previous reports of the Bureau, are not included in this table.

The information contained in this table has been drawn from various sources, but chiefly from original records, pay rolls, etc., placed at the disposal of this office. Some of the statistics have appeared in Volume II., Tenth Census of the United States, in the special report on the Factory System.* Averages for the industry, by periods of years, are carried forward to their proper place in the tables that follow.

In this table, male operatives are indicated by m, and females by f, following the designation of the occupation. When the wages given are the actual amounts paid, the fact is denoted by the letters ac, which follow the letter indicating the sex of the operatives; while " average" wages are indicated by the use of the letters av in the same manner. For instance, mac, following the name of an occupation, indicates that men in that employment received the actual sum given in the table; on the other hand, mav indicates that the amount presented was the "average" wage paid to men.

In numerous instances more than one wage appears in connection with a given occupation. This is caused by variations in prices between different establishments, or between different departments of the same establishment, and will enable the reader to note the range between high and low wages paid at a given period in the same occupation.

---

* By Carroll D. Wright, special agent.

Wages: Cotton Mill Operatives.

Years and Occupations.	Ba-sis.	Amount.	Years and Occupations.	Ba-sis.	Amount.
1828.			*Spinning—Con.*		
Carding.			Spinners, section hands, *mac*	wk.	$4.50
Carders, *fav*	wk.	$2.55	Spinners, section hands, *mac*	wk.	4.20
			Spinners, *mac* . . .	wk.	5.52
Spinning.			Spinners, *mac* . . .	wk.	4.50
Spinners, *fav* . . .	wk.	2.58	Spinners, spare, *fac* .	wk.	2.76
			Spinners, spare, *fac* .	wk.	2.52
Dressing.			Spinners, spare, *fac* .	wk.	2.25
Dressers, *fav* . . .	wk.	2.82	Spinners, filling, *fav* (high)	wk.	3.50
			Spinners, filling, *fav* (medium)	wk.	3.44
Weaving.			Spinners, filling, *fav* (low)	wk.	2.13
Weavers, *fav* . . .	wk.	2.61	Spinners, warp, *fav* (high)	wk.	4.24
			Spinners, warp, *fav* (medium)	wk.	3.45
All Departments.			Spinners, warp, *fav* (low) .	wk.	2.21
All departments, *fav*	wk.	2.62	*Dressing.*		
1836.			Drawers-in, *fav* (high) .	wk.	4.43
Carding.			Drawers-in, *fav* (medium)	wk.	3.99
Carders, overseers, *mac* .	wk.	14.00	Drawers-in, *fav* (low) .	wk.	3.78
Carders, overseers, *mac* .	wk.	13.50	Dressers, overseers, *mac* .	wk.	12.00
Carders, overseers, *mac* .	wk.	12.00	Dressers, overseers, *mac* .	wk.	10.50
Carders, second hands, *mac* .	wk.	8.52	Dressers, second hands, *mac* .	wk.	7.50
Carders, second hands, *mac* .	wk.	7.50	Dressers, second hands, *mac* .	wk.	6.00
Carders, second hands, *mac* .	wk.	7.00	Dressers, third hands, *mac* .	wk.	4.50
Carders, third hands, *mac* .	wk.	6.00	Dressers, boys, *mac* .	wk.	3.00
Carders, spare, *mac* .	wk.	4.98	Dressers, *fav* (high) .	wk.	7.20
Carders, spare, *mac* .	wk.	4.20	Dressers, *fav* (medium) .	wk.	5.28
Card grinders, *mac* . .	wk.	6.60	Dressers, *fav* (med. low)	wk.	4.44
Card grinders, *mac* . .	wk.	6.00	Dressers, *fav* (low) .	wk.	3.11
Doublers, *mac* . .	wk.	4.20	Warpers, *fav* (high) .	wk.	5.07
Doublers, *mac* . .	wk.	3.60	Warpers, *fav* (medium) .	wk.	4.64
Drawers, *fac* . . .	wk.	3.18	Warpers, *fav* (med. low)	wk.	3.38
Drawers, *fac* . . .	wk.	3.00	Warpers, *fav* (low)	wk.	2.43
Drawers, *fac* . . .	wk.	2.94			
Drawers, *fac* . . .	wk.	2.88	*Weaving.*		
Drawers, *fav* . . .	wk.	*1.87	Weavers, overseers, *mac* .	wk.	12.00
Drawers and speeders, spare, *fac*	wk.	3.00	Weavers, overseers, *mac* .	wk.	10.50
			Weavers, second hands, *mac* .	wk.	7.50
Drawers and speeders, spare, *fac*	wk.	2.25	Weavers, second hands, *mac* .	wk.	7.00
			Weavers, third hands, *mac* .	wk.	6.00
Drawers and speeders, spare, *fav*	wk.	2.41	Weavers, third hands, *mac* .	wk.	5.50
Lap boys, *mac* . . .	wk.	3.00	Weavers, third hands, *mac* .	wk.	4.80
Lap boys, *mac* . . .	wk.	2.52	Weavers, third hands, *mac* .	wk.	4.20
Pickers, *mac* . . .	wk.	6.00	Weavers, *fav* (high) .	wk.	5.17
Pickers, *mac* . . .	wk.	4.98	Weavers, *fav* (medium) .	wk.	4.33
Speeders, *fac* . . .	wk.	4.26	Weavers, *fav* (med. low) .	wk.	3.75
Speeders, *fac* . . .	wk.	3.60	Weavers, *fav* (low) . .	wk.	2.05
Speeders, *fav* (high) .	wk.	4.06	Weavers, spare, *fac* .	wk.	4.26
Speeders, *fav* (low) .	wk.	2.44	Weavers, spare, *fac* .	wk.	2.15
Strippers, *mac* . .	wk.	6.00	Weavers, spare, *fav*	wk.	2.65
Strippers, *mac* . .	wk.	4.50			
Strippers, *mac* . .	wk.	4.20	*Cloth Room.*		
Winders, overseers, *mac*	wk.	4.98	Cloth room hands, overseer, *mac*	wk.	12.00
Winders, *mac* . .	wk.	5.52	Cloth room hands, *mac* .	wk.	6.60
Winders, *fav* (high) .	wk.	4.71	Cloth room hands, *mac* .	wk.	6.48
Winders, *fav* (low) .	wk.	4.19	Cloth room hands, *mac* .	wk.	4.98
Winders, spare, *fac* .	wk.	2.89	Cloth room hands, *fac* .	wk.	3.78
			Cloth room hands, *fac* .	wk.	3.00
Spinning.			Cloth room hands, *fac* .	wk.	2.76
Doffers, *fav* (high) .	wk.	3.46	Cloth room boys, *mac* .	wk.	2.52
Doffers, *fav* (low) .	wk.	3.42			
Reelers, *fac* . .	wk.	5.23	*Repair Hands.*		
Reelers, *fav* . .	wk.	4.82	Repair hands, overseer, *mac* .	wk.	15.00
Spinners, overseers, *mac*	wk.	13.00	Repair hands, *mac* . .	wk.	10.50
Spinners, overseers, *mac*	wk.	12.00	Repair hands, *mac* . .	wk.	3.75
Spinners, second hands, *mac* .	wk.	7.50	Repair hands, *mav* . .	wk.	7.75
Spinners, second hands, *mac* .	wk.	6.60			
Spinners, third hands, *mac* .	wk.	6.50	**1837.**		
Spinners, third hands, *mac* .	wk.	5.52	*Carding.*		
Spinners, section hands, *mac*	wk.	4.98	Carders, overseers, *mac* .	wk.	14.00
			Carders, overseers, *mac* .	wk.	13.50

* This amount is a low "average" wage reported by one establishment, and has no connection with the actual wages given for the same sex and occupation.

Wages: Cotton Mill Operatives — CONTINUED.

Years and Occupations.	Basis.	Amount.	Years and Occupations.	Basis.	Amount.
Carding — Con.			*Dressing* — Con.		
Carders, overseers, *mac*	wk.	$12.00	Drawers-in, *fav* (med. low)	wk.	$3.40
Carders, second hands, *mac*	wk.	8.52	Drawers-in, *fav* (low)	wk.	3.16
Carders, second hands, *mac*	wk.	7.50	Dressers, overseers, *mac*	wk.	12.00
Carders, third hands, *mac*	wk.	6.00	Dressers, second hands, *mac*	wk.	7.50
Carders, spare, *mac*	wk.	5.52	Dressers, second hands, *mac*	wk.	7.02
Carders, spare, *mac*	wk.	4.80	Dressers, second hands, *mac*	wk.	6.00
Carders, spare, *mac*	wk.	4.50	Dressers, third hands, *mac*	wk.	4.98
Carders, spare, *mav*	wk.	3.42	Dressers, third hands, *mac*	wk.	4.80
Card grinders, *mac*	wk.	7.00	Dressers, boys, *mac*	wk.	3.00
Card grinders, *mac*	wk.	6.60	Dressers, *fav* (high)	wk.	6.36
Card grinders, *mac*	wk.	6.50	Dressers, *fav* (medium)	wk.	5.34
Card grinders, *mav*	wk.	6.00	Dressers, *fav* (med. low)	wk.	4.64
Doublers, *mac*	wk	4.98	Dressers, *fav* (low)	wk.	2.76
Doublers, *mac*	wk.	4.20	Warpers, *fav* (high)	wk.	5.14
Drawers, *fac*	wk.	3.48	Warpers, *fav* (medium)	wk.	4.67
Drawers, *fac*	wk.	2.88	Warpers, *fav* (med. low)	wk.	3.89
Drawers, *fav*	wk.	3.19	Warpers, *fav* (low)	wk.	3.42
Drawers and speeders, spare, *fac*	wk.	3.12			
Drawers and speeders, spare, *fac*	wk.	2.37	*Weaving.*		
Drawers and speeders, spare, *fav*	wk.	2.68	Weavers, overseers, *mac*	wk.	12.00
Lap boys, *mac*	wk.	3.18	Weavers, overseers, *mac*	wk.	10.50
Lap boys, *mac*	wk.	3.00	Weavers, second hands, *mac*	wk.	9.00
Pickers, *mac*	wk.	6.00	Weavers, second hands, *mac*	wk.	7.50
Pickers, (breakers and openers) *mav*	wk.	4.98	Weavers, third hands, *mac*	wk.	6.00
Pickers, (openers) *mav*	wk.	4.80	Weavers, third hands, *mac*	wk.	4.98
Speeders, *fac*	wk.	4.68	Weavers, third hands, *mac*	wk.	4.80
Speeders, *fac*	wk.	3.50	Weavers, *man* (high)	wk.	5.52
Speeders, *fav* (high)	wk.	3.96	Weavers, *mav* (medium)	wk.	4.52
Speeders, *fav* (low)	wk.	3.06	Weavers, *mav* (low)	wk.	3.60
Strippers, *mac*	wk.	6.00	Weavers, *fav* (high)	wk.	5.00
Strippers, *mac*	wk.	4.80	Weavers, *fav* (medium)	wk.	3.77
Strippers, *mac*	wk.	4.50	Weavers, *fav* (low)	wk.	2.80
Strippers, *mav*	wk.	5.52	Weavers, spare, *fac*	wk.	4.32
Winders, overseers, *mac*	wk	6.00	Weavers, spare, *fac*	wk.	2.37
Winders, *mac*	wk.	5.52	Weavers, spare, *fav*	wk.	2.89
Winders, *mac*	wk.	4.20			
Winders, *fav* (high)	wk.	5.76	*Cloth Room.*		
Winders, *fav* (medium)	wk.	4.68	Cloth room hands, overseer, *mac*	wk.	12.00
Winders, *fav* (low)	wk.	3.00	Cloth room hands, overseer, *mac*	wk.	10.50
Winders, spare, *fac*	wk.	3.24	Cloth room hands, *mac*	wk.	6.00
Winders, spare, *fac*	wk.	2.79	Cloth room hands, *mac*	wk.	4.80
Winders, spare, *fac*	wk.	2.37	Cloth room hands, *mac*	wk.	3.50
			Cloth room hands, *mac*	wk.	3.30
Spinning.			Cloth room hands, *fac*	wk.	3.50
Doffers, *fav* (high)	wk.	3.42	Cloth room hands, *fac*	wk.	3.12
Doffers, *fav* (low)	wk.	3.24			
Reelers, *fac*	wk.	6.42	*Repair Hands, etc.*		
Spinners, overseers, *mac*	wk.	13.00	Laborers, *mac*	wk.	4.98
Spinners, overseers, *mac*	wk.	12.00	Masons, *mac*	wk.	10.50
Spinners, overseers, *mac*	wk.	10.50	Repair hands, overseer, *mac*	wk.	13.50
Spinners, second hands, *mac*	wk.	7.50	Repair hands, overseer, *mac*	wk.	10.00
Spinners, third hands, *mac*	wk.	6.50	Repair hands, overseer, *mac*	wk.	8.00
Spinners, third hands, *mac*	wk.	5.52	Repair hands, *mac*	wk.	10.50
Spinners, section hands, *mac*	wk.	4.98	Repair hands, *mac*	wk.	3.00
Spinners, section hands, *mac*	wk.	4.80	Repair hands, *mav*	wk.	7.08
Spinners, section hands, *mac*	wk.	4.50	Teamsters, *mac*	wk.	6.00
Spinners, *mac*	wk.	3.48	Waste pickers, *fac*	wk.	2.64
Spinners, spare, *fac*	wk.	2.88	Watchmen, *mac*	wk.	12.00
Spinners, spare, *fac*	wk.	2.13	Watchmen, *mac*	wk.	6.84
Spinners, spare, *fav*	wk.	2.54	Watchmen, *mac*	wk.	6.60
Spinners, filling, *fav* (high)	wk.	3.50			
Spinners, filling, *fav* (medium)	wk.	3.45			
Spinners, filling, *fav* (low)	wk.	3.00	**1838.**		
Spinners, warp, *fav* (high)	wk.	4.20			
Spinners, warp, *fav* (medium)	wk.	3.47	*Carding.*		
Spinners, warp, *fav* (low)	wk.	3.00	Carders, overseers, *mac*	wk.	14.00
			Carders, overseers, *mac*	wk.	13.50
Dressing.			Carders, overseers, *mac*	wk.	12.00
Drawers-in, *fav* (high)	wk.	3.97	Carders, second hands, *mac*	wk.	7.50
Drawers-in, *fav* (medium)	wk.	3.70	Carders, second hands, *mac*	wk.	7.00
			Carders, spare, *mac*	wk.	5.52
			Carders, spare, *mac*	wk.	4.80

Wages: Cotton Mill Operatives—CONTINUED.

Years and Occupations.	Basis.	Amount.	Years and Occupations.	Basis.	Amount.
Carding—Con.			*Dressing*—Con.		
Carders, spare, *mac*	wk.	$4.50	Warpers, *fav* (medium)	wk.	$3.92
Card grinders, *mac*	wk.	7.00	Warpers, *fav* (low)	wk.	3.51
Card grinders, *mac*	wk.	6.60			
Card grinders, *mac*	wk.	6.50	*Weaving.*		
Card grinders, *mac*	wk.	6.00	Weavers, overseers, *mac*	wk.	12.00
Doublers, *mac*	wk.	4.98	Weavers, overseers, *mac*	wk.	9.00
Doublers, *mac*	wk.	4.20	Weavers, second hands, *mac*.	wk.	7.00
Drawers, *fac*	wk.	2.94	Weavers, third hands, *mac*	wk.	6.60
Drawers, *fac*	wk.	2.67	Weavers, *mac*	wk.	5.70
Drawers, *fav*	wk.	2.80	Weavers, *mac*	wk.	3.90
Drawers and speeders, spare, *fac*	wk.	2.88	Weavers, *fav* (high)	wk.	4.36
Drawers and speeders, spare, *fac*	wk.	2.25	Weavers, *fav* (medium)	wk.	3.65
Drawers and speeders, spare, *fav*	wk.	2.49	Weavers, *fav* (low)	wk.	3.26
Lap boys, *mac*	wk.	3.00	Weavers, spare, *fac*	wk.	4.32
Pickers, *mac*	wk.	6.00	Weavers, spare, *fac*	wk.	2.10
Pickers, *mac*	wk.	5.52	Weavers, spare, *fav*	wk.	2.72
Pickers, *mac*	wk.	4.20	*Cloth Room.*		
Speeders, *fac*	wk.	3.33	Cloth room hands, overseer, *mac*	wk.	12.00
Speeders, *fac*	wk.	3.00	Cloth room hands, *mac*	wk.	6.00
Speeders, *fav*	wk.	3.18	Cloth room hands, *mac*	wk.	5.10
Strippers, *mac*	wk.	6.00	Cloth room hands, *mac*	wk.	4.98
Strippers, *mac*	wk.	4.80	Cloth room hands, *fac*	wk.	3.18
Strippers, *mac*	wk.	4.50	Cloth room hands, *fac*	wk.	2.88
Winders, overseers, *mac*	wk.	7.00	Cloth room hands, *fac*	wk.	2.37
Winders, *mac*	wk.	5.52	Cloth room boys, *mac*	wk.	3.72
Winders, *mac*	wk.	3.90	Cloth room boys, *mac*	wk.	2.40
Winders, *fav* (high)	wk.	5.91	Cloth room boys, *mac*	wk.	1.98
Winders, *fav* (low)	wk.	4.37			
Winders, spare, *fac*	wk.	4.50	*Repair Hands, etc.*		
Winders, spare, *fac*	wk.	2.37	Repair hands, overseer, *mac* .	wk.	12.00
Winders, spare, *fav*	wk.	3.40	Repair hands, *mac*	wk.	9.00
			Repair hands, *mac*	wk.	4.50
Spinning.			Repair hands, *mav*	wk.	7.90
Doffers, *fav* (high)	wk.	2.94	Watchmen, *mac*	wk.	12.00
Doffers, *fav* (medium)	wk.	2.71	Watchmen, *mac*	wk.	6.60
Doffers, *fav* (low)	wk.	2.10	Watchmen, *mac*	wk.	6.00
Reelers, *fac*	wk.	4.73			
Reelers, *fav*	wk.	3.88	**1840.**		
Spinners, overseers, *mac*	wk.	13.00			
Spinners, overseers, *mac*	wk.	12.00	*Carding.*		
Spinners, second hands, *mac*.	wk.	7.50	Carders, overseers, *mac*	wk.	12.00
Spinners, second hands, *mac*.	wk.	6.60	Carders, *mav*	wk.	4.50
Spinners, third hands, *mac*	wk.	6.50	Carders, *mfav*	wk.	3.50
Spinners, section hands, *mac*.	wk.	4.98	Card grinders, *mav*	wk.	4.75
Spinners, section hands, *mac*.	wk.	4.32	Drawers, *fav*	wk.	2.50
Spinners, spare, *fac*	wk.	2.79	Lap tenders, *mav*	wk.	4.00
Spinners, spare, *fac*	wk.	2.10	Pickers, *mav*	wk.	4.68
Spinners, spare, *fav*	wk.	2.40	Pickers, (scutchers) *mav*	wk.	5.00
Spinners, filling, *fav* (high)	wk.	3.48	Pickers, (willow hands) *mav*.	wk.	4.00
Spinners, filling, *fav* (medium)	wk.	2.94	Speeders, *fav*	wk.	3.00
Spinners, filling, *fav* (low)	wk.	2.88	Strippers, *mav*	wk.	4.00
Spinners, warp, *fav* (high)	wk.	3.12			
Spinners, warp, *fav* (medium)	wk.	3.03	*Spinning.*		
Spinners, warp, *fav* (low)	wk.	2.98	Spinners, overseers, *mac*	wk.	12.00
			Spinners, *fav*	wk.	3.00
Dressing.					
Drawers-in, *fav* (high)	wk.	3.45	*Weaving.*		
Drawers-in, *fav* (medium)	wk.	3.37	Weavers, overseers, *mac*	wk.	12.00
Drawers-in, *fav* (low)	wk.	3.21	Weavers, *fav*	wk.	2.75
Dressers, overseers, *mac*	wk.	12.00			
Dressers, overseers, *mac*	wk.	9.00	*Cloth Room.*		
Dressers, second hands, *mac*.	wk.	7.50	Cloth room hands, *fav*	wk.	2.25
Dressers, second hands, *mac*.	wk.	6.00			
Dressers, third hands, *mac*	wk.	4.98	*Repair Hands, etc.*		
Dressers, third hands, *mac*	wk.	4.20	Repair hands, *mav*	wk.	9.00
Dressers, boys, *mac*	wk.	3.00	Watchmen, *mav*	wk.	5.00
Dressers, *fav* (high)	wk.	5.95	Watchmen and yard hands, *mav*	wk.	6.60
Dressers, *fav* (medium)	wk.	4.93			
Dressers, *fav* (low)	wk.	4.35	All departments, *fav*	wk.	2.84
Warpers, *fav* (high)	wk.	4.50			

Wages: Cotton Mill Operatives—CONCLUDED.

Years and Occupations.	Basis.	Amount.	Years and Occupations.	Basis.	Amount.
1843.*			*Dressing.*		
Carding.			Dresser tenders, *mav*	wk.	$9.79
Carders, *mav*	wk.	$5.10			
Carders, *fav*	wk.	2.72	*Weaving.*		
			Weavers, *mav*	wk.	6.00
Spinning.			Weavers, *fav* (high)	wk.	4.99
Spinners, *mav*	wk.	6.66	Weavers, *fav* (low)	wk.	3.52
Spinners, *fav*	wk.	2.64			
			Dyeing.		
Dressing.			Dyers, *mav*	wk.	6.21
Dressers, *mav*	wk.	7.74			
Dressers, *fav*	wk.	2.98	*Repair Hands, etc.*		
			Laborers, *mav*	wk.	5.52
Weaving.			Repair hands, *mav*	wk.	8.58
Weavers, *mav*	wk.	7.14	Watchmen and yard hands, *mav*	wk.	6.36
Weavers, *fav*	wk.	2.84	All departments, *fav*	wk.	3.62
Cloth Room.					
Cloth room hands, *mav*	wk.	7.14	**1860.**		
Cloth room hands, *fav*	wk.	2.96			
			Carding.		
Repair Hands, etc.			Carders, *mav* (high)	wk.	4.98
Repair hands, *mav*	wk.	8.58	Carders, *mav* (medium)	wk.	4.56
Overseers, all departments, *mav*	wk.	12.00	Carders, *mav* (low)	wk.	3.75
Watchmen and yard hands, *mav*	wk.	6.42	Pickers, *mav* (high)	wk.	6.00
			Pickers, *mav* (medium)	wk.	4.98
1848.			Pickers, *mav* (low)	wk.	3.75
Carding.					
Carders, *mav*	wk.	4.50	*Spinning.*		
Pickers, *mav*	wk.	6.00	Spinners, *mav* (high)	wk.	5.58
			Spinners, *mav* (low)	wk.	5.12
Spinning.			Spinners, *fav*	wk.	3.21
Spinners, *mfav*	wk.	2.63			
			Dressing.		
Dressing.			Dresser tenders, *mav*	wk.	11.04
Dresser tenders, *mav*	wk.	7.02			
			Weaving.		
Weaving.			Weavers, *mav* (high)	wk.	5.68
Weavers, *mav*	wk.	4.20	Weavers, *mav* (low)	wk.	4.00
Weavers, *fav*	wk.	4.61	Weavers, *fav* (high)	wk.	4.54
			Weavers, *fav* (medium)	wk.	3.73
Dyeing.			Weavers, *fav* (low)	wk.	3.05
Dyers, *mav*	wk.	6.25			
			Dyeing.		
Watchmen, etc.			Dyers, *mav*	wk.	6.15
Watchmen and yard hands, *mav*	wk.	6.00			
All departments, *fav*	wk.	4.11	*Repair Hands, etc.*		
			Laborers, *mav* (high)	wk.	6.00
1850.			Laborers, *mav* (low)	wk.	4.99
Carding.			Repair hands, *mav* (high)	wk.	9.00
Carders, *mav* (high)	wk.	4.98	Repair hands, *mav* (medium)	wk.	8.70
Carders, *mav* (low)	wk.	4.50	Repair hands, *mav* (low)	wk.	8.40
Pickers, *mav* (high)	wk.	7.02	Watchmen and yard hands, *mav* (high)	wk.	7.00
Pickers, *mav* (low)	wk.	4.80	Watchmen and yard hands, *mav* (medium)	wk.	6.00
			Watchmen and yard hands, *mav* (low)	wk.	5.64
Spinning.			All departments, *fav* (high)	wk.	3.78
Spinners, *mfav*	wk.	2.63	All departments, *fav* (medium)	wk.	3.26
			All departments, *fav* (low)	wk.	3.00

* In the case of females the wages for 1843, as obtained by the Bureau, were net average weekly wages, the operatives in each department being given their board in addition thereto. The amounts presented in the table have been obtained by adding to the actual *net* average wages the estimated amount of $1.25 per week for board, the sum thus obtained being presented as the *gross* average weekly wages.

We also present, as a matter of historical interest, the following table of wages and prices for certain occupations and articles for various years included in the period from 1630 to 1777. These wages and prices were obtained from quotations of decrees of the General Court (published in Felt's "History of Massachusetts Currency"), by which the wages to be paid for work performed were regulated from time to time, and the prices established for which the articles designated should be accepted either as a part of the circulating medium of the times or received at the treasury in payment of public dues.

The wages and prices quoted in this table, in accordance with the customs and usages of the time, were also considered to be indicative of the price to be paid in proportion for a day's labor at seasons of the year other than those specified for the given occupation, or for better or less desirable qualities of any given article. This is especially the case as regards the wages and prices given for 1777, the price paid to farm laborers being taken as the standard from which the wages paid to mechanics, tradesmen, and other laborers were to be computed. In the same year, also, the amounts stated for wood, pine boards, and lumber generally were the prices paid upon delivery at Boston; for cotton, sugar, and other imported articles, at port where first landed, and for bloomery iron, etc., at place of manufacture, due allowance being made and charged for transportation therefrom to various parts of the State.

Table of Occupations and Articles.   PRICES CURRENT.

OCCUPATIONS AND ARTICLES.	Year.	Basis.	Amount.	OCCUPATIONS AND ARTICLES.	Year.	Basis.	Amount.
OCCUPATIONS.				*Occupations* — Con.			
				Laborers,	1630	day	$0.167
Carpenters and joiners, (master workmen; with board) . . .	1630	day	$0.223	(with board) .	1630	day	.083
				(best) . .	1633	day	.25
Carpenters and joiners, (inferior workmen; with board) . . .	1630	day	.167	(best; with board) .	1633	day	.111
Carpenters and joiners, (master workmen) .	1633	day	.333	(from Oct. 1 to Apr. 1) .	1672	day	.209
Carpenters and joiners, (master workmen; with board) . . .	1633	day	.195	(from Apr. 1 to July 1) .	1672	day	.278
Carpenters and joiners, (Mar. 1 to Oct. 10) .	1672	day	.333	(from July 1 to Oct. 1, with board only)	1672	day	.333
	1712	day	.833	Laborers, agricultural (cutting peas) . .	1672	acre	.50
Coopers, (piece work, for tight bbl. of 32 gal.)	1672	bbl.	.444	Laborers, agricultural (mowing English grass)	1672	acre	.333
				Laborers, agricultural (mowing salt marsh) .	1672	acre	.333

Table of Occupations and Articles.   PRICES CURRENT — Con.

Occupations and Articles.	Year.	Basis.	Amount.	Occupations and Articles.	Year.	Basis.	Amount.
Occupations — Con.				*Articles* — Con.			
Laborers, agricultural (mowing fresh meadow)	1672	acre	$0.25	Beaver, (sold) . . .	1635	lb.	$1.67
				Beef, merchantable .	1727	bbl.	10.00
Laborers, agricultural (reaping wheat) . .	1672	acre	.667	(240 lbs. in bbl.) .	1777	bbl.	12.41
				(stall-fed) .	1777	lb.	.056
Laborers, agricultural (reaping rye) . .	1672	acre	.50	(grass-fed) .	1777	lb.	.042
				Boards, merchantable white pine . .	1777	M.ft.	8.00
Laborers, agricultural (reaping barley) . .	1672	acre	.167	Butter, ...	1777	lb.	.139
				(by the firkin) .	1777	lb.	.125
Laborers, agricultural (reaping oats) . .	1672	acre	.167	sweet firkin	1727	lb.	.167
				Calfskins, raw . .	1777	lb.	.083
Laborers, agricultural (cutting wood) . .	1672	cd.	.209	Charcoal, (by the basket)	1777	b'k't	.167
				Cheese, (manufactured in America) . .	1777	lb.	.083
Laborers, agricultural (summer; with board)	1777	day	.50	Chocolate, (manufactured in America) .	1777	lb.	.278
Masons and bricklayers, (master workmen; with board) . .	1630	day	.223	Cloth, tow (yard wide) .	1777	yd.	.375
				homespun cotton and linen (yard wide) .	1777	yd.	.583
Masons and bricklayers, (inferior workmen; with board) . .	1630	day	.167	Cocoa, best . . .	1777	cwt.	21.67
				Codfish, merchantable dry . . .	1727	q't'l	5.00
Masons and bricklayers, (master workmen)	1633	day	.333	Coffee, ...	1777	lb.	.223
				Corn, ...	1642	bu.	.416
Masons and bricklayers, (master workmen; with board) . .	1633	day	.195		1645	bu.	.444
					1647	bu.	.50
Masons and bricklayers, (Mar. 1 to Oct. 10.)	1672	day	.333		1658	bu.	.444
					1662	bu.	.50
Stone layers, (Mar. 1 to Oct. 10.) . .	1672	day	.333		1681	bu.	.583
					1690	bu.	.583
Tailors, (master workmen; with board) .	1633	day	.167		1694	bu.	.375
				Indian (rates) .	1635	bu.	.833
(inferior workmen; with board) .	1633	day	.111	Indian (sold) .	1635	bu.	1.00
				Indian . .	1636	bu.	.833
(master workmen; 12 hours per day) .	1672	day	.278	Indian . .	1640	bu.	.667
				Indian . .	1648	bu.	.50
(apprentices — first 4 years) .	1672	day	.167	Indian . .	1649	bu.	.50
				Indian . .	1650	bu.	.50
				Indian (Oct. 17 to Mar. 10)	1654	bu.	.444
				Indian (thereafter)	1654	bu.	.50
ARTICLES.				Indian . .	1655	bu.	.416
				Indian . .	1664	bu.	.50
Barley, . . .	1640	bu.	$0.833	Indian . .	1667	bu.	.444
	1642	bu.	.667	Indian . .	1670	bu.	.50
	1645	bu.	.667	Indian . .	1671	bu.	.444
	1647	bu.	.667	Indian . .	1680	bu.	.583
	1648	bu.	.833	Indian . .	1685	bu.	.50
	1649	bu.	.916	Indian . .	1688	bu.	.195
	1650	bu.	.833	Indian . .	1727	bu.	.667
	1654	bu.	.833	Indian . .	1777	bu.	.667
	1655	bu.	.75	Cotton, . .	1777	lb.	.611
	1658	bu.	.667	(by the bag) .	1777	lb.	.50
	1662	bu.	.916	Duck, dunghill .	1777	lb.	.07
	1664	bu.	.75	Flannel, striped (yard wide) . .	1777	yd.	.583
	1667	bu.	.667	Flax, . . .	1727	lb.	.223
	1680	bu.	.583	good merchantable	1777	lb.	.167
	1681	bu.	.667	Flour, (from Southern States) .	1777	cwt.	5.00
	1685	bu.	.667	(manufactured in Mass.) .	1777	cwt.	4.16
	1688	bu.	.416	Fowl, dunghill .	1777	lb.	.07
	1690	bu.	.667	Geese, . . .	1777	lb.	.056
	1727	bu.	1.00	Hay, best English .	1777	cwt	.833
Barley malt, . .	1658	bu.	.667	Hemp, . . .	1727	lb.	.125
	1662	bu.	.916	Hides, dry . .	1727	lb.	.083
	1664	bu.	.75	raw . .	1777	lb.	.042
	1667	bu.	.667	tanned . .	1777	lb.	.209
	1670	bu.	.667	Iron, merchantable bar .	1727	cwt.	8.00
	1671	bu.	.916	bloomery .	1777	cwt.	5.00
	1680	bu.	.583	refined .	1777	cwt.	8.34
	1681	bu.	.667	Lamb, . . .	1777	lb.	.056
	1685	bu.	.667	Leather, tanned .	1727	lb.	.167
	1688	bu.	.416	Mackerel, . .	1727	bbl.	5.00
	1690	bu.	.667	Meal, Indian . .	1777	bu.	.667
	1694	bu.	.375				
Beans, . . .	1777	bu.	1.00				

Table of Occupations and Articles.   PRICES CURRENT — Con.

Occupations and Articles.	Year.	Basis.	Amount.	Occupations and Articles.	Year.	Basis.	Amount.
Articles — Con.				*Articles — Con.*			
Meal, rye . . .	1777	bu.	$0.833	Rye, ...	1727	bu.	$1.00
Milk, ...	1777	qt.	.035		1777	bu.	.833
Molasses, best quality .	1777	gal.	.667	Rum, New England .	1777	gal.	.75
(by the hhd., including cask) . .	1772	gal.	.556	New England (by the hhd. or bbl., exclusive of 13s. for hhd. or 4s. for bbl.) .	1777	gal.	.639
(by the bbl., exclusive of 3s. for bbl.) .	1777	gal.	.611	West India . .	1777	qt.	.333
Mutton, . . .	1777	lb.	.056	West India . .	1777	gal.	1.28
Oats, ...	1680	bu.	.278	West India (by the hhd., including cask) . .	1777	gal.	1.11
	1681	bu.	.333	West India (by the bbl., exclusive of bbl.) . .	1777	gal.	1.14
	1685	bu.	.333	Salt, (imported) . .	1777	bu.	1.67
	1688	bu.	.139	(manufactured in Mass.) . .	1777	bu.	2.00
	1690	bu.	.25	Shoes, men's (sizes eleven and twelve)	1672	pr.	.833
	1694	bu.	.223	women's (sizes seven and eight)	1672	pr.	.611
	1727	bu.	.416	men's neat's leather	1777	pr.	1.33
	1777	bu.	.333	Stockings, men's best yarn . . .	1777	pr.	1.00
Oil, ...	1727	bbl.	8.34	Sugar, best Muscovado .	1777	lb.	.111
blubber refined .	1777	bbl.	5.00	best Muscovado .	1777	cwt.	10.00
liver (by the bbl.) .	1777	gal.	.667	best Muscovado (by the hhd.) .	1777	cwt.	9.00
Peas, ...	1640	bu.	1.00	Tallow, tried . .	1727	lb.	.111
	1642	bu.	.556	tried . .	1777	lb.	.104
	1645	bu.	.583	rough . .	1777	lb.	.07
	1648	bu.	.667	Turkey, . . .	1777	lb.	.07
	1649	bu.	.667	Turpentine, full bound .	1727	cwt.	2.17
	1650	bu.	.667	Tobacco, well cured .	1727	lb.	.056
	1655	bu.	.667	Veal, . . .	1777	lb.	.056
	1658	bu.	.667	Wheat, (summer) . .	1640	bu.	1.00
	1662	bu.	.75		1642	bu.	.667
	1664	bu.	.667		1645	bu.	.667
	1667	bu.	.583		1647	bu.	.75
	1670	bu.	.667		1648	bu.	.833
	1671	bu.	.833		1649	bu.	.833
	1680	bu.	.667		1650	bu.	.833
	1681	bu.	.667		1654	bu.	.833
	1685	bu.	.667		1655	bu.	.75
	1688	bu.	.50		1658	bu.	.833
	1690	bu.	.667		1662	bu.	.916
	1694	bu.	.583		1664	bu.	.833
	1727	bu.	1.50		1667	bu.	.833
	1777	bu.	1.33		1670	bu.	.833
Pork, good merchantable	1727	bbl.	18.34		1671	bu.	.916
fresh (well fatted)	1777	lb.	.063		1680	bu.	.833
salted (220 lbs. in bbl.) . .	1777	bbl.	15.33		1681	bu.	1.00
Potatoes, Spanish (high)	1777	bu.	.333*		1685	bu.	.833
Spanish (low)	1777	bu.	.223*		1688	bu.	.458
Pots and kettles, cast iron . . .	1727	cwt.	8.00		1690	bu.	.833
Rye, ...	1640	bu.	.833		1694	bu.	.833
	1642	bu.	.556	(summer) . .	1727	bu.	1.17
	1645	bu.	.583	(winter) . .	1727	bu.	1.33
	1647	bu.	.583		1777	bu.	1.25
	1648	bu.	.667	Wood, Eastern . .	1777	cd.	3.66
	1649	bu.	.667	good walnut (high)	1777	cd.	5.00†
	1650	bu.	.667	good walnut (low)	1777	cd.	4.66‡
	1654	bu.	.667	good oak . .	1777	cd.	4.00
	1655	bu.	.583	green oak . .	1777	cd.	4.66
	1658	bu.	.667	Wool, merchantable sheep's . . .	1777	lb.	.333
	1662	bu.	.75	Wax, bayberry . .	1727	lb.	.223
	1664	bu.	.667	bee's . .	1727	lb.	.416
	1667	bu.	.667				
	1670	bu.	.667				
	1671	bu.	.833				
	1680	bu.	.50				
	1681	bu.	.75				
	1685	bu.	.667				
	1688	bu.	.333				
	1690	bu.	.667				
	1694	bu.	.458				

* Prices varied according to season.   † Delivered at door of buyer.
‡ Delivered at wharf in Boston.

THE OCCUPATIONS AND ARTICLES TABLES, BY PERIODS OF YEARS.

In the tables which follow, we present averages drawn from the preceding tables of occupations and articles, by name, for the various periods of years from 1752 to 1860, the time covered by the investigation, and by the use of the wages and prices already published in previous reports of the Bureau from 1860 forward to 1883.

Following the tables of occupations and articles, by periods of years, we present wage and price fluctuations, also by periods of years, for certain occupations and articles brought forward into a separate table, using only those bases which are common to the particular occupation or article considered.

For the purpose of presenting these averages, the whole number of years comprehended by the tables, from 1752 to 1883, has been divided by decades, so far as possible, into the following periods of years : —

1752 to 1760;	1801 to 1810;	1851 to 1860;
1761 to 1770;	1811 to 1820;	1861 to 1880;
1771 to 1780;	1821 to 1830;	1881 to 1883.
1781 to 1790;	1831 to 1840;	
1791 to 1800;	1841 to 1850;	

With the exception of the first period beginning with 1752 and ending with 1760, and the periods from 1861 to 1880 and 1881 to 1883, each period covers ten years, and all periods include both the year with which they begin and the year with which they end. The period from 1861 to 1880 has been made to include twenty years, there being no wages or prices reported for any year included in the decade ending with 1870. The period from 1881 to 1883 presents figures for the years 1881 and 1883 only.

The wages used as the basis of the averages presented for the periods from 1861 to 1880 and from 1881 to 1883 have been taken, as has been stated, from previous reports of the Bureau, as follows : —

WAGES. — For the year 1860, from Part III., of the Report for 1879 ; for the year 1872, from Parts II. and IV., of the Report for 1874 ; for the year 1875, from Part I., of the Report

for 1876, and from Vol. II., Census of Massachusetts for 1875; for the year 1878, from Part III., of the Report for 1879; for the year 1880, from Part II., of the Report for 1883; for the year 1881, from Part IV., of the Report for 1882; for the year 1883, from Part II., of the Report for 1884. For 1883, also, wages for paper-mill operatives, ship and boat builders, and tanners and curriers are included in the averages given for the period ending with 1883, wages for these occupations, although used in Part III., not being included in Part II. of the report for 1884, from which averages for the other occupations were drawn.

PRICES. — For the years 1860, 1872, 1878, 1881, and 1883, from Part IV., of the Report for 1884.

In the occupations and articles tables, by periods of years, only those bases are used for which averages are given in more than one period for the same occupation or article.

In the occupations table, by periods of years, for purposes of exact comparison so far as possible, all wages given by the week have been brought to the basis of day, and wages given by the year to the basis of month, wages being presented in the period showings by the day and month only. The prices paid to clothing makers and shoemakers for piece work, where the basis was pair or piece, have not been used, although the bases appear for more than one period.

The wages paid to ship and boat builders for the periods ending with 1860, 1880, and 1883 are high as compared with the averages obtained for the same occupation for other periods, the wages presented for the periods named being the amounts paid, for the given basis, for general shipbuilding work, and including undoubtedly higher-priced labor than that for which wages were obtained for the periods preceding 1860.

In the table of articles, by periods of years, the term " wholesale " represents, for any given basis, the average price obtained for any article, when sold in large quantities, although this fact may have been indicated by the use of some other term in the occupations and articles tables, by name. This does not apply, of course, to articles which are usually sold both in large and small quantities, as, for instance, flour by the pound and barrel, or fish by the pound and quintal. Hose, socks, and stockings, although presented separately in the preceding tables, are combined in the table by periods of years.

The averages given, for the period ending with 1883, for dress goods, dry goods, etc., and all articles of clothing were taken from a table printed in Part IV. of the Report for 1884, where the prices, by reason of the nature of the articles quoted, were divided into grades, and designated either as "high," "medium high," "medium," "medium low," or "low." In presenting averages for such articles for the period ending with 1883, the three lower grades only have been used, except in the case of alpaca, beige, galloon, handkerchiefs, pins, satin, shirtings, and ticking, for which all grades are included in the averages, the range of prices for these articles corresponding in most respects to those obtained for the preceding periods.

In the consideration of the averages presented by periods of years, reference should always be had to the occupations and articles tables, by name, to determine the exact data used as the basis for these averages. For instance, an average wage presented for a certain occupation, for any particular period, might be influenced either by the fact that wages obtained for the years included in that period were generally for very high or very low priced labor, or that wages for that period were given for but one or two years only. The same is also true as regards prices, extremely high or low prices for certain years or for the entire period, or quotations of prices for but one year only, making a proportionately high or low average for that period, as compared with the averages obtained, for the same article, for other periods.

THE OCCUPATIONS AND ARTICLES TABLES, BY PERIODS OF YEARS.

Occupations: By Periods of Years.

Occupations and Periods.	Basis.	Amount.	Occupations and Periods.	Basis.	Amount.
Agricultural Laborers.			*Bookbinders* — Con.		
1752 to 1760, . . .	day	$0.311	1861 to 1880, ...	day	$1.91
(with oxen) .	day	1.33	1881 to 1883, ...	day	1.49
1761 to 1770, . . .	day	.33			
(with oxen) .	day	1.66	*Brewery and Distillery Employés.*		
1771 to 1780, . . .	day	.315			
(with oxen) .	day	1.50	1851 to 1860, . . .	day	2.02
1781 to 1790, . . .	day	.396	1861 to 1880, . . .	day	2.13
1791 to 1800, . . .	day	.478	1881 to 1883, . . .	day	2.45
1801 to 1810, . . .	day	.779			
1811 to 1820, . . .	day	.782	*Butchers.*		
	mo.	13.50	1771 to 1780, . . .	day	.333
(with board) .	day	.56	1801 to 1810, . . .	day	.50
(with board and lodging) . .	mo.	8.00	1811 to 1820, . . .	day	.75
			1821 to 1830, . . .	day	.917
(with two meals a day) . .	mo.	10.00	1861 to 1880, . . .	day	2.03
(with oxen) .	day	2.25	1881 to 1883, . . .	day	1.36
1821 to 1830, . . .	day	.803			
	mo.	16.50	*Carpenters.*		
(with board) .	day	.58	1771 to 1780, . . .	day	.522
(with board and lodging) . .	mo.	11.00	1781 to 1790, . . .	day	.539
			1791 to 1800, . . .	day	.736
(with two meals a day) . .	mo.	13.50	1801 to 1810, . . .	day	1.09
(with oxen) .	day	1.82	1811 to 1820, . . .	day	1.13
1831 to 1840, . . .	day	.875	(with board)	day	.833
	mo.	16.50	1821 to 1830, . . .	day	1.07
(with board) .	day	.55	(with board)	day	.648
(with board and lodging) . .	mo.	11.00	1831 to 1840, . . .	day	1.40
			(with board)	day	.71
(with two meals a day) . .	mo.	13.50	1841 to 1850, . . .	day	1.37
1841 to 1850, . . .	day	.95	(with board)	day	.748
	mo.	17.50	1851 to 1860, . . .	day	2.03
(with board and lodging) . .	mo.	11.00	(with board)	day	1.00
			1861 to 1880, . . .	day	2.42
(with two meals a day) . .	mo.	13.50	1881 to 1883, . . .	day	2.41
1851 to 1860, . . .	day	1.01			
	mo.	21.50	*Carriage Makers.*		
(with board) .	mo.	11.88	1831 to 1840, . . .	day	1.34
1861 to 1880, . . .	day	1.31	1841 to 1850, . . .	day	1.59
(with board) .	day	.888	1851 to 1860, . . .	day	1.85
1881 to 1883, . . .	mo.	15.72	1861 to 1880, . . .	day	2.40
	day	1.37	1881 to 1883, . . .	day	2.27
(with board) .	mo.	18.00			
Blacksmiths.			*Clockmakers.*		
1781 to 1790, . . .	day	.694	1811 to 1820, . . .	day	1.13
1811 to 1820, . . .	day	.842	1821 to 1830, . . .	day	1.29
(with board) .	day	.538	1831 to 1840, . . .	day	1.29
1821 to 1830, . . .	day	1.12	1841 to 1850, . . .	day	1.29
(with board) .	day	.50	1851 to 1860, . . .	day	1.96
1831 to 1840, . . .	day	1.40	1861 to 1880, . . .	day	2.30
(with board) .	day	.60			
1841 to 1850, . . .	day	1.47	*Clothing Makers.*		
(with board) .	day	.55	1811 to 1820, . . .	day	1.00
1851 to 1860, . . .	day	1.69	(with board)	day	.50
(with board) .	day	.667	1821 to 1830, . . .	day	1.27
1861 to 1880, . . .	day	2.28	(with board)	day	.50
(with board) .	day	.666	1831 to 1840, . . .	day	.896
1881 to 1883, . . .	day	1.92	1841 to 1850, . . .	day	1.38
Bookbinders.			1851 to 1860, . . .	day	1.43
			1861 to 1880, . . .	day	1.93
1831 to 1840, . . .	day	.917	1881 to 1883, . . .	day	1.99
1841 to 1850, . . .	day	1.46	*Cordage Makers.*		
1851 to 1860, . . .	day	1.38	1821 to 1830, . . .	day	1.12
			1831 to 1840, . . .	day	1.21
			1841 to 1850, . . .	day	.914
			1861 to 1880, . . .	day	1.52

Occupations: By Periods of Years—CONTINUED.

Occupations and Periods.	Basis.	Amount.	Occupations and Periods.	Basis.	Amount.
Cotton Mill Operatives.			*Masons*—Con.		
1821 to 1830, . . .	day	$0.439	1811 to 1820, (with board) .	day	$0.754
1831 to 1840, . . .	day	.897	1821 to 1830, .	day	1.22
1841 to 1850, . . .	day	.92	(with board) .	day	.833
1851 to 1860, . . .	day	1.03	1831 to 1840, .	day	1.37
1861 to 1880, . . .	day	1.40	(with board) .	day	.893
1881 to 1883, . . .	day	1.27	1841 to 1850, .	day	1.33
			(with board) .	day	.875
Glass Makers.			1851 to 1860, . . .	day	1.53
1821 to 1830, . . .	day	1.13	1861 to 1880, . . .	day	2.79
1831 to 1840, . . .	day	1.62	1881 to 1883, . . .	day	2.14
1841 to 1850, . . .	day	2.44			
1851 to 1860, . . .	day	2.96	*Metal Workers.*		
1861 to 1880, . . .	day	1.79	1811 to 1820, . . .	day	1.05
1881 to 1883, . . .	day	2.01	1821 to 1830, . . .	day	1.23
			1831 to 1840, . . .	day	1.54
Gold and Silver Workers.			1841 to 1850, . . .	day	1.42
1831 to 1840, . . .	day	.974	1851 to 1860, . . .	day	1.35
1841 to 1850, . . .	day	1.28	1861 to 1880, . . .	day	2.16
1851 to 1860, . . .	day	1.69	1881 to 1883, . . .	day	2.00
1861 to 1880, . . .	day	1.53			
1881 to 1883, (gold workers			*Millwrights.*		
only)	day	3.21	1791 to 1800, . . .	day	1.09
			1811 to 1820, . . .	day	1.13
Harness Makers.			1821 to 1830, . . .	day	1.21
1811 to 1820, . . .	day	.88	1831 to 1840, . . .	day	1.39
(with board) .	day	.45	1841 to 1850, . . .	day	1.39
1821 to 1830, . . .	day	1.13	1851 to 1860, . . .	day	1.66
(with board) .	day	.45	1861 to 1880, . . .	day	2.65
1831 to 1840, . . .	day	1.25	1881 to 1883, . . .	day	2 54
1841 to 1850, . . .	day	1.46			
1851 to 1860, . . .	day	1.65	*Nail Makers.*		
			1781 to 1790, . . .	day	.481
Hat Makers.			1811 to 1820, . . .	day	1.00
1841 to 1850, . . .	day	2.08		mo.	18.00
1851 to 1860, . . .	day	2.54	1821 to 1830, . . .	day	1.39
1861 to 1880, . . .	day	1.96	1831 to 1840, . . .	day	.86
1881 to 1883, . . .	day	1.68		mo.	43.55
			1841 to 1850, . . .	day	1.50
Laborers.				mo.	47.42
1752 to 1760, . . .	day	.29	1851 to 1860, . . .	mo.	62.12
1761 to 1770, . . .	day	.325	1861 to 1880, . . .	mo.	60.42
	mo.	6.00	1881 to 1883, . . .	day	1.84
1771 to 1780, . . .	day	.376			
1781 to 1790, . . .	day	.428	*Painters.*		
(with team) .	day	1.33	1801 to 1810, . . .	day	1.15
1791 to 1800, . . .	day	.623	1811 to 1820, . . .	day	1.34
	mo.	13.33	1821 to 1830, . . .	day	1.25
(with team) .	day	1.83	1831 to 1840, . . .	day	1.32
1801 to 1810, . . .	day	.817	1841 to 1850, . . .	day	1.47
	mo.	12.25	1851 to 1860, . . .	day	1.85
1811 to 1820, . . .	day	.91	1861 to 1880, . . .	day	2.32
(with team) .	day	1.50	1881 to 1883, . . .	day	1.97
1821 to 1830, . . .	day	.796			
	mo.	10.50	*Paper Mill Operatives.*		
1831 to 1840, . . .	day	.872	1811 to 1820, . . .	day	1.09
1841 to 1850, . . .	day	.852	1821 to 1830, . . .	day	.666
1851 to 1860, . . .	day	.975	1831 to 1840, . . .	day	.749
	mo.	20.00	1841 to 1850, . . .	day	.842
1861 to 1880, . . .	day	1.48	1851 to 1860, . . .	day	1.17
	mo.	34.49	1861 to 1880, . . .	day	1.71
1881 to 1883, . . .	day	1.31	1881 to 1883, . . .	day	1.71
Machinists.			*Printers.*		
1831 to 1840, . . .	day	1.35	1811 to 1820, . . .	day	1.13
1841 to 1850, . . .	day	1.62	1821 to 1830, . . .	day	1 25
1851 to 1860, . . .	day	2.15	1831 to 1840, . . .	day	1.38
1861 to 1880, . . .	day	2.49	1841 to 1850, . . .	day	1.17
1881 to 1883, . . .	day	2.25	1851 to 1860, . . .	day	1.75
			1861 to 1880, . . .	day	2.18
Masons.			1881 to 1883, . . .	day	2.14
1771 to 1780, . . .	day	.666			
1781 to 1790, . . .	day	1.00	*Ship and Boat Builders.*		
1801 to 1810, . . .	day	1.41	1781 to 1790, . . .	day	.889
1811 to 1820, . . .	day	1.52	1811 to 1820, . . .	day	1.25

Occupations: By Periods of Years — Concluded.

Occupations and Periods.	Basis.	Amount.	Occupations and Periods.	Basis.	Amount.
Ship and Boat Builders–Con.			*Tanners and Curriers* — Con.		
1811 to 1820, (with board) .	day	$0.50	1861 to 1880, ...	day	$2.09
1821 to 1830, ...	day	1.40	1881 to 1883, ...	day	1.86
(with board) .	day	.50			
1831 to 1840, ...	day	1.33	*Teachers.*		
(with board) .	day	66	1791 to 1800, ...	mo.	34.22
1841 to 1850, ...	day	1.35	1801 to 1810, ...	mo.	47.50
(with board) .	day	.58	1861 to 1880, ...	mo.	58.74
1851 to 1860, (general ship-building) .	day	3.65	*Teamsters.*		
1861 to 1880, (general ship-building) .	day	2.49	1831 to 1840, ...	day	1.16
			1841 to 1850, ...	day	1.30
1881 to 1883, (general ship-building) . . .	day	3.25	1851 to 1860, ...	day	1.45
			1861 to 1880, ...	day	1.44
Shoemakers.			1881 to 1883, ...	day	1.77
1791 to 1800, ...	day	.733			
1821 to 1830, ...	day	1.06	*Watchmen.*		
1831 to 1840, ...	day	.873	1831 to 1840, ...	day	.923
1841 to 1850, ...	day	1.12	1851 to 1860, ...	day	.954
1851 to 1860, ...	day	1.70			
1861 to 1880, ...	day	1.76	*Wooden Goods Makers.*		
1881 to 1883, ...	day	1.87	1801 to 1810, ...	day	.66
			1811 to 1820, ...	day	1.26
Stone Quarrymen and Cutters.			1821 to 1830, ...	day	1.25
1831 to 1840, ...	day	1.29	1831 to 1840, ...	day	1.36
1841 to 1850, ...	day	1.45	1841 to 1850, ...	day	1.11
1851 to 1860, ...	day	1.40	1851 to 1860, ...	day	1.72
1861 to 1880, ...	day	2.33	1861 to 1880, ...	day	2.01
1881 to 1883, ...	day	2.01	1881 to 1883, ...	day	2.28
			Woollen Mill Operatives.		
Tanners and Curriers.			1821 to 1830, ...	day	1.12
1811 to 1820, ...	day	1.00	1831 to 1840, ...	day	.995
1821 to 1830, ...	day	1.13	1841 to 1850, ...	day	.865
1831 to 1840, ...	day	1.46	1851 to 1860, ...	day	.873
1841 to 1850, ...	day	1.13	1861 to 1880, ...	day	1 31
1851 to 1860, ...	day	1.67	1881 to 1883, ...	day	1.24

Articles: By Periods of Years.

Articles and Periods.	Basis.	Amount.	Articles and Periods.	Basis.	Amount.
AGRICULTURAL PRODUCTS.			*Barley.*		
Apples.			1791 to 1800, ...	pk.	$0.209
1752 to 1760, ...	bu.	$0.319		bu.	.688
1761 to 1770, ...	bu.	.183	1801 to 1810, ...	pk.	.25
1771 to 1780, ...	bu.	.152		bu.	.965
1781 to 1790, ...	bu.	.17	1811 to 1820, ...	pk.	.50
1791 to 1800, ...	bu.	.259		bu.	1.00
1801 to 1810, ...	bu.	.344	1821 to 1830, ...	pk.	.18
	bbl.	1.50	1851 to 1860, ...	bu.	.80
1811 to 1820, ...	pk.	.075			
	bu.	.526	*Beans.*		
	bbl.	2.50	1752 to 1760, ...	qt.	.033
1821 to 1830, ...	pk.	.153		bu.	.80
	bu.	.439	1761 to 1770, ...	qt.	.042
	bbl.	1.20		pk.	.25
1831 to 1840, ...	pk.	.263		bu.	.80
	bu.	.708	1771 to 1780, ...	qt.	.042
	bbl.	1.85	1781 to 1790, ...	qt.	.041
1841 to 1850, ...	pk.	.271		pk.	.389
	bu.	.876	1791 to 1800, ...	qt.	.049
	bbl.	1.72		bu.	1.05
(wholesale) .	bbl.	1.60	1801 to 1810, ...	qt.	.051
1851 to 1860, ...	pk.	.269		pk.	.444
	bu.	.995		bu.	1.48
	bbl.	1.96	1811 to 1820, ...	qt.	.109
(wholesale) .	bbl.	1.37		pk.	.648

Articles: By Periods of Years—Continued.

Articles and Periods.	Basis.	Amount.	Articles and Periods.	Basis.	Amount.
Beans—Con.			*Oats.*		
1811 to 1820, . . .	bu.	$2.36	1752 to 1760, . . .	bu.	$0.333
1821 to 1830, . . .	qt.	.085	1761 to 1770, . . .	bu.	.333
	pk.	.406	1781 to 1790, . . .	bu.	.494
	bu.	1.49	1791 to 1800, . . .	bu.	.451
1831 to 1840, . . .	qt.	.081	1801 to 1810, . . .	bu.	.554
	pk.	.667	1811 to 1820, . . .	bu.	.737
	bu.	1.91	(wholesale)	bu.	.40
1841 to 1850, . . .	qt.	.067	1821 to 1830, . . .	bu.	.426
	pk.	.492	(wholesale)	bu.	.36
	bu.	1.89	1831 to 1840, . . .	bu.	.544
1851 to 1860, . . .	qt.	.088	1841 to 1850, . . .	bu.	.545
	pk.	.537			
	bu.	2.60	*Onions.*		
1861 to 1880, . . .	qt.	.089	1761 to 1770, . . .	bu.	1.00
1881 to 1883, . . .	qt.	.123	1821 to 1830, . . .	pk.	.22
			1841 to 1850, . . .	pk.	.158
Buckwheat.				bu.	.643
1841 to 1850, . . .	bu.	.755	1851 to 1860, . . .	pk.	.25
1851 to 1860, . . .	bu.	1.00		bu.	.94
			Parsnips.		
Corn.			1752 to 1760, . . .	pk.	.167
1752 to 1760, . . .	pk.	.222	1761 to 1770, . . .	pk.	.126
	bu.	.574	1831 to 1840, . . .	pk.	.193
1761 to 1770, . . .	pk.	.167	1841 to 1850, . . .	pk.	.17
	bu.	.558			
1771 to 1780, . . .	bu.	.703	*Peas.*		
1781 to 1790, . . .	pk.	.167	1761 to 1770, . . .	pk.	.277
	bu.	.725	1771 to 1780, . . .	qt.	.055
1791 to 1800, . . .	bu.	.90	1781 to 1790, . . .	pk.	.514
(wholesale)	bu.	.805	1801 to 1810, . . .	pk.	.409
1801 to 1810, . . .	pk.	.28		bu.	1.34
	bu.	1.04	1811 to 1820, . . .	qt.	.06
(wholesale)	bu.	.948		pk.	.683
1811 to 1820, . . .	pk.	.28	1821 to 1830, . . .	bu.	1.09
	bu.	1.31	1831 to 1840, . . .	pk.	.20
(wholesale)	bu.	1.13	1841 to 1850, . . .	qt.	.086
1821 to 1830, . . .	bu.	.817		pk.	.571
(wholesale)	bu.	.546		bu.	2.52
1831 to 1840, . . .	bu.	.782			
1841 to 1850, . . .	pk.	.293	*Potatoes.*		
	bu.	.721	1752 to 1760, . . .	pk.	.098
(wholesale)	bu.	.663		bu.	.371
1851 to 1860, . . .	bu.	.992	1761 to 1770, . . .	pk.	.106
(wholesale)	bu.	.796		bu.	.354
			1771 to 1780, . . .	bu.	.30
Cranberries.			1781 to 1790, . . .	bu.	.279
1781 to 1790, . . .	pk.	.218	1791 to 1800, . . .	bu.	.302
1801 to 1810, . . .	pk.	.313	1801 to 1810, . . .	pk.	.197
1811 to 1820, . . .	pk.	.25		bu.	.501
1821 to 1830, . . .	pk.	.273	(wholesale)	bu.	.458
1831 to 1840, . . .	pk.	.52	1811 to 1820, . . .	bu.	.485
	bu.	1.63	(wholesale)	bu.	.28
1841 to 1850, . . .	pk.	.635	1821 to 1830, . . .	pk.	.10
	bu.	1.90		bu.	.369
			1831 to 1840, . . .	pk.	.193
Flax.				bu.	.492
1761 to 1770, . . .	lb.	.132	(wholesale)	bu.	.25
1771 to 1780, . . .	lb.	.113	1841 to 1850, . . .	pk.	.28
1781 to 1790, . . .	lb.	.125		bu.	.783
1791 to 1800, . . .	lb.	.169	(wholesale)	bu.	.532
1801 to 1810, . . .	lb.	.212	1851 to 1860, . . .	pk.	.357
1811 to 1820, . . .	lb.	.21		bu.	.86
1821 to 1830, . . .	lb.	.152	(wholesale)	bu.	.648
			1861 to 1880, . . .	bu.	.999
Flaxseed.			1881 to 1883, . . .	bu.	1.00
1752 to 1760, . . .	bu.	.444			
1781 to 1790, . . .	bu.	.392	*Rice.*		
1791 to 1800, . . .	bu.	.936	1781 to 1790, . . .	lb.	.055
			1791 to 1800, . . .	lb.	.037
Hops.			(wholesale)	lb.	.032
1801 to 1810, . . .	lb.	.19	1801 to 1810, . . .	lb.	.058
1811 to 1820, . . .	lb.	.248	(wholesale)	lb.	.048
1831 to 1840, . . .	lb.	.159	1811 to 1820, . . .	lb.	.063
1841 to 1850, . . .	lb.	.188	(wholesale)	lb.	.056
1851 to 1860, . . .	lb.	.289			

Articles: By Periods of Years — Continued.

Articles and Periods.	Basis.	Amount.
Rice — Con.		
1821 to 1830,	lb.	$0.044
1831 to 1840,	lb.	.056
1841 to 1850,	lb.	.049
1851 to 1860,	lb.	.06
1861 to 1880,	lb.	.103
1881 to 1883,	lb.	.092
Rye.		
1752 to 1760,	pk.	.195
	bu.	.622
1761 to 1770,	bu.	.663
1771 to 1780,	pk.	.25
	bu.	1.00
1781 to 1790,	pk.	.29
	bu.	.967
(wholesale)	bu.	.75
1791 to 1800,	pk.	.237
	bu.	1.14
(wholesale)	bu.	1.06
1801 to 1810,	pk.	.416
	bu.	1.27
(wholesale)	bu.	1.30
1811 to 1820,	pk.	.338
	bu.	1.44
(wholesale)	bu.	.863
1821 to 1830,	pk.	.25
	bu.	.882
(wholesale)	bu.	.634
1831 to 1840,	bu.	1.03
1841 to 1850,	bu.	1.00
1851 to 1860,	bu.	1.50
Squashes.		
1841 to 1850,	lb.	.015
1851 to 1860,	lb.	.016
Sweet Potatoes.		
1831 to 1840,	lb.	.023
1841 to 1850,	lb.	.039
	pk.	.306
1851 to 1860,	lb.	.032
	pk.	.647
Turnips.		
1752 to 1760,	bu.	.262
1761 to 1770,	pk.	.076
	bu.	.264
1771 to 1780,	pk.	.178
	bu.	.252
1781 to 1790,	bu.	.242
1791 to 1800,	bu.	.50
1801 to 1810,	pk.	.167
	bu.	.417
1811 to 1820,	bu.	.475
1821 to 1830,	pk.	.07
	bu.	.33
1831 to 1840,	bu.	.25
1841 to 1850,	bu.	.333
1851 to 1860,	bu.	.335
Wheat.		
1761 to 1770,	bu.	.999
1771 to 1780,	bu.	.916
Wool.		
1781 to 1790,	lb.	.325
1801 to 1810,	lb.	.39
1811 to 1820,	lb.	.785
BOOTS, SHOES, AND LEATHER.		
Boots.		
1791 to 1800,	pr.	6.00
1801 to 1810,	pr.	4.45
1811 to 1820,	pr.	6.14

Articles and Periods.	Basis.	Amount.
Boots — Con.		
1821 to 1830,	pr.	$4.75
1831 to 1840,	pr.	3.72
1841 to 1850,	pr.	2.49
1851 to 1860,	pr.	2.21
Calamanco.		
1781 to 1790,	yd.	.331
1791 to 1800,	yd.	.457
Leather.		
1791 to 1800,	lb.	.194
1801 to 1810,	lb.	.235
1811 to 1820,	lb.	.207
1821 to 1830,	lb.	.255
Rubbers.		
1821 to 1830,	pr.	1.25
1831 to 1840,	pr.	1.17
1841 to 1850,	pr.	.719
1851 to 1860,	pr.	.753
Shoes.		
1752 to 1760,	pr.	1.00
1761 to 1770,	pr.	1.11
1771 to 1780,	pr.	.837
1781 to 1790,	pr.	.958
1791 to 1800,	pr.	.97
(wholesale)	pr.	.671
1801 to 1810,	pr.	1.29
(wholesale)	pr.	.878
1811 to 1820,	pr.	1.25
(wholesale)	pr.	.919
1821 to 1830,	pr.	1.26
1831 to 1840,	pr.	1.35
1841 to 1850,	pr.	1.06
1851 to 1860,	pr.	1.09
Slippers.		
1791 to 1800,	pr.	.556
(wholesale)	pr.	.709
1811 to 1820, (wholesale)	pr.	.81
1821 to 1830,	pr.	.935
1831 to 1840,	pr.	.947
1841 to 1850,	pr.	1.00
1851 to 1860,	pr.	.945
1881 to 1883,	pr.	1.56
Taps.		
1761 to 1770,	pr.	.167
1791 to 1800,	pr.	.139
1811 to 1820,	pr.	.12
BUTTONS AND DRESS TRIMMINGS.		
Braid.		
1821 to 1830,	yd.	.013
	p'ce	.078
1831 to 1840,	p'ce	.04
1851 to 1860,	yd.	.056
	p'ce	.073
1881 to 1883,	yd.	.033
Buttons.		
1781 to 1790,	doz.	.314
1791 to 1800,	doz.	.29
	gro.	1.55
1801 to 1810,	doz.	.141
	gro.	1.26
1811 to 1820,	doz.	.239
	gro.	.62
1821 to 1830,	doz.	.141
1831 to 1840,	doz.	.131
1841 to 1850,	doz.	.101
1851 to 1860,	doz.	.381

Articles: By Periods of Years — Continued.

Articles and Periods.	Basis.	Amount.	Articles and Periods.	Basis.	Amount.
Galloon.			*Mittens* — Con.		
1801 to 1810,	yd.	$0.042	1831 to 1840,	pr.	$0.402
1811 to 1820,	yd.	.051	1841 to 1850,	pr.	.458
1841 to 1850,	yd.	.03	1851 to 1860,	pr.	.609
1851 to 1860,	yd.	.055			
1881 to 1883,	yd.	.047	*Mitts.*		
			1791 to 1800,	pr.	.833
Tape.			1841 to 1850,	pr.	.75
1781 to 1790,	yd.	.021	1851 to 1860,	pr.	1.00
1801 to 1810,	yd.	.041			
	p'ce	.172	*Overalls.*		
1811 to 1820,	yd.	.053	1841 to 1850,	pr.	.60
	p'ce	.121	1851 to 1860,	pr.	.535
1821 to 1830,	p'ce	.118			
1831 to 1840,	p'ce	.077	*Vests.*		
1841 to 1850,	p'ce	.057	1791 to 1800,	ea.	2.23
1851 to 1860,	p'ce	.057	1811 to 1820,	ea.	4.50
1881 to 1883,	p'ce	.039	1841 to 1850,	ea.	3.75
			1851 to 1860,	ea.	2.46
CLOTHING.					
Gloves.			*Waistcoats.*		
1781 to 1790,	pr.	.464	1801 to 1810,	ea.	1.67
1791 to 1800,	pr.	.63	1831 to 1840,	ea.	1.38
1801 to 1810,	pr.	.687			
1811 to 1820,	pr.	.458	CLOTHS.		
1821 to 1830,	pr.	.517	*Broadcloth.*		
1831 to 1840,	pr.	.466	1771 to 1780,	yd.	1.33
1841 to 1850,	pr.	.404	1781 to 1790,	yd.	2.36
1851 to 1860,	pr.	.594	1791 to 1800,	yd.	2.94
1881 to 1883,	pr.	.648	1801 to 1810,	yd.	3.25
			1811 to 1820,	yd.	4.99
Handkerchiefs.			1821 to 1830,	yd.	4.36
1761 to 1770,	doz.	.95	1831 to 1840,	yd.	2.83
1771 to 1780,	ea.	.367	1851 to 1860,	yd.	2.23
1781 to 1790,	ea.	.593			
	doz.	15.32	*Cassimere.*		
1791 to 1800,	ea.	.728	1791 to 1800,	yd.	2.01
	doz.	2.83	1801 to 1810,	yd.	2.39
1801 to 1810,	ea.	.448	1811 to 1820,	yd.	1.94
	doz.	5.50	1821 to 1830,	yd.	1.91
1811 to 1820,	ea.	.66	1831 to 1840,	yd.	1.92
1821 to 1830,	ea.	.441	1841 to 1850,	yd.	1.13
1831 to 1840,	ea.	.442	1851 to 1860, (mostly cotton)	yd.	.316
1841 to 1850,	ea.	.491			
1851 to 1860,	ea.	.414	*Circassian Cloth.*		
1881 to 1883,	ea.	.525	1821 to 1830,	yd.	.491
			1831 to 1840,	yd.	.396
Hats.					
1761 to 1770,	ea.	6.67	*Corduroy.*		
1781 to 1790,	ea.	2.51	1781 to 1790,	yd.	.836
1791 to 1800,	ea.	2.63	1791 to 1800,	yd.	.721
1801 to 1810,	ea.	2.55			
1811 to 1820,	ea.	2.68	*Durant.*		
1821 to 1830,	ea.	2.61	1781 to 1790,	yd.	.56
1831 to 1840,	ea.	2.84	1791 to 1800,	yd.	.389
1841 to 1850,	ea.	1.90			
1851 to 1860,	ea.	1.45	*Erminet.*		
			1841 to 1850,	yd.	.664
Hose, Socks, and Stockings.			1851 to 1860,	yd.	.384
1761 to 1770,	pr.	.978			
1781 to 1790,	pr.	.734	*Florentine.*		
1791 to 1800,	pr.	1.35	1791 to 1800,	yd.	.822
(wholesale)	pr.	1.05	1811 to 1820,	yd.	.761
	doz.	10.67			
1801 to 1810,	pr.	1.23	*Fustian.*		
(wholesale)	pr.	.916	1791 to 1800,	yd.	.361
	doz.	12.67	1801 to 1810,	yd.	.33
1811 to 1820,	pr.	.932	1821 to 1830,	yd.	.30
1821 to 1830,	pr.	.59			
1831 to 1840,	pr.	.523	*Lambskin.*		
1841 to 1850,	pr.	.38	1781 to 1790,	yd.	1.17
1851 to 1860,	pr.	.445	1791 to 1800,	yd.	1.06
1881 to 1883,	pr.	.49			
			Mixed Cloth.		
Mittens.			1791 to 1800,	yd.	1.83
1811 to 1820,	pr.	.20	1801 to 1810,	yd.	1.08
1821 to 1830,	pr.	.221			

Articles: By Periods of Years—Continued.

Articles and Periods.	Basis.	Amount.	Articles and Periods.	Basis.	Amount.
Plain Blue Cloth.			**Milk — Con.**		
1791 to 1800,	yd.	$0.543	1811 to 1820,	qt.	$0.047
1801 to 1810,	yd.	1.16	1821 to 1830,	qt.	.044
1811 to 1820,	yd.	1.36	1831 to 1840,	qt.	.049
			1841 to 1850,	qt.	.05
Plain Cloth.			(wholesale)	qt.	.037
1791 to 1800,	yd.	1.18	1851 to 1860,	qt.	.052
1801 to 1810,	yd.	1.00	(wholesale)	qt.	.043
			1861 to 1880,	qt.	.067
Ratteen.			1881 to 1883,	qt.	.066
1781 to 1790,	yd.	.969			
1791 to 1800,	yd.	.556	**DRESS GOODS.**		
1801 to 1810,	yd.	.96	*Alepine.*		
			1831 to 1840,	yd.	1.98
DAIRY PRODUCTS.			1851 to 1860,	yd.	1.25
Butter.					
1761 to 1770,	lb.	.167	*Alpaca.*		
1771 to 1780,	lb.	.11	1841 to 1850,	yd.	.513
1781 to 1790,	lb.	.114	1851 to 1860,	yd.	.484
1791 to 1800,	lb.	.185	1881 to 1883,	yd.	.509
(wholesale)	lb.	.163			
1801 to 1810,	lb.	.213	*Barège.*		
(wholesale)	lb.	.176	1841 to 1850,	yd.	.50
1811 to 1820,	lb.	.24	1851 to 1860,	yd.	.389
(wholesale)	lb.	.204			
1821 to 1830,	lb.	.186	*Batiste.*		
(wholesale)	lb.	.139	1821 to 1830,	yd.	.623
1831 to 1840,	lb.	.22	1831 to 1840,	yd.	.334
1841 to 1850,	lb.	.196			
(wholesale)	lb.	.148	*Beige.*		
1851 to 1860,	lb.	.262	1791 to 1800,	yd.	.424
(wholesale)	lb.	.164	1801 to 1810,	yd.	.665
1861 to 1880,	lb.	.323	1881 to 1883,	yd.	.737
1881 to 1883,	lb.	.325			
			Bombazet.		
Cheese.			1801 to 1810,	yd.	.608
1752 to 1760,	lb.	.084	1811 to 1820,	yd.	.496
1761 to 1770,	lb.	.087	1821 to 1830,	yd.	.354
1771 to 1780,	lb.	.133	1831 to 1840,	yd.	.383
1781 to 1790,	lb.	.081	1841 to 1850,	yd.	.30
1791 to 1800,	lb.	.096			
(wholesale)	lb.	.103	*Calico.*		
1801 to 1810,	lb.	.14	1781 to 1790,	yd.	.579
(wholesale)	lb.	.103	1791 to 1800,	yd.	.394
1811 to 1820,	lb.	.123	(wholesale)	yd.	.387
(wholesale)	lb.	.107	1801 to 1810,	yd.	.385
1821 to 1830,	lb.	.089	(wholesale)	yd.	.356
(wholesale)	lb.	.075	1811 to 1820,	yd.	.36
1831 to 1840,	lb.	.096	1821 to 1830,	yd.	.292
1841 to 1850,	lb.	.096	1831 to 1840,	yd.	.243
1851 to 1860,	lb.	.117	1841 to 1850,	yd.	.163
(wholesale)	lb.	.081	1851 to 1860,	yd.	.105
1861 to 1880,	lb.	.149			
1881 to 1883,	lb.	.16	*Cambric.*		
			1771 to 1780,	yd.	1.02
Eggs.			1781 to 1790,	yd.	1.24
1752 to 1760,	doz.	.078	1791 to 1800,	yd.	1.28
1771 to 1780,	doz.	.056	1801 to 1810,	yd.	.805
1781 to 1790,	doz.	.085	1811 to 1820,	yd.	.796
1791 to 1800,	doz.	.07	1821 to 1830,	yd.	.359
1801 to 1810,	doz.	.235	1831 to 1840,	yd.	.254
1811 to 1820,	doz.	.206	1841 to 1850,	yd.	.212
1821 to 1830,	doz.	.15	1851 to 1860,	yd.	.193
1831 to 1840,	doz.	.19			
1841 to 1850,	doz.	.19	*Camlet.*		
1851 to 1860,	doz.	.22	1781 to 1790,	yd.	.329
1861 to 1880,	doz.	.275	1791 to 1800,	yd.	.403
1881 to 1883,	doz.	.343	1801 to 1810,	yd.	.26
			1841 to 1850,	yd.	.562
Milk.					
1771 to 1780,	qt.	.029	*Cashmere.*		
1781 to 1790,	qt.	.025	1811 to 1820,	yd.	1.50
1791 to 1800,	qt.	.034	1851 to 1860,	yd.	1.02
1801 to 1810,	qt.	.042			

Articles: By Periods of Years — CONTINUED.

ARTICLES AND PERIODS.	Basis.	Amount.	ARTICLES AND PERIODS.	Basis.	Amount.
Crape.			*Muslin.*		
1801 to 1810,	yd.	$0.56	1791 to 1800,	yd.	$0.528
1821 to 1830,	yd.	.927	1801 to 1810,	yd.	.793
1831 to 1840,	yd.	.683	1811 to 1820,	yd.	.697
1881 to 1883,	yd	1.67	1821 to 1830,	yd.	.585
			1831 to 1840,	yd.	.541
			1841 to 1850,	yd.	.36
Dimity.			1851 to 1860,	yd.	.263
1801 to 1810,	yd.	.531	1881 to 1883,	yd.	.216
1811 to 1820,	yd.	.685			
1821 to 1830,	yd.	.477	*Muslin de Laine.*		
1831 to 1840,	yd.	.479	1831 to 1840,	yd.	.503
1851 to 1860,	yd.	.437	1841 to 1850,	yd.	.304
			1851 to 1860,	yd.	.176
Gauze.					
1781 to 1790,	yd	.578	*Nankeen.*		
1791 to 1800,	yd.	.315	1781 to 1790,	yd.	.80
1801 to 1810,	yd.	.352	1791 to 1800,	yd.	.537
1821 to 1830,	yd.	.98	1801 to 1810,	yd.	.408
			1811 to 1820,	yd.	.267
			1821 to 1830,	yd.	.176
Gingham.			1851 to 1860,	yd.	.181
1791 to 1800,	yd.	.556			
(wholesale)	yd.	.362	*Plaid.*		
1801 to 1810,	yd.	.337	1811 to 1820,	yd.	.651
1811 to 1820,	yd.	.451	1821 to 1830,	yd.	.538
(wholesale)	yd.	.409	1831 to 1840,	yd.	.568
1821 to 1830,	yd.	.317	1851 to 1860,	yd.	.496
1831 to 1840,	yd.	.249			
1841 to 1850,	yd.	.203	*Poplin.*		
1851 to 1860,	yd.	.192	1781 to 1790,	yd.	.443
			1791 to 1800,	yd.	.458
Lawn.			1851 to 1860,	yd.	.254
1771 to 1780,	yd.	.903			
1781 to 1790,	yd.	.734	*Sarcenet.*		
1811 to 1820,	yd.	.538	1781 to 1790,	yd.	.50
1821 to 1830,	yd.	.644	1791 to 1800,	yd.	.433
1831 to 1840,	yd.	.559			
1841 to 1850,	yd.	.452	*Satin.*		
1851 to 1860,	yd.	.228	1771 to 1780,	yd.	.731
			1781 to 1790,	yd.	1.10
Linsey-woolsey.			1801 to 1810,	yd.	2.45
1821 to 1830,	yd.	.583	1881 to 1883,	yd.	2.16
1851 to 1860,	yd.	.20			
			Satinet.		
Lustring.			1781 to 1790,	yd.	.75
1791 to 1800,	yd.	1.18	1791 to 1800,	yd.	.753
1801 to 1810,	yd.	1.13	1811 to 1820,	yd.	1.31
1811 to 1820,	yd.	.668	1821 to 1830,	yd.	.745
1821 to 1830,	yd.	.708	1831 to 1840,	yd.	.737
1831 to 1840,	yd.	.762	1841 to 1850,	yd.	.792
			1851 to 1860,	yd.	.461
Merino.					
1831 to 1840,	yd.	.948	*Serge.*		
1841 to 1850,	yd.	.868	1791 to 1800,	yd.	.833
			(wholesale)	yd.	.764
Millinet.			1801 to 1810,	yd.	.805
1781 to 1790,	yd.	.389	(wholesale)	yd.	.785
1801 to 1810,	yd.	.198	1811 to 1820,	yd.	.833
1811 to 1820,	yd.	.25	1821 to 1830,	yd.	2.47
1821 to 1830,	yd.	.22	1831 to 1840,	yd.	.717
			1841 to 1850,	yd.	.333
Mode.			1881 to 1883,	yd.	.75
1781 to 1790,	yd.	.897			
1791 to 1800,	yd.	.704	*Shalloon.*		
(wholesale)	ell.	.678	1771 to 1780,	yd.	.40
1801 to 1810,	yd.	.918	1781 to 1790,	yd.	.477
(wholesale)	ell.	.667	1801 to 1810,	yd.	.50
1811 to 1820,	yd.	1.00	1811 to 1820,	yd.	.625
1821 to 1830,	yd.	.75	1831 to 1840,	yd.	.63
Moreen.			*Silk.*		
1781 to 1790,	yd.	.413	1781 to 1790,	yd.	.868
1841 to 1850,	yd.	.297	1791 to 1800,	yd.	1.00
1851 to 1860,	yd.	.283	1801 to 1810,	yd.	1.08

Articles: By Periods of Years — CONTINUED.

Articles and Periods.	Ba-sis.	Amount.	Articles and Periods.	Ba-sis.	Amount.
Silk — Con.			*Copperplate.*		
1811 to 1820, ...	yd.	$1.58	1791 to 1800, ...	yd.	$0.419
1821 to 1830, ...	yd.	.799	1811 to 1820, ...	yd.	.25
1831 to 1840, ...	yd.	.659	1821 to 1830, ...	yd.	.40
1841 to 1850, ...	yd.	.832	*Cotton Batting.*		
1851 to 1860, ...	yd.	.989	1771 to 1780, ...	lb.	.277
1881 to 1883, ...	yd.	1.00	1821 to 1830, ...	lb.	.11
			1831 to 1840, ...	lb.	.10
Swan's-down.			1841 to 1850, ...	lb.	.105
1791 to 1800, ...	yd.	1.17	1851 to 1860, ...	lb.	.11
1811 to 1820, ...	yd.	.375	*Cotton Cloth.*		
			1781 to 1790, ...	yd.	.884
Tammy.			1791 to 1800, ...	yd.	.339
1771 to 1780, ...	yd.	.36	1801 to 1810, ...	yd.	.328
1781 to 1790, ...	yd.	.28	1811 to 1820, ...	yd.	.415
			1821 to 1830, ...	yd.	.21
Velvet.			1831 to 1840, ...	yd.	.148
1781 to 1790, ...	yd.	.889	1841 to 1850, ...	yd.	.129
1791 to 1800, ...	yd.	.917	1851 to 1860, ...	yd.	.118
1801 to 1810, ...	yd.	1.61			
1811 to 1820, ...	yd.	1.13	*Cotton Flannel.*		
1821 to 1830, ...	yd.	1.00	1821 to 1830, ...	yd.	.22
1831 to 1840, ...	yd.	1.69	1831 to 1840, ...	yd.	.201
1841 to 1850, ...	yd.	.59	1841 to 1850, ...	yd.	.155
1851 to 1860, ...	yd.	.50	1851 to 1860, ...	yd.	.126
1881 to 1883, ...	yd.	1.87	*Cotton Wool.*		
			1761 to 1770, ...	lb.	.50
Velveteen.			1771 to 1780, ...	lb.	.666
1791 to 1800, ...	yd.	1.33	1781 to 1790, ...	lb.	.465
1801 to 1810, ...	yd.	.828	1791 to 1800, ...	lb.	.32
1881 to 1883, ...	yd.	1.00	1801 to 1810, ...	lb.	.222
			1811 to 1820, ...	lb.	.125
DRY GOODS.					
Baize.			*Crash.*		
1781 to 1790, ...	yd.	.405	1811 to 1820, ...	yd.	.14
1791 to 1800, ...	yd.	.346	1821 to 1830, ...	yd.	.12
1801 to 1810, ...	yd.	.333	1831 to 1840, ...	yd.	.11
1811 to 1820, ...	yd.	.333	1841 to 1850, ...	yd.	.086
1831 to 1840, ...	yd.	.46	1851 to 1860, ...	yd.	.112
1841 to 1850, ...	yd.	.295			
			Damask.		
Binding.			1821 to 1830, ...	yd.	.835
1781 to 1790, ...	gro.	1.25	1831 to 1840, ...	yd.	.584
1791 to 1800, ...	gro.	1.19	1841 to 1850, ...	yd.	.62
1801 to 1810, ...	gro.	1.53	1851 to 1860, ...	yd.	.726
Blankets.			*Denim.*		
1781 to 1790, ...	ea.	1.17	1781 to 1790, ...	yd.	.144
1791 to 1800, ...	ea.	2.33	1791 to 1800, ...	yd.	.111
	pr.	5.28	1851 to 1860, ...	yd.	.147
1801 to 1810, ...	pr.	7.50			
1811 to 1820, ...	pr	7.50	*Diaper.*		
1831 to 1840, ...	ea.	1.78	1811 to 1820, ...	yd.	.35
1841 to 1850, ...	pr.	4.25	1841 to 1850, ...	yd.	.21
1851 to 1860, ...	ea.	1.00	1851 to 1860, ...	yd.	.167
	pr.	3.88	*Dowlas.*		
1881 to 1883, ...	pr.	4.67	1791 to 1800, ...	yd.	.156
			1821 to 1830, ...	yd.	.333
Buckram.			*Drilling.*		
1781 to 1790, ...	yd.	.246	1821 to 1830, ...	yd.	.542
1791 to 1800, ...	yd.	.275	1831 to 1840, ...	yd.	.353
1801 to 1810, ...	yd.	.35	1841 to 1850, ...	yd.	.294
1821 to 1830, ...	yd.	.278	1851 to 1860, ...	yd.	.119
1831 to 1840, ...	yd.	.20			
			Duck.		
Canvas.			1791 to 1800, ...	yd.	.288
1831 to 1840, ...	yd.	.335	1801 to 1810, ...	yd.	.416
1851 to 1860, ...	yd.	.20	1811 to 1820, ...	yd.	.404
Chintz.			1821 to 1830, ...	yd.	.345
1771 to 1780, ...	yd.	.545	1831 to 1840, ...	yd.	.278
1781 to 1790, ...	yd.	.593	1841 to 1850, ...	yd.	.20
1791 to 1800, ...	yd.	.557			

Articles: By Periods of Years — CONTINUED.

ARTICLES AND PERIODS.	Basis.	Amount.
Flannel.		
1791 to 1800,	yd.	$0.423
(wholesale)	yd.	.356
1801 to 1810,	yd.	.713
(wholesale)	yd.	.395
1811 to 1820,	yd.	.657
(wholesale)	yd.	.167
1821 to 1830,	yd.	.57
1831 to 1840,	yd.	.435
1841 to 1850,	yd.	.388
1851 to 1860,	yd.	.405
1881 to 1883,	yd.	.326
Holland.		
1781 to 1790,	yd.	.56
1791 to 1800,	yd.	.21
1801 to 1810,	yd.	.353
1811 to 1820,	yd.	.446
1821 to 1830,	yd.	.375
Huckaback.		
1831 to 1840,	yd.	.45
1841 to 1850,	yd.	.236
Jean.		
1781 to 1790,	yd.	.351
1801 to 1810,	yd.	.445
1811 to 1820,	yd.	.495
1821 to 1830,	yd.	.297
1831 to 1840,	yd.	.197
1851 to 1860,	yd.	.26
Lasting.		
1781 to 1790,	yd.	.695
1791 to 1800,	yd.	.466
1821 to 1830,	yd.	1.05
Linen.		
1781 to 1790,	yd.	.449
1791 to 1800,	yd.	.369
(wholesale)	yd.	.306
1801 to 1810,	yd.	.605
(wholesale)	yd.	.498
1811 to 1820,	yd.	.526
1821 to 1830,	yd.	.453
1831 to 1840,	yd.	.578
1841 to 1850,	yd.	.379
1851 to 1860,	yd.	.531
Lining.		
1781 to 1790,	yd.	.508
1791 to 1800,	yd.	.361
1801 to 1810,	yd.	.42
Napkins.		
1821 to 1830,	doz.	1.25
1851 to 1860,	doz.	1.82
1881 to 1883,	doz.	2.07
Oiled Silk.		
1821 to 1830,	yd.	1.33
1841 to 1850,	yd.	1.00
Patch.		
1791 to 1800,	yd.	.583
1811 to 1820,	yd.	.383
1821 to 1830,	yd.	.205
1831 to 1840,	yd.	.182
1841 to 1850,	yd.	.112
1851 to 1860,	yd.	.121
Sheetings.		
1791 to 1800,	yd.	.51
1801 to 1810,	yd.	.426
1811 to 1820,	yd.	.523
1821 to 1830,	yd.	.281

ARTICLES AND PERIODS.	Basis.	Amount.
Sheetings — Con.		
1831 to 1840,	yd.	$0.206
1841 to 1850,	yd.	.105
1851 to 1860,	yd.	.124
1881 to 1883,	yd.	.162
Shirtings.		
1801 to 1810,	yd.	.458
1811 to 1820,	yd.	.386
(wholesale)	yd.	.405
1821 to 1830,	yd.	.223
(wholesale)	yd.	.135
1831 to 1840,	yd.	.135
1841 to 1850,	yd.	.114
1851 to 1860,	yd.	.107
1881 to 1883,	yd.	.12
Silesia.		
1831 to 1840,	yd.	.211
1841 to 1850,	yd.	.123
1851 to 1860,	yd.	.12
Ticking.		
1791 to 1800,	yd.	.904
1801 to 1810,	yd.	.75
1811 to 1820,	yd.	.615
1821 to 1830,	yd.	.367
1831 to 1840,	yd.	.254
1841 to 1850,	yd.	.169
1851 to 1860,	yd.	.16
1881 to 1883,	yd.	.155
Tow Cloth.		
1752 to 1760,	yd.	.15
1761 to 1770,	yd.	.299
1781 to 1790,	yd.	.214
(wholesale)	yd.	.16
1791 to 1800,	yd.	.201
1801 to 1810,	yd.	.278
(wholesale)	yd.	.18
1811 to 1820,	yd.	.292
1821 to 1830,	yd.	.173
1831 to 1840,	yd.	.147
1851 to 1860,	yd.	.128
Towelling.		
1791 to 1800,	yd.	.111
1831 to 1840,	yd.	.417
1851 to 1860,	yd.	.17
1881 to 1883,	yd.	.145
FISH.		
Clams.		
1801 to 1810,	pk.	.133
1811 to 1820,	pk.	.262
1821 to 1830,	pk.	.186
1831 to 1840,	pk.	.233
1841 to 1850,	pk.	.239
Cod.		
1841 to 1850,	lb.	.039
1851 to 1860,	lb.	.05
Codfish.		
1781 to 1790,	lb.	.034
1801 to 1810,	lb.	.034
(by the quintal)	q't'l	4.92
1811 to 1820,	lb.	.033
(by the quintal)	q't'l	5.50
1821 to 1830,	lb.	.031
1831 to 1840,	lb.	.038
1841 to 1850,	lb.	.034
1851 to 1860,	lb.	.053
1861 to 1880,	lb.	.072
1881 to 1883,	lb.	.089

Articles: By Periods of Years—CONTINUED.

ARTICLES AND PERIODS.	Basis.	Amount.
Eels.		
1801 to 1810, ...	lb.	$0.062
1811 to 1820, ...	lb.	.067
1821 to 1830, ...	lb.	.062
1831 to 1840, ...	lb.	.067
1841 to 1850, ...	lb.	.071
Fish.		
1752 to 1760, (wholesale)	lb.	.004
1761 to 1770, (wholesale)	lb.	.006
1791 to 1800, ...	lb.	.034
(wholesale)	lb.	.02
(by the quintal) .	q't'l	4.30
1801 to 1810, .	lb.	.052
(wholesale)	lb.	.048
(by the quintal) .	q't'l	4.73
1811 to 1820, ...	lb.	.057
(wholesale)	lb.	.043
(by the quintal) .	q't'l	4.93
1821 to 1830, ...	lb.	.039
(wholesale)	lb.	.04
1831 to 1840, ...	lb.	.041
1841 to 1850, ...	lb.	.055
(wholesale)	lb.	.023
1851 to 1860, ...	lb.	.049
Haddock.		
1811 to 1820, ...	lb.	.037
1821 to 1830, ...	lb.	.029
1831 to 1840, ...	lb.	.033
1841 to 1850, ...	lb.	.038
Halibut.		
1801 to 1810, . . .	lb.	.045
1811 to 1820, . . .	lb.	.048
1821 to 1830, . . .	lb.	.048
1831 to 1840, . . .	lb.	.053
1841 to 1850, . . .	lb.	.059
1851 to 1860, . . .	lb.	.105
Herring.		
1761 to 1770, ...	doz.	.25
1781 to 1790, ...	doz.	.083
1791 to 1800, ...	C.	.667
1801 to 1810, ...	doz.	.15
1811 to 1820, ...	doz.	.176
	C.	1.13
1821 to 1830, ...	doz.	.083
	C.	.694
1831 to 1840, ...	doz.	.09
1841 to 1850, ...	doz.	.118
1851 to 1860, ...	doz.	.08
Mackerel.		
1752 to 1760, ...	bbl.	5.33
1801 to 1810, ...	lb.	.055
1811 to 1820, ...	lb.	.084
	bbl.	7.18
1821 to 1830, ...	lb.	.038
	bbl.	5.10
1831 to 1840, ...	lb.	.066
	bbl.	6.66
1841 to 1850, ...	lb.	.071
1851 to 1860, ...	lb.	.085
1861 to 1880, ...	lb.	.13
1881 to 1883, ...	lb.	.133
Oysters.		
1801 to 1810, ...	pk.	.50
1811 to 1820, ...	pk.	.50
1821 to 1830, ...	pk.	.50
1831 to 1840, ...	qt.	.50
	pk.	.50
1841 to 1850, ...	qt.	.233

ARTICLES AND PERIODS.	Basis.	Amount.
Pollock.		
1801 to 1810, ...	lb.	$0.029
1811 to 1820, ...	lb.	.027
1821 to 1830, ...	lb.	.026
1831 to 1840, ...	lb.	.026
Salmon.		
1801 to 1810, ...	lb.	.167
1811 to 1820, ...	lb.	.163
1821 to 1830, ...	lb.	.20
1831 to 1840, ...	lb.	.219
1841 to 1850, ...	lb.	.21
1851 to 1860, ...	lb.	.125
Salt Fish.		
1791 to 1800, ...	lb.	.044
1811 to 1820, ...	lb.	.056
1821 to 1830, ...	lb.	.061
1831 to 1840, ...	lb.	.05
1841 to 1850, ...	lb.	.049
1851 to 1860, ...	lb.	.052
Shad.		
1811 to 1820, ...	lb.	.03
1831 to 1840, ...	lb.	.167
1841 to 1850, ...	lb.	.167
FLOUR AND MEAL.		
Bolted Rye Meal.		
1801 to 1810, . . .	bbl.	4.50
1811 to 1820, . . .	bbl.	6.58
1821 to 1830, . . .	bbl.	3.00
Buckwheat Flour.		
1841 to 1850, . . .	lb.	.033
1851 to 1860, . . .	lb.	.038
Flour.		
1752 to 1760, . . .	lb.	.044
1781 to 1790, . . .	lb.	.047
	bbl.	5.96
1791 to 1800, . . .	lb.	.063
	cwt.	5.33
	bbl.	8.25
(wholesale)	bbl.	6.40
1801 to 1810, . . .	lb.	.065
	cwt.	7.33
	bbl.	8.78
1811 to 1820, . . .	lb.	.07
	bbl.	11.67
(wholesale)	bbl.	5.00
1821 to 1830, . . .	lb.	.038
	bbl.	7.08
(wholesale)	bbl.	5.44
1831 to 1840, . . .	lb.	.045
	bbl.	8.16
1841 to 1850, . . .	lb.	.036
	bbl.	6.78
1851 to 1860, . . .	lb.	.044
	bbl.	8.92
1861 to 1880, . . .	lb.	.051
1881 to 1883, . . .	lb.	.043
Graham Flour.		
1831 to 1840, . . .	bbl.	8.25
1841 to 1850, . . .	lb.	.035
	bbl.	7.24
1851 to 1860, . . .	lb.	.048
	bbl.	9.50
Indian Meal.		
1791 to 1800, . . .	bu.	.814
1801 to 1810, . . .	bu.	1.08
1811 to 1820, . . .	lb.	.039
	pk.	.33
	bu.	1.35

Articles: By Periods of Years — Continued.

Articles and Periods.	Ba- sis.	Amount.	Articles and Periods.	Ba- sis.	Amount.
Indian Meal — Con.			*Bread (by the loaf).*		
1821 to 1830, ...	lb.	$0.016	1801 to 1810, ...	ea.	$0.125
	bu.	.788	1811 to 1820, ...	ea.	.148
1831 to 1840, ...	lb.	.02	1821 to 1830, ...	ea.	.079
	pk.	.261	1831 to 1840, ...	ea.	.072
	bu.	1.02	1841 to 1850, ...	ea.	.072
1841 to 1850, ...	lb.	.016	1851 to 1860, ...	ea.	.075
	pk.	.243			
	bu.	.831	*Chocolate.*		
(wholesale)	bu.	.63	1781 to 1790, ...	lb.	.278
1851 to 1860, ...	lb.	.021	1791 to 1800, ...	lb.	.291
	pk.	.339	(wholesale)	lb.	.262
	bu.	.982	1801 to 1810, ...	lb.	.338
(wholesale)	bu.	.70	(wholesale)	lb.	.264
1861 to 1880, ...	lb.	.019	1811 to 1820, ...	lb.	.271
1881 to 1883, ...	lb.	.029	(wholesale)	lb.	.228
			1821 to 1830, ...	lb.	.245
Meal.			1831 to 1840, ...	lb.	.20
1761 to 1770, ...	bu.	.50	1841 to 1850, ...	lb.	.20
1771 to 1780, ...	pk.	.25	1851 to 1860, ...	lb.	.235
1781 to 1790, ...	pk.	.209			
	bu.	.778	*Cocoa.*		
1791 to 1800, ...	bu.	.847	1791 to 1800, (wholesale)	lb.	.255
1801 to 1810, ...	pk.	.358	1801 to 1810, (wholesale)	lb.	.189
	bu.	.998	1811 to 1820, ...	lb.	.334
(wholesale)	bu.	1.09	(wholesale)	lb.	.17
1811 to 1820, ...	lb.	.027	1831 to 1840, ...	lb.	.221
	pk.	.51	1841 to 1850, ...	lb.	.209
	bu.	1.55	1851 to 1860, ...	lb.	.219
(wholesale)	bu.	1.20			
1821 to 1830, ...	lb.	.016	*Cocoa and Shells.*		
	pk.	.26	1841 to 1850, ...	lb.	.16
	bu.	.956	1851 to 1860, ...	lb.	.118
1831 to 1840, ...	lb.	.026			
	pk.	.23	*Cocoa Shells.*		
	bu.	1.21	1791 to 1800, ...	lb.	.10
1841 to 1850, ...	pk.	.265	1801 to 1810, ...	lb.	.202
	bu.	.871	(wholesale)	lb.	.128
1851 to 1860, ...	lb.	.023	1811 to 1820, ...	lb.	.166
	pk.	.36	(wholesale)	lb.	.128
	bu.	.965	1821 to 1830, ...	lb.	.151
Oatmeal.			1831 to 1840, ...	lb.	.141
1801 to 1810, ...	lb.	.125	1841 to 1850, ...	lb.	.141
1811 to 1820, ...	lb.	.131	1851 to 1860, ...	lb.	.166
1831 to 1840, ...	lb.	.102			
1841 to 1850, ...	lb.	.096	*Coffee.*		
1851 to 1860, ...	lb.	.088	1781 to 1790, ...	lb.	.23
			1791 to 1800, ...	lb.	.213
Rice Meal.			(wholesale)	lb.	.219
1841 to 1850, ...	lb.	.011	1801 to 1810, ...	lb.	.273
1851 to 1860, ...	lb.	.011	(wholesale)	lb.	.258
			1811 to 1820, ...	lb.	.256
Rye Meal.			(wholesale)	lb.	.192
1771 to 1780, ...	pk.	.167	1821 to 1830, ...	lb.	.206
1791 to 1800, ...	bu.	1.03	(wholesale)	lb.	.13
1801 to 1810, ...	bu.	1.36	1831 to 1840, ...	lb.	.14
1811 to 1820, ...	lb.	.042	(wholesale)	lb.	.11
	pk.	.30	1841 to 1850, ...	lb.	.115
	bu.	1.38	(wholesale)	lb.	.101
1821 to 1830, ...	lb.	.018	1851 to 1860, ...	lb.	.163
	bu.	.853	1861 to 1880, ...	lb.	.318
1831 to 1840, ...	lb.	.03	1881 to 1883, ...	lb.	.214
	pk.	.275			
	bu.	1.17	*Corn Starch.*		
1841 to 1850, ...	lb.	.021	1841 to 1850, ...	lb.	.121
	pk.	.277	1851 to 1860, ...	lb.	.114
	bu.	.913			
1851 to 1860, ...	lb.	.026	*Crackers.*		
	pk.	.273	1811 to 1820, ...	bbl.	6.44
	bu.	1.24	1821 to 1830, ...	doz.	.083
FOOD PREPARATIONS.			1831 to 1840, ...	lb.	.125
Biscuit.				doz.	.111
1771 to 1780, ...	ea.	.009		bbl.	3.25
1781 to 1790, ...	ea.	.013	1841 to 1850, ...	lb.	.093
1791 to 1800, ...	doz.	.111		bbl.	3.44
1811 to 1820, ...	doz.	.10	1851 to 1860, ...	lb.	.11

Articles: By Periods of Years — CONTINUED.

ARTICLES AND PERIODS.	Basis.	Amount.	ARTICLES AND PERIODS.	Basis.	Amount.
Cream of Tartar.			*Saleratus.*		
1811 to 1820, ...	oz.	$0.063	1821 to 1830, ...	lb.	$0.133
	lb.	.50	1831 to 1840, ...	lb.	.097
1821 to 1830, ...	lb.	.489	1841 to 1850, ...	lb.	.088
1831 to 1840, ...	oz.	.04	1851 to 1860, ...	lb.	.082
	lb.	.32			
1841 to 1850, ...	lb.	.255	*Salt.*		
1851 to 1860, ...	lb.	.407	1752 to 1760, ...	pk.	.222
				bu.	.767
Farina.			1761 to 1770, ...	qt.	.021
1841 to 1850, ...	lb.	.12		bu.	.556
1851 to 1860, ...	lb.	.136	1771 to 1780, ...	bu.	.50
			1781 to 1790, ...	pk.	.143
Honey.				bu.	.611
1801 to 1810, ...	lb.	.167	1791 to 1800, ...	qt.	.028
1821 to 1830, ...	lb.	.125		pk.	.278
1831 to 1840, ...	lb.	.12		bu.	1.04
				hhd.	6.00
Lard.			1801 to 1810, ...	pk.	.297
1791 to 1800, (wholesale) .	lb.	.125		bu.	1.02
1801 to 1810, ...	lb.	.125		hhd.	5.00
(wholesale) .	lb.	.10	1811 to 1820, ...	qt.	.05
1811 to 1820, ...	lb.	.196		pk.	.29
1821 to 1830, ...	lb.	.108		bu.	.893
1831 to 1840, ...	lb.	.122		bag	4.50
1841 to 1850, ...	lb.	.097	1821 to 1830, ...	qt.	.063
(wholesale) .	lb.	.079		pk.	.204
1851 to 1860, ...	lb.	.137		bu.	.717
1861 to 1880, ...	lb.	.128	1831 to 1840, ...	qt.	.028
1881 to 1883, ...	lb.	.136		pk.	.185
				bu.	.668
Macaroni.			1841 to 1850, ...	lb.	.01
1831 to 1840, ...	lb.	.17		qt.	.025
1851 to 1860, ...	lb.	.179		pk.	.183
				bu.	.613
Molasses.				bag	1.69
1752 to 1760, ...	gal.	.555	1851 to 1860, ...	qt.	.029
1761 to 1770, ...	qt.	.111		pk.	.187
	gal.	.50		bu.	.669
(wholesale) . .	gal.	.201		bag	1.73
1771 to 1780, ...	qt.	.083	*Soda.*		
	gal.	.393	1831 to 1840, ...	lb.	.093
1781 to 1790, ...	qt.	.143	1841 to 1850, ...	lb.	.086
	gal.	.382	1851 to 1860, ...	lb.	.10
1791 to 1800, ...	qt.	.153			
	gal.	.583	*Starch.*		
(wholesale) . .	gal.	.488	1791 to 1800, ...	lb.	.248
1801 to 1810, ...	qt.	.176	1801 to 1810, ...	lb.	.21
	gal.	.612	1811 to 1820, ...	lb.	.238
(wholesale) . .	gal.	.496	1821 to 1830, ...	lb.	.16
1811 to 1820, ...	qt.	.227	1831 to 1840, ...	lb.	.151
	gal.	.851	1841 to 1850, ...	lb.	.114
(wholesale) . .	gal.	.45	1851 to 1860, ...	lb.	.12
1821 to 1830, ...	gal.	.386	1861 to 1880, ...	lb.	.109
(wholesale) . .	gal.	.292	1881 to 1883, ...	lb.	.10
1831 to 1840, ...	qt.	.103			
	gal.	.445	*Suet.*		
1841 to 1850, ...	qt.	.093	1801 to 1810, ...	lb.	.113
	gal.	.302	1811 to 1820, ...	lb.	.131
(wholesale) . .	gal.	.21	1821 to 1830, ...	lb.	.10
1851 to 1860, ...	qt.	.11			
	gal.	.43	*Sugar.*		
1861 to 1880, (Porto Rico and New Orleans) .	gal.	.679	1752 to 1760, ...	lb.	.133
			1761 to 1770, ...	lb.	.111
1881 to 1883, (Porto Rico and New Orleans) .	gal.	.646	1771 to 1780, ...	lb.	.122
			1781 to 1790, ...	lb.	.11
			1791 to 1800, ...	lb.	.187
Pearl Barley.			(wholesale) .	lb.	.142
1801 to 1810, ...	lb.	.334	1801 to 1810, ...	lb.	.158
1811 to 1820, ...	lb.	.375	(wholesale) .	lb.	.14
			1811 to 1820, ...	lb.	.183
Sago.			(wholesale) .	lb.	.142
1841 to 1850, ...	lb.	.107	1821 to 1830, ...	lb.	.146
1851 to 1860, ...	lb.	.106	1831 to 1840, ...	lb.	.134
			(wholesale) .	lb.	.089

Articles: By Periods of Years—Continued.

Articles and Periods.	Basis.	Amount.	Articles and Periods.	Basis.	Amount.
Sugar — Con.			*Lemons — Con.*		
1841 to 1850, . . .	lb.	$0.108	1821 to 1830, . . .	ea.	$0.06
(wholesale)	lb.	.07		doz.	.302
1851 to 1860, . . .	lb.	.093	1831 to 1840, . . .	doz.	.257
(wholesale)	lb.	.073	1841 to 1850, . . .	ea.	.019
1861 to 1880, . . .	lb.	.102		doz.	.253
1881 to 1883, . . .	lb.	.094	1851 to 1860, . . .	doz.	.277
Syrup.			*Oranges.*		
1851 to 1860, . . .	gal.	.578	1811 to 1820, . . .	ea.	.062
1861 to 1880, . . .	gal.	.807		doz.	.60
1881 to 1883, . . .	gal.	.775	1821 to 1830, . . .	doz.	.50
			1831 to 1840, . . .	doz.	.396
Tapioca.			1841 to 1850, . . .	ea.	.026
1831 to 1840, . . .	lb.	.10		doz.	.24
1841 to 1850, . . .	lb.	.117	1851 to 1860, . . .	doz.	.281
1851 to 1860, . . .	lb.	.145			
			Prunes.		
Tea.			1801 to 1810, . . .	lb.	.25
1752 to 1760, . . .	lb.	1.33	1841 to 1850, . . .	lb.	.112
1771 to 1780, . . .	lb.	.625	1851 to 1860, . . .	lb.	.107
1781 to 1790, . . .	lb.	.83			
(wholesale)	lb.	.528	*Raisins.*		
1791 to 1800, . . .	lb.	.796	1781 to 1790, . . .	lb.	.187
(wholesale)	lb.	.559	1791 to 1800, . . .	lb.	.133
1801 to 1810, . . .	lb.	.936	1801 to 1810, . . .	lb.	.173
(wholesale)	lb.	.884	1811 to 1820, . . .	lb.	.202
1811 to 1820, . . .	lb.	1.13	1821 to 1830, . . .	lb.	.139
(wholesale)	lb.	.71	1831 to 1840, . . .	lb.	.106
1821 to 1830, . . .	lb.	.825	1841 to 1850, . . .	lb.	.102
(wholesale)	lb.	.575	1851 to 1860, . . .	lb.	.143
1831 to 1840, . . .	lb.	.557			
1841 to 1850, . . .	lb.	.546			
1851 to 1860, . . .	lb.	.529	*FUEL.*		
1861 to 1880, . . .	lb.	.647	*Bark.*		
1881 to 1883, . . .	lb.	.56	1801 to 1810, . . .	cd.	6.18
			1811 to 1820, . . .	cd.	6.19
Fruits.			1821 to 1830, . . .	cd.	6.00
Citron.			*Charcoal.*		
1821 to 1830, . . .	lb.	.418	1791 to 1800, . . .	bu.	.063
1831 to 1840, . . .	lb.	.76	1801 to 1810, . . .	b'k't	.25
1841 to 1850, . . .	lb.	.307	1811 to 1820, . . .	bu.	.163
1851 to 1860, . . .	lb.	.349		b'k't	.27
			Coal.		
Currants.			1831 to 1840, . . .	ton	8.45
1801 to 1810, . . .	lb.	.183	1851 to 1860, . . .	bu.	.302
1811 to 1820, . . .	lb.	.175		ton	7.00
1821 to 1830, . . .	lb.	.213	1861 to 1880, . . .	bu.	.28
1831 to 1840, . . .	lb.	.143	1881 to 1883, . . .	bu.	.264
1841 to 1850, . . .	lb.	.136			
1851 to 1860, . . .	lb.	.219	*Wood.*		
			1752 to 1760, . . .	ft.	.147
Dried Apple.			1761 to 1770, . . .	ft.	.195
1791 to 1800, . . .	bu.	.833		cd.	1.64
1801 to 1810, . . .	bu.	1.03	1771 to 1780, . . .	ft.	.261
1811 to 1820, . . .	bu.	1.17		cd.	2.00
1821 to 1830, . . .	lb.	.049	1781 to 1790, . . .	ft.	.29
1831 to 1840, . . .	lb.	.069		cd.	1.55
1841 to 1850, . . .	lb.	.069	1791 to 1800, . . .	ft.	.467
1851 to 1860, . . .	lb.	.108		cd.	2.47
			(wholesale)	cd.	2.20
Figs.			1801 to 1810, . . .	ft.	.323
1801 to 1810, . . .	lb.	.25		cd.	5.00
1811 to 1820, . . .	lb.	.184	(wholesale)	cd.	3.22
1821 to 1830, . . .	lb.	.123	1811 to 1820, . . .	ft.	.505
1831 to 1840, . . .	lb.	.13		cd.	4.35
1841 to 1850, . . .	lb.	.131	(wholesale)	cd.	3.67
1851 to 1860, . . .	lb.	.168		cd.	3.59
			1821 to 1830, . . .	ft.	.454
Lemons.			1831 to 1840, . . .	ft.	.827
1781 to 1790, . . .	ea.	.05		cd.	3.81
1801 to 1810, . . .	ea.	.05	1841 to 1850, . . .	ft.	.61
	doz.	.487		cd.	3.93
1811 to 1820, . . .	doz.	.487	(wholesale)	cd.	2.91

Articles: By Periods of Years—CONTINUED.

ARTICLES AND PERIODS.	Basis.	Amount.	ARTICLES AND PERIODS.	Basis.	Amount.
Wood — Con.			*Rum — Con.*		
1851 to 1860,	ft.	$0.705	1791 to 1800,	gal.	$1.01
	cd.	5.58	(wholesale)	gal.	1.01
1861 to 1880,	ft.	.903	1801 to 1810,	qt.	.264
1881 to 1883,	ft.	.877		gal.	.915
			(wholesale)	gal.	.732
LIQUORS AND BEVERAGES.			1811 to 1820,	qt.	.267
Aniseed.				gal.	1.13
1801 to 1810,	gal.	.726	(wholesale)	gal.	.867
1811 to 1820,	gal.	.80	1821 to 1830,	qt.	.236
Beer.				gal.	.754
1811 to 1820,	gal.	.233	1831 to 1840,	qt.	.183
1841 to 1850,	gal.	.315			
Brandy.			*Snakeroot.*		
1781 to 1790,	qt.	.315	1801 to 1810,	gal.	.80
1791 to 1800,	qt.	.38	1811 to 1820,	gal.	.90
	gal.	1.47			
(wholesale)	gal.	1.35	*Wine.*		
1801 to 1810,	qt.	.372	1781 to 1790,	qt.	.334
	gal.	1.54	1791 to 1800,	gal.	1.50
(wholesale)	gal.	1.07	(wholesale)	gal.	1.16
1811 to 1820,	qt.	.66	1801 to 1810,	qt.	.416
	gal.	2.08		gal.	1.56
(wholesale)	gal.	1.50	(wholesale)	gal.	1.28
1821 to 1830,	qt.	.365	1811 to 1820,	qt.	.58
	gal.	1.48		gal.	1.77
(wholesale)	gal.	1.15	(wholesale)	gal.	1.54
1831 to 1840,	qt.	.56	1821 to 1830,	qt.	.27
1841 to 1850,	gal.	2.00		gal.	1.33
1851 to 1860,	qt.	.875	1831 to 1840,	qt.	.369
Cider.			1841 to 1850,	qt.	.364
1752 to 1760,	bbl.	.778		gal.	1.25
1761 to 1770,	bbl.	.974			
1771 to 1780,	gal.	.089	LUMBER.		
	bbl.	.863	*Shingles.*		
1781 to 1790,	bbl.	1.00	1791 to 1800,	M.	2.82
1791 to 1800,	gal.	.056	1801 to 1810,	M.	2.77
	bbl.	3.00	1811 to 1820,	M.	3.75
1801 to 1810,	gal.	.084	1821 to 1830,	M.	2.00
	bbl.	3.44	*Timber.*		
1811 to 1820,	gal.	.258	1791 to 1800,	C.ft.	2.64
	bbl.	2.31	1801 to 1810,	C.ft.	3.22
1821 to 1830,	qt.	.04			
	gal.	.20	MEATS.		
1831 to 1840,	qt.	.039	*Bacon.*		
	gal.	.145	1811 to 1820,	lb.	.155
1841 to 1850,	qt.	.037	1821 to 1830,	lb.	.10
	gal.	.154	1831 to 1840,	lb.	.102
1851 to 1860,	qt.	.045	1841 to 1850,	lb.	.091
	gal.	.10			
Gin.			*Beef.*		
1781 to 1790,	qt.	.443	1752 to 1760,	lb.	.033
1791 to 1800,	gal.	1.25	1761 to 1770,	lb.	.039
(wholesale)	gal.	.997	1771 to 1780,	lb.	.074
1801 to 1810,	qt.	.333	1781 to 1790,	lb.	.044
	gal.	1.28	(wholesale)	lb.	.042
(wholesale)	gal.	1.07	1791 to 1800,	lb.	.047
1811 to 1820,	gal.	1.06	(wholesale)	lb.	.047
(wholesale)	gal.	.965	1801 to 1810,	lb.	.084
1821 to 1830,	qt.	.224	(wholesale)	lb.	.047
	gal.	1.20	1811 to 1820,	lb.	.089
1831 to 1840,	qt.	.272	(wholesale)	lb.	.052
	gal.	1.30	1821 to 1830,	lb.	.076
Rum.			(wholesale)	lb.	.054
1761 to 1770,	pt.	.106	1831 to 1840,	lb.	.081
	gal.	.50	(wholesale)	lb.	.055
1771 to 1780,	gal.	.444	1841 to 1850,	lb.	.09
1781 to 1790,	qt.	.221	(wholesale)	lb.	.052
	gal.	.407	1851 to 1860,	lb.	.126
1791 to 1800,	pt.	.13	(wholesale)	lb.	.074
	qt.	.209	1861 to 1880,	lb.	.144
			1881 to 1883,	lb.	.142

Articles: By Periods of Years — CONTINUED.

ARTICLES AND PERIODS.	Basis.	Amount.	ARTICLES AND PERIODS.	Basis.	Amount.
Ham.			*Tripe.*		
1781 to 1790,	lb.	$0.215	1831 to 1840,	lb.	$0.098
1821 to 1830,	lb.	.095	1841 to 1850,	lb.	.086
1831 to 1840,	lb.	.101			
1841 to 1850,	lb.	.105	*Veal.*		
1851 to 1860,	lb.	.125	1752 to 1760,	lb.	.029
1861 to 1880,	lb.	.13	1761 to 1770,	lb.	.035
1881 to 1883,	lb.	.152	1771 to 1780,	lb.	.039
			1781 to 1790,	lb.	.042
Lamb.			1791 to 1800,	lb.	.058
1791 to 1800,	lb.	.072	1801 to 1810,	lb.	.085
1801 to 1810,	lb.	.072	1811 to 1820,	lb.	.096
1811 to 1820,	lb.	.069	1821 to 1830,	lb.	.075
1821 to 1830,	lb.	.059	1831 to 1840,	lb.	.084
1831 to 1840,	lb.	.076	1841 to 1850,	lb.	.085
1841 to 1850,	lb.	.078	(wholesale)	lb.	.08
1851 to 1860,	lb.	.123	1851 to 1860,	lb.	.13
			(wholesale)	lb.	.089
Mutton.			1861 to 1880,	lb.	.169
1752 to 1760,	lb.	.056	1881 to 1883,	lb.	.153
1761 to 1770,	lb.	.046			
1771 to 1780,	lb.	.081	NUTS.		
1781 to 1790,	lb.	.043	*Almonds.*		
1791 to 1800,	lb.	.056	1801 to 1810,	lb.	.419
1801 to 1810,	lb.	.074	1811 to 1820,	lb.	.22
1811 to 1820,	lb.	.069	1821 to 1830,	lb.	.29
1821 to 1830,	lb.	.064	1831 to 1840,	lb.	.197
1831 to 1840,	lb.	.069	1841 to 1850,	lb.	.163
1841 to 1850,	lb.	.078	1851 to 1860,	lb.	.151
1851 to 1860,	lb.	.118			
1861 to 1880,	lb.	.151	*Filberts.*		
1881 to 1883,	lb.	.153	1801 to 1810,	lb.	.25
			1831 to 1840,	lb.	.08
Pork.			*Walnuts.*		
1752 to 1760,	lb.	.08	1801 to 1810,	bu.	1.38
1761 to 1770,	lb.	.086	1811 to 1820,	bu.	1.90
1771 to 1780,	lb.	.096	1821 to 1830,	bu.	1.25
1781 to 1790,	lb.	.105	OILS AND ILLUMINATING FLUIDS.		
1791 to 1800,	lb.	.109	*Burning Oils and Fluids.*		
(wholesale)	lb.	.07	1781 to 1790,	gal.	1.08
	bbl.	22.00	1791 to 1800,	gal.	.778
1801 to 1810,	lb.	.115	(wholesale)	gal.	.583
(wholesale)	lb.	.101	1801 to 1810,	qt.	.404
	bbl.	25.50		gal.	1.11
1811 to 1820,	lb.	.136	(wholesale)	gal.	.927
(wholesale)	lb.	.104	1811 to 1820,	qt.	.315
	bbl.	35.00		gal.	1.37
1821 to 1830,	lb.	.088	(wholesale)	gal.	1.10
(wholesale)	lb.	.068	1821 to 1830,	qt.	.301
1831 to 1840,	lb.	.105		gal.	.814
(wholesale)	lb.	.078	(wholesale)	gal.	.665
1841 to 1850,	lb.	.091	1831 to 1840,	qt.	.257
(wholesale)	lb.	.063		gal.	1.11
1851 to 1860,	lb.	.114	1841 to 1850,	qt.	.297
(wholesale)	lb.	.085		gal.	1.05
1861 to 1880,	lb.	.108	1851 to 1860,	qt.	.236
1881 to 1883,	lb.	.125		gal.	1.05
			1861 to 1880, (kerosene)	gal.	.30
Sausages.			1881 to 1883, (kerosene)	gal.	.186
1811 to 1820,	lb.	.133			
1821 to 1830,	lb.	.114	*Linseed Oil.*		
1831 to 1840,	lb.	.117	1781 to 1790,	gal.	1.27
1841 to 1850,	lb.	.088	1791 to 1800,	gal.	.771
1851 to 1860,	lb.	.115			
1861 to 1880,	lb.	.119	PAPER.		
1881 to 1883,	lb.	.133	*Letter Paper.*		
			1781 to 1790,	qr.	.184
Tongue.			(by the sheet)	ea.	.015
1801 to 1810,	lb.	.082	1791 to 1800,	qr.	.208
1811 to 1820,	lb.	.113		r'm	1.50
1821 to 1830,	lb.	.085	(by the sheet)	ea.	.01
1831 to 1840,	lb.	.073			
1841 to 1850,	lb.	.112			

Articles: By Periods of Years — CONTINUED.

ARTICLES AND PERIODS.	Basis	Amount.
Letter Paper — Con.		
1801 to 1810,	qr.	$0.359
	r'm	1.87
1811 to 1820,	qr.	.156
	r'm	2.32
(by the sheet)	ea.	.012
1821 to 1830,	qr.	.296
	r'm	2.95
1831 to 1840,	qr.	.258
	r'm	2.15
1841 to 1850,	qr.	.209
	r'm	2.17
(by the sheet)	ea.	.015
1851 to 1860,	qr.	.192
	r'm	1.54
(by the sheet)	ea.	.01
Wrapping Paper.		
1791 to 1800,	r'm	1.17
1801 to 1810,	qr.	.375
	r'm	1.06
1811 to 1820,	r'm	.966
POULTRY AND GAME.		
Chicken.		
1811 to 1820,	lb.	.09
1821 to 1830,	lb.	.058
1831 to 1840,	lb.	.087
Fowl.		
1752 to 1760,	lb.	.111
1821 to 1830,	lb.	.08
1831 to 1840,	lb.	.125
1841 to 1850,	lb.	.128
Goose.		
1801 to 1810,	lb.	.08
1811 to 1820,	lb.	.083
1821 to 1830,	lb.	.065
1831 to 1840,	lb.	.091
1841 to 1850,	lb.	.078
Poultry.		
1811 to 1820,	lb.	.125
1831 to 1840,	lb.	.125
1841 to 1850,	lb.	.12
Turkey.		
1752 to 1760,	lb.	.055
1781 to 1790,	lb.	.056
1791 to 1800,	lb.	.055
1801 to 1810,	lb.	.103
1811 to 1820,	lb.	.107
1821 to 1830,	lb.	.083
1831 to 1840,	lb.	.118
1841 to 1850,	lb.	.116
1851 to 1860,	lb.	.152
RIBBONS AND LACES.		
Lace.		
1801 to 1810,	yd.	.59
1811 to 1820,	yd.	.708
1821 to 1830,	yd.	.595
1831 to 1840,	yd.	.207
1841 to 1850,	yd.	.275
1851 to 1860,	yd.	.298
1881 to 1883,	yd.	.274
Ribbon.		
1781 to 1790,	yd.	.15
1791 to 1800,	yd.	.275
1801 to 1810,	yd.	.171
1811 to 1820,	yd.	.15

ARTICLES AND PERIODS.	Basis	Amount.
Ribbon — Con.		
1821 to 1830,	yd.	$0.153
1831 to 1840,	yd.	.173
1841 to 1850,	yd.	.141
1851 to 1860,	yd.	.235
SMALL WARES.		
Knitting Cotton.		
1811 to 1820,	lb.	1.58
1831 to 1840,	lb.	.887
Needles.		
1801 to 1810,	pap.	.10
	C.	.416
1811 to 1820,	pap.	.125
	C.	.487
1821 to 1830,	C.	.366
1831 to 1840,	pap.	.091
1851 to 1860,	pap.	.058
1881 to 1883,	pap.	.05
Pins.		
1781 to 1790,	pap.	.141
1791 to 1800,	pap.	.111
	lb.	.833
1801 to 1810,	pap.	.167
1811 to 1820,	pap.	.114
1821 to 1830,	pap.	.162
	lb.	.73
1831 to 1840,	pap.	.157
1851 to 1860,	pap.	.089
1881 to 1883,	pap.	.115
Sewing Cotton.		
1801 to 1810,	sk.	.083
	lb.	1.97
1811 to 1820,	sk.	.062
	lb.	2.38
1821 to 1830,	sk.	.054
	sp.	.086
	lb.	2.60
1831 to 1840,	sk.	.08
	sp.	.064
	lb.	1.06
1841 to 1850,	sk.	.054
	sp.	.058
	lb.	.913
1851 to 1860,	sp.	.037
1881 to 1883,	sp.	.046
Sewing and Embroidering Silk.		
1781 to 1790,	sk.	.057
1791 to 1800,	sk.	.056
	oz.	.31
	lb.	5.42
1801 to 1810,	sk.	.079
	lb.	6.08
1811 to 1820,	sk.	.085
	oz.	.508
	lb.	8.50
1821 to 1830,	sk.	.049
	lb.	2.00
1831 to 1840,	sk.	.042
	sp.	.063
1841 to 1850,	sk.	.046
	oz.	.56
1851 to 1860,	sk.	.034
	oz.	.759
Thread (Cotton and Linen).		
1771 to 1780,	sk.	.015
1781 to 1790,	sk.	.032
1791 to 1800,	sk.	.143

Articles: By Periods of Years—Continued.

Articles and Periods.	Basis.	Amount.	Articles and Periods.	Basis.	Amount.
Thread (Cotton and Linen) —Con.			*Cloves.*		
			1781 to 1790, . . .	oz.	$0.041
1791 to 1800, . . .	oz.	$0.153	1791 to 1800, . . .	oz.	.165
	lb.	1.81	1801 to 1810, ; . .	oz.	.125
1801 to 1810, . . .	sk.	.011		lb.	1.00
	oz.	.084	1811 to 1820,	lb.	1.40
	lb.	1.35	1821 to 1830, . . .	oz.	.10
1811 to 1820, . . .	sk.	.159		lb.	1.07
	oz.	.125	1831 to 1840, . . .	oz.	.044
	lb.	.80		lb.	.418
1831 to 1840, . . .	sk.	.01	1841 to 1850, . . .	oz.	.026
	sp.	.08		lb.	.423
	lb.	1.50	1851 to 1860, . . .	oz.	.03
1841 to 1850, . . .	oz.	.125		lb.	.403
	lb.	.745	*Ginger.*		
1851 to 1860, . . .	sk.	.036	1781 to 1790, . . .	lb.	.333
	sp.	.044	1791 to 1800, . . .	lb.	.25
Twist.			(wholesale)	lb.	.147
1781 to 1790, (by the stick)	ea.	.099	1801 to 1810, . . .	lb.	.247
1791 to 1800, . . .	sk.	.054	(wholesale)	lb.	.105
	lb.	7.34	1811 to 1820, . . .	lb.	.319
(by the stick)	ea.	.049	(wholesale)	lb.	.111
1801 to 1810, . . .	sk.	.042	1821 to 1830, . . .	lb.	.145
	lb.	8.17	1831 to 1840, . . .	lb.	.149
(by the stick)	ea.	.06	1841 to 1850, . . .	lb.	.126
1811 to 1820, (by the stick)	ea.	.093	1851 to 1860, . . .	lb.	.133
1821 to 1830, . . .	sk.	.051	*Mace.*		
(by the stick)	ea.	.13	1801 to 1810, . . .	oz.	.71
1831 to 1840, (by the stick)	ea.	.062	1821 to 1830, . . .	lb.	3.00
1841 to 1850, (by the stick)	ea.	.05	1831 to 1840, . . .	oz.	.25
1851 to 1860, . . .	sk.	.05	1841 to 1850, . . .	oz.	.138
(by the stick)	ea.	.045		lb.	2.32
			1851 to 1860, . . .	oz.	.133
Spices and Condiments.				lb.	1.71
Allspice.			*Mustard.*		
1781 to 1790, . . .	oz.	.05	1801 to 1810, . . .	lb.	.52
1791 to 1800, . . .	lb.	.299	1811 to 1820, . . .	lb.	.61
1801 to 1810, . . .	lb.	.426	1821 to 1830, . . .	lb.	.432
1811 to 1820, . . .	lb.	.423	1831 to 1840, . . .	box	.174
1821 to 1830, . . .	oz.	.025		lb.	.405
	lb.	.39	1841 to 1850, . . .	box	.16
1831 to 1840, . . .	oz.	.03		lb.	.402
	lb.	.273	1851 to 1860, . . .	box	.16
1841 to 1850, . . .	lb.	.221		lb.	.351
1851 to 1860, . . .	lb.	.236	*Nutmegs.*		
Cassia.			1781 to 1790, . . .	ea.	.08
				oz.	.333
1801 to 1810, . . .	lb.	.472	1791 to 1800, . . .	ea.	.097
1811 to 1820, . . .	lb.	.766		lb.	5.00
1821 to 1830, . . .	lb.	.538	1801 to 1810, . . .	ea.	.078
1831 to 1840, . . .	lb.	.33		oz.	.521
1841 to 1850, . . .	lb.	.382		lb.	6.00
1851 to 1860, . . .	lb.	.466	1811 to 1820, . . .	ea.	.10
Cayenne Pepper.				oz.	.50
1821 to 1830, . . .	oz.	.10	1821 to 1830, . . .	oz.	.152
	lb.	1.50		lb.	2.19
1831 to 1840, . . .	lb.	.736	1831 to 1840, . . .	oz.	.127
1841 to 1850, . . .	oz.	.06		lb.	1.88
	lb.	.834	1841 to 1850, . . .	oz.	.111
1851 to 1860, . . .	lb.	.76		lb.	1.65
			1851 to 1860, . . .	oz.	.091
Cinnamon.				lb.	1.24
			Pepper.		
1781 to 1790, . . .	oz.	.195	1781 to 1790, . . .	oz.	.061
1791 to 1800, . . .	oz.	.111	1791 to 1800, . . .	oz.	.04
1801 to 1810, . . .	oz.	.192		lb.	.528
	lb.	.80	(wholesale)	lb.	.416
1811 to 1820, . . .	oz.	.122	1801 to 1810, . . .	lb.	.449
	lb.	1.59	(wholesale)	lb.	.245
1821 to 1830, . . .	oz.	.036	1811 to 1820, . . .	lb.	.42
	lb.	.60	(wholesale)	lb.	.17
1831 to 1840, . . .	oz.	.138	1821 to 1830, . . .	lb.	.321
	lb.	.328	1831 to 1840, . . .	lb.	.245
1841 to 1850, . . .	lb.	.425	1841 to 1850, . . .	lb.	.228
			1851 to 1860, . . .	lb.	.205

Articles: By Periods of Years — Continued.

Articles and Periods.	Basis.	Amount.	Articles and Periods.	Basis.	Amount.
Pimento.			*Soap.*		
1791 to 1800, (wholesale)	lb.	$0.139	1781 to 1790, . . .	lb.	$0.16
1801 to 1810, (wholesale)	lb.	.27	1791 to 1800, . . .	lb.	.111
1811 to 1820, (wholesale)	lb.	.28	(wholesale)	lb.	.139
1831 to 1840, . . .	lb.	.21	1801 to 1810, . . .	lb.	.10
1841 to 1850, . . .	lb.	.241	1811 to 1820, . . .	lb.	.121
1851 to 1860, . . .	lb.	.243	(wholesale)	lb.	.10
Vinegar.			1821 to 1830, . . .	lb.	.109
1761 to 1770, . . .	gal.	.126	1831 to 1840, . . .	lb.	.113
1771 to 1780, . . .	gal.	.122	(wholesale)	lb.	.056
1781 to 1790, . . .	qt.	.051		bar	.283
	gal.	.125	1841 to 1850, . . .	lb.	.086
1791 to 1800, . . .	gal.	.209	(wholesale)	lb.	.054
(wholesale)	gal.	.141		bar	.21
1801 to 1810, . . .	qt.	.082	1851 to 1860, . . .	lb.	.114
	gal.	.224		bar	.212
(wholesale)	gal.	.175	1861 to 1880, . . .	lb.	.08
1811 to 1820, . . .	qt.	.07	1881 to 1883, . . .	lb.	.074
	gal.	.288			
(wholesale)	gal.	.165	*Tallow.*		
1821 to 1830, . . .	qt.	.05	1752 to 1760, . . .	lb.	.117
	gal.	.189	1761 to 1770, . . .	lb.	.122
(wholesale)	gal.	.15	1771 to 1780, . . .	lb.	.111
1831 to 1840, . . .	qt.	.047	1781 to 1790, . . .	lb.	.174
	gal.	.194	1791 to 1800, . . .	lb.	.153
1841 to 1850, . . .	qt.	.047	(wholesale)	lb.	.096
	gal.	.167	1811 to 1820, . . .	lb.	.146
1851 to 1860, . . .	gal.	.169	(wholesale)	lb.	.11
(wholesale)	gal.	.125	1821 to 1830, . . .	lb.	.127
			(wholesale)	lb.	.06
Tacks, Brads, and Nails.			1831 to 1840, . . .	lb.	.06
4d. Nails.			1841 to 1850, . . .	lb.	.08
1791 to 1800, . . .	M.	.32			
1801 to 1810, . . .	lb.	.108	**Tobacco and Snuff.**		
	M.	.333	*Snuff.*		
1811 to 1820, . . .	lb.	.105	1781 to 1790, . . .	oz.	.05
1821 to 1830, . . .	lb.	.08	1791 to 1800, . . .	oz.	.028
			1821 to 1830, . . .	oz.	.015
10d. Nails.				lb.	.40
1791 to 1800, . . .	M.	1.41	1831 to 1840, . . .	lb.	.294
1801 to 1810, . . .	lb.	.108	1841 to 1850, . . .	lb.	.259
	M.	1.46	1851 to 1860, . . .	lb.	.26
1811 to 1820, . . .	lb.	.094			
			Tobacco.		
20d. Nails.			1761 to 1770, . . .	lb.	.06
1791 to 1800, . . .	M.	2.25	1771 to 1780, . . .	lb.	.064
1811 to 1820, . . .	lb.	.104	1781 to 1790, . . .	lb.	.091
	M.	2.08	1791 to 1800, . . .	lb.	.15
1821 to 1830, . . .	lb.	.10	(wholesale)	lb.	.154
			1801 to 1810, . . .	lb.	.125
			(wholesale)	lb.	.171
Tallow, Candles, Soap, etc.			1811 to 1820, . . .	lb.	.304
Candles.			1821 to 1830, . . .	lb.	.20
1752 to 1760, . . .	lb.	.108	1831 to 1840, . . .	lb.	.181
1761 to 1770, . . .	lb.	.133	1841 to 1850, . . .	lb.	.226
1771 to 1780, . . .	lb.	.223	1851 to 1860, . . .	lb.	.285
1781 to 1790, . . .	lb.	.245			
1791 to 1800, . . .	lb.	.199	**Tools and Implements.**		
(wholesale)	lb.	.167	*Files.*		
1801 to 1810, . . .	lb.	.199	1791 to 1800, . . .	doz.	.962
(wholesale)	lb.	.155	1801 to 1810, . . .	doz.	.75
1811 to 1820, . . .	lb.	.24			
(wholesale)	lb.	.165	*Hoes.*		
1821 to 1830, . . .	lb.	.163	1801 to 1810, . . .	ea.	.565
1831 to 1840, . . .	lb.	.139	1811 to 1820, . . .	ea.	.54
1841 to 1850, . . .	lb.	.134	1821 to 1830, . . .	ea.	.467
(wholesale)	lb.	.12	1841 to 1850, . . .	ea.	.56
1851 to 1860, . . .	lb.	.274			
			Scythes.		
Castile Soap.			1791 to 1800, . . .	ea.	.887
			1801 to 1810, . . .	ea.	1.00
1841 to 1850, . . .	bar	.25	1811 to 1820, . . .	ea.	.92
1851 to 1860, . . .	bar	.147	1821 to 1830, . . .	ea.	1.00

Articles: By Periods of Years — CONCLUDED.

ARTICLES AND PERIODS.	Basis.	Amount.	ARTICLES AND PERIODS.	Basis.	Amount.
Shoe Knives.			*Cotton* — Con.		
1791 to 1800, ...	doz.	$0.896	1791 to 1800, (wholesale) .	lb.	$0.305
1801 to 1810, ...	doz.	.813	1801 to 1810, ...	lb.	.377
1841 to 1850, ...	doz.	1.60	(wholesale) .	lb.	.258
			1821 to 1830, ...	lb.	.15
Shovels.					
1791 to 1800, ...	ea.	1.08	*Iron.*		
	doz.	7.50	1752 to 1760, ...	lb.	.055
1801 to 1810, ...	doz.	9.80	1761 to 1770, ...	lb.	.045
1811 to 1820, ...	doz.	10.75	1821 to 1830, ...	lb.	.055
1821 to 1830, ...	ea.	.25			
1841 to 1850, ...	ea.	.88	*Matches.*		
1851 to 1860, ...	ea.	.96	1831 to 1840, ...	¼gro.	.175
			1841 to 1850, ...	¼gro.	.234
NOT CLASSIFIED.			1851 to 1860, ...	¼gro.	.157
Brick.			*Tumblers.*		
1752 to 1760, ...	M.	2.07	1781 to 1790, ...	doz.	2.50
1761 to 1770, ...	M.	2.75	1801 to 1810, ...	doz.	1.63
1801 to 1810, ...	M.	10.00	1811 to 1820, ...	doz.	1.33
			1821 to 1830, ...	doz.	1.70
Brooms.			1831 to 1840, ...	doz.	.972
1781 to 1790, ...	ea.	.129	1841 to 1850, ...	doz.	1.36
1801 to 1810, ...	ea.	.268	1851 to 1860, ...	doz.	.953
1811 to 1820, ...	ea.	.23			
1821 to 1830, ...	ea.	.192	*Wafers.*		
1831 to 1840, ...	ea.	.245	1801 to 1810, ...	lb.	1.50
1841 to 1750, ...	ea.	.235	1811 to 1820, ...	lb.	2.00
1851 to 1860, ...	ea.	.25			
			Wine Glasses.		
Cotton.			1801 to 1810, ...	doz.	1.03
1781 to 1790, ...	lb.	.50	1811 to 1820, ...	doz.	1.75
1791 to 1800, ...	lb.	.329	1821 to 1830, ...	doz.	.88

From the occupations and articles tables, by periods of years, we now bring forward into the following table the averages for those occupations and articles for which we show wage and price fluctuations. In this table, we present average wages by the day only for occupations, and for articles average retail prices for the basis or bases only by which the articles are commonly bought and sold.

Occupations and Articles,

OCCUPATIONS AND ARTICLES.	Basis.	PERIOD ENDING WITH —			
		1760	1770	1780	1790
OCCUPATIONS.					
Agricultural laborers,	day	$0.311	$0.33	$0.315	$0.396
Blacksmiths,	day	–	–	–	.694
Bookbinders,	day	–	–	–	–
Butchers,	day	–	–	.333	–
Carpenters,	day	–	–	.522	.539
Carriage makers,	day	–	–	–	–
Clockmakers,	day	–	–	–	–
Clothing makers,	day	–	–	–	–
Cotton mill operatives,	day	–	–	–	–
Glass makers,	day	–	–	–	–
Gold and silver workers,	day	–	–	–	–
Harness makers,	day	–	–	–	–
Laborers,	day	.29	.325	.376	.428
Machinists,	day	–	–	–	–
Masons,	day	–	–	.666	1.00
Metal workers,	day	–	–	–	–
Millwrights,	day	–	–	–	–
Nail makers,	day	–	–	–	.481
Painters,	day	–	–	–	–
Paper mill operatives,	day	–	–	–	–
Printers,	day	–	–	–	–
Ship and boat builders,	day	–	–	–	.889
Shoemakers,	day	–	–	–	–
Stone quarrymen and cutters,	day	–	–	–	–
Tanners and curriers,	day	–	–	–	–
Wooden goods makers,	day	–	–	–	–
Woollen mill operatives,	day	–	–	–	–
ARTICLES.					
Agricultural Products.					
Apples,	bu.	.319	.183	.152	.17
Beans,	qt.	.033	.042	.042	.041
	bu.	.80	.80	–	–
Corn,	bu.	.574	.558	.703	.725
Oats,	bu.	.333	.333	–	.494
Potatoes,	bu.	.371	.354	.30	.279
Rice,	lb.	–	–	–	.055
Rye,	bu.	.622	.663	1.00	.967
Turnips,	bu.	.262	.264	.252	.242
Boots, Shoes, and Leather.					
Boots,	pr.	–	–	–	–
Shoes,	pr.	1.00	1.11	.837	.958
Slippers,	pr.	–	–	–	–
Clothing.					
Gloves,	pr.	–	–	–	.464
Handkerchiefs,	ea.	–	–	.367	.593
Hose, socks, and stockings,	pr.	–	.978	–	.734
Dairy Products.					
Butter,	lb.	–	.167	.11	.114
Cheese,	lb.	.084	.087	.133	.081
Eggs,	doz.	.078	–	.056	.085
Milk,	qt.	–	–	.029	.025
Dress Goods.					
Calico,	yd.	–	–	–	.579
Cambric,	yd.	–	–	1.02	1.24
Gingham,	yd.	–	–	–	–
Lawn,	yd.	–	–	.903	.734
Muslin,	yd.	–	–	–	–
Silk,	yd.	–	–	–	.868
Dry Goods.					
Cotton cloth,	yd.	–	–	–	.884
Flannel,	yd.	–	–	–	–
Linen,	yd.	–	–	–	.449
Sheetings,	yd.	–	–	–	–
Shirtings,	yd.	–	–	–	–
Ticking,	yd.	–	–	–	–
Tow cloth,	yd.	.15	.299	–	.214

By Periods of Years.

			PERIOD ENDING WITH—					
1800	**1810**	**1820**	**1830**	**1840**	**1850**	**1860**	**1880**	**1883**
$0.478	$0.779	$0.782	$0.803	$0.875	$0.95	$1.01	$1.31	$1.37
–	–	.842	1.12	1.40	1.47	1.69	2.28	1.92
–	–	–	–	.917	1.46	1.38	1.91	1.49
–	.50	.75	.917	–	–	–	2.03	1.36
.736	1.09	1.13	1.07	1.40	1 37	2.03	2.42	2.41
–	–	–	–	1.34	1.59	1.85	2.40	2.27
–	–	1.13	1.29	1.29	1.29	1.96	2.30	–
–	–	1.00	1.27	.896	1.38	1.43	1.93	1.99
–	–	–	.439	.897	.92	1.03	1.40	1.27
–	–	–	1.13	1.62	2.44	2.96	1.79	2.01
–	–	–	–	.974	1.28	1.69	1.53	3.21
–	–	.88	1.13	1.25	1.46	1.65	–	–
.623	.817	.91	.796	.872	.852	.975	1.48	1.31
–	–	–	–	1.35	1.62	2.15	2.49	2.25
–	1.41	1.52	1.22	1.37	1.33	1.53	2.79	2.14
–	–	1.05	1.23	1.54	1.42	1.35	2.16	2.00
1.09	–	1.13	1.21	1.39	1.39	1.66	2.65	2.54
–	–	1.00	1.39	.86	1.50	–	–	1.84
–	1.15	1.34	1.25	1.32	1.47	1.85	2.32	1.97
–	–	1.09	.666	.749	.842	1.17	1.71	1.71
–	–	1.13	1.25	1.38	1.17	1.75	2.18	2.14
.733	–	1.25	1.40	1.33	1.35	3.65	2.49	3 25
–	–	–	1.06	.873	1.12	1.70	1.76	1.87
–	–	–	–	1.29	1.45	1.40	2.33	2.01
–	–	1.00	1.13	1.46	1.13	1.67	2.09	1.86
–	.66	1.26	1.25	1.36	1.11	1.72	2.01	2.28
–	–	–	1.12	.995	.865	.873	1.31	1.24
.259	.344	.526	.439	.708	.876	.995	–	–
.049	.051	.109	.085	.081	.067	.088	.089	.123
1.05	1.48	2.36	1.49	1.91	1.89	2.60	–	–
.90	1.04	1.31	.817	.782	.721	.992	–	–
.451	.554	.737	.426	.544	.545	–	–	–
.302	.501	.485	.369	.492	.783	.86	.999	1.00
.037	.058	.063	.044	.056	.049	.06	.103	.092
1.14	1.27	1.44	.882	1.03	1.00	1.50	–	–
.50	.417	.475	.33	.25	.333	.335	–	–
6.00	4.45	6.14	4.75	3.72	2.49	2.21	–	–
.97	1.29	1.25	1.26	1.35	1.06	1.09	–	–
.556	–	–	.935	.947	1.00	.945	–	1.56
.63	.687	.458	.517	.466	.404	.594	–	.648
.728	.448	.66	.441	.442	.491	.414	–	.525
1.35	1.23	.932	.59	.523	.38	.445	–	.49
.185	.213	.24	.186	.22	.196	.262	.323	.325
.096	.14	.123	.089	.096	.096	.117	.149	.16
.07	.235	.206	.15	.19	.19	.22	.275	.343
.034	.042	.047	.044	.049	.05	.052	.067	.066
.394	.385	.36	.292	.243	.163	.105	–	–
1.28	.805	.796	.359	.254	.212	.193	–	–
.556	.337	.451	.317	.249	.203	.192	–	–
–	–	.538	.644	.559	.452	.228	–	–
.528	.793	.697	.585	.541	.36	.263	–	.216
1.00	1.08	1.58	.799	.659	.832	.989	–	1.00
.339	.328	.415	.21	.148	.129	.118	–	–
.423	.713	.657	.57	.435	.388	.405	–	.326
.369	.605	.526	.453	.578	.379	.531	–	–
.51	.426	.523	.281	.206	.105	.124	–	.162
–	.458	.386	.223	.135	.114	.107	–	.12
.904	.75	.615	.367	.254	.169	.16	–	.155
.201	.278	.292	.173	.147	–	.128	x	–

Occupations and Articles,

OCCUPATIONS AND ARTICLES.	Basis.	PERIOD ENDING WITH —			
		1760	1770	1780	1790
Fish.					
Codfish,	lb.	–	–	–	$0.034
Fish,	lb.	–	–	–	–
Halibut,	lb.	–	–	–	–
Herring,	doz.	–	$0.25	–	.083
Mackerel,	lb.	–	–	–	–
Salmon,	lb.	–	–	–	–
Saltfish,	lb.	–	–	–	–
Flour and Meal.					
Flour,	lb.	$0.044	–	–	.047
	bbl.	–	–	–	5.96
Indian meal,	lb.	–	–	–	–
	bu.	–	–	–	–
Rye meal,	lb.	–	–	–	–
	bu.	–	–	–	–
Food Preparations.					
Chocolate,	lb.	–	–	–	.278
Coffee,	lb.	–	–	–	.23
Lard,	lb.	–	–	–	–
Molasses,	gal.	.555	.50	$0.393	.382
Salt,	qt.	–	.021	–	–
	bu.	.767	.556	.50	.611
Starch,	lb.	–	–	–	–
Sugar,	lb.	.133	.111	.122	.11
Tea,	lb.	1.33	–	.625	.83
Fruits.					
Raisins,	lb.	–	–	–	.187
Fuel.					
Wood,	ft.	.147	.195	.261	.29
	cd.	–	1.64	2.00	1.55
Liquors and Beverages.					
Brandy,	gal.	–	–	–	–
Cider,	gal.	–	–	.089	–
Gin,	gal.	–	–	–	–
Rum,	gal.	–	.50	.444	.407
Wine,	gal.	–	–	–	–
Meats.					
Beef,	lb.	.033	.039	.074	.044
Ham,	lb.	–	–	–	.215
Lamb,	lb.	–	–	–	–
Mutton,	lb.	.056	.046	.081	.043
Pork,	lb.	.08	.086	.096	.105
Sausages,	lb.	–	–	–	–
Veal,	lb.	.029	.035	.039	.042
Oils and Illuminating Fluids.					
Burning oils and fluids,	gal.	–	–	–	1.08
Paper.					
Letter paper,	qr.	–	–	–	.184
	r'm	–	–	–	–
Poultry and Game.					
Turkey.	lb.	.055	–	–	.056
Spices and Condiments.					
Allspice,	lb.	–	–	–	–
Cassia,	lb.	–	–	–	–
Cinnamon,	lb.	–	–	–	–
Cloves,	lb.	–	–	–	–
Ginger,	lb.	–	–	–	.333
Mustard,	lb.	–	–	–	–
Nutmegs,	oz.	–	–	–	.333
	lb.	–	–	–	–
Pepper,	lb.	–	–	–	–
Vinegar,	gal.	–	.126	.122	.125
Tallow, Candles, Soap, etc.					
Candles,	lb.	.108	.133	.223	.245
Soap,	lb.	–	–	–	.16
Tallow,	lb.	.117	.122	.111	.174

By Periods of Years — Concluded.

	PERIOD ENDING WITH—							
1800	**1810**	**1820**	**1830**	**1840**	**1850**	**1860**	**1880**	**1883**
–	$0.034	$0.033	$0.031	$0.038	$0.034	$0.053	$0.072	$0.089
$0.034	.052	.057	.039	.041	.055	.049	–	–
–	.045	.048	.048	.053	.059	.105	–	–
–	.15	.176	.083	.09	.118	.08	.13	.133
–	.055	.084	.038	.066	.071	.085	–	–
–	.167	.163	.20	.219	.21	.125	–	–
.044	–	.056	.061	.05	.049	.052	–	–
.063	.065	.07	.038	.045	.036	.044	.051	.043
8.25	8.78	11.67	7.08	8.16	6.78	8.92	–	–
–	–	.039	.016	.02	.016	.021	.019	.029
.814	1.08	1.35	.788	1.02	.831	.982	–	–
–	–	.042	.018	.03	.021	.026	–	–
1.03	1.36	1.38	.853	1.17	.913	1.24	–	–
.291	.338	.271	.245	.20	.20	.235	–	–
.213	.273	.256	.206	.14	.115	.163	.318	.214
–	.125	.196	.108	.122	.097	.137	.128	.136
.583	.612	.851	.386	.445	.302	.43	.679	.646
.028	–	.805	.063	.028	.025	.029	–	–
1.04	1.02	.893	.717	.668	.613	.669	–	–
.248	.21	.238	.16	.151	.114	.12	.109	.10
.187	.158	.183	.146	.134	.108	.093	.102	.094
.796	.936	1.13	.825	.557	.546	.529	.647	.56
.133	.173	.202	.139	.106	.102	.143	–	–
.467	.323	.505	.454	.827	.61	.705	.903	.877
2.47	5.00	4.35	3.59	3.81	3.93	5.58	–	–
1.47	1.54	2.08	1.48	–	2.00	–	–	–
.056	.084	.258	.20	.145	.154	.10	–	–
1.25	1.28	1.06	1.20	1.30	–	–	–	–
1.01	.915	1.13	.754	–	–	–	–	–
1.50	1.56	1.77	1.33	–	1.25	–	–	–
.047	.084	.089	.076	.081	.09	.126	.144	.142
–	–	–	.095	.101	.105	.125	.13	.152
.072	.072	.069	.059	.076	.078	.123	–	–
.056	.074	.069	.064	.069	.078	.118	.151	.153
.109	.115	.136	.088	.105	.091	.114	.108	.125
–	–	.133	.114	.117	.088	.115	.119	.133
.058	.085	.096	.075	.084	.085	.13	.169	.153
.778	1.11	1.37	.814	1.11	1.05	1.05	.30	.186
.208	.359	.156	.296	.258	.209	.192	–	–
1.50	1.87	2.32	2.95	2.15	2.17	1.54	–	–
.055	.103	.107	.083	.118	.116	.152	–	–
.299	.426	.423	.39	.273	.221	.236	–	–
–	.472	.766	.538	.33	.382	.466	–	–
–	.80	1.50	.60	.328	.425	–	–	–
–	1.00	1.40	1.07	.418	.423	.403	–	–
.25	.247	.319	.145	.149	.126	.133	–	–
–	.52	.61	.432	.405	.402	.351	–	–
–	.521	.50	.152	.127	.111	.091	–	–
5.00	6.00	–	2.19	1.88	1.65	1.24	–	–
.528	.449	.42	.321	.245	.228	.205	–	–
.209	.224	.288	.189	.194	.167	.169	–	–
.199	.199	.24	.163	.139	.134	.274	–	–
.111	.10	.121	.109	.113	.086	.114	.08	.074
.153	–	.146	.127	.06	.08	–	–	–

We present next, by occupations and articles, wage and price fluctuation tables, showing for each occupation and article, together with the amounts, the period in which the highest and lowest wage or price was reported for the basis indicated; we then give the general average wage or price for all periods, and show the excess of the highest wage or price over both the lowest and the general average wage or price.

Wage Fluctuations. By Occupations.

OCCUPATIONS.	Basis.	Highest Wage.		Lowest Wage.		General Average Wage.	Excess of Highest Wage—	
		Period ending with —	Amount.	Period ending with —	Amount.		Over Lowest.	Over Average.
Agricultural laborers, .	day	1883	$1.37	1760	$0.311	$0.747	$1.06	$0.623
Blacksmiths, .	day	1880	2.28	1790	.694	1.43	1.59	.85
Bookbinders, .	day	1880	1.91	1840	.917	1.43	.993	.48
Butchers, .	day	1880	2.03	1780	.333	.982	1.70	1.05
Carpenters, .	day	1880	2.42	1780	.522	1.34	1.90	1.08
Carriage makers, .	day	1880	2.40	1840	1.34	1.89	1.06	.51
Clockmakers, .	day	1880	2.30	1820	1.13	1.54	1.17	.76
Clothing makers, .	day	1883	1.99	1840	.896	1.41	1.09	.58
Cotton mill operatives, .	day	1880	1.40	1830	.439	.993	.961	.407
Glass makers, .	day	1860	2.96	1830	1.13	1.99	1.83	.97
Gold and silver workers, .	day	1883	3.21	1840	.974	1.74	2.24	1.47
Harness makers, . . .	day	1860	1.65	1820	.88	1.27	.77	.38
Laborers, .	day	1880	1.48	1760	.29	.773	1.19	.707
Machinists, .	day	1880	2.49	1840	1.35	1.97	1.14	.52
Masons, .	day	1880	2.79	1780	.666	1.50	2.12	1.29
Metal workers, .	day	1880	2.16	1820	1.05	1.54	1.11	.62
Millwrights, .	day	1880	2.65	1800	1.09	1.63	1.56	1.02
Nail makers, .	day	1883	1.84	1790	.481	1.18	1.36	.66
Painters, .	day	1880	2.32	1810	1.15	1.58	1.17	.74
Paper mill operatives, .	day	1880 1883	1.71	1830	.666	1.13	1.04	.58
Printers, .	day	1880	2.18	1820	1.13	1.57	1.05	.61
Ship and boat builders, .	day	1860	3.65	1790	.889	1.95	2.76	1.70
Shoemakers, .	day	1883	1.87	1800	.733	1.30	1.14	.57
Stone quarrymen and cutters,	day	1880	2.33	1840	1.29	1.70	1.04	.63
Tanners and curriers, .	day	1880	2.09	1820	1.00	1.48	1.09	.61
Wooden goods makers, .	day	1883	2.28	1810	.66	1.46	1.62	.82
Woollen mill operatives, .	day	1880	1.31	1850	.865	1.07	.445	.24

Price Fluctuations. By Articles.

ARTICLES.	Basis.	Highest Price.		Lowest Price.		General Average Price.	Excess of Highest Price—	
		Period ending with —	Amount.	Period ending with —	Amount.		Over Lowest.	Over Average.
Agricultural Products.								
Apples, .	bu.	1860	$0.995	1780	$0.152	$0.452	$0.843	$0.543
Beans, .	qt.	1883	.123	1760	.033	.069	.09	.054
	bu.	1860	2.60	1760 1770	.80	1.60	1.80	1.00
Corn, .	bu.	1820	1.31	1770	.558	.829	.752	.481
Oats, .	bu.	1820	.737	1760 1770	.333	.491	.404	.246
Potatoes, .	bu.	1883	1.00	1790	.279	.546	.721	.454
Rice, .	lb.	1880	.103	1800	.037	.062	.066	.041
Rye, .	bu.	1860	1.50	1760	.622	1.05	.878	.45
Turnips, .	bu.	1800	.50	1790	.242	.333	.258	.167

Price Fluctuations.   By Articles — *Con.*

ARTICLES.	Basis.	Highest Price.		Lowest Price.		General Average Price.	Excess of Highest Price —	
		Period ending with —	Amount.	Period ending with —	Amount.		Over Lowest.	Over Average.
Boots, Shoes, and Leather.								
Boots, ...	pr.	1820	$6.14	1860	$2.21	$4.25	$3.93	$1.89
Shoes, ...	pr.	1840	1.35	1780	.837	1.11	.513	.24
Slippers, ...	pr.	1883	1.56	1800	.556	.991	1.00	.569
Clothing.								
Gloves, ...	pr.	1810	.687	1850	.404	.541	.283	.146
Handkerchiefs, . . .	ea.	1800	.728	1780	.367	.511	.361	.217
Hose, socks, and stockings, .	pr.	1800	1.35	1850	.38	.765	.97	.585
Dairy Products.								
Butter, ...	lb	1883	.325	1780	.11	.212	.215	.113
Cheese, ...	lb.	1883	.16	1790	.081	.112	.079	.048
Eggs, ...	doz.	1883	.343	1780	.056	.175	.287	.168
Milk, ...	qt.	1880	.067	1790	.025	.046	.042	.021
Dress Goods.								
Calico, ...	yd.	1790	.579	1860	.105	.315	.474	.264
Cambric, ...	yd.	1800	1.28	1860	.193	.684	1.09	.596
Gingham, ...	yd.	1800	.556	1860	.192	.329	.364	.227
Lawn, ...	yd.	1780	.903	1860	.228	.58	.675	.323
Muslin, ...	yd.	1810	.793	1883	.216	.498	.577	.295
Silk, ...	yd.	1820	1.58	1840	.659	.979	.921	.601
Dry Goods.								
Cotton cloth, ...	yd.	1790	.884	1860	.118	.321	.766	.563
Flannel, ...	yd.	1810	.713	1883	.326	.49	.387	.223
Linen, ...	yd.	1810	.605	1800	.369	.486	.236	.119
Sheetings, ...	yd.	1820	.523	1850	.105	.292	.418	.231
Shirtings, ...	yd.	1810	.458	1860	.107	.22	.351	.238
Ticking, ...	yd.	1800	.904	1883	.155	.422	.749	.482
Tow cloth, ...	yd.	1770	.299	1860	.128	.209	.171	.09
Fish.								
Codfish, ...	lb.	1883	.089	1830	.031	.046	.058	.043
Fish, ...	lb.	1820	.057	1800	.034	.047	.023	.01
Halibut, ...	lb.	1860	.105	1810	.045	.06	.06	.045
Herring, ...	doz.	1770	.25	1860	.08	.129	.17	.121
Mackerel, ...	lb.	1883	.133	1830	.038	.083	.095	.05
Salmon, ...	lb.	1840	.219	1860	.125	.181	.094	.038
Saltfish	lb.	1830	.061	1800	.044	.052	.017	.009
Flour and Meal.								
Flour, ...	lb.	1820	.07	1850	.036	.05	.034	.02
	bbl.	1820	11.67	1790	5.96	8.20	5.71	3.47
Indian meal, ...	lb.	1820	.039	{ 1830 1850 }	.016	.03	.023	.009
	bu.	1820	1.35	1830	.788	.981	.562	.369
Rye meal, ...	lb.	1820	.042	1830	.018	.027	.024	.015
	bu.	1820	1.38	1830	.853	1.14	.527	.24
Food Preparations.								
Chocolate, ...	lb.	1810	.338	{ 1840 1850 }	.20	.257	.138	.081
Coffee, ...	lb.	1880	.318	1850	.115	.213	.203	.105
Lard, ...	lb.	1820	.196	1850	.097	.131	.099	.065
Molasses, ...	gal.	1820	.851	1850	.302	.52	.549	.331
Salt, ...	qt.	1830	.063	1770	.021	.035	.042	.028
	bu.	1800	1.04	1780	.50	.732	.54	.308
Starch, ...	lb.	1800	.248	1883	.10	.161	.148	.087
Sugar, ...	lb.	1800	.187	1860	.093	.129	.094	.058
Tea, ...	lb.	1760	1.33	1860	.529	.776	.801	.554
Fruits.								
Raisins, ...	lb.	1820	.202	1850	.102	.148	.10	.054
Fuel.								
Wood, ...	ft.	1880	.903	1760	.147	.505	.756	.398
	cd.	1860	5.58	1790	1.55	3.39	4.03	2.19
Liquors and Beverages.								
Brandy, ...	gal.	1820	2.08	1800	1.47	1.71	.61	.37
Cider, ...	gal.	1820	.258	1800	.056	.136	.202	.122
Gin, ...	gal.	1840	1.30	1820	1.06	1.22	.24	.08
Rum, ...	gal.	1820	1.13	1790	.407	.737	.723	.393
Wine, ...	gal.	1820	1.77	1850	1.25	1.48	.52	.29

Price Fluctuations.

ARTICLES.	Ba-sis.	Highest Price.		Lowest Price.		General Average Price.	Excess of Highest Price —	
		Period ending with —	Amount.	Period ending with —	Amount.		Over Lowest.	Over Aver-age.
Meats.								
Beef,	lb.	1880	.144	1760	.033	.082	.111	.062
Ham,	lb.	1790	.215	1830	.095	.132	.12	.083
Lamb,	lb.	1860	.123	1830	.059	.078	.064	.045
Mutton,	lb.	1883	.153	1790	.043	.081	.11	.072
Pork,	lb.	1820	.136	1760	.08	.104	.056	.032
Sausages,	lb.	1820 } 1883 }	.133	1850	.088	.117	.045	.016
Veal,	lb.	1880	.169	1760	.029	.083	.14	.086
Oils and Illuminating Fluids.								
Burning oils and fluids,	gal.	1820	1.37	1883	.186	.885	1.18	.485
Paper.								
Letter paper,	qr.	1810	.359	1820	.156	.233	.203	.126
	r'm	1830	2.95	1800	1.50	2.07	1.45	.88
Poultry and Game.								
Turkey,	lb.	1860	.152	1760 } 1800 }	.055	.094	.097	.058
Spices and Condiments.								
Allspice,	lb.	1810	.426	1850	.221	.324	.205	.102
Cassia,	lb.	1820	.766	1840	.33	.492	.436	.274
Cinnamon,	lb.	1820	1.59	1840	.328	.749	1.26	.841
Cloves,	lb.	1820	1.40	1860	.403	.786	.997	.614
Ginger,	lb.	1790	.333	1850	.126	.213	.207	.12
Mustard,	lb.	1820	.61	1860	.351	.453	.259	.157
Nutmegs,	oz.	1810	.521	1860	.091	.262	.43	.259
	lb.	1810	6.00	1860	1.24	2.99	4.76	3.01
Pepper,	lb.	1800	.528	1860	.205	.342	.323	.186
Vinegar,	gal.	1820	.288	1780	.122	.181	.166	.107
Tallow, Candles, Soap, etc.								
Candles,	lb.	1860	.274	1760	.108	.187	.166	.087
Soap,	lb.	1790	.16	1883	.074	.107	.086	.053
Tallow,	lb.	1790	.174	1840	.06	.121	.114	.053

We show next wage and price fluctuations, by periods of years, giving for each period the whole number of occupations and articles for which average wages and prices have been presented, and, in addition, the number reporting highest and the number reporting lowest wages or prices, also for each period.

Wage and Price Fluctuations.   By PERIODS OF YEARS.

PERIOD ENDING WITH —	OCCUPATIONS.			ARTICLES.		
	Whole Number.	Highest.	Lowest.	Whole Number.	Highest.	Lowest.
1760,	2	–	2	25	1	10
1770,	2	–	–	28	2	4
1780,	5	–	3	29	1	7
1790,	7	–	3	51	6	8
1800,	5	–	2	69	10	9
1810,	7	–	2	77	10	1
1820,	18	–	5	83	27	2
1830,	22	–	3	86	3	8
1840,	26	–	6	83	3	5
1850,	26	–	1	83	–	14
1860,	25	3	–	79	8	17
1880,	25	18	–	26	6	–
1883,	25	7	–	36	10	6

SUMMARY.

Contrasting, in summing up, the present with the past, we find :

Instead of a few industries struggling for existence, every kind of manufacturing industry well established, covering a wide range of products formerly unknown but now deemed essential to the comfort and convenience of man. The multiplication of industries has broadened the avenues of employment, and their subdivision has given opportunity for the exercise of special skill and talent, while the manner of conducting the industries under the factory system has immensely increased the productive capacity of the workman, cheapening the product to the consumer, increasing profits to the manufacturer and wages to the employé, and, in the aggregated industries, giving to labor a larger relative share of product.

Machinery of every kind has come to the assistance of the workman, and, with the advent of machinery, new products have been introduced, thus putting at command of the consumer a wider range of comforts and creating new channels of industry.

Under the new system of labor, working time has been reduced 12 to 24 per cent.

The household comforts and conveniences possessed by the workingman to-day are so far beyond what the workingman had in the first quarter of the century that the difference in scale of living between the employer class and the laborer of the early period was far less than that between the workman of to-day and his predecessor.

The educational and social privileges free to the laborer to-day give him wide opportunities of self-culture and enjoyment, and are such as to raise his children to higher levels of employment, and therefore tend to put them on an equality with the children of the wealthy as to getting on in the world.

The improvements in internal communication — the railroad and the electric telegraph — bind together industrial communities widely separated geographically, enabling the laborer to quickly and cheaply seek new localities if deprived of employment in any particular place, permitting workmen to unite in a

common effort to better their condition, adding to the certainty and security of industrial operations, thus protecting the laborer in his employment, besides cheapening the price of commodities by facilitating exchanges.

As regards the course of wages and prices during the century the statistics presented in the tables are so complete as to require little comment here. Carefully studied, in connection with the explanatory text and notes which accompany them, they afford an interesting view of the economic conditions surrounding the workingman, so far as these conditions depend on the money reward received for his labor. They will be found of value to the student, who may be left to make whatever deductions occur to him without extended summarizing of results in these pages.

A brief review of the more obvious points may be permitted.

From various causes, chief among which were excessive importations, the spirit of speculation, and the abuse of the credit system, two violent commercial revulsions occurred between 1830 and 1860. These took place in 1837 and 1857. The first was prolonged by a failure of the grain crop during 1837–8. Breadstuffs temporarily rose in price. There was a steady drain of specie from the country. Wages temporarily declined. Banks everywhere suspended. Bankruptcies were general. After the modification of the tariff in 1842, importations were checked, manufactures revived, and, the commercial atmosphere having been purified, business generally recovered. The same general features were repeated after the panic of 1857. Many large establishments were closed for months, while others ran only on half time.

The question at once arises what influence, if any, had these commercial depressions upon the general tendency of wages? So far as the answer may be gathered from the tables it does not appear that such influence was material. Whatever changes occurred, either reductions in wages or fluctuations in prices, were temporary only and were not sufficiently important to affect the averages for the decades ending with 1840 and 1860 respectively. By a reference to the table, "Occupations and Articles, by Periods of Years," pages 184 to 187, it will be seen that the wages of the following occupations only show a decrease for the period ending with 1840 as compared

with that ending with 1830 : clothing makers, nail makers, ship and boat builders, shoemakers, and woollen mill operatives.

A decrease is also shown in the woollen industry at the close of the next decade, and, undoubtedly, is apparent merely from the fact that the wage presented for the period ending with 1830 is based principally upon the amounts paid to overseers, and does not include the medium and low priced labor of the factory. The decrease shown in the four other industries is slight and more than recovered during the next decade.

For the period ending with 1860, but three occupations, book-binders, metal workers, and stone quarrymen and cutters, show a decrease as compared with the previous decade, and in all instances the decrease is very slight. From this it appears that during these periods of business depression the nominal rates of wages were but slightly reduced, although the aggregate earnings of wage workers may have been considerably diminished on account of reductions in working time.

As a rule, wages show an upward tendency from the earliest recorded period to the present time, the progress being broken at certain intervals, as relates to certain industries, by fluctuations temporary only and therefore not materially affecting the onward current. The whole movement is clearly shown in the table to which we have just referred, pages 184 to 187. In accordance with this rule, wages for the decade ending with 1830 for all occupations were higher than during any previous decennial period, except for carpenters, laborers, masons, painters, paper mill operatives, and wooden goods makers, all of which show a slightly higher average at the close of the previous decade. A comparison of wages for the decade ending with 1830 and those for the decade ending with 1860 shows at a glance the advance that has been made. We are able to make such a comparison for twenty leading occupations and now bring forward for that purpose data supplied by the table, "Occupations and Articles, by Periods of Years." We present this comparison in the following table, showing at the same time, for each occupation, the percentage of increase or decrease for the period ending with 1860 as compared with the period ending with 1830 :

Comparison of Wages by Periods: 1830 and 1860.

OCCUPATIONS.	Average Daily Wages for the Period ending with 1830.	Average Daily Wages for the Period ending with 1860.	Percentage of Increase or Decrease.
Agricultural laborers,	$0.803	$1.01	+ 25.8
Blacksmiths,	1.12	1.69	+ 50.9
Carpenters,	1.07	2.03	+ 89.7
Clockmakers,	1.29	1.96	+ 51.9
Clothing makers,	1.27	1.43	+ 12.6
Cotton mill operatives,*	.886	1.03	+ 16.3
Glass makers,	1.13	2.96	+161.9
Harness makers,	1.13	1.65	+ 46.0
Laborers,	.796	.975	+ 22.5
Masons,	1.22	1.53	+ 25.4
Metal workers,	1.23	1.35	+ 9.8
Millwrights,	1.21	1.66	+ 37.2
Painters,	1.25	1.85	+ 48.0
Paper mill operatives,	.666	1.17	+ 75.7
Printers,	1.25	1.75	+ 40.0
Ship and boat builders,	1.40	3.65	+160.7
Shoemakers,	1.06	1.70	+ 60.4
Tanners and curriers,	1.13	1.67	+ 47.8
Wooden goods makers,	1.25	1.72	+ 37.6
Woollen mill operatives,*	.946	.873	— 7.7

* As the wages of cotton mill operatives presented for the period ending with 1830 are for females only, the average daily wage for 1836, which includes both sexes, is used in this comparison. Similarly, as the wages of woollen mill operatives for the period ending with 1830 are for overseers principally, the average daily wage for 1837 is used in this table, the latter affording a fairer basis of comparison.

But after all, it is not the rate of money wages that most nearly concerns the workingman but rather what may be termed real wages, that is, the amount of subsistence obtainable at a given period for a given expenditure. Has this increase in money wages been more than counterbalanced by an increase in prices so that, after all, the workingman's real wages have declined? To determine this, having made a comparison of wages in leading occupations in the decades ending respectively with 1830 and 1860, we now present a similar comparison between the prices paid for the leading articles of household consumption during the same periods:

Comparison of Prices by Periods: 1830 and 1860.

ARTICLES.	Basis.	Average Prices for the Period ending with 1830.	Average Prices for the Period ending with 1860.	Percentage of Increase or Decrease.
Agricultural Products.				
Apples,	bu.	$0.439	$0.995	+126.7
Beans,	qt.	.085	.088	+ 3.5
Corn,	bu.	.817	.992	+ 21.4
Potatoes,	bu.	.369	.86	+133.1
Rice,	lb.	.044	.06	+ 36.4
Rye,	bu.	.882	1.50	+ 70.1
Turnips,	bu.	.33	.335	+ 1.5

Comparison of Prices by Periods: 1830 and 1860—Con.

ARTICLES.	Basis.	Average Prices for the Period ending with 1830.	Average Prices for the Period ending with 1860.	Percentage of Increase or Decrease.
Boots and Shoes.				
Boots,	pr.	$4.75	$2.21	— 53.5
Shoes,	pr.	1.26	1.09	— 13.5
Slippers,	pr.	.935	.945	+ 1.1
Clothing.				
Gloves,	pr.	.517	.594	+ 14.9
Handkerchiefs,	ea.	.441	.414	— 6.1
Hose, socks, and stockings,	pr.	.59	.445	— 24.6
Dairy Products.				
Butter,	lb.	.186	.262	+ 40.9
Cheese,	lb.	.089	.117	+ 31.5
Eggs,	doz.	.15	.22	+ 46.7
Milk,	qt.	.044	.052	+ 18.2
Dress Goods.				
Calico,	yd.	.292	.105	— 64.0
Cambric,	yd.	.359	.193	— 46.2
Gingham,	yd.	.317	.192	— 39.4
Lawn,	yd.	.644	.228	— 64.6
Muslin,	yd.	.585	.263	— 55.0
Silk,	yd.	.799	.989	+ 23.8
Dry Goods.				
Cotton cloth,	yd.	.21	.118	— 43.8
Flannel,	yd.	.57	.405	— 28.9
Linen,	yd.	.453	.531	+ 17.2
Sheetings,	yd.	.281	.124	— 55.9
Shirtings,	yd.	.223	.107	— 52.0
Ticking,	yd.	.367	.16	— 56.4
Tow cloth,	yd.	.173	.128	— 26.0
Fish.				
Codfish,	lb.	.031	.053	+ 71.0
Fish,	lb.	.039	.049	+ 25.6
Halibut,	lb.	.048	.105	+118.8
Herring,	doz.	.083	.08	— 3.6
Mackerel,	lb.	.038	.085	+123.7
Salmon,	lb.	.20	.125	— 37.5
Saltfish,	lb.	.061	.052	— 14.8
Flour and Meal.				
Flour,	bbl.	7.08	8.92	+ 26.0
Indian meal,	lb.	.016	.021	+ 31.3
Rye meal,	lb.	.018	.026	+ 44.4
Food Preparations.				
Chocolate,	lb.	.245	.235	— 4.1
Coffee,	lb.	.206	.163	— 20.9
Lard,	lb.	.108	.137	+ 26.9
Molasses,	gal.	.386	.43	+ 11.4
Salt,	qt.	.063	.029	— 54.0
Starch,	lb.	.16	.12	— 25.0
Sugar,	lb.	.146	.093	— 36.3
Tea,	lb.	.825	.529	— 35.9
Fruits.				
Raisins,	lb.	.139	.143	+ 2.9
Fuel.				
Wood,	cd.	3.59	5.58	+ 55.4
Meats.				
Beef,	lb.	.076	.126	+ 65.8
Ham,	lb.	.095	.125	+ 31.6
Lamb,	lb.	.059	.123	+108.5
Mutton,	lb.	.064	.118	+ 84.4
Pork,	lb.	.088	.114	+ 29.5
Sausages,	lb.	.114	.115	+ 0.9
Veal,	lb.	.075	.13	+ 73.3
Oils and Illuminating Fluids.				
Burning oils and fluids,	gal.	.814	1.05	+ 29.0

Comparison of Prices by Periods: 1830 and 1860 — Con.

ARTICLES.	Basis.	Average Prices for the Period ending with 1830.	Average Prices for the Period ending with 1860.	Percentage of Increase or Decrease.
Paper.				
Letter paper, ...	qr.	$0.296	$0.192	— 35.1
Poultry and Game.				
Turkey, ...	lb.	.083	.152	+ 83.1
Spices and Condiments.				
Allspice, ...	lb.	.39	.236	— 39.5
Cassia, ...	lb.	.538	.466	— 13.4
Cloves, ...	lb.	1.07	.403	— 62.3
Ginger, ...	lb.	.145	.133	— 8.3
Mustard, ...	lb.	.432	.351	— 18.8
Nutmegs, ...	oz.	.152	.091	— 40.1
Pepper, ...	lb.	.321	.205	— 36.1
Vinegar, ...	gal.	.189	.169	— 10.6
Tallow, Candles, Soap, etc.				
Candles, ...	lb.	.163	.274	+ 68.1
Soap, ...	lb.	.109	.114	+ 4.6

The foregoing comparison shows that to a certain extent prices have increased, but not uniformly. Certain staple articles, chiefly those produced by the factory system of labor in its completest form, such as boots, shoes, calico, cambric, cotton cloth, shirtings, sheetings, flannels, and dry goods and dress goods generally, show an almost constant decline during the century. A few articles show no material increase. Food preparations, under which term is included, as will be noticed, certain staple groceries, have declined, while flour, fish, and meats have risen in price.

Consolidating and averaging the wages shown in our comparison it appears that, for all the occupations compared, the general average increase in wages shown for the decade ending with 1860 as compared with that ending with 1830 is 52.3 per cent.

From a comparison of the prices given for the same periods, it appears that :

Agricultural products	advanced 62.8 per cent.
Burning oils and fluids	advanced 29.0 per cent.
Candles and soap	advanced 42.6 per cent.
Dairy products	advanced 38.8 per cent.
Fish	advanced 9.8 per cent.
Flour and meal	advanced 26.0 per cent.
Fuel (wood only)	advanced 55.4 per cent.
Meats, etc. (turkey added)	advanced 53.0 per cent.

Boots and shoes	declined 38.9 per cent.
Clothing and dress goods	declined 24.7 per cent.
Dry goods	declined 30.9 per cent.
Food preparations (raisins added)	declined 17.5 per cent.
Letter paper	declined 35.1 per cent.
Spices and condiments	declined 36.5 per cent.

By a consolidation of the percentages showing either an advance or decline in prices for the fourteen classes of articles represented in the comparison, the general average percentage of increase in prices is found to be 9.6 per cent. If, on the other hand, we consider, for the same classes of articles, the averages, and not the percentages, obtained for each class, we find the general average increase in prices to be 15.7 per cent. The mean of these two percentages is 12.7 per cent, which figure is presented as indicating, for the fourteen classes of articles considered, the general average increase in prices shown for the decade ending with 1860 as compared with that ending with 1830. In the absence of budgets showing the expenses of workingmen for the periods under consideration, no results can be arrived at which will accurately indicate the percentage of increased cost of living to the workingman for the decade ending with 1860 as compared with that ending with 1830.

The percentages of advance or decline in prices, however, considered in connection with the material advance in wages from 1830 to 1860, are sufficiently indicative of the improved condition financially of the workingman.

It should be noted that in but three classes of articles, agricultural products, fuel, and meats, etc., has the increase in prices been so great as the increase in wages.

These results indicate better than can any words of ours the change in the pecuniary status of the workingman between 1830 and 1860. In an elaborate review of wages and prices in 1860, 1872, and 1878, contained in the tenth annual report of this Bureau, pages 59 to 95, it was remarked, page 95, that the ascertained relations of wages and prices show "in 1878 an advance over 1860 of twenty-four and four-tenths per cent in average weekly wages, and an average advance in cost of living of fourteen and a half per cent, — which means a pecuniary betterment of ten per cent in the general condition of the workingman in Massachusetts in 1878 as compared with 1860, no

account being made of the decrease in the hours of labor in many industries." And it is sufficient to add here, that subsequent investigations of the Bureau have shown no decline in the condition of the workingman since 1878.

All occupations show their highest wage during the decade ending with 1860 or subsequently. Six classes of workmen, agricultural laborers, clothing makers, gold and silver workers, nail makers, shoe makers, and wooden goods makers, appear to have received their highest wage during the decade ending with 1883. Paper mill operatives report highest wage received for both the decades ending with 1880 and 1883. Glass makers, harness makers, and ship and boat builders show their highest wage during the decade ending with 1860, and all others, except those just noted, during the decade ending with 1880.

If the period in which appears the largest proportion of highest or lowest wage rates to the whole number returned be taken as indicating the highest or lowest wage level for the century, as the case may be, then it appears from the table showing wage and price fluctuations by periods of years, page 190, that the level of highest wages was reached in 1880, eighteen of the twenty-five industries presented in that year returning their highest recorded wage. The level of highest prices seems to be during 1820, twenty-seven out of eighty-three articles having in that year their highest recorded prices. On the other hand, the largest proportion of lowest prices appears in 1860, seventeen out of seventy-nine articles having then their lowest recorded prices.

Thus directly the laborer profits by increased wages for his work, and indirectly by the advanced standard of civilization in the benefits of which he shares equally with his employer and without direct cost to himself. In the free schools, the free library, well-lighted streets, public water supplies, and improved tenements, are seen important ways in which he shares with capital, few of which were open to his predecessors from 1800 to 1830.

It is undoubtedly true that each age brings its own problems, and that the industrial changes of the century, which have amounted to an industrial revolution, have not been effected without individual cases of hardship. The transition from

manual to machine labor has been a serious matter to many workmen who have not been able at once to adapt themselves to the new industrial conditions.

The sharp competition of the present day renders it necessary for employers to watch carefully that important element in production, the cost of labor as represented in wages, and, in considering the question of labor cost, the rate of wages is generally taken as the standard. We venture the suggestion, however, that it is the *sum* of wages and not the *rate* which constitutes the true money standard of cost of labor, and we carry this suggestion to its logical outcome in the following proposition : — In proportion as capital, through machinery, becomes more effective, the relative number of laborers is decreased in proportion to product, the rate of wages is increased, and the sum of wages is reduced ; that is, lower cost is compassed by way of higher wages.

The direct contact of employer with employé, possible and necessary under the old, has, it is true, largely passed away under the new organization of labor. But in any broad view of the labor question it must be admitted that from the purely material standpoint of money reward for a given outlay of time and effort, labor as a whole has gained not only directly in the absolute amount of wages paid but indirectly in the general rise of the standard of living under the new régime.

The wants of man constantly tend to exceed the fulfilment of his desires, and thus there will always be a labor question while human nature remains. The condition of the laborer to-day is not an ideal one, but that so much advance has been made, that it is constantly easier to secure respectful attention to, and, finally, just action upon the claims of labor, is, of itself, an index of progress. In the heat of discussion what has been accomplished is often forgotten. Whatever changes the future may bring in the industrial organization, the tendency is upward toward better social conditions, not downward, as is sometimes assumed. In this upward trend lies labor's hope.

COMPARATIVE WAGES, PRICES, AND COST OF LIVING:

MASSACHUSETTS AND GREAT BRITAIN.

1860-1883.

COMPARATIVE WAGES AND PRICES:

MASSACHUSETTS AND GREAT BRITAIN.

1860-1883.

In the Fifteenth Annual Report of this bureau, published in July, 1884, we devoted more than three hundred pages to a consideration of comparative wages in Massachusetts and Great Britain for 1883, and for the period from 1860 to 1883, and the comparative prices and cost of living in the same countries for the same period.

The direct consideration of these important subjects took but little space, but in order that a complete basis might be given for the conclusions stated, we were obliged to carry the presentation of details to the extent named. Such presentations, and the accompanying consideration, constituted Parts II., III., and IV., of our last annual report.

The great interest on the part of the public in the wages question caused the edition of 1884 to be exhausted in about ten days' time, and we have been unable since to answer calls for the statistics of wages presented. We have, therefore, condensed the three hundred and odd pages of last year's report into one Part of about fifty pages in order that those parties who were unable to secure copies of the first edition may still be able to obtain the valuable facts presented. This condensation preserves every fact stated in the full presentation, but we have left out the long tables of details from which the tables of aggregates, and the summaries have been drawn.

We have preserved all the important text, but have elimi-

nated that essential only to the description of the detail tables. This Part, in condensed form, is particularly appropriate in this volume because we follow it with a history of prices and wages in Massachusetts for over a hundred years.

With this work on wages, a subject which has claimed a good share of the attention of the bureau for several years, we shall drop the presentation of rates of wages, giving, of course, at intervals, when there is permanency in rates, the facts necessary to preserve the history of fluctuations of wages in this Commonwealth. These periodical presentations, with wage statistics drawn from Census returns, will give the State a continuous record of wages paid in all our industries. We shall, however, make reports on the labor cost of production involving the economic value of wages in production, statistics relating to which, at the present time, are exceedingly meagre.

[From Part II., Fifteenth Annual Report, for 1884.]

COMPARATIVE WAGES: 1883.

MASSACHUSETTS AND GREAT BRITAIN.

In various reports of this bureau there will be found statistics of wages both American and European. In the Fifth Annual Report, 1874, we gave quite elaborate data gathered from original sources by Dr. Edward Young, but these statistics were not in such shape as to allow of our ascertaining the exact percentage of difference of wages between this and other countries. In more recent reports, especially for 1879 and 1882, while giving the American side with great fullness, we were unable to present foreign wages with any completeness. So with the wage statements made to the United States government by consuls; while a great many valuable tables have been presented by them, they have not been so specifically arranged that the line could be clearly drawn by which the differences could be ascertained.

An investigation which would bring the rates of wages paid in industries common to this country and European countries into clear comparison has not yet been undertaken, although

the results of such an investigation have been called for constantly and earnestly on all sides by the press and the people.*

The resources of this office have not allowed us to undertake an investigation reaching all the great industries common to the United States and foreign countries, and in fact, had our resources been ample for this purpose, we should not have felt at liberty to undertake so broad an investigation ; but to ascertain the results of such an investigation so far as Massachusetts and her leading competitor abroad, Great Britain, are concerned, we have undertaken to bring into comparison the rates of wages paid in these two communities, and in so far as Massachusetts and Great Britain may be representative States supply the needed information.

To accomplish this result, in the fall of 1883, we started upon an original investigation, through personal agents of the bureau, in Massachusetts and Great Britain, and through these agents we have gathered from original sources (meaning by original sources the pay rolls of great manufacturing establishments, the official wage lists agreed upon in England, so far as England is concerned, between trade societies and employers, and from other reliable sources) the rates of wages paid in the following industries which are common to Massachusetts and Great Britain.

1 Agricultural Implements.	14 Hats : Fur, Wool, and Silk.
2 Artisans' Tools.	15 Hosiery.
3 Boots and Shoes.	16 Liquors : Malt and Distilled.
4 Brick.	17 Machines and Machinery.
5 Building Trades.	18 Metals and Metallic Goods.
6 Carpetings.	19 Printing and Publishing.
7 Carriages and Wagons.	20 Printing,Dyeing,Bleaching,and Finishing, Cotton Textiles.
8 Clothing.	
9 Cotton Goods.	21 Stone.
10 Flax and Jute Goods.	22 Wooden Goods.
11 Food Preparations.	23 Woollen Goods.
12 Furniture.	24 Worsted Goods.
13 Glass.	

It is perfectly easy to collect wage statistics from the counting rooms of factories and manufacturing establishments in

* The Honorable Secretary of State, since the publication of our Report in 1884, has published, in a letter to Congress, an elaborate statement of wages in Europe, constituting an exceedingly valuable compilation of wage statistics.

Massachusetts, but it is quite a different matter when a collection of such information is attempted in Great Britain; very many proprietors will give no information at all regarding their industry, yet we have been peculiarly fortunate in finding a sufficient number to give such information as to make our report quite as trustworthy for Great Britain as for Massachusetts, wherever facts are given for the former country.

The absence of industrial censuses in countries other than the United States is a serious drawback to any scientific comparison on a grand scale.

The industries covered by this special comparison for 1883, and for which statistics were gathered during the last four months of the year just closed (1883), involve 74.9 per cent of the total products of the manufacturing industries of Massachusetts. This statement shows the complete representative character of our statistics.

It should be remembered that since the information has been gathered wages in many industries in Massachusetts have been reduced on an average, as near as we can judge, ten per cent. This reduction would of course, wherever it has been made, affect the percentage of difference shown by the tables.

The statistics presented in these Parts, relating to wages in Massachusetts and Great Britain, have been collected with the greatest care, and have been tabulated and presented in such a manner as to bring out all the relations involved in them, and while it is true that a "comparison of wages is worthless as a gauge of relative cost (of production) unless all the conditions are identical in the establishments compared,"[*] a comparison of rates only is exceedingly valuable, when such rates simply are to be determined, and the relative purchasing power of the earnings in such rates is sought. This latter result is the main one aimed at in the investigation; that is, we have sought simply to determine with mathematical accuracy the percentage of difference in the rates of wages paid in Massachusetts and Great Britain, in industries common to each.

It was, of course, impossible to show the wages for all the employés in any industry in either country. The investigation was intended to cover about ten per cent of those engaged in the various industries considered in Massachusetts as com-

* Edward Atkinson.

pared with the totals shown by the census of 1880. In some instances the wages for more than ten per cent of the workers in an industry were secured, and in other instances less. For Great Britain the proportion obtained can not be shown owing to the absence of official figures giving the numbers employed in the various industries, and also from the fact that many of our Great Britain returns were not for definite numbers of employés.

It will, therefore, be plainly seen and should be clearly understood that these tables relate only to the employés included in our investigation, and that the tables are not claimed to show, in any instance, the whole number employed in any industry considered in either country.

GRAND COMPARISON.

We present first, consolidations showing the highest average weekly wage, the lowest average weekly wage, the average weekly wage, and the general average weekly wage for day, piece, and day and piece hands. Each table is composed of three parts, the first showing the amounts, that is, wages paid; the second, percentages, indicating the higher rate of wage in Massachusetts or Great Britain, and the third, a summary, in which, on the industry basis, the average highest, average lowest, average, and general average weekly wages are shown for men, women, young persons, and children.

The letter " h " preceding a wage figure indicates that the wages having been returned on more than one basis, the highest figure has been made use of. This occurs only once in Massachusetts, in the case of the Hosiery industry.

The double dash ($=$), used in the percentage tables, indicates that there was a wage figure in the amount tables but no corresponding wage figure for the other country, so that a percentage could not be figured.

GRAND COMPARISON. *Highest Average Weekly Wage.* • **AMOUNTS.**

INDUSTRIES.	MASSACHUSETTS.				GREAT BRITAIN.			
	Men.	Wo-men.	Young Persons.	Chil-dren.	Men.	Wo-men.	Young Persons.	Chil-dren.
Agricultural implements,	$18 20	–	$8 80	–	$14 60	–	–	–
Artisans' tools,	18 00	–	6 00	–	11 13	–	$2 98	–
Boots and shoes,	18 75	$12 00	7 00	–	7 31	$3 65	2 92	–
Brick,	22 14	–	–	–	7 30	2 92	2 68	–
Building trades,	21 00	–	–	–	10 83	–	3 65	–
Carpetings,	10 43	6 34	5 05	–	7 84	4 67	2 92	–
Carriages and wagons,	25 00	–	5 60	–	9 31	–	2 44	–
Clothing,	39 17	18 12	5 67	–	12 33	5 45	1 95	–
Cotton goods,	30 00	8 69	7 00	$5 29	12 17	5 68	3 90	$1 10
Flax and jute goods,	21 00	6 79	4 54	3 25	8 76	5 35	2 58	49
Food preparations,	30 00	7 33	7 40	5 00	8 67	2 69	3 16	–
Furniture,	30 00	8 00	8 00	4 00	8 15	–	–	–
Glass,	25 18	5 00	5 41	5 21	13 39	2 92	2 92	–
Hats: fur, wool, and silk,	25 00	10 00	8 25	–	11 92	4 09	2 68	–
Hosiery,	24 00	8 27	7 50	–	7 68	4 20	2 43	–
Liquors: malt and distilled,	25 00	–	–	–	19 46	–	–	–
Machines and machinery,	37 00	5 50	7 00	5 70	13 39	–	3 65	–
Metals and metallic goods,	25 00	8 40	10 27	5 00	15 82	2 80	5 48	–
Printing and publishing,	35 00	10 67	8 33	3 50	18 25	3 39	2 43	–
Printing, dyeing, bleaching, and finishing, cotton textiles,	32 00	6 00	9 24	4 50	14 60	5 25	4 14	97
Stone,	18 60	–	7 50	–	10 16	–	–	–
Wooden goods,	19 83	–	6 00	–	9 00	–	2 11	–
Woollen goods,	21 00	7 57	5 85	6 00	12 77	4 62	2 43	–
Worsted goods,	38 46	8 46	5 34	3 60	7 79	3 89	3 41	1 63

GRAND COMPARISON. *Highest Average Weekly Wage.* **PERCENTAGES.**

Industry				
Agricultural implements,	24 7	–	=	–
Artisans' tools,	61.7	–	101.3	–
Boots and shoes,	156.5	228.8	139.7	–
Brick,	203.3	–	–	=
Building trades,	93.9	–	–	–
Carpetings,	33.0	35.8	72.9	–
Carriages and wagons,	168.5	–	129.5	–
Clothing,	217.7	232.5	190.8	–
Cotton goods,	146.5	53.0	79.5	380.9
Flax and jute goods,	139.6	26.9	76.0	563.3
Food preparations,	243.5	172.5	134.2	=
Furniture,	268.1	=	=	=
Glass,	88.1	71.2	85.3	=
Hats: fur, wool, and silk,	109.7	144.5	207.8	–
Hosiery,	212.5	96.9	208.6	–
Liquors: malt and distilled,	28.5	–	–	–
Machines and machinery,	176.3	=	91.8	–
Metals and metallic goods,	58.0	200.0	87.4	=
Printing and publishing,	91.8	214.7	242.8	=
Printing, dyeing, bleaching, and finishing, cotton textiles,	119.2	14.3	122.7	363.9
Stone,	83.1	–	=	–
Wooden goods,	120.3	–	184.4	–
Woollen goods,	64.4	63.9	140.7	=
Worsted goods,	393.7	117.5	56.6	120.9

SUMMARY. *Average Highest Weekly Wage.*

CLASSIFICATION.	MASSACHUSETTS.			GREAT BRITAIN.		
	Number of Industries.	Average Highest Weekly Wage.	Higher in Mass. Per cent.	Number of Industries.	Average Highest Weekly Wage.	Higher in Great Britain. Per cent.
Men,	24	$25 41	123.66	24	$11 36	–
Women,	16	8 57	108.85	15	4 10	–
Young Persons,	21	6 94	128.06	20	3 04	–
Children,	11	4 64	343.05	4	1 05	–

GRAND COMPARISON.   *Lowest Average Weekly Wage.*   AMOUNTS.

INDUSTRIES.	LOWEST AVERAGE WEEKLY WAGE.							
	MASSACHUSETTS.				GREAT BRITAIN.			
	Men.	Women.	Young Persons.	Children.	Men.	Women.	Young Persons.	Children.
Agricultural implements,	$7 67	–	$6 00	–	$5 35	–	–	–
Artisans' tools,	8 40	–	4 50	–	4 06	–	$1 46	–
Boots and shoes,	8 00	$4 50	2 25	–	6 76	$1 95	1 95	–
Brick,	6 52	–	–	–	4 91	2 31	2 54	–
Building trades,	6 73	–	–	–	4 38	–	1 23	–
Carpetings,	6 30	4 10	3 50	–	4 38	3 04	2 92	–
Carriages and wagons,	9 00	–	5 60	–	3 29	–	97	–
Clothing,	9 00	4 45	2 50	–	4 87	1 83	1 22	–
Cotton goods,	6 00	4 37	3 00	$1 89	3 51	1 70	1 22	$0 49
Flax and jute goods,	6 64	3 60	3 81	2 64	2 31	1 89	1 28	49
Food preparations,	6 00	5 50	4 64	3 30	1 70	2 31	1 22	–
Furniture,	5 00	4 20	5 00	4 00	7 66	–	–	–
Glass,	9 00	4 50	5 41	4 00	6 81	2 92	1 83	–
Hats: fur, wool, and silk,	7 50	7 43	3 82	–	5 36	2 68	2 07	–
Hosiery,	5 70	4 80	4 19	–	4 90	2 99	1 46	–
Liquors: malt and distilled,	10 93	–	–	–	5 42	–	–	–
Machines and machinery,	7 60	5 00	4 50	3 00	3 21	–	1 46	–
Metals and metallic goods,	7 50	4 46	3 71	3 50	4 38	2 31	1 83	–
Printing and publishing,	5 00	5 00	3 00	–	5 68	1 16	1 22	–
Printing, dyeing, bleaching, and finishing, cotton textiles,	6 75	5 07	4 06	3 13	4 28	2 19	1 36	79
Stone,	9 00	–	7 50	–	5 72	–	–	–
Wooden goods,	7 00	–	6 00	–	5 62	–	2 11	–
Woollen goods,	5 82	3 90	3 50	3 30	4 87	2 43	1 94	–
Worsted goods,	3 00	3 00	3 00	2 16	3 87	2 31	1 95	64

GRAND COMPARISON.   *Lowest Average Weekly Wage.*   PERCENTAGES.

INDUSTRIES.								
Agricultural implements,	43.4	–	=	–	–	–	–	–
Artisans' tools,	106.9	–	208.2	–	–	–	–	–
Boots and shoes,	18.3	130.8	15.4	–	–	–	–	–
Brick,	32.8	–	–	–	–	–	–	–
Building trades,	53.7	–	–	–	–	=	=	–
Carpetings,	43.8	34.9	19.9	–	–	–	=	–
Carriages and wagons,	173.6	–	477.3	–	–	–	–	–
Clothing,	84.8	143.2	104.9	–	–	–	–	–
Cotton goods,	70.9	157.1	145.9	285.7	–	–	–	–
Flax and jute goods,	187.4	90.5	197.7	438.8	–	–	–	–
Food preparations,	252.9	138.1	280.3	–	–	–	–	–
Furniture,	–	=	=	=	53.2	–	–	–
Glass,	32.2	54.1	195.6	–	–	–	–	–
Hats: fur, wool, and silk,	39.9	177.2	84.5	–	–	–	–	–
Hosiery,	16.3	60.5	186.9	–	–	–	–	–
Liquors: malt and distilled,	101.7	–	–	–	–	–	–	–
Machines and machinery,	136.8	=	208.2	–	–	–	–	–
Metals and metallic goods,	71.2	93.1	102.7	=	–	–	–	–
Printing and publishing,	–	331.0	145.9	–	13.6	–	–	–
Printing, dyeing, bleaching, and finishing, cotton textiles,	57.7	131.5	198.5	298.7	–	–	–	–
Stone,	57.3	–	–	–	–	–	–	–
Wooden goods,	24.6	–	184.4	–	–	–	–	–
Woollen goods,	19.5	60.5	80.4	–	–	–	–	–
Worsted goods,	–	29.9	105.1	237.5	29 0	–	–	–

SUMMARY.   *Average Lowest Weekly Wage.*

CLASSIFICATION.	MASSACHUSETTS.			GREAT BRITAIN.		
	Number of Industries.	Average Lowest Weekly Wage	Higher in Mass. Per cent.	Number of Industries.	Average Lowest Weekly Wage.	Higher in Great Britain. Per cent.
Men,	24	$7 09	50.10	24	$4 72	–
Women,	16	4 62	103.57	15	2 27	–
Young Persons,	21	4 26	156.38	20	1 66	–
Children,	11	3 09	412.13	4	60	–

GRAND COMPARISON.   *Average Weekly Wage.*   AMOUNTS.

INDUSTRIES.	AVERAGE WEEKLY WAGE.							
	MASSACHUSETTS.				GREAT BRITAIN.			
	Men.	Women.	Young Persons.	Children.	Men.	Women.	Young Persons.	Children.
Agricultural implements,	$10 36	–	$7 09	–	$8 85	–	h$2 65	–
Artisans' tools,	12 02	–	5 00	–	h 7 11	–	h 2 69	–
Boots and shoes,	13 75	$8 66	4 63	–	h 7 30	h$3 63	2 58	–
Brick,	8 63	–	–	–	5 45	2 51	2 58	–
Building trades,	14 99	–	–	–	h 7 81	–	1 91	–
Carpetings,	8 22	5 51	4 02	–	6 11	3 71	2 92	–
Carriages and wagons,	13 88	–	5 60	–	h 8 53	–	h 2 44	–
Clothing,	17 37	7 51	3 86	–	h 7 52	h 4 70	h 3 04	h $0 89
Cotton goods,	9 44	5 90	4 30	$3 38	h 7 52	h 4 59	h 3 04	h $0 89
Flax and jute goods,	8 69	5 03	4 00	2 88	h 6 79	h 2 61	h 1 53	49
Food preparations,	10 95	5 72	5 55	3 43	h 5 49	2 57	1 40	–
Furniture,	11 31	6 10	5 52	4 00	7 96	–	–	–
Glass,	15 03	4 67	5 41	5 08	h 9 56	2 92	h 3 08	–
Hats: fur, wool, and silk,	14 20	7 64	4 68	–	h 8 22	h 3 57	h 2 53	–
Hosiery,	h 9 15	h 5 99	h 5 44	–	6 63	4 07	2 20	–
Liquors: malt and distilled,	12 87	–	–	–	h19 46	–	–	–
Machines and machinery,	12 04	5 12	5 76	5 31	h 8 07	–	h 2 52	–
Metals and metallic goods,	12 38	5 41	4 67	4 32	h10 51	h 2 80	2 45	–
Printing and publishing,	15 58	6 30	4 73	3 25	h 9 08	h 2 93	h 2 31	–
Printing, dyeing, bleaching, and finishing, cotton textiles,	10 05	5 28	4 64	3 31	h 7 96	h 3 28	h 3 14	h 97
Stone,	14 44	–	7 50	–	h10 16	–	–	–
Wooden goods,	12 46	–	6 00	–	6 89	–	2 11	–
Woollen goods,	7 67	6 54	4 93	3 81	h 7 64	h 3 19	2 10	–
Worsted goods,	8 82	6 10	3 80	3 18	h 6 17	h 3 40	h 2 72	81

GRAND COMPARISON.   *Average Weekly Wage.*   PERCENTAGES.

INDUSTRIES.	Men.	Women.	Young Persons.	Children.	Men.	Women.	Young Persons.	Children.
Agricultural implements,	17.1	–	=	–	–	–	–	–
Artisans' tools,	69.1	–	88.7	–	–	–	–	–
Boots and shoes,	88.4	138.6	72.1	–	–	=	–	–
Brick,	58.3	–	–	–	–	–	–	–
Building trades,	91.9	–	–	–	–	–	–	–
Carpetings,	34.5	48.5	37.7	–	–	–	–	–
Carriages and wagons,	62.7	–	129.5	–	–	–	–	–
Clothing,	95.4	59.7	142.8	–	–	–	–	–
Cotton goods,	25.5	28.5	41.4	279.8	–	–	–	–
Flax and jute goods,	28.0	92.7	161.4	487.8	–	–	–	–
Food preparations,	99.5	122.6	296.4	–	–	–	–	–
Furniture,	42.1	=	=	–	–	–	–	–
Glass,	57.2	59.9	75.6	–	–	–	–	–
Hats: fur, wool, and silk,	72.7	114.0	85.0	–	–	–	–	–
Hosiery,	38.0	47.2	147.3	–	51.2	–	–	–
Liquors: malt and distilled,								
Machines and machinery,	49.2	=	128.6	–	–	–	–	–
Metals and metallic goods,	17.8	93.2	90.6	=	–	–	–	–
Printing and publishing,	71.6	115.0	104.8	=	–	–	–	–
Printing, dyeing, bleaching, and finishing, cotton textiles,	26.3	61.0	47.8	241.2	–	–	–	–
Stone,	42.1	–	=	–	–	–	–	–
Wooden goods,	80.8	–	184.4	–	–	–	–	–
Woollen goods,	.4	105.0	134.8	=	–	–	–	–
Worsted goods,	43.1	79.4	39.7	292.6	–	–	–	–

SUMMARY.   *Average Weekly Wage.*

CLASSIFICATION.	MASSACHUSETTS.			GREAT BRITAIN.		
	Number of Industries.	Average Weekly Wage.	Higher in Mass. Per cent.	Number of Industries.	Average Weekly Wage.	Higher in Great Britain. Per cent.
Men,	24	$11 85	43.47	24	$8 26	–
Women,	16	6 09	81.04	15	3 37	–
Young Persons,	21	5 10	112.99	20	2 40	–
Children,	11	3 81	382.66	4	79	–

GRAND COMPARISON. *General Average Weekly Wage: Day and Piece.*
AMOUNTS.

| INDUSTRIES. | GENERAL AVERAGE WEEKLY WAGE PAID TO DAY, PIECE, AND DAY AND PIECE EMPLOYES. | | | | | |
| | MASSACHUSETTS. | | | GREAT BRITAIN. | | |
	Day Hands.	Piece Hands.	Day and Piece Hands.	Day Hands.	Piece Hands.	Day and Piece Hands.
Agricultural implements,	$9 94	$14 27	–	$8 85	–	–
Artisans' tools,	11 88	10 81	–	h 6 94	–	–
Boots and shoes,	14 53	11 42	–	h 4 93	h $5 42	–
Brick,	8 63	–	–	4 16	–	–
Building trades,	14 99	–	–	h 7 81	h 9 49	–
Carpetings,	5 96	6 56	–	4 11	–	–
Carriages and wagons,	12 80	14 90	–	h 8 53	–	–
Clothing,	9 17	10 46	$10 43	h 9 73	5 78	–
Cotton goods,	6 61	6 31	–	h 7 28	h 6 08	h $4 72
Flax and jute goods,	6 48	5 55	–	h 3 27	–	2 78
Food preparations,	10 08	6 65	–	h 3 74	–	–
Furniture,	11 16	11 35	7 69	7 96	–	–
Glass,	12 83	9 62	–	h10 95	–	h 9 92
Hats: fur, wool, and silk,	9 73	11 75	9 00	h 7 30	8 66	5 87
Hosiery,	8 69	h 6 48	–	7 22	–	4 44
Liquors: malt and distilled,	12 86	13 13	–	h 19 46	–	–
Machines and machinery,	11 96	–	9 43	h 7 40	7 16	h 8 62
Metals and metallic goods,	11 55	10 74	11 92	h 10 51	h 6 91	–
Printing and publishing,	11 36	11 40	–	h 9 48	h 10 07	h 7 14
Printing, dyeing, bleaching, and finishing, cotton textiles,	8 68	7 63	–	h 4 83	h 4 97	h 6 32
Stone,	13 54	15 01	–	h 4 83	–	–
Wooden goods,	13 51	8 55	–	h 10 16	–	–
Woollen goods,	6 79	7 01	–	5 67	–	–
Worsted goods,	7 39	7 21	–	h 5 49	–	–
				2 55	–	h 4 27

GRAND COMPARISON. *General Average Weekly Wage: Day and Piece.*
PERCENTAGES.

Agricultural implements,	12.3	=	–	–	–	–
Artisans' tools,	71.2	=	–	–	–	–
Boots and shoes,	194.7	110.7	–	–	–	–
Brick,	107.4	–	–	–	–	–
Building trades,	91.9	–	–	–	–	–
Carpetings,	45.0	=	–	–	=	–
Carriages and wagons,	50.1	=	–	–	–	–
Clothing,	–	81.0	=	6.1	–	–
Cotton goods,	–	3.8	=	10.1	–	=
Flax and jute goods,	98.2	=	–	–	–	=
Food preparations,	169.5	=	–	–	–	–
Furniture,	40.2	=	=	–	–	–
Glass,	17.2	=	–	–	–	=
Hats: fur, wool, and silk,	33.3	35.7	53.3	–	–	=
Hosiery,	20.4	=	–	–	–	=
Liquors: malt and distilled,	–	=	–	51.3	–	–
Machines and machinery,	61.6	–	9.4	–	–	=
Metals and metallic goods,	9.9	55.4	–	–	=	–
Printing and publishing,	19.8	13.2	=	–	–	–
Printing, dyeing, bleaching, and finishing, cotton textiles,	79.7	53.5	–	–	–	=
Stone,	33.3	=	–	–	–	=
Wooden goods,	138.3	=	–	–	–	–
Woollen goods,	23.7	=	–	–	–	–
Worsted goods,	189.8	=	–	–	–	=

SUMMARY. *General Average Weekly Wage: Day and Piece.*

| CLASSIFICATION. | MASSACHUSETTS. | | | GREAT BRITAIN. | | |
	Number of Industries.	General Average Weekly Wage.	Higher in Mass. Per cent.	Number of Industries.	General Average Weekly Wage.	Higher in Great Britain. Per cent.
Day hands,	24	$10 46	40.82	24	$7 43	–
Piece hands,	21	9 85	37.33	9	7 17	–
Day and Piece hands,	5	9 69	61.35	9	6 01	–

We next present a table showing the general average weekly wage paid to all employés.

GRAND COMPARISON. *General Average Weekly Wage paid to All Employés.*
AMOUNTS.

INDUSTRIES.	General Average Weekly Wage paid to All Employés.	
	Massachusetts.	Great Britain.
Agricultural implements, ...	$10 25	$8 85
Artisans' tools, ...	11 80	h 6 94
Boots and shoes, ...	11 63	h 5 08
Brick, ...	8 63	4 16
Building trades, ...	14 99	h 7 83
Carpetings, ...	6 08	4 11
Carriages and wagons, ...	13 80	h 8 53
Clothing, ...	10 01	h 7 30
Cotton goods, ...	6 45	h 5 72
Flax and jute goods, ...	6 46	h 3 17
Food preparations, ...	9 81	h 3 74
Furniture, ...	11 04	7 96
Glass, ...	12 28	h 8 80
Hats: fur, wool, and silk, ...	11 01	h 5 89
Hosiery, ...	h 6 63	4 67
Liquors: malt and distilled, ...	12 87	h 19 46
Machines and machinery, ...	11 75	h 8 07
Metals and metallic goods, ...	11 25	h 8 89
Printing and publishing, ...	11 37	h 6 78
Printing, dyeing, bleaching, and finishing, cotton textiles, . .	8 67	h 5 55
Stone, ...	14 39	h 10 16
Wooden goods, ...	12 19	5 67
Woollen goods, ...	6 90	h 5 49
Worsted goods, ...	7 32	h 4 27

We next show the percentage of employés receiving more than, or the same or less than, the general average weekly wage.

GRAND COMPARISON.   *Wage Percentages.*

| INDUSTRIES. | Percentage of employés receiving more than, or the same or less than, the general average weekly wage. | | | |
| | Massachusetts. | | Great Britain. | |
	More than.	The same or less than.	More than.	The same or less than.
Agricultural implements,	36.5	63.5	37.5	62.5
Artisans' tools,	48.9	51.1	ℏ 62.1	ℏ 37.9
Boots and shoes,	48.1	51.9	ℏ 50.0	ℏ 50.0
Brick,	35.6	64.4	55.3	44.7
Building trades,	60.7	39.3	ℏ 48.9	ℏ 51.1
Carpetings,	39.2	60.8	33.2	66.8
Carriages and wagons,	49.0	51.0	ℏ 57.5	ℏ 42.5
Clothing,	31.6	68.4	ℏ 41.0	ℏ 59.0
Cotton goods,	38.4	61.6	ℏ 46.9	ℏ 53.1
Flax and jute goods,	67.6	32.4	ℏ 42.1	ℏ 57.9
Food preparations,	55.7	44.3	ℏ 47.0	ℏ 53.0
Furniture,	58.6	41.4	50.0	50 0
Glass,	44.9	55.1	ℏ 50.0	ℏ 50.0
Hats : fur, wool, and silk,	42.7	57.3	ℏ 50.2	ℏ 49.8
Hosiery,	ℏ 48.9	ℏ 51.1	32.6	67.4
Liquors : malt and distilled,	48.6	51.4	ℏ 33.3	ℏ 66.7
Machines and machinery,	33.5	66 5	ℏ 48.9	ℏ 51.1
Metals and metallic goods,	50.1	49.9	ℏ 39.4	ℏ 60.6
Printing and publishing,	46.4	53.6	ℏ 69.5	ℏ 30.5
Printing, dyeing, bleaching, and finishing, cotton textiles,	51.5	48.5	ℏ 47.7	ℏ 52.3
Stone,	73.4	26.6	ℏ 55.8	ℏ 44 2
Wooden goods,	42.3	57.7	84.9	15.1
Woollen goods,	47.9	52.1	ℏ 44.4	ℏ 55.6
Worsted goods,	39.0	61.0	ℏ 43.8	ℏ 56.2

The amounts contained in the second table preceding, which shows the general average weekly wage paid to all employés, are reduced to percentages in the following table.

GRAND COMPARISON.   *Massachusetts and Great Britain.*   RESULT.

| INDUSTRIES. | General Average Weekly Wage higher in — | |
| | Massachusetts. | Great Britain. |
	Percentages.	Percentages.
Agricultural implements,	15.8	–
Artisans' tools,	70.0	–
Boots and shoes,	128.9	–
Brick,	107.5	–
Building trades,	91.5	–
Carpetings,	47.9	–
Carriages and wagons,	61.8	–
Clothing,	37.1	–
Cotton goods,	12.8	–
Flax and jute goods,	103.8	–
Food preparations,	162.3	–
Furniture,	38.7	–
Glass,	39.5	–
Hats : fur, wool, and silk,	86.9	–
Hosiery,	42.0	–
Liquors : malt and distilled,	–	51.2
Machines and machinery,	45.6	–
Metals and metallic goods,	26.5	–
Printing and publishing,	67.7	–
Printing, dyeing, bleaching, and finishing, cotton textiles,	56.2	–
Stone,	41.6	–
Wooden goods,	115.0	–
Woollen goods,	25.7	–
Worsted goods,	71.4	–

...ee that in twenty-three industries the general average
...ly wage is higher in Massachusetts than in Great Britain;
...one industry the general average weekly wage is higher in
Great Britain than in Massachusetts.

From the comparison aggregations of the various industries,
we are enabled to prepare a grand consolidation of all the
industries.

ALL INDUSTRIES.   *Grand Comparison.*

CLASSIFICATION.	Massachu-setts.	Great Britain.
Average *highest* weekly wage paid to Men, ...	$25 41	$11 36
Average *highest* weekly wage paid to Women, ...	8 57	4 10
Average *highest* weekly wage paid to Young Persons, . . .	6 94	3 04
Average *highest* weekly wage paid to Children, ...	4 64	1 05
Average *lowest* weekly wage paid to Men, ...	7 09	4 72
Average *lowest* weekly wage paid to Women, ...	4 62	2 27
Average *lowest* weekly wage paid to Young Persons, . . .	4 26	1 66
Average *lowest* weekly wage paid to Children, ...	3 09	60
Average weekly wage paid to Men, ...	11 85	8 26
Average weekly wage paid to Women, ...	6 09	3 37
Average weekly wage paid to Young Persons, ...	5 10	2 40
Average weekly wage paid to Children, ...	3 81	79
General Average weekly wage paid to employés working by the *Day*,	10 46	7 43
General Average weekly wage paid to employés working by the *Piece*,	9 85	7 17
General Average weekly wage paid to employés working by the *Day* and *Piece*, ...	9 69	6 01
General Average weekly wage paid to *All Employés*, ...	10 32	6 96
Percentage of employés receiving *more than* the general average weekly wage, ...	47.5%	48.8%
Percentage of employés receiving *the same* or *less than* the general average weekly wage, ...	52.5%	51.2%
RESULT. — *General Average* weekly wage higher in Massachusetts, by	**48.28%**	–

The table is so explicit it is unnecessary to repeat in text
what the figures so plainly show. *The grand result is that, in
the twenty-four industries considered, the general average weekly
wage is higher in Massachusetts by 48.28 per cent.*

The wage returns from Great Britain were made to us in
three different ways; first, for a definite number of employés,
second, by percentage returns; and third, by general returns,
both the latter being for an indefinite number of employés.
Where more than one basis was used we have heretofore invariably used the highest figure for Great Britain and indicated
it by prefixing the letter " *h.*" The influence that the use of
this highest figure has had upon the grand result may be seen
in the following table.

Great Britain — " High."

INDUSTRIES.	"Number" Average.	"Percentage" Average.	"General" Average.	Great Britain — "High."	
				Classification used.	Amount.
Agricultural implements, . .	–	$8 85	–	Percentage	$8 85
Artisans' tools, ...	$6 94	6 28	$1 46	Number	6 94
Boots and shoes, . . .	–	5 08	3 66	Percentage	5 08
Brick, ...	4 16	–	–	Number	4 16
Building trades, ...	6 24	7 83	7 56	Percentage	7 83
Carpetings, ...	–	4 11	–	Percentage	4 11
Carriages and wagons, . .	3 70	8 53	2 44	Percentage	8 53
Clothing, ...	7 00	5 83	7 30	General	7 30
Cotton goods, ...	3 26	5 72	4 99	Percentage	5 72
Flax and jute goods, . . .	2 51	–	3 17	General	3 17
Food preparations, . . .	3 74	–	1 70	Number	3 74
Furniture, ...	–	–	7 96	General	7 96
Glass, ...	–	8 80	5 07	Percentage	8 80
Hats: fur, wool, and silk, .	5 89	5 12	–	Number	5 89
Hosiery, ...	4 67	–	–	Number	4 67
Liquors: malt and distilled, .	–	5 86	19 46	General	19 46
Machines and machinery, . .	6 26	8 07	6 47	Percentage	8 07
Metals and metallic goods, .	5 71	8 89	7 61	Percentage	8 89
Printing and publishing, . .	3 55	6 78	6 22	Percentage	6 78
Printing, dyeing, bleaching, and finishing, cotton textiles, .	4 44	5 55	4 83	Percentage	5 55
Stone, ...	5 72	10 16	9 85	Percentage	10 16
Wooden goods, ...	5 67	–	–	Number	5 67
Woollen goods, ...	–	4 23	5 49	General	5 49
Worsted goods, ...	2 55	4 27	3 98	Percentage	4 27

This "high" figure has been used in eighteen industries, and in some instances it will be seen it was much higher than the result obtained from the other kinds of returns.

In order to show more fully the influence exerted. by the use of this highest wage, we have prepared other tables in which for Great Britain, instead of the *high* wage, we have used the *average* of the two or more bases upon which returns were made. One table shows the average weekly wage paid to men, women, young persons, and children, and the general average weekly wage paid to day hands, piece hands, and day and piece hands respectively. The second table is in two parts, one showing the general average weekly wage paid to all employés, and the other showing the resulting percentages.

Great Britain — "*Average.*"

INDUSTRIES.	AVERAGE WEEKLY WAGE.				GENERAL AVERAGE WEEKLY WAGE.		
	Men.	Women.	Young Persons.	Children.	Day Hands	Piece Hands.	Day and Piece Hands.
Agricultural implements, . .	$8 85	–	–	–	$8 85	–	–
Artisans' tools, ...	6 70	–	$2 06	–	4 89	–	–
Boots and shoes, ...	7 22	$2 79	2 32	–	4 42	$4 17	–
Brick, ...	5 45	2 51	2 58	–	4 16	–	–
Building trades, ...	7 29	–	1 91	–	7 18	8 65	–
Carpetings, ...	6 11	3 71	2 92	–	4 11	–	–
Carriages and wagons, . . .	7 00	–	1 85	–	4 89	–	–
Clothing, ...	7 85	4 10	1 59	–	8 01	5 78	–
Cotton goods, ...	7 45	3 80	2 59	$0 86	5 46	3 99	$3 71
Flax and jute goods, . . .	5 94	2 60	1 30	49	2 89	–	2 78
Food preparations, . . .	3 60	2 57	1 40	–	2 72	–	–
Furniture, ...	7 96	–	–	–	7 96	–	–
Glass, ...	9 35	2 92	2 88	–	7 91	–	6 91
Hats: fur, wool, and silk, . .	7 76	3 55	2 50	–	6 08	8 66	5 87
Hosiery, ...	6 63	4 07	2 20	–	7 22	–	4 44
Liquors : malt and distilled, .	12 66	–	–	–	12 66	–	–
Machines and machinery, . .	7 48	–	2 26	–	6 76	7 16	7 34
Metals and metallic goods, . .	8 28	2 58	2 45	–	8 92	6 20	–
Printing and publishing, . .	8 33	2 40	1 87	–	6 14	6 94	5 15
Printing, dyeing, bleaching, and finishing, cotton textiles, .	6 37	3 12	2 76	88	4 35	4 72	5 45
Stone, ...	8 58	–	–	–	8 58	–	–
Wooden goods, ...	6 89	–	2 11	–	5 67	–	–
Woollen goods, ...	6 65	2 99	2 10	–	4 86	–	–
Worsted goods, ...	5 89	3 10	2 45	81	2 55	–	4 13

GRAND COMPARISON. *General Average Weekly Wage paid to All Employés.* AMOUNTS.

INDUSTRIES.	General Average Weekly Wage paid to All Employés.	
	Massachusetts.	Great Britain.*
Agricultural implements, ...	$10 25	$8 85
Artisans' tools, ...	11 80	4 89
Boots and shoes, ...	11 63	4 37
Brick, ...	8 63	4 16
Building trades, ...	14 99	7 21
Carpetings, ...	6 08	4 11
Carriages and wagons, ...	13 80	4 89
Clothing, ...	10 01	6 71
Cotton goods, ...	6 45	4 66
Flax and jute goods, ...	6 46	2 84
Food preparations, ...	9 81	2 72
Furniture, ...	11 04	7 96
Glass, ...	12 28	6 94
Hats : fur, wool, and silk, ...	11 01	5 51
Hosiery, ...	6 49	4 67
Liquors : malt and distilled, ...	12 87	12 66
Machines and machinery, ...	11 75	6 93
Metals and metallic goods, ...	11 25	7 40
Printing and publishing, ...	11 37	5 52
Printing, dyeing, bleaching, and finishing, cotton textiles, . .	8 67	4 94
Stone, ...	14 39	8 58
Wooden goods, ...	12 19	5 67
Woollen goods, ...	6 90	4 86
Worsted goods, ...	7 32	3 60
All industries, ...	$10 31	$5 86

* "Average" instead of "High" wage rates for Great Britain.

INDUSTRIES.	General Average Weekly Wage higher in —	
	Massachusetts.	Great Britain.
	Percentages.*	Percentages.
Agricultural implements, ...	15.8	–
Artisans' tools, ...	141.3	–
Boots and shoes, ...	166.1	–
Brick, ...	107.5	–
Building trades, ...	107.9	–
Carpetings, ...	47.9	–
Carriages and wagons, ...	182.2	–
Clothing, ...	49.1	–
Cotton goods, ...	38.4	–
Flax and jute goods, ...	127.5	–
Food preparations, ...	260.7	–
Furniture, ...	38.7	–
Glass, ...	76.9	–
Hats : fur, wool, and silk, ...	99.8	–
Hosiery, ...	39.0	–
Liquors : malt and distilled, ...	1 7	–
Machines and machinery, ...	69.6	–
Metals and metallic goods, ...	52.0	–
Printing and publishing, ...	106.0	–
Printing, dyeing, bleaching, and finishing, cotton textiles, .	75.5	–
Stone, ...	67.7	–
Wooden goods, ...	115.0	–
Woollen goods, ...	42.0	–
Worsted goods, ...	103.3	–
All industries, ...	75.94	

* "Average" instead of "High" wage rates used for Great Britain in determining percentages.

It will be noticed that by thus crediting Great Britain with the *average* instead of the *high* weekly wage, the point is brought out that, in each of the twenty-four industries, the general average weekly wage is higher in Massachusetts than in Great Britain.

We find that the average percentage in favor of Massachusetts, in the 24 industries considered, consolidated by the use of the " average" as explained, is 75.94.

To indicate the true percentage which will show, for all industries, the higher rate of average weekly wages in Massachusetts requires that we should settle upon a figure between the two extremes already given, namely : 48.28 per cent derived from those tables in which Great Britain is credited with the *high* wage, and 75.94 per cent drawn from those tables in which Great Britain is credited only with the *average* of the returns made upon the different bases.

The mean of these two figures is *62.11* per cent, and we consider this figure to be *the result of the investigation*, which we formulate as follows : —

The general average weekly wage paid to employés in 24 manufacturing and mechanical industries in Massachusetts is 62 + per cent higher than the general average weekly wage paid in the same industries in Great Britain.

Of the 210 establishments in Massachusetts making returns, 92 supplied us with weekly pay rolls showing the number of persons employed during the week in question, and the whole amount of the pay roll for that week, from which we could easily arrive at an average weekly wage for each emlpoyé. Of the 110 establishments in Great Britain but 11 supplied us with such pay rolls.

In the 92 establishments in Massachusetts, comprehending 16 of the 24 industries considered, 9,648 employés received an average weekly wage of $10.82.

In the 11 establishments in Great Britain, representing 9 of the 24 industries considered, 7,115 employés received an average weekly wage of $5.48. *This shows that, comparing these establishments, the average weekly wage in Massachusetts was higher by 97.39 per cent.*

We present this figure as another strong indication that the mean figure we have adopted, namely, 62 + per cent, is fully sustained by the wage statistics in our possession. All computations have been refigured, and it is impossible for an error of sufficient importance to have occurred to materially affect the result.

The average number of working days in the year in Massachusetts, in the 23 industries considered, is 309.29, while in Great Britain, in 14 industries, it is 305.29, or 4 days less in the year in Great Britain than in Massachusetts. As the employés are only paid for the time when actually employed, this would indicate a slight advantage gained in Massachusetts by virtue of this small excess in working days in the year.

In Massachusetts the average number of working hours in the week is 60.17, while in Great Britain it is 53.50, being 6.67 hours less in the week in Great Britain than in Massachusetts; that is, the weekly working time in Massachusetts is 12 + per cent longer than in Great Britain.

This percentage is based upon returns from 159 out of 210 establishments in Massachusetts and 61 establishments out of

110 in Great Britain. We present a table showing by industries the number of establishments reporting weekly working hours, and the average number of weekly working hours in the various industries in the two countries.

Average Weekly Working Hours.

INDUSTRIES.	MASSACHUSETTS.		GREAT BRITAIN.	
	Number of Establishments.	Average Weekly Working Hours.	Number of Establishments.	Average Weekly Working Hours.
Agricultural implements, ...	4	60	1	54
Artisans' tools, ...	3	60	1	54
Boots and shoes, ...	11	59.45	1	52.50
Brick, ...	3	64	–	–
Building trades, ...	8	60	13	51.50
Carpetings, ...	–	–	–	–
Carriages and wagons, ...	11	60	3	54
Clothing, ...	8	58.38	4	53.63
Cotton goods, ...	8	60	4	56
Flax and jute goods, ...	2	60	2	54
Food preparations, ...	5	60	2	55.75
Furniture, ...	10	59.50	1	52.50
Glass, ...	1	60	–	–
Hats : fur, wool, and silk, ...	2	60	1	54
Hosiery, ...	4	60	2	54.25
Liquors : malt and distilled, ...	9	69.33	–	–
Machines and machinery, ...	12	59.58	7	52 29
Metals and metallic goods, ...	25	59.48	6	53.75
Printing and publishing, ...	12	58.13	5	53.65
Printing, dyeing, bleaching, and finishing, cotton textiles, ...	3	60	3	54
Stone, ...	10	59.70	–	–
Wooden goods, ...	4	60	–	–
Woollen goods, ...	3	60	2	56
Worsted goods, ...	1	60	3	56
Totals, ...	159	60.17	61	53.50

This table supplies to a certain extent information of value in considering the cause of higher wages in Massachusetts as compared with Great Britain.

The fairest way to institute a comparison is to bring the wages paid to the basis of the *hour*, which we do, so far as our statistics will enable us, in the following table.

Average Wages by the Hour.

INDUSTRIES.	MASSACHUSETTS.				GREAT BRITAIN.				General Average Weekly Wage higher in Massachusetts. Per cent.
	Average Weekly Working Hours.	Average Weekly Wage paid to all employés.	Average Wages per Hour.	Wages by the hour higher in Mass. Per cent.	Average Weekly Working Hours.	Average Weekly Wage paid to all employes.	Average Wages per Hour.	Wages by the hour higher in Great Britain. Per cent.	
			Cents.				Cents.		
Agricultural implements, . . .	60	$10 25	17.08	4.2	54	$8 85	16.39	–	15.8
Artisans' tools, . .	60	11 80	19.67	117.1	54	4 89	9.06	–	141.3
Boots and shoes, . .	59.45	11 63	19.56	135.1	52.50	4 37	8.32	–	166.1
Brick, ...	64	8 63	13.48	–	–	4 16	–	–	107.5
Building trades, . .	60	14 99	24.98	78.4	51.50	7 21	14.00	–	107.9
Carpetings, . . .	–	6 08	–	–	–	4 11	–	–	47.9
Carriages and wagons,	60	13 80	23.00	153.9	54	4 89	9.06	–	182.2
Clothing, . . .	58.38	10 01	17.15	37.1	53.63	6 71	12.51	–	49.1
Cotton goods, . .	60	6 45	10.75	29.2	56	4 66	8.32	–	38.4
Flax and jute goods, .	60	6 46	10.77	104.8	54	2 84	5.26	–	127.5
Food preparations, .	60	9 81	16.35	217.5	55.75	2 72	4.88	–	260.7
Furniture, . . .	59.50	11 04	18.55	22.4	52.50	7 96	15.16	–	38.7
Glass, ...	60	12 28	20.47	–	–	6 94	–	–	76.9
Hats: fur, wool, and silk, ...	60	11 01	18.35	79.9	54	5 51	10.20	–	99.8
Hosiery, . . .	60	6 49	10.82	25.7	54.25	4 67	8.61	–	39.0
Liquors: malt and distilled, ...	69.33	12 87	18.56	–	–	12 66	–	–	1.7
Machines and machinery, . . .	59.58	11 75	19.72	48.8	52.29	6 93	13.25	–	69.6
Metals and metallic goods, . . .	59.48	11 25	18.91	37.3	53.75	7 40	13.77	–	52.0
Printing and publishing, ...	58.13	11 37	19.56	90.1	53.65	5 52	10.29	–	106.0
Printing, dyeing, bleaching, and finishing, cotton textiles, .	60	8 67	14.45	57.9	54	4 94	9.15	–	75.5
Stone, ...	59.70	14 39	24.10	–	–	8 58	–	–	67.7
Wooden goods, . .	60	12 19	20.32	–	–	5 67	–	–	115.0
Woollen goods, . .	60	6 90	11.50	32.5	56	4 86	8.68	–	42.0
Worsted goods, . .	60	7 32	12.20	89.7	56	3 60	6.43	–	103.3

In this table Great Britain is credited with the *average* and not the *high* wage. Taking the average for all the industries supplying rates, *we find that wages by the hour in Massachusetts exceed those in Great Britain by 70.88 per cent, and the excess is shown to exist in every industry considered.* This percentage still further sustains the result drawn from the average weekly wage returns. The industry percentages, drawn from the average weekly wage result in which Great Britain is credited with the " average," are given in the right hand column for purposes of ready comparison.

In order to show the higher average weekly wage in Massachusetts as regards related industries, we present a table showing such consolidated percentages for textiles, clothing, building trades, metallic work of all kinds, wood work, etc. In this table Great Britain is credited with the *average* and not the *high* wage.

Related Industries.

INDUSTRIES.	General Average Weekly Wage paid to All Employés in—		Higher in Massachusetts Per cent.
	Massachusetts.	Great Britain.	
Textiles.			
Carpetings, ...	$6 08	$4 11	47.9
Cotton goods, ...	6 45	4 66	38.4
Flax and jute goods, ...	6 46	2 84	127.5
Hosiery, ...	6 49	4 67	39.0
Printing, dyeing, bleaching, and finishing, cotton textiles, ...	8 67	4 94	75.5
Woollen goods, ...	6 90	4 86	42.0
Worsted goods, ...	7 32	3 60	103.3
Clothing.			
Boots and shoes, ...	11 63	4 37	166.1
Clothing, ...	10 01	6 71	49.1
Hats: fur, wool, and silk, ...	11 01	5 51	99.8
Building.			
Brick, ...	8 63	4 16	107.5
Building trades, ...	14 99	7 21	107.9
Stone, ...	14 39	8 58	67.7
Metallic Work.			
Agricultural implements, ...	10 25	8 85	15.8
Artisans' tools, ...	11 80	4 89	141.3
Machines and machinery, ...	11 75	6 93	69.6
Metals and metallic goods, ...	11 25	7 40	52.0
Wood Work.			
Carriages and wagons, ...	13 80	4 89	182.2
Furniture, ...	11 04	7 96	38.7
Wooden goods, ...	12 19	5 67	115.0
Other Industries.			
Food preparations, ...	9 81	2 72	260.7
Glass, ...	12 28	6 94	76.9
Liquors: malt and distilled, ...	12 87	12 66	1.7
Printing and publishing, ...	11 37	5 52	106.0

Recapitulation.

	Massachusetts.	Great Britain.	Higher Per cent.
Textiles, ...	$6 91	$4 24	62.9
Clothing, ...	10 88	5 53	96.7
Building, ...	12 67	6 65	90.5
Metallic work, ...	11 26	7 02	60.4
Wood work, ...	12 34	6 17	100.0
Other industries, ...	11 59	6 96	66.5
All industries, ...	$10 31	$5 86	75.94

From the grand comparison table, including all industries, by comparing the general average weekly wages paid to men, women, young persons, and children, we are enabled to arrive at the ratio of wages paid to women, young persons, and children to those paid to men. Taking the average wages paid to men as 100, in Massachusetts the ratio of those paid to women is as 51.39 to 100 (that is, the average wages of women are a little more than one-half as much as those paid to men), those paid to young persons 43.04 to 100, and those paid to children 32.15 to 100. In Great Britain the ratio for women

is 40.92 (men's wages considered as the unit, or 100), for young persons 29.06 to 100, and for children 9.56 to 100. In Massachusetts, on the average, one woman, one young person, and one child working together would earn as much combined as 1.26 men; in Great Britain they could earn only .79 as much as a man, or 59.4 per cent in favor of the women, young persons, and children of Massachusetts.

These results will be of value in comparing wage returns in future, and will also enable one to form an intelligent estimate of the wages paid to women, young persons, and children, when only those for men are actually known.

If we bring forward the percentages resulting from the comparisons made upon the bases previously explained we secure the following

GRAND RESULT.

1.   If Massachusetts is credited with the *average* wages paid, and Great Britain is credited with the *high* wages paid, — the Massachusetts wages are higher in 23 out of the 24 industries considered, the percentage in favor of Massachusetts, in all the industries, being 48.28.

2.   If both Massachusetts and Great Britain are credited with the *average* wages paid, — the wages in Massachusetts are higher in each of the 24 industries considered, the percentage in favor of Massachusetts, in all industries, being 75.94.

3.   On an industry basis, the average percentage in favor of Massachusetts, in 23 industries, is 65.05.

4.   Taking the wages paid per hour as the basis, — the average in Massachusetts is higher in each of the 24 industries, the percentage in favor of Massachusetts, in all the industries, being 70.88.

5.   On the basis of establishment pay rolls, — the percentage in favor of Massachusetts is 97.39.

The percentage that will truly and fairly indicate the higher rate of wages paid in Massachusetts in the industries considered, as compared with the wages paid in the same industries in Great Britain, must be found somewhere between the extremes as here given, namely: 48.28 per cent, and 97.39 per cent. The results shown in sections 4 and 5 are not based upon as complete data as those shown in sections 1, 2, and 3, and neither percentage can be fairly used in determining the grand

result. The mean of 48.28 per cent and 75.94 per cent, as we have previously shown, is 62.11 per cent, and this approximates so closely to the general average 65.05 as shown in section 3, that we state, as the grand result of the comparative weekly wages investigation in Massachusetts and Great Britain for the year 1883,

That the general average weekly wage of the employés in 24 industries in Massachusetts is **62 +** *per cent higher than the general average weekly wage of the employés in the same industries in Great Britain.*

[From Part III., Fifteenth Annual Report, for 1884.]

COMPARATIVE WAGES: 1860—1883.

MASSACHUSETTS AND GREAT BRITAIN.

The design of the present Part is to bring forward into a compact form for direct comparison all the statistics of wages, for Massachusetts and Great Britain, that have been previously presented in the Reports of the Bureau, including the returns for 1883 given in Part II. of this report, together with such additional statistics of wages in Great Britain, in past years, as we have been able to secure.

We are able to present wage statistics for the years 1860, 1872, 1874, 1875, 1878, 1880, 1881, and 1883 for Massachusetts, and for the years 1872, 1877, 1880, and 1883 for Great Britain. These statistics are drawn from various sources, — census or official reports and from personal investigations by the Bureau agents, and others. The following statements for Massachusetts and Great Britain will show the sources from which the wage statistics used have been derived.

Massachusetts Wage Statistics.

1860.   Massachusetts wage statistics for 1860 were first presented in the Report for 1879, Part III.   They were obtained by our agents in 34 cities and towns and represented 63,515 employés.

1872.   Wage statistics for 1872 were first presented in Part IV. of the Report for 1874.   They were obtained by the Bureau agents.   The number of employés represented was 271,970, or about three-quarters of all at that time employed in agricul-

tural, mechanical, manufacturing, and mining occupations in the
State.

1874. The Report for 1875, Part IV., supplies the wages
for 1874 for 397 men, all heads of families. These 397 families
contained 2,041 persons, of whom 734 were at work.

1875. The wage statistics for 1875 are drawn from the State
Census returns for that year. The wages for 71,339 employés,
engaged in 950 different occupations, were given in Part I., of
the Report for 1876. In Vol. II., "Manufactures and Occupations," Census of Massachusetts for 1875, the wages for
266,339 employés were given out of a grand total of 297,042
persons employed. The Report statistics were supplied by employés, and those in the Census volume by employers.

1878. The statistics for 1878 appear in the Report for 1879
in direct comparison with those for 1860, being obtained by the
Bureau agents for 63,515 employés.

1880. The Report for 1883, Parts II. and III., contains the
wage statistics for 1880, they being drawn from the United
States Census of 1880, and representing 207,793 employés.

1881. Wage statistics for 1881 were given in Part IV. of
the Report for 1882 for an indefinite number of employés in
21 industries. They were brought into direct comparison with
those for 1860, 1872, and 1878.

1883. The statistics given for 35,902 employés in Part II.
of the present Report are brought forward.

Great Britain Wage Statistics.

1872. Statistics of wages paid in Great Britain in 1872
were first given in Part IV. of the Report for 1874 where they
were brought into direct comparison with Massachusetts statistics for the same year. It is impossible to state how many employés they represent.

1877. Wages in Great Britain in 1877 were obtained from
"Miscellaneous Statistics of the United Kingdom," presented
to both Houses of Parliament in 1879. They were compiled
from returns made to the statistical department of the Board of
Trade by the Council and Secretaries of the several Chambers
of Commerce, etc., and covered 28 of the principal industries.
No mention is made of the number of employés represented in
the returns.

1880. As in the year 1877, from "Miscellaneous Statistics" presented to Parliament in 1883. The returns are similar to those for 1877, from the same official sources, and represent an indefinite number of employés in 39 industries.

1883. The statistics for 17,430 employés, as given in Part II. of the present Report, are brought forward. We are unable to state how many employés are represented by the percentage and general returns.

From a careful examination of these sources and estimates based upon our original returns we obtain the following result:

In the ninety industries, in Massachusetts and Great Britain, supplying statistics of average weekly wages for the period between the years 1860 and 1883 the wages of at least one and a quarter millions (1,250,000) of employés are represented.

GRAND COMPARISON.

Our first analysis table brings forward from the comparison table under each industry head the general average weekly wage paid to all employés in each country in the years specified.

GRAND COMPARISON.   *General Average Weekly Wage.*

	INDUSTRIES.	1860.		1872.		1874.	
		Mass.	G. B.	Mass.	G. B.	Mass.	G. B.
	Domestic and Personal Office.						
1	Domestic service, ...	–	–	–	–	–	–
	Trade and Transportation.						
2	Carriers on roads, . . .	–	–	–	–	$12 44	–
	Agriculture.						
3	Agriculture, ...	$4 28	–	$5 33	$2 26	–	–
	Fisheries.						
4	Fisheries, ...	–	–	–	–	11 67	–
	Mines.						
5	Mining, ...	–	–	–	–	–	–
	Manufactures and Mechanical Industries.						
6	Agricultural implements, . .	–	–	–	–	–	–
7	Arms and ammunition, . .	14 15	–	–	–	–	–
8	Artificial teeth and dental work,	–	–	–	–	–	–
9	Artisans' tools, ...	8 45	–	–	–	–	–
10	Awnings and tents, . . .	–	–	–	–	–	–
11	Bags and bagging, . . .	–	–	–	–	–	–
12	Bookbinderies, ...	–	–	–	–	–	–
13	Boots and shoes, ...	11 42	–	14 73	5 65	10 75	–
14	Boxes, ...	6 80	–	8 74	4 72	–	–
15	Brick, ...	5 01	–	11 25	5 86	–	–
16	Brooms and brushes, . . .	10 58	–	11 67	5 30	–	–
17	Building trades, ...	9 87	–	15 64	6 64	13 59	–
18	Burial cases, caskets, coffins, etc.,	–	–	–	–	–	–
19	Buttons and dress trimmings, .	–	–	–	–	–	–
20	Carpetings, ...	6 62	–	12 76	3 92	–	–
21	Carriages and wagons, . .	10 74	–	17 11	6 55	14 42	–
22	Cement, kaolin, lime, and plaster,	–	–	–	–	–	–
23	Charcoal, ...	–	–	–	–	–	–
24	Chemical preparations, . .	–	–	–	–	–	–
25	Clocks and watches, . . .	–	–	13 78	7 44	14 02	–
26	Clothing, ...	8 26	–	12 37	5 79	13 90	–
27	Concrete walks, paving, etc., .	–	–	–	–	–	–
28	Cooking, lighting, and heating apparatus, ...	–	–	–	–	–	–

MASSACHUSETTS AND GREAT BRITAIN—1860–1883.

1875.		1877.		1878.		1880.		1881.		1883.		
Mass.	G. B.	Mass.	G. B.	Mass.	G. B.	Mass.	G. B.	Mass.	G. B.	Mass.	G. B.	
$3 03	–			–	–	–	–			–	–	1
–				–	–	–	–			–	–	2
7 84	–	–	–	$5 57	–		–	$6 19	–	–	–	3
–				–	–	–	–			–	–	4
–	–	–	$4 71	–	–	–	$5 38	–		–	–	5
14 80	–	–	–		–	$7 75	–		–	$10 25	$8 85	6
14 03	–	–	–	16 95	–	9 55	6 86	–	–	11 04	–	7
15 75	–	–	–		–	11 87	–		–	–	–	8
13 73	–	–	–	11 67	–	8 57	–		–	11 80	4 89	9
16 11	–	–	–		–	7 83	–		–	–	–	10
5 16	–	–	–		–	–	–		–	–	–	11
10 66	–	–	–		–	–	–		–	–	–	12
11 75	–	–	4 68	12 02	–	9 60	3 78	11 54	–	11 63	4 37	13
11 00	–	–	–	7 55	–	8 04	–		–	–	–	14
10 26	–	–	–	5 43	–	7 77	–		–	8 63	4 16	15
9 44	–	–	–	11 90	–	6 08	–		–	–	–	16
15 41	–	–	5 56	12 63	–	10 54	5 73	13 29	–	14 99	7 21	17
14 19	–	–	–	–	–	12 60	–		–	–	–	18
7 71	–	–	–		–	6 33	–		–	–	–	19
6 70	–	–	–	8 20	–	5 87	4 51	7 00	–	6 08	4 11	20
13 88	–	–	7 14	14 03	–	10 23	7 33	13 27	–	13 80	4 89	21
10 43	–	–	–		–	7 01	–		–	–	–	22
9 74	–	–	–		–	9 28	–		–	–	–	23
–	–	–	–		–	8 78	–		–	–	–	24
14 38	–	–	–		–	11 46	–		–	11 28	–	25
10 03	–	–	3 75	9 48	–	8 31	4 09	12 16	–	10 19	6 22	26
13 95	–	–	–		–	9 44	–		–	–	–	27
–	–	–	–		–	10 22	–		–	–	–	28

GRAND COMPARISON.   *General Average Weekly Wage.*

	INDUSTRIES.	1860.		1872.		1874.	
		Mass.	G. B.	Mass.	G. B.	Mass.	G. B.
29	Cordage and twine, ...	–	–	–	–		
30	Corks, ...	–	–	–	–		
31	Cotton goods, ...	$6 50	–	$8 14	$5 36	–	–
32	Cotton and woollen textiles, .	–	–	–	–		
33	Crayons, pencils, crucibles, etc.,		–	–	–		
34	Drugs and medicines, . . .	–	–	–	–		
35	Dyeing and finishing textiles, .			–	–		
36	Dyestuffs, ...	–	–	–	–	–	–
37	Earthen and stone ware, . .	–	–	–	–		
38	Electroplating, ...	–	–	–	–		
39	Emery and sand paper, cloth, etc., .		–	–	–		
40	Fancy articles, ...	–	–		–		
41	Fertilizers, ...	–	–	–	–		
42	Fireworks and matches, . .	–	–	–	–		
43	Flax, linen, hemp, and jute goods, .	4 63	–	7 69	3 27	–	–
44	Food preparations, . . .	8 81	–	9 68	4 58	–	–
45	Furniture, ...	11 77	–	13 24	7 97	$16 42	–
46	Gas works, ...	–	–	–	–		
47	Glass, ...	–	–	11 39	6 95		
48	Glue, isinglass, and starch, .	–	–	–	–		
49	Hair work, ...	–	–	–	–		
50	Hose : rubber, linen, etc., .	–	–	–	–		
51	Hosiery, ...	–	–	–	–		
52	Ink, mucilage, and paste, . .	–	–	–	–		
53	Ivory, bone, and horn goods, .	–	–	–	–		
54	Jewelry burnishing and lapidary work, ...	–	–	–	–	–	–
55	Leather, ...	10 01	–	11 65	6 38	11 02	–
56	Liquors and beverages, . .	–	–	–	–		
57	Liquors : malt and distilled, .	10 73	–	13 83	5 97	–	–
58	Lumber, ...	–	–	–	–		
59	Machines and machinery, . .	7 90	–	13 51	6 77	13 35	–
60	Metals and metallic goods, .	9 07	–	15 52	6 84	12 64	–
61	Mixed textiles, ...	–	–	–	–	9 57	–
62	Models and patterns, . . .	–	–	–	–	–	–
63	Musical instruments and materials, .	10 94	–	–	–	–	–
64	Oils and illuminating fluids, .	–	–	–	–	–	–
65	Paints, colors, and chemicals, .	8 95	–	13 29	5 98	–	–

MASSACHUSETTS AND GREAT BRITAIN — 1860–1883 — *Con.*

1875.		1877.		1878.		1880.		1881.		1883.		
Mass.	G. B.	Mass.	G. B.	Mass.	G. B.	Mass.	G. B.	Mass.	G. B.	Mass.	G. B.	
$9 17	–	–	–	–	–	$6 39	–	–	–	–	–	29
8 85	–	–	–	–	–	6 14	–	–	–	–	–	30
7 01	–	–	$4 87	$7 78	–	7 37	$3 57	$8 19	–	$6 45	$4 66	31
7 70	–	–	–	–	–	6 53	–	–	–	–	–	32
10 06	–	–	–	–	–	10 14	–	–	–	–	–	33
9 32	–	–	–	–	–	9 62	–	–	–	–	–	34
12 72	–	–	–	–	–	7 56	–	–	–	–	–	35
–	–	–	–	–	–	9 65	–	–	–	–	–	36
13 04	–	–	–	–	–	9 11	–	–	–	–	–	37
14 35	–	–	–	–	–	8 74	–	–	–	–	–	38
12 72	–	–	–	–	–	9 29	–	–	–	–	–	39
11 80	–	–	–	–	–	4 24	–	–	–	–	–	40
11 67	–	–	–	–	–	9 05	–	–	–	–	–	41
7 01	–	–	–	5 25	–	7 52	–	–	–	–	–	42
6 25	–	–	3 63	5 31	–	4 82	3 54	–	–	6 46	2 84	43
12 00	–	–	7 66	10 97	–	10 01	5 78	–	–	9 81	2 72	44
12 10	–	–	–	12 63	–	9 95	–	12 42	–	11 04	7 96	45
15 54	–	–	7 24	–	–	–	6 79	–	–	14 58	–	46
11 44	–	–	6 11	10 59	–	8 57	5 78	11 95	–	12 28	6 94	47
12 53	–	–	–	–	–	7 35	–	–	–	–	–	48
7 35	–	–	–	–	–	5 56	–	–	–	–	–	49
12 30	–	–	–	–	–	5 81	–	–	–	–	–	50
–	–	–	–	8 89	–	–	4 42	10 09	–	6 49	4 67	51
10 98	–	–	–	–	–	10 05	–	–	–	–	–	52
11 19	–	–	–	–	–	6 78	–	–	–	–	–	53
17 05	–	–	–	–	–	9 89	–	–	–	–	–	54
11 90	–	–	3 65	12 89	–	9 63	–	13 52	–	10 65	–	55
–	–	–	–	–	–	8 76	–	–	–	–	–	56
13 25	–	–	–	12 40	–	9 70	–	–	–	12 87	12 66	57
11 26	–	–	–	–	–	5 13	–	–	–	–	–	58
13 98	–	–	4 77	10 05	–	10 40	5 93	12 27	–	11 75	6 93	59
13 16	–	–	6 40	11 75	–	10 23	5 77	13 96	–	11 25	7 40	60
7 46	–	–	5 75	–	–	6 95	6 16	–	–	–	6 10	61
18 05	–	–	–	–	–	9 52	–	–	–	–	–	62
17 94	–	–	–	11 96	–	12 32	–	13 55	–	14 73	–	63
11 33	–	–	–	–	–	8 41	–	–	–	–	–	64
11 78	–	–	6 66	11 46	–	10 86	5 76	–	–	–	–	65

	INDUSTRIES.	1860.		1872.		1874.	
		Mass.	G. B.	Mass.	G. B.	Mass.	G. B.
66	Paper, ...	$8 63	–	$9 77	$3 60	–	–
67	Perfumes and toilet preparations, .	–	–	–	–	–	–
68	Photographs and photographic materials, ...	–	–	–	–	–	–
69	Polishes and dressings, . . .	–	–	–	–	–	–
70	Printing and publishing, . . .	11 06	–	12 84	6 54	–	–
71	Printing, dyeing, bleaching, and finishing, cotton textiles, . . .	9 90	–	12 89	6 19	–	–
72	Railroad construction, ...	–	–	–	–	–	–
73	Rubber and elastic goods, . . .	–	–	10 21	4 32	–	–
74	Salt, ...	–	–	–	–	–	–
75	Scientific instruments and appliances, ...	–	–	–	–	–	–
76	Seed crushing, ...	–	–	–	–	–	–
77	Shipbuilding, ...	20 84	–	16 17	6 76	$14 23	–
78	Silk and silk goods, ...	5 91	–	–	–	–	–
79	Sporting goods, ...	–	–	–	–	–	–
80	Stone, ...	8 01	–	–	–	13 93	–
81	Straw goods, ...	–	–	–	–	–	–
82	Tallow, candles, soap, and grease, .	9 00	–	10 63	3 54	–	–
83	Tobacco and cigars, ...	10 00	–	12 89	4 50	16 28	–
84	Toys and games, ...	–	–	–	–	–	–
85	Trunks and valises, ...	–	–	–	–	–	–
86	Whips, ...	–	–	–	–	13 16	–
87	Wooden goods, ...	–	–	10 00	2 07	–	–
88	Woollen goods, ...	5 38	–	7 28	4 64	–	–
89	Worsted goods, ...	6 10	–	–	–	–	–
	Laborers.						
90	Laborers, ...	–	–	–	–	8 07	–

MASSACHUSETTS AND GREAT BRITAIN — 1860–1883 — *Con.*

1875.		1877.		1878.		1880.		1881.		1883.		
Mass.	G. B.	Mass.	G. B.	Mass.	G. B.	Mass.	G. B.	Mass.	G. B.	Mass.	G. B.	
$8 89	–	–	$3 87	$9 51	–	$8 17	$4 57	$10 44	–	$8 11	–	66
7 70	–	–	–	–	–	7 85	–	–	–	–	–	67
11 41	–	–	–	–	–	7 64	–	–	–	–	–	68
10 85	–	–	–	–	–	9 52	–	–	–	–	–	69
12 79	–	–	6 26	13 58	–	11 02	4 94	14 39	–	11 37	$5 52	70
9 36	–	–	5 35	9 58	–	7 01	4 92	–	–	8 67	4 94	71
13 93	–	–	–	–	–	8 84	–	–	–	–	–	72
9 43	–	–	–	9 66	–	8 15	–	9 61	–	6 96	–	73
–	–	–	–	–	–	2 63	–	–	–	–	–	74
12 81	–	–	–	–	–	10 57	–	–	–	–	–	75
–	–	–	6 64	–	–	–	5 73	–	–	–	–	76
17 05	–	–	6 19	10 75	–	12 47	6 10	–	–	20 44	8 14	77
6 12	–	–	–	8 32	–	5 87	–	–	–	7 58	–	78
11 28	–	–	–	–	–	5 75	–	–	–	–	–	79
15 12	–	–	–	8 69	–	10 25	–	10 11	–	14 39	8 58	80
10 33	–	–	–	11 37	–	5 01	–	11 25	–	9 91	–	81
12 54	–	–	6 21	10 24	–	9 19	5 50	–	–	–	–	82
12 65	–	–	–	11 89	–	9 45	–	–	–	–	–	83
13 10	–	–	–	–	–	6 37	–	–	–	–	–	84
13 70	–	–	–	–	–	10 37	–	–	–	–	–	85
11 58	–	–	–	–	–	9 38	–	–	–	–	–	86
12 46	–	–	–	–	–	9 24	–	–	–	12 19	5 67	87
7 76	–	–	5 63	6 89	–	7 93	5 25	7 32	–	6 90	4 86	88
7 59	–	–	4 47	7 41	–	5 66	4 36	–	–	7 32	3 60	89
9 79	–	–	–	–	–	–	–	–	–	13 37	–	90

We present second a table showing by industries, and countries, the wage fluctuations from year to year since 1860. We give the years, in this range, in which the highest and lowest average weekly wages were paid, compare these averages with the general average of all years, and then show the excess of the highest average weekly wage first over the lowest average weekly wage and then over the general average weekly wage. Only those industries appear, in either country, which gave general averages for at least two different years.

MASSACHUSETTS. *Wage Fluctuations.* BY INDUSTRIES.

INDUSTRIES.	Highest Average Weekly Wage.		Lowest Average Weekly Wage.		General Average Weekly Wage.	Excess of Highest Average Weekly Wage—	
	Year.	Amount.	Year.	Amount.		Over Lowest.	Over Average.
Agriculture, ...	1875	$7 84	1860	$4 28	$6 59	$3 56	$1 25
Agricultural implements, . .	1875	14 80	1880	7 75	11 42	7 05	3 38
Arms and ammunition, . .	1878	16 95	1880	9 55	13 62	7 40	3 33
Artificial teeth and dental work, .	1875	15 75	1880	11 87	12 65	3 88	3 10
Artisans' tools, ...	1875	13 73	1860	8 45	10 32	5 28	3 41
Awnings and tents, . .	1875	16 11	1880	7 83	13 69	8 28	2 42
Boots and shoes, ...	1872	14 73	1880	9 60	10 34	5 13	4 39
Boxes, ...	1875	11 00	1860	6 80	8 80	4 20	2 20
Brick, ...	1872	11 25	1860	5 01	8 59	6 24	2 66
Brooms and brushes, . . .	1878	11 90	1880	6 08	9 42	5 82	2 48
Building trades, ...	1872	15 64	1860	9 87	12 54	5 77	3 10
Burial cases, caskets, coffins, etc.,	1875	14 19	1880	12 60	13 34	1 59	85
Buttons and dress trimmings, .	1875	7 71	1880	6 33	6 93	1 38	78
Carpetings, ...	1872	12 76	1880	5 87	7 76	6 89	5 00
Carriages and wagons, . . .	1872	17 11	1880	10 23	12 48	6 88	4 63
Cement, kaolin, lime, and plaster,	1875	10 43	1880	7 01	8 46	3 42	1 97
Charcoal, ...	1875	9 74	1880	9 28	9 71	46	03
Clocks and watches, . . .	1875	14 38	1883	11 28	12 99	3 10	1 39
Clothing, ...	1874	13 90	1860	8 26	9 23	5 64	4 67
Concrete walks, paving, etc., .	1875	13 95	1880	9 44	13 83	4 51	12
Cordage and twine, . . .	1875	9 17	1880	6 39	7 73	2 78	1 44
Corks, ...	1875	8 85	1880	6 14	7 14	2 71	1 71
Cotton goods, ...	1881	8 19	1860	6 50	7 14	1 69	1 05
Cotton and woollen textiles, . .	1875	7 70	1880	6 53	7 00	1 17	70
Crayons, pencils, crucibles, etc., .	1880	10 14	1875	10 06	10 10	08	04
Drugs and medicines, . . .	1880	9 62	1875	9 32	9 53	30	09
Dyeing and finishing textiles, .	1875	12 72	1880	7 56	7 56	5 16	5 16
Earthen and stone ware, . .	1875	13 04	1880	9 11	11 14	3 93	1 90
Electroplating, ...	1875	14 35	1880	8 74	10 91	5 6?	3 44
Emery and sand paper, cloth, etc.,	1875	12 72	1880	9 29	10 30	3 43	2 42
Fancy articles, ...	1875	11 80	1880	4 24	6 23	7 56	5 57
Fertilizers, ...	1875	11 67	1880	9 05	10 04	2 62	1 63
Fireworks and matches, . .	1880	7 52	1878	5 25	7 20	2 27	32
Flax, linen, hemp and jute goods, .	1872	7 69	1860	4 63	5 99	3 06	1 70
Food preparations, . . .	1875	12 00	1860	8 81	10 66	3 19	1 34
Furniture, ...	1874	16 42	1880	9 95	10 99	6 47	5 43
Gas works, ...	1875	15 54	1883	14 58	15 06	96	48
Glass, ...	1883	12 28	1880	8 57	10 84	3 71	1 44
Glue, isinglass, and starch, . .	1875	12 53	1880	7 35	9 91	5 18	2 62
Hair work, ...	1875	7 35	1880	5 56	6 67	1 79	68
Hose: rubber, linen, etc., . .	1875	12 30	1880	5 81	8 85	6 49	3 45
Hosiery, ...	1881	10 09	1883	6 49	7 49	3 60	2 60
Ink, mucilage, and paste, . .	1875	10 98	1880	10 05	10 50	93	48
Ivory, bone, and horn goods, .	1875	11 19	1880	6 78	8 46	4 41	2 73
Jewelry burnishing and lapidary work, ...	1875	17 05	1880	9 89	13 73	7 16	3 32
Leather, ...	1881	13 52	1880	9 63	10 44	3 89	3 08
Liquors: malt and distilled, . .	1872	13 83	1880	9 70	11 94	4 13	1 89
Lumber, ...	1875	18 40	1880	5 13	7 80	13 27	10 60
Machines and machinery, . .	1875	13 98	1860	7 90	10 16	6 08	3 82
Metals and metallic goods, . .	1872	15 52	1860	9 07	11 36	6 45	4 16

MASSACHUSETTS. *Wage Fluctuations.* By INDUSTRIES. — *Con.*

INDUSTRIES.	Highest Average Weekly Wage.		Lowest Average Weekly Wage.		General Average Weekly Wage.	Excess of Highest Average Weekly Wage—	
	Year.	Amount.	Year.	Amount.		Over Lowest.	Over Average.
Mixed textiles,	1874	$9 57	1880	$6 95	$7 10	$2 62	$2 47
Models and patterns,	1875	18 05	1880	9 52	13 46	8 53	4 59
Musical instruments and materials,	1875	17 94	1860	10 94	13 53	7 00	4 41
Oils and illuminating fluids,	1875	11 33	1880	8 41	10 93	2 92	40
Paints, colors, and chemicals,	1872	13 29	1860	8 95	11 85	4 34	1 44
Paper,	1881	10 44	1883	8 11	8 65	2 33	1 79
Perfumes and toilet preparations,	1880	7 85	1875	7 70	7 81	15	04
Photographs and photographic materials,	1875	11 41	1880	7 64	8 93	3 77	2 48
Polishes and dressings,	1875	10 85	1880	9 52	9 96	1 33	89
Printing and publishing,	1881	14 39	1880	11 02	11 68	3 37	2 71
Printing, dyeing, bleaching, and finishing, cotton textiles,	1872	12 89	1880	7 01	9 94	5 88	2 95
Railroad construction,	1875	13 93	1880	8 84	11 26	5 09	2 67
Rubber and elastic goods,	1872	10 21	1883	6 96	8 60	3 25	1 61
Scientific instruments and appliances,	1875	12 81	1880	10 57	11 44	2 24	1 37
Shipbuilding,	1860	20 84	1878	10 75	15 59	10 09	5 25
Silk and silk goods,	1878	8 32	1880	5 87	6 68	2 45	1 64
Sporting goods,	1875	11 28	1880	5 75	6 01	5 53	5 27
Stone,	1875	15 12	1860	8 01	12 02	7 11	3 10
Straw goods,	1878	11 37	1880	5 01	8 97	6 36	2 40
Tallow, candles, soap, and grease,	1875	12 54	1860	9 00	10 28	3 54	2 26
Tobacco and cigars,	1874	16 84	1880	9 45	10 53	7 39	6 31
Toys and games,	1875	13 10	1880	6 37	7 96	6 73	5 14
Trunks and valises,	1875	13 70	1880	10 37	12 07	3 33	1 63
Whips,	1874	13 16	1880	9 38	10 56	3 78	2 60
Wooden goods,	1875	12 46	1880	9 24	10 39	3 22	2 07
Woollen goods,	1880	7 93	1860	5 38	6 75	2 55	1 18
Worsted goods,	1875	7 59	1880	5 66	6 83	1 93	76
Laborers,	1883	13 37	1874	8 07	11 57	5 30	1 80

GREAT BRITAIN. *Wage Fluctuations.* By INDUSTRIES.

INDUSTRIES.	Year.	Amount.	Year.	Amount.	General Average Weekly Wage.	Over Lowest.	Over Average.
Mining,	1880	$5 38	1877	$4 71	$5 14	$0 67	$0 24
Boots and shoes,	1872	5 65	1880	3 78	4 90	1 87	75
Brick,	1872	5 86	1883	4 16	5 01	1 70	85
Building trades,	1883	7 21	1877	5 56	6 61	1 65	60
Carpetings,	1880	4 51	1872	3 92	4 11	59	40
Carriages and wagons,	1880	7 33	1883	4 89	6 45	2 44	88
Clothing,	1883	6 22	1877	3 75	5 46	2 47	76
Cotton goods,	1872	5 36	1880	3 57	4 60	1 79	76
Flax, linen, hemp, and jute goods,	1877	3 63	1883	2 84	3 01	79	62
Food preparations,	1877	7 66	1883	2 72	4 79	4 94	2 87
Furniture,	1872	7 97	1883	7 96	7 96	01	01
Gas works,	1877	7 24	1880	6 79	6 92	45	32
Glass,	1872	6 95	1880	5 78	6 54	1 17	41
Hosiery,	1883	4 67	1880	4 42	4 55	25	12
Leather,	1872	6 38	1877	3 65	5 69	2 73	69
Liquors : malt and distilled,	1883	12 66	1872	5 97	6 24	6 69	6 42
Machines and machinery,	1883	6 93	1877	4 77	6 73	2 16	20
Metals and metallic goods,	1883	7 40	1880	5 77	6 90	1 63	50
Mixed textiles,	1880	6 16	1877	5 75	6 04	41	12
Paints, colors, and chemicals,	1877	6 66	1880	5 76	6 22	90	44
Paper,	1880	4 57	1872	3 60	4 13	97	44
Printing and publishing,	1872	6 54	1880	4 94	5 42	1 60	1 12
Printing, dyeing, bleaching, and finishing, cotton textiles,	1872	6 19	1880	4 92	5 10	1 27	1 09
Seed crushing,	1877	6 64	1880	5 73	6 17	91	47
Shipbuilding,	1883	8 14	1880	6 10	6 73	2 04	1 41
Tallow, candles, soap, and grease,	1877	6 21	1872	3 54	5 74	2 67	47
Wooden goods,	1883	5 67	1872	2 07	3 87	3 60	1 80
Woollen goods,	1877	5 63	1872	4 64	4 79	99	84
Worsted goods,	1877	4 47	1883	3 60	3 75	87	72

By a consolidation we obtain the following table showing the wage fluctuations by years in both countries.

Wage Fluctuations.   By Years.

| | NUMBER OF INDUSTRIES. | | | |
| YEARS. | MASSACHUSETTS. | | GREAT BRITAIN. | |
	Highest.	Lowest.	Highest.	Lowest.
1860	1	16		
1872	11	–		
1874	5	1		
1875	45	3		
1878	4	2		
1880	5	51		
1881	5	–		
1883	2	5		
1872			8	6
1877			8	6
1880			5	11
1883			8	6
Totals, ...	78	78	29	29

This table will bear careful study. We see that one industry in Massachusetts, Shipbuilding, paid its highest wages in 1860. Two industries, Glass and Laborers, reached their highest point in 1883. Forty-five, or 57 + per cent, reached their highest figure in 1875. In Massachusetts, sixteen industries were at their lowest point in 1860, and fifty-one in 1880. Five industries, Clocks and Watches, Gas Works, Hosiery, Paper, and Rubber and Elastic Goods, paid their lowest wage in 1883.

In Great Britain there is a very even distribution among the four years as regards the highest wage point, and a plain indication that more industries were at a low wage level in 1880 than in any other year.

A further investigation of these fluctuations shows in Massachusetts, during the eight wage periods from 1860 to 1883, that 110 industries advanced as regards wages while 128 showed a falling off at some period. In Great Britain 28 advanced and 35 fell off. These results were gained by comparisons with previous years in each country and not by comparison of one country with another. Massachusetts has advanced on a high general average wage and Great Britain has advanced on a comparatively low general average wage. The result, in both countries, was obtained irrespective of amounts, a small industry with a small gain counting as much, that is, as an industry,

as a great industry with a marked advance in wages. Reduced to percentages the results show, as regards the industries considered, an advance in 46.21 per cent and a falling off in 53.79 per cent in Massachusetts; an advance in 44.42 per cent and a falling off in 55.58 per cent in Great Britain.

We next bring into direct comparison fourteen leading industries for which we have wage statistics in both countries for 1872, 1880, and 1883. In this table we have also included Great Britain wages for 1877 and Massachusetts wages for 1878, they furnishing, in our opinion, a thoroughly trustworthy basis for comparisons.

GRAND COMPARISON.   FOURTEEN LEADING INDUSTRIES.

Massachusetts and Great Britain.

INDUSTRIES AND COUNTRIES.	GENERAL AVERAGE WEEKLY WAGE PAID TO ALL EMPLOYES.				General Average Weekly Wage. 1872-1883.	Higher in Mass. PERCENTAGES.
	1872.	1877-8.	1880.	1883.		
BOOTS AND SHOES.						
Mass..	$14 73	$12 02	$9 60	$11 63	$9 73	98.57
G. B..	5 65	4 68	3 78	4 37	4 90	
BUILDING TRADES.						
Mass..	15 64	12 63	10 54	14 99	10 91	65.05
G. B..	6 64	5 56	5 73	7 21	6 61	
CARRIAGES AND WAGONS.						
Mass..	17 11	14 03	10 23	13 80	11 82	83.26
G. B..	6 55	7 14	7 33	4 89	6 45	
CLOTHING.						
Mass..	12 37	9 48	8 31	10 19	8 58	57.14
G. B..	5 79	3 75	4 09	6 22	5 46	
COTTON GOODS.						
Mass..	8 14	7 78	7 37	6 45	7 68	66.96
G. B..	5 36	4 87	3 57	4 66	4 60	
FLAX, LINEN, HEMP, AND JUTE GOODS.						
Mass..	7 69	5 31	4 82	6 46	5 96	98.01
G. B..	3 27	3 63	3 54	2 84	3 01	
FOOD PREPARATIONS.						
Mass..	9 68	10 97	10 01	9 81	10 02	109.19
G. B..	4 58	7 66	5 78	2 72	4 79	
GLASS.						
Mass..	11 39	10 59	8 57	12 28	10 11	54.59
G. B..	6 95	6 11	5 78	6 94	6 54	
MACHINES AND MACHINERY.						
Mass..	13 51	10 05	10 40	11 75	10 67	58.54
G. B..	6 77	4 77	5 93	6 93	6 73	
METALS AND METALLIC GOODS.						
Mass..	15 52	11 75	10 23	11 25	10 42	51.01
G. B..	6 84	6 40	5 77	7 40	6 90	
PRINTING AND PUBLISHING.						
Mass..	12 84	13 58	11 02	11 37	11 27	107.93
G. B..	6 54	6 26	4 94	5 52	5 42	

GRAND COMPARISON. FOURTEEN LEADING INDUSTRIES — *Con.*

Massachusetts and Great Britain.

INDUSTRIES AND COUNTRIES.	GENERAL AVERAGE WEEKLY WAGE PAID TO ALL EMPLOYES.				General Average Weekly Wage. 1872–1883.	Higher in Mass. PERCENTAGES.
	1872.	1877–8.	1880.	1883.		
PRINTING, DYEING, BLEACHING, AND FINISHING, COTTON TEXTILES.						
Mass..	$12 89	$9 58	$7 01	$8 67	$9 52	86.67
G. B..	6 19	5 35	4 92	4 94	5 10	
SHIPBUILDING.						
Mass. (Wooden ships) . . .	16 17	10 75	12 47	20 44	13 64	102.67
G. B. (Iron ships)	6 76	6 19	6 10	8 14	6 73	
WOOLLEN GOODS.						
Mass..	7 28	6 89	7 93	6 90	6 92	44.47
G. B..	4 64	5 63	5 25	4 86	4 79	

In the case of each industry Massachusetts shows a much higher general average wage than does Great Britain. The percentage of excess in one industry in Massachusetts is under 50, in four from 50 to 60, in six from 60 to 100, and in three above 100 per cent.

We are now ready to present the Grand Comparison showing the general average weekly wage paid to all employés, in both countries, by industries, for all the wage periods considered from 1860 to 1883, the consolidation being for eight different years or less in Massachusetts and for four different years or less in Great Britain, the varying number of years, as regards particular industries, being shown in the case of each.

GRAND COMPARISON.   BY INDUSTRIES.

General Average Weekly Wage paid to All Employés. — 1860–1883.

	INDUSTRIES.	MASSACHUSETTS.			GREAT BRITAIN.		
		Number of different years represented.	General average Weekly Wage.	Higher in Mass. Per cent.	Number of different years represented.	General average Weekly Wage.	Higher in G. B. Per cent.
	Domestic and Personal Office.						
1	Domestic service, ...	1	$3 03	–	–	–	–
	Trade and Transportation.						
2	Carriers on roads, ...	1	12 44	–	–	–	–
	Agriculture.						
3	Agriculture, ...	5	6 59	191.6	1	$2 26	–

GRAND COMPARISON.   BY INDUSTRIES. — *Con.*

General Average Weekly Wage paid to All Employés. — 1860–1883.

	INDUSTRIES.	MASSACHUSETTS.			GREAT BRITAIN.		
		Number of different years represented.	General average Weekly Wage.	Higher in Mass. Per cent.	Number of different years represented.	General average Weekly Wage.	Higher in G. B. Per cent.
	Fisheries.						
4	Fisheries, ...	1	$11 67	–	–	–	–
	Mines.						
5	Mining, ...	–	–	–	2	$5 14	–
	Manufactures and Mechanical Industries.						
6	Agricultural implements, . .	3	11 42	33.6	1	8 85	–
7	Arms and ammunition, .	5	13 62	98.5	1	6 86	–
8	Artificial teeth and dental work, .	2	12 65	–	–	–	–
9	Artisans' tools, . . .	5	10 32	111.0	1	4 89	–
10	Awnings and tents, . . .	2	13 69	–	–	–	–
11	Bags and bagging, ...	1	5 16	–	–	–	–
12	Bookbinderies, ...	1	10 66	–	–	–	–
13	Boots and shoes, ...	8	10 34	111.0	4	4 90	–
14	Boxes, ...	5	8 80	86.4	1	4 72	–
15	Brick, ...	6	8 59	71.5	2	5 01	–
16	Brooms and brushes, . . .	5	9 42	77.7	1	5 30	–
17	Building trades, ...	8	12 54	89.7	4	6 61	–
18	Burial cases, caskets, coffins, etc.,	2	13 34	–	–	–	–
19	Buttons and dress trimmings, .	2	6 93	–	–	–	–
20	Carpetings, ...	7	7 76	88.8	3	4 11	–
21	Carriages and wagons, . .	8	12 48	93.5	4	6 45	–
22	Cement, kaolin, lime, and plaster,	2	8 46	–	–	–	–
23	Charcoal, ...	2	9 71	–	–	–	–
24	Chemical preparations, . .	1	8 78	–	–	–	–
25	Clocks and watches, . . .	5	12 99	74.6	1	7 44	–
26	Clothing, ...	8	9 23	69.0	4	5 46	–
27	Concrete walks, paving, etc., .	2	13 83	–	–	–	–
28	Cooking, lighting, and heating apparatus, ...	1	10 22	–	–	–	–
29	Cordage and twine, . . .	2	7 73	–	–	–	–
30	Corks, ...	2	7 14	–	–	–	–
31	Cotton goods, ...	7	7 14	55.2	4	4 60	–
32	Cotton and woollen textiles, .	2	7 00	–	–	–	–
33	Crayons, pencils, crucibles, etc., .	2	10 10	–	–	–	–
34	Drugs and medicines, . . .	2	9 53	–	–	–	–
35	Dyeing and finishing textiles, .	2	7 56	–	–	–	–
36	Dyestuffs, ...	1	9 65	–	–	–	–
37	Earthen and stone ware, . .	2	11 14	–	–	–	–
38	Electroplating, ...	2	10 91	–	–	–	–
39	Emery and sand paper, cloth, etc.,	2	10 30	–	–	–	–
40	Fancy articles, ...	2	6 23	–	–	–	–
41	Fertilizers, ...	2	10 04	–	–	–	–
42	Fireworks and matches, . .	3	7 20	–	–	–	–
43	Flax, linen, hemp, and jute goods,	6	5 99	99.0	4	3 01	–
44	Food preparations, . . .	6	10 66	122.5	4	4 79	–
45	Furniture, ...	8	10 99	38.1	2	7 96	–
46	Gas works, ...	2	15 06	117.6	2	6 92	–
47	Glass, ...	6	10 84	65.7	4	6 54	–
48	Glue, isinglass, and starch, .	2	9 91	–	–	–	–
49	Hair work, ...	2	6 67	–	–	–	–
50	Hose: rubber, linen, etc., .	2	8 85	–	–	–	–
51	Hosiery, ...	3	7 49	64.6	2	4 55	–
52	Ink, mucilage, and paste, .	2	10 50	–	–	–	–
53	Ivory, bone, and horn goods, .	2	8 46	–	–	–	–
54	Jewelry burnishing and lapidary work, ...	2	13 73	–	–	–	–
55	Leather, ...	8	10 44	83.5	2	5 69	–

GRAND COMPARISON.   BY INDUSTRIES. — *Con.*

General Average Weekly Wage paid to All Employés. — 1860-1883.

	INDUSTRIES.	MASSACHUSETTS.			GREAT BRITAIN.		
		Number of different years represented.	General average Weekly Wage.	Higher in Mass. Per cent.	Number of different years represented.	General average Weekly Wage.	Higher in G. B. Per cent.
56	Liquors and beverages,	1	$8 76	–	–	–	–
57	Liquors: malt and distilled,	6	11 94	91.3	2	$6 24	–
58	Lumber,	2	7 80	–	–	–	–
59	Machines and machinery,	8	10 16	51.0	4	6 73	–
60	Metals and metallic goods,	8	11 36	64.6	4	6 90	–
61	Mixed textiles,	3	7 10	17.5	3	6 04	–
62	Models and patterns,	2	13 46	–	–	–	–
63	Musical instruments and materials,	6	13 53	–	–	–	–
64	Oils and illuminating fluids,	2	10 93	–	–	–	–
65	Paints, colors, and chemicals,	5	11 85	90.5	3	6 22	–
66	Paper,	7	8 65	109.4	3	4 13	–
67	Perfumes and toilet preparations,	2	7 81	–	–	–	–
68	Photographs and photographic materials,	2	8 93	–	–	–	–
69	Polishes and dressings,	2	9 96	–	–	–	–
70	Printing and publishing,	7	11 68	115.5	4	5 42	–
71	Printing, dyeing, bleaching, and finishing, cotton textiles,	6	9 94	94.9	4	5 10	–
72	Railroad construction,	2	11 26	–	–	–	–
73	Rubber and elastic goods,	6	8 60	99.1	1	4 32	–
74	Salt,	1	2 63	–	–	–	–
75	Scientific instruments and appliances,	2	11 44	–	–	–	–
76	Seed crushing,	–	–	–	2	6 17	–
77	Shipbuilding,	7	15 59	131.6	4	6 73	–
78	Silk and silk goods,	5	6 68	–	–	–	–
79	Sporting goods,	2	6 01	–	–	–	–
80	Stone,	7	12 02	40.1	1	8 58	–
81	Straw goods,	5	8 97	–	–	–	–
82	Tallow, candles, soap, and grease,	5	10 28	79.1	3	5 74	–
83	Tobacco and cigars,	6	10 53	134.0	1	4 50	–
84	Toys and games,	2	7 96	–	–	–	–
85	Trunks and valises,	2	12 07	–	–	–	–
86	Whips,	3	10 56	–	–	–	–
87	Wooden goods,	4	10 39	168.5	2	3 87	–
88	Woollen goods,	7	6 75	40.9	4	4 79	–
89	Worsted goods,	5	6 83	82.1	3	3 75	–
	Laborers.						
90	Laborers,	3	11 57	–	–	–	–

Summary.

Domestic and personal office,	1	$3 03	–	–	–	–
Trade and transportation,	1	12 44	–	–	–	–
Agriculture,	5	6 59	191.6	1	$2 26	–
Fisheries,	1	11 67	–	–	–	–
Mines,	–	–	–	2	5 14	–
Manufactures and mechanical industries,	*3.80	9 81	73.0	*2.68	5 67	–
Laborers,	3	11 57	–	–	–	–
All industries,	*3.70	$9 77	**75.40**	*2.62	$5 57	–

* Average.

From the preceding table we secure our first grand comparison, and result.

In the 90 industries considered, from 1860 to 1883, the general average weekly wage was 75.40 per cent higher in Massachusetts than in Great Britain.

If we examine the *manufacturing and mechanical industries* by themselves, 84 in Massachusetts and 35 in Great Britain, we find, in these industries, *That the general average weekly wage, from 1860 to 1883, was 73.02 per cent higher in Massachusetts than in Great Britain.* If we confine our comparison to the 37 industries which supply an exact comparison, that is, an average figure in both countries for the same industry, we discover that the general average weekly wage in these 37 industries in Massachusetts, from 1860 to 1883, was $10.17, while in Great Britain it was $5.57, or, *The general average weekly wage was 82.59 per cent higher in Massachusetts than in Great Britain.* A further examination of these 37 fully comparative industries shows that in 8 the percentage in favor of Massachusetts was less than 60, in 7 from 60 to 80, in 11 from 80 to 100, and in 11 over 100 per cent, reaching as high as 191.6 per cent.

For a final grand comparison we show the general average weekly wage paid to all employés, in both countries, by years, presenting also the number of industries considered in each year.

GRAND COMPARISON.   BY YEARS.

General Average Weekly Wage paid to All Employés.

YEARS.	GENERAL AVERAGE WEEKLY WAGE PAID TO ALL EMPLOYES.				PERCENTAGES.	
	MASSACHUSETTS.		GREAT BRITAIN.		General Average Weekly Wage higher in—	
	No. of Industries considered.	Amounts.	No. of Industries considered.	Amounts.	Massachusetts.	Great Britain.
1860	31	$8 18	–	–	–	–
1872	29	11 10	29	$5 34	107.86	–
1874	17	10 98	–	–	–	–
1875	80	10 05	–	–	–	–
1877	–	–	23	5 59	–	–
1878	36	9 51	–	–	–	–
1880	79	9 45	25	5 51	71.51	–
1881	20	10 40	–	–	–	–
1883	34	10 50	25	5 86	79.18	–
All years, . .	88	$10 02	39	$5 58	79.57	–

By the industry presentation the percentage in favor of Massachusetts in 90 industries, from 1860 to 1883, was shown to be 75.40 per cent; by the yearly consolidation (on nine yearly bases instead of ninety industry bases) we find it to result in 79.57 per cent in favor of Massachusetts. The mean of these two percentages is 77.49 per cent. The result of the comparative wages investigation, for 1860 to 1883, is —

That the general average weekly wage of the employés, in the industries considered, was 77.49 per cent higher in Massachusetts than in Great Britain.

From the grand comparison by years we are enabled to derive a table which shows, for both countries, the money advance or decline, and the percentages of increase or decrease, from year to year, and which also supplies comparisons between more widely separated periods, as regards the general average weekly wage in all the industries considered.

GRAND COMPARISON.   BY YEARS AND PERIODS.

Massachusetts and Great Britain.

YEARS AND PERIODS.		MASSACHUSETTS.		GREAT BRITAIN.	
From —	To —	Amounts.	Percentages.	Amounts.	Percentages.
1860	1872	+ $2 92	+ 35.70		
1872	1874	− 0 12	− 1.08		
1874	1875	− 0 93	− 8.47		
1875	1878	− 0 54	− 5.37		
1878	1880	− 0 06	− 0.63		
1880	1881	+ 0 95	+ 10.05		
1881	1883	+ 0 10	+ 0.96		
1872	1877			+ $0 25	+ 4.68
1877	1880			− 0 08	− 1.43
1880	1883			+ 0 35	+ 6.35
1860	1883	+ 2 32	+ 28.36	-	-
1872	1883	− 0 60	− 5.41	+ 0 52	+ 9.74

This table shows the comparison of one country with itself, as regards wages in different years, and in no way affects the percentages showing the higher rates of wages in Massachusetts as compared with Great Britain.

We see, in Massachusetts, a great advance from 1860 to 1872; then a continual falling off until 1880; then a rally, and continued improvement to 1883. From 1860 to 1883 the advance was 28.36 per cent.

In Great Britain, wages advanced from 1872 to 1877, fell off between 1877 and 1880, and advanced again between 1880 and 1883. From 1872 to 1883 the advance was 9.74 per cent. In Massachusetts, wages in 1883 were 5.41 per cent lower than in 1872.

In all the wage tables in this Part it will be seen that wages reached their lowest level in Massachusetts in 1880. The close approximation of the 1880 wages to those for 1878 denotes an unmistakable downward tendency from 1872. At the same time it is worthy of mention and remembrance that in Massachusetts, in 1875 and 1880, the wage statistics were drawn from Census returns which practically covered all the employés engaged in manufacturing and mechanical industries in the State. In such Census returns the general average is always lower than in returns of special investigations, for the Census returns include the small establishments, and also the lowest paid employés. Again, the Census returns are usually yearly earnings, which divided by 52 (weeks) will usually give a lower rate than the average weekly wage, owing to loss of time for various reasons. The last table shows conclusively that 1880 was a turning point in Massachusetts wages which are now (1883) but five per cent lower than the highest point which was reached in 1872.

From the preceding tables we are now able to formulate in concise language the —

GRAND RESULT.

1. The number of employés whose average weekly wages are represented in the comparisons from 1860 to 1883 is at least one and a quarter millions (1,250,000).

2. In the comparisons, 88 industries in Massachusetts and 39 in Great Britain were represented. The Massachusetts wages were higher in all the industries compared, the percentage in favor of Massachusetts, on an industry basis, being 75.40.

3. The purely manufacturing industries entering into this comparison numbered 84 in Massachusetts and 37 in Great Britain. In these industries the percentage in favor of Massachusetts was 73.02.

4. Complete comparisons were possible in the case of 37 industries having wage statistics for both countries. In these industries the percentage in favor of Massachusetts was 82.59.

5. On the yearly basis, Massachusetts from 1860 to 1883, and Great Britain from 1872 to 1883, the percentage in favor of Massachusetts is 79.57.

6. Wages in Massachusetts are 28.36 per cent higher than they were in 1860.

7. Wages in Great Britain are 9.74 per cent higher than they were in 1872.

The mean of the percentages shown on the industry basis in section 2 (75.40) and on the yearly basis in section 5 (79.57) is 77.49, which figure is the result of the comparisons from 1860 to 1883. This result not only verifies beyond question the result shown on page 217, viz., 62+ per cent, but it also shows that the extreme figure, for 1883 alone, also shown on page 217, viz., 75.94 per cent, is less than the average per cent in favor of Massachusetts from 1860 to 1883.

The grand result of the comparative wages investigation in Massachusetts and Great Britain for the years 1860 to 1883 is —

That the general average weekly wage of the employés in the industries considered in Massachusetts was 77+ *per cent higher than the general average weekly wage of the employés in the industries considered in Great Britain.*

[From Part IV., Fifteenth Annual Report, for 1884.]

COMPARATIVE PRICES AND COST OF LIVING.

1860-1883.

MASSACHUSETTS AND GREAT BRITAIN.

The question of wages forms but one side of the working-man's account. On the other is the question of cost of living. This fact has always been fully recognized by this Bureau, for presentations of wages in past reports have been accompanied by statistics of the prices of commodities in use by working-men and of the cost of living. The publications of the Bureau on this point may be summarized, by years, since 1874, as follows:

1872. In the Report for 1874, Part VI. was devoted to the Prices of Provisions, etc , in Massachusetts and Europe, and the Purchase Power of Money, for 1872. The statistics for Great Britain were very full, being obtained in fifteen cities and towns in the kingdom.

1874. Part IV. of the Report for 1875 was devoted to the Condition of Workingmen's Families, and included statistics of the cost of living of 397 workingmen's families in Massachusetts. The analysis of the statistics sustained Engel's law relative to the expenditures of workingmen's families in most particulars.

1878. Wages and prices in 1860, 1872, and 1878 were presented in Part III. of the Report for 1879. The figures for 1872 were brought forward from the Report for 1874, but the prices in 1860 and 1878 were obtained by the Bureau agents in the last named year from 345 retail dealers in different parts of the Commonwealth.

1881. In the Report for 1882, Part IV., the statistics of prices for 1860, 1872, and 1878 were again brought forward and put in comparison with the prices of commodities in 1881.

1883. The same agents who obtained the wage statistics for Massachusetts and Great Britain, presented in Parts II. and III., of this Report, also secured statistics of prices of articles used by and entering into the cost of living of workingmen in both countries.

ANALYSES OF THE PRICES TABLES.

To secure the quotations given in detail in the twelve prices tables, about 75 retail stores in 10 cities and towns were visited in Massachusetts and 150 retail stores in 20 cities and towns in Great Britain. In addition, the printed price lists of leading retail houses in Boston and the " supply books " of the large workingmen's stores in Great Britain were consulted and used for verifications and to complete the grading of prices.

We have undertaken from a consideration of the prices tables to secure averages and percentages which will indicate as nearly as may be, when all qualifying circumstances are taken into account at their full weight, the higher cost of living in Massachusetts. That the cost of living is higher in Mas-

sachusetts than in Great Britain is generally acknowledged. Our aim is to show in what way and to what degree.

Groceries, Provisions, Fuel. — The advance or decline, in Massachusetts alone, by years, and by periods, is shown in the subjoined summary.

SUMMARY. *Prices in Massachusetts — 1860-1883.*

YEARS.		PERCENTAGES.		
From —	To —	Groceries.	Provisions.	Fuel.
1860	1872	+ 32.24	+ 50.60	+ 55.12
1872	1878	— 13.04	— 15.41	— 31.12
1878	1881	— .25	+ 19.91	+ 34.37
1881	1883	— 4.10	— 11.43	— 23.52
1860	1878	+ 15.00	+ 27.40	+ 6.84
1860	1883	+ 10.01	+ 35.30	+ 9.79
1872	1883	— 16.81	— 10.16	— 29.22

NOTE. The plus sign (+) indicates an advance and the minus sign (—) a decline in price to the extent shown by the percentages for each class of commodities.

The great advance from 1860 to 1872 will be noticed, and then the gradual decline to 1883. From 1860 to 1883 an advance is shown, but from 1872 to 1883 a marked decline from the high figures of 1872 is apparent.

In Massachusetts the decline as regards 1883 has just been shown. In Great Britain in 1883, groceries were .83 per cent higher than in 1872, provisions 10.32 per cent lower, and fuel 41.26 per cent lower. Comparing Massachusetts and Great Britain for the year 1872 we find that groceries were 23.03 per cent higher in Massachusetts, provisions 25.74 per cent higher in Great Britain, and fuel 60.19 per cent higher in Massachusetts.

Comparisons for 1883 between Massachusetts and Great Britain enable us to secure the following results: groceries were 16.18 per cent higher in Massachusetts, provisions were 23.08 per cent higher in Great Britain, while fuel was 104.96 per cent higher in Massachusetts.

Dry Goods. — From the high, medium high, medium, medium low, and low prices for dry goods, we secure two percentages, both in favor of Great Britain. If all goods in all grades are compared we find that dry goods were 13.26 per cent higher in Massachusetts in 1883 than in Great Britain. If

the comparison is made on the basis of all goods in the medium, medium low, and low grades, from which workingmen obtain their supplies, the figure in favor of Great Britain is .9 or less than 1 per cent.

Boots, Shoes, and Slippers. — In 1883, if all goods in all grades are included, boots, shoes, and slippers were 62.59 per cent higher in Massachusetts than in Great Britain. If the comparison is confined to the medium, medium low, and low grades, then these articles were 42.75 per cent higher in Massachusetts than in Great Britain.

Clothing. — If all goods in all grades are considered, the specified articles of clothing were 45.06 per cent higher in Massachusetts in 1883 than in Great Britain. If the comparison covers only the medium, medium low, and low grades, then the articles considered were 27.36 per cent higher in Massachusetts. The low grade alone shows that prices in Massachusetts were 18 per cent higher, while the high and medium high grades indicate that prices in Massachusetts were 56.57 per cent higher.

Rents. — A very full showing of rents for Massachusetts and Great Britain in 1883 supplies the following result: rents were, on the average, 89.62 per cent higher in Massachusetts than in Great Britain. The average rent of *one room* in Massachusetts was 66 cents per week, $2.86 per month, and $34.38 per year. The average rent for various sized tenements can be easily computed on this basis. In Great Britain the average rent for *one room* was 35 cents per week, $1.51 per month, and $18.02 per year. Computations for tenements can be made as in the case of Massachusetts.

Board and Lodging. — The board and lodging returns are also very complete. The result is that board and lodging, on the average, were 39.01 per cent higher in Massachusetts in 1883 than in Great Britain. The average price for *board and lodging* in Massachusetts, in 1883, for men, per week, was $4.79, for women $3.19; per month, men $20.76, women $13.82; per year, men $249.08, and women $165.88. Considering *board* alone the average rates for men, per week, were $3.84, for women $2.56; per month, men $16.68, women $11.09; per year, men $199.68, and women $133.12. Taking *lodging* by itself, the average rates, per week, for men were

$2.20, for women $1.46 ; per month, for men $9.53, for women $6.33 ; per year, for men $114.40, and for women $75.92.

Comparative figures for *board and lodging*, in 1883, in Great Britain, are as follows: per week, for men $3.37, for women $2.37 ; per month, men $14.58, women $10.28 ; per year, men $174.98, and women $123.41. Women pay about two-thirds as much for board and lodging as men. Parties lodging in one house and boarding in another pay more than those who secure board and lodging together. For this reason the averages for *board* added to those for *lodging* make more than the averages given for *board and lodging*.

The preceding percentages we consolidate in tabular form :

SUMMARY. *Prices in Massachusetts and Great Britain —1883.*

ARTICLES.	PERCENTAGES.	
	Higher in Massachusetts.	Higher in Great Britain.
Groceries,	16.18	–
Provisions,	–	23.08
Fuel,	104.96	–
Dry goods, all grades,	13.26	–
three lower grades,	.90	–
Boots, shoes, and slippers, all grades,	62.59	–
three lower grades,	42.75	–
Clothing, all grades,	45.06	–
three lower grades,	27.36	–
lowest grade,	18.00	–
two highest grades,	56.57	–
Rents,	89.62	–
Board and lodging,	39.01	–

COST OF LIVING.

The application of the percentages just arrived at to the various elements of a workingman's expenses will enable us to arrive at the comparative cost of living in Massachusetts and Great Britain in 1883. To do this it is first essential to know the proportionate parts of a workingman's income required for groceries, provisions, etc. These proportions were first arrived at and propounded as an economic law by Dr. Engel, chief of the Royal Prussian Bureau of Statistics at Berlin. The investigations of the Massachusetts Bureau, in the same line in 1875 and 1879, supported and confirmed Engel's law in all important particulars, due allowance being made for the difference in standard of living in Massachusetts and Germany.

Dr. Engel's law was based upon an unknown number of

workingmen's budgets, or annual accounts of all items of expense in detail. The Bureau corroboration of his propositions was founded upon 397 budgets collected in 1874 and printed in 1875. Ten years having passed we considered it essential to obtain some fresh budgets to see if there had been any material change in the manner of living in Massachusetts, and also to supply comparisons for 1883 between Massachusetts and Great Britain. We secured 19 budgets, or annual accounts of expenditures, in Massachusetts and 16 in Great Britain which we present in a series of tables.

WORKINGMEN'S BUDGETS. *Size of Family, Persons at Work, Earnings and Expenses.* MASSACHUSETTS.

No.	Persons in Family.			At Work.			Earnings of head of Family.	Earnings of members of Family.	Total earnings.	Total expenses.	Surplus or Debt.
	Adults.	Children.	Total.	Adults.	Children.	Total.					
1	2	4	6	1	1	2	$616	$224	$840	$661	+$179
2	2	4	6	1	2	3	572	364	936	936	–
3	2	2	4	1	–	1	616	–	616	649	—33
4	3	3	6	1	2	3	624	390	1,014	1,014	–
5	2	4	6	2	–	2	450	156	606	432	+174
6	2	5	7	1	2	3	390	456	846	846	–
7	2	4	6	1	2	3	385	358	743	743	–
8	3	3	6	1	2	3	416	195	611	611	–
9	2	4	6	1	1	2	520	184	704	653	+51
10	2	4	6	1	2	3	608	282	890	890	–
11	2	4	6	1	1	2	624	300	924	924	–
12	3	–	3	2	–	2	520	780	1,300	1,185	+115
13	2	3	5	1	1	2	614	260	874	874	–
14	2	1	3	1	–	1	1,040	–	1,040	834	+206
15	2	–	2	2	–	2	520	260	780	540	+240
16	2	4	6	1	1	2	494	156	650	650	–
17	2	2	4	1	1	2	470	156	626	626	–
18	2	3	5	1	1	2	520	130	650	650	–
19	2	4	6	1	–	1	616	–	616	616	–

WORKINGMEN'S BUDGETS. *Size of Family, Persons at Work, Earnings and Expenses.* GREAT BRITAIN.

No.	Persons in Family.			At Work.			Earnings of head of Family.	Earnings of members of Family.	Total earnings.	Total expenses.	Surplus or Debt.
	Adults.	Children.	Total.	Adults.	Children.	Total.					
1	2	4	6	1	–	1	$282 24	–	$282 24	$282 24	–
2	2	3	5	1	2	3	126 52	$666 64	793 16	647 18	+$145 98
3	2	3	5	1	2	3	243 30	209 24	452 54	452 54	–
4	2	2	4	1	1	2	277 36	101 21	378 57	378 57	–
5	2	5	7	1	2	3	326 02	192 21	518 23	518 23	–
6	1	6	7	1	1	2	227 73	88 56	316 29	316 29	–
7	2	4	6	1	2	3	253 03	253 04	506 07	506 07	–
8	3	5	8	1	3	4	291 96	340 62	632 58	632 58	–
9	2	5	7	1	2	3	248 17	327 49	575 66	575 66	–
10	2	4	6	1	1	2	417 50	151 82	569 32	569 32	–
11	2	6	8	1	2	3	399 01	272 50	671 51	671 51	–
12	2	3	5	1	2	3	462 27	321 16	783 43	783 43	–
13	2	4	6	1	2	3	301 69	128 95	430 64	430 64	–
14	2	4	6	1	–	1	379 55	–	379 55	379 55	–
15	2	2	4	1	1	2	341 59	88 56	430 15	430 15	–
16	2	5	7	1	2	3	379 55	180 04	559 59	559 59	–

WORKINGMEN'S BUDGETS. *Expense Details.* MASSACHUSETTS.

No.	Total Expenses.	Rent.	Groceries.	Meat.	Fish.	Milk.	Fuel.	Clothing.	Boots and Shoes.	Dry Goods.	Sundry Expenses.
1	$661	$144	$150	$85	$30	–	$40	$60	$30	$12	$110
2	936	192	300	100	30	$30	40	150	50	15	29
3	649	owned.	250	104	30	25	40	60	25	15	100
4	1,014	240	300	150	40	30	40	100	40	15	59
5	432	72	200	50	20	30	–	20	15	5	20
6	846	150	260	125	20	25	30	90	40	12	94
7	743	96	200	100	30	30	30	100	30	10	117
8	611	144	200	75	25	25	30	50	20	10	32
9	653	66	200	75	30	20	–	100	50	–	112
10	890	168	280	156	10	25	40	100	24	30	57
11	924	180	300	156	25	30	40	75	26	15	77
12	1,185	400	200	75	30	20	80	150	–	40	190
13	874	150	240	100	20	25	40	50	25	20	204
14	834	168	250	100	30	25	40	100	30	20	71
15	540	156	150	75	15	12	15	40	20	8	49
16	650	120	156	156	20	13	20	75	20	10	60
17	626	96	200	75	20	25	25	40	25	20	100
18	650	144	220	80	20	30	26	60	25	15	30
19	616	144	175	75	30	25	40	60	25	15	27

WORKINGMEN'S BUDGETS. *Expense Details.* GREAT BRITAIN.

No.	Total Expenses.	Rent.	Groceries.	Meat.	Fish.	Milk.	Fuel.	Clothing.	Boots and Shoes.	Dry Goods.	Sundry Expenses.
1	$282 24	$48 66	$99 75	$24 33	$14 60	$17 03	$8 76	$29 20	$12 17	$9 73	$18 01
2	647 18	owned.	145 98	*121 65	–	24 33	24 33	58 39	34 06	38 93	199 51
3	452 54	50 60	194 64	–	14 60	12 17	17 03	77 85	12 17	–	73 48
4	378 57	94 89	126 51	60 82	24 33	9 73	12 17	35 52	–	14 60	–
5	518 23	63 26	145 98	72 99	9 73	19 46	14 60	48 66	29 20	19 46	94 89
6	316 29	43 79	87 59	48 66	4 87	19 46	9 73	38 93	14 60	14 60	34 06
7	506 07	63 26	194 64	121 65	29 20	19 46	19 46	43 80	14 60	–	–
8	632 58	75 91	145 98	*75 42	–	9 73	21 90	87 59	24 33	68 12	123 60
9	575 66	56 93	234 06	58 88	16 79	19 46	29 20	48 66	11 92	24 33	75 43
10	569 32	77 86	194 64	97 32	14 60	14 60	24 33	68 12	19 46	19 46	38 93
11	671 51	107 05	243 30	145 98	19 46	19 47	19 47	58 39	24 33	–	34 06
12	783 43	99 27	170 31	*97 32	–	7 30	19 46	24 33	24 33	48 66	219 46
13	430 64	63 26	145 98	48 66	12 17	9 73	19 46	34 06	9 73	9 73	77 86
14	379 55	75 42	145 98	48 66	–	17 03	14 60	48 66	17 03	–	12 17
15	430 15	69 58	145 98	38 92	9 73	18 98	12 17	58 39	12 17	9 73	54 50
16	559 15	107 05	194 64	58 39	9 73	24 33	18 25	82 72	19 47	–	45 01

* Includes Fish.

WORKINGMEN'S BUDGETS. *Averages.* MASSACHUSETTS AND GREAT BRITAIN.

CLASSIFICATION.	MASSACHUSETTS.		GREAT BRITAIN.	
	Average.	Per cent.	Average.	Per cent.
Persons in family,	5.21	–	6.06	–
Adults,	2.16	41.46	2.00	33.00
Children,	3.05	58.54	4.06	67.00
Number at work,	2.16	–	2.56	–
Adults,	1.16	53.70	1.00	39.06
Children,	1.00	46.30	1.56	60.94
Total earnings,	$803 47	–	$517 47	–
Earnings of head of family,	558 68	69.53	309 84	59.88
Earnings of members of family,	244 79	30.47	207 63	40.12
Total expenses,	$754 42	93.89	$508 35	98.24
Surplus,	49 05	6.11	9 12	1.76

These averages show, as regards the families considered, that the average Great Britain family was slightly larger but had a fraction more persons at work, and, for this reason, matches the average Massachusetts family. As regards total earnings, the Massachusetts family, on an average, earned 55.27 per cent more than the average Great Britain family. The average earnings of the head of the family in Massachusetts were 80.31 per cent higher than in Great Britain; that is, the advantage of wages, as shown in Part II., is 75.94 per cent, while the advantage of earnings, owing to increased yearly working time in Massachusetts, is 80.31 per cent. The average earnings of members of the family were 17.90 per cent higher in Massachusetts than in Great Britain. The total family expenses in Massachusetts were 48.41 per cent *greater* (not higher) than in Great Britain. The average Massachusetts family expended 93.89 per cent of its total income and had 6.11 per cent surplus. The average Great Britain family expended 98.24 per cent of its income and had 1.76 per cent surplus.

WORKINGMEN'S BUDGETS.   *Percentages of Expenditure.* MASSACHU-
SETTS AND GREAT BRITAIN.

CLASSIFICATION.	MASSACHUSETTS.		GREAT BRITAIN.	
	Average.	Per cent.	Average.	Per cent.
Rent, ...	$148 95	19.74	$68 55	13.48
Groceries, ...	222 68	29.52	163 50	32.16
Meat, ...	100 63	13.34	69 98	13.77
Fish, ...	25 00	3.31	11 24	2.21
Milk, ...	23 42	3.11	16 39	3.22
Fuel, ...	32 42	4.30	17 81	3.50
Clothing, ...	77 89	10.32	57 27	11.27
Boots and shoes, ...	27 37	3.63	17 47	3.44
Dry goods, ...	15 11	2.00	17 33	3.41
Sundry expenses, ...	80 95	10.73	68 81	13.54

We have now arrived at the percentages of expenditure as drawn from the 19 budgets obtained in Massachusetts and the 16 obtained in Great Britain. We must next bring these percentages into comparison with those secured by Dr. Engel, and also with those arrived at by the Bureau.

Engel's law was first printed by the Bureau in the Sixth Annual Report, for 1875; as the edition of that report is exhausted, we reproduce the table and Dr. Engel's conclusions.

Engel's Law.

ITEMS OF EXPENDITURE.	PERCENTAGE OF THE EXPENDITURE OF THE FAMILY OF—		
	A workingman with an Income of from $225 to $300 a year.	A man of the intermediate class ("Mittel-standes") with an Income of from $450 to $600 a year.	A person in easy circumstan-ces ("des Wohl-standes") with an Income of from $750 to $1,100 a year.
	Per cent.	Per cent.	Per cent.
1. Subsistence,	62.0 ⎫	55.0 ⎫	50.0 ⎫
2. Clothing,	16.0 ⎬ 95.0	18.0 ⎬ 90.0	18.0 ⎬ 85.0
3. Lodging,	12.0 ⎮	12 0 ⎮	12.0 ⎮
4. Firing and lighting,	5.0 ⎭	5.0 ⎭	5.0 ⎭
5. Education, public worship, etc.,	2.0 ⎫	3.5 ⎫	5.5 ⎫
6. Legal protection,	1.0 ⎬ 5.0	2.0 ⎬ 10.0	3.0 ⎬ 15.0
7. Care of health,	1.0 ⎮	2.0 ⎮	3.0 ⎮
8. Comfort, mental and bodily recreation,	1.0 ⎭	1.5 ⎭	3.5 ⎭
Total,	100.0	100.0	100.0

"The foregoing table demonstrates the points upon the strength of which Dr. Engel propounds an economic law.

The distinct propositions are, —

First. That the greater the income, the smaller the relative percentage of outlay for subsistence.

Second. That the percentage of outlay for clothing is approximately the same, whatever the income.

Third. That the percentage of outlay for lodging, or rent, and for fuel and light, is invariably the same, whatever the income.

Fourth. That as the income increases in amount, the percentage of outlay for 'sundries' becomes greater."

We also reprint the Bureau table from the same report.

Percentages of Expenditure. BUREAU TABLE.

ITEMS OF EXPENDITURE.	PERCENTAGE OF THE EXPENDITURE OF THE FAMILY OF A WORKINGMAN WITH AN INCOME—				
	From $300 to $450.	From $450 to $600.	From $600 to $750.	From $750 to $1,200.	Above $1,200.
	Per cent.	Per cent.	Per cent.	Per cent.	Per cent.
Subsistence,	64 ⎫	63 ⎫	60 ⎫	56 ⎫	51 ⎫
Clothing,	7 ⎬ 97	10.5 ⎬ 95	14 ⎬ 94	15 ⎬ 94	19 ⎬ 90
Rent,	20 ⎮	15.5 ⎮	14 ⎮	17 ⎮	15 ⎮
Fuel,	6 ⎭	6 ⎭	6 ⎭	6 ⎭	5 ⎭
Sundry expenses,	3 ⎰ 3	5 ⎰ 5	6 ⎰ 6	6 ⎰ 6	10 ⎰ 10
Totals,	100	100	100	100	100

We have seen that the average annual family expenditure in Massachusetts, as shown by the budgets for 1883, was $754.42 and in Great Britain, for the same year, $508.35. For purposes of comparison we bring together, for the average Massachusetts family and also for the average Great Britain family, the percentages of expenditure as drawn from the budgets, and the percentages for the same sized incomes, from Engel's law and the Bureau table.

MASSACHUSETTS. *Percentages of Expenditure, Amount, $754.42.*

ITEMS OF EXPENDITURE.	Mass. Budgets. 1883.	Engel's Prussian law.	Mass. Bureau table. 1875.	Average.
Subsistence, ...	49.28	50.00	56.00	51.76
Clothing, ...	15.95	18.00	15.00	16.32
Rent, ...	19.74	12.00	17.00	16.25
Fuel, ...	4.30	5.00	6.00	5.10
Sundry expenses, ...	10.73	15.00	6.00	10.57
Totals, ...	100.00	100.00	100.00	100.00

GREAT BRITAIN. *Percentages of Expenditure, Amount, $508.35.*

ITEMS OF EXPENDITURE.	Gt. Britain Budgets. 1883.	Engel's Prussian law.	Mass. Bureau table. 1875.	Average.
Subsistence, ...	51.36	55.00	63.00	56.45
Clothing, ...	18.12	18.00	10.50	15.54
Rent, ...	13.48	12.00	15.50	13.66
Fuel, ...	3.50	5.00	6.00	4.83
Sundry expenses, ...	13.54	10.00	5.00	9.52
Totals, ...	100.00	100.00	100.00	100.00

The remarkable harmony in the items of expenditure shown by a percentage of total expenditure must establish the soundness of the economic law propounded by Dr. Engel.* The column of averages should, therefore, be taken as the very best result of that law sustained by a wide range of data from three great countries, and this law would stand for Massachusetts on a total annual expenditure, for instance, of $750, as follows: — Subsistence, 51.76%; Clothing, 16.32%; Rent,

---

* This same harmony is found to exist in other localities and verifies beyond question the results of previous efforts in establishing the law relative to the division of income as regards the various items of living expenses. The following tables are taken from the Third Biennial Report of the Bureau of Labor Statistics of Illinois. The Secretary,

16.25%; Fuel, 5.10%; Sundry expenses, 10.57%; total, 100%; and for Great Britain on a total expenditure, for

Mr. John S. Lord, has brought into direct comparison the results previously obtained by this Bureau, for Massachusetts, Great Britain, and Prussia, and the results for 1,769 families in Illinois. The average expenditures per family in Massachusetts, Illinois, and Great Britain as shown in this table are not to be taken as indicating the *relative cost of living* in the different communities. No attempt has been made to make the basis of comparison identical in each case, which of course would be necessary if it were desired to determine the relative cost of living. The data are presented solely for the purpose of showing the accuracy of Dr. Engel's law, when applied to families incurring different amounts of total expenditure, and presumably living upon different social levels.

Percentages of Expenditure by the Families of Workingmen in Illinois, Massachusetts, and Great Britain.

CLASSIFICATION.	ILLINOIS.		MASSACHUSETTS.		GREAT BRITAIN.	
	Average.	Per cent.	Average.	Per cent.	Average.	Per cent.
Rent, ...	$96 83	17.42	$148 95	19.74	$68 55	13.48
Groceries, . . .	*161 37	29.14	222 68	29.52	163 50	32.16
Meat, ...	67 90	12.24	100 63	13.34	69 98	13.77
Fish, ...	–	–	25 00	3.31	11 24	2.21
Milk, ...	–	–	23 42	3.11	16 39	3.22
Fuel, ...	31 22	5.63	32 42	4.30	17 81	3.50
Clothing, . . .	55 45	10.00	77 89	10.32	57 27	11.27
Boots and shoes, .	25 71	4.65	27 37	3.63	17 47	3.44
Dry goods, . . .	35 26	6.35	15 11	2.00	17 33	3.41
Sundries, . . .	†80 84	14.57	80 95	10.73	68 81	13.54
Totals, . . .	$554 58	100.00	$754 42	100.00	$508 35	100.00

    * Fish included.   † Milk included.

Comparative Percentages of Expenditures in Illinois, Massachusetts, Great Britain, and Prussia.

ITEMS.	ILLINOIS. Per cent.	MASSACHU-SETTS. Per cent.	GREAT BRITAIN. Per cent.	PRUSSIA. Per cent.	AVERAGE. Per cent.
Subsistence, . . .	41.38	49.28	51.36	55.00	49.25
Clothing, . . .	21.00	15.95	18.12	18.00	18.27
Rent, ...	17.42	19.74	13.48	12.00	15.66
Fuel, ...	5.63	4.30	3.50	5.00	4.61
Sundries, . . .	14.57	10.73	13.54	10.00	12.21
Totals, . . .	100.00	100.00	100.00	100.00	100.00

Comparative Percentages of Expenditures in the United States and Europe.

ITEMS OF EXPENDITURE.	UNITED STATES. Per cent.	EUROPE. Per cent.
Subsistence, ...	45.33	53.18
Clothing, ...	18.47	18.06
Rent, ...	18.58	12.74
Fuel, ...	4.97	4.25
Sundries, ...	12.65	11.77
Totals, ...	100.00	100.00

instance, of $500 per annum, as follows: — Subsistence, 56.45%; Clothing, 15.54%; Rent, 13.66%; Fuel, 4.83%; Sundry expenses, 9.52%; total, 100%.

In examining the two preceding tables it will be seen that in Great Britain, in accordance with the Massachusetts Bureau table of 1875, 63 per cent of an annual expenditure of $508.35 was for subsistence. This figure, which seems out of proportion to percentages of subsistence established by other data, is really in harmony with the economic law stated, for in all cases, so far as we have been able to examine, the percentage of expenditure for subsistence increases and that for clothing decreases, of course within certain limits, as the total annual expenditure for family support decreases.

We have now but to apply the percentages indicating higher prices in either country to a uniform basis for both countries in order to ascertain the higher cost of living in Massachusetts.

As this basis is necessarily an arbitrary one, we adopt $1000 and apply to this basis the various percentages. Any uniform basis for both countries would do as well as $1000, as the object is only to secure money equivalents for established percentages as shown on page 249, *ante*.

Supposing a family in Massachusetts and a family in Great Britain were each to expend $1000 in a given time (not necessarily a year) the elements of such expense would be as shown below in the column headed "Basis," which, it will be seen, foots up $1000. The column headed "Increased" contains the basis figures increased by the percentages indicating the higher prices in each country.

GRAND COMPARISON.   *Cost of Living — 1883.*   MASSACHUSETTS AND GREAT BRITAIN.

Articles.	Massachusetts.		Great Britain.	
	Basis.	Increased.	Basis.	Increased.
Groceries,	$295 20	$373 63	$321 60	$321 60
Provisions,	197 60	197 60	192 00	243 21
Fuel,	43 00	71 74	35 00	35 00
Dry goods,	20 00	34 41	34 10	34 10
Boots, shoes, and slippers,	36 30	49 11	34 40	34 40
Clothing,	103 20	143 53	112 70	112 70
Rents,	197 40	255 61	134 80	134 80
Sundries,	107 30	107 30	135 40	135 40
Totals,	$1000 00	$1232 93	$1000 00	$1051 21

This table means that $1000 worth of the specified " articles " (in the proportions stated) in Great Britain, if purchased in Massachusetts would cost $1232.93, while, with the same conditions, $1000 worth of " articles " in Massachusetts would cost $1051.21 in Great Britain. That is, the ratio of cost of living in Massachusetts and Great Britain is as $1232.93 to $1051.21, or, reduced to a simple decimal, the ratio would stand 1.23 to 1.05. By comparing these grand results we find —

That, on any basis of yearly expenditure, the prices of articles entering into the cost of living were, on the average, 17.29 per cent higher in Massachusetts, in 1883, than in Great Britain; that of this figure 11.49 per cent was due to higher rents in Massachusetts, leaving 5.80 per cent as indicative of the higher cost of living in Massachusetts, as compared with Great Britain, as regards the remaining elements of expense.

We have seen, on page 249, *ante*, that the Massachusetts workingman expends 48.41 per cent more for the support of his family than the workingman in Great Britain. (The average families referred to (page 249) are virtually of the same size, for the slightly increased size of the average Great Britain family is compensated for by a greater proportion at work in Great Britain, and this proportion is the same as the ratio between Massachusetts and Great Britain as regards size of family and persons at work.) Of this 48.41 per cent, 5.80 per cent is paid extra for articles which could be purchased 5.80 per cent cheaper in Great Britain; 11.49 per cent is paid extra to secure more and larger rooms and more air space than the workingman in Great Britain enjoys, while the remainder, 31.12 per cent, indicates also an extra amount expended by the Massachusetts workingman to secure better home surroundings and to maintain the same higher standard of living, as shown for rent, as regards other expenses, which standard is higher than that secured by the workingman in Great Britain.

Distinguishing the figures indicating the greater expenditure for living in Massachusetts (48.41 per cent) from those indicating the higher cost of living (17.29 per cent) we find, as a grand result —

That, the higher prices in Massachusetts are represented by 5.80 per cent; that increased accommodations in housing and the general higher standard of living maintained by Massachusetts workingmen as compared with the standard of living of workingmen in Great Britain is represented by 42.61 (11.49+ 31.12) per cent out of the total GREATER COST of 48.41 per cent, or, stated as a direct ratio, the standard of living of Massachusetts workingmen is to that of the workingmen of Great Britain as 1.42 is to 1.